REDATING
THE NEW TESTAMENT

BOOKS BY JOHN A. T. ROBINSON

Published by The Westminster Press

Redating the New Testament

The Human Face of God

The Difference in Being a Christian Today

Christian Freedom in a Permissive Society

The New Reformation?

Christian Morals Today

Liturgy Coming to Life

Honest to God

On Being the Church in the World

REDATING THE NEW TESTAMENT

John A. T. Robinson

THE WESTMINSTER PRESS
Philadelphia

Unless otherwise stated, biblical quotations are normally taken from the New English Bible, and the place of publication of books quoted is London.

PUBLISHED BY THE WESTMINSTER PRESS ®
PHILADELPHIA, PENNSYLVANIA

PRINTED IN THE UNITED STATES OF AMERICA

Library of Congress Cataloging in Publication Data

Robinson, John Arthur Thomas, Bp., 1919–
Redating the New Testament.

Includes bibliographical references and indexes.
1. Bible — Authorship — Date of authorship. I. Title.
BS2315.5.R67 225.1'4 76-17554
ISBN 0-664-21336-7

For my father
ARTHUR WILLIAM ROBINSON
who began at Cambridge just one hundred years ago
to learn from Lightfoot, Westcott and Hort,
whose wisdom and scholarship remain the fount
of so much in this book

and my mother
MARY BEATRICE ROBINSON
who died as it was being finished
and shared and cared to the end.

Remember that through your parents you were born;
What can you give back to them that equals their gift to you?
Ecclus. 7.28.

All Souls Day, 1975

CONTENTS

PREFACE

I really have no more to say than thank you – to my long-suffering secretary Stella Haughton and her husband; to Professor C. F. D. Moule from whose New Testament seminar so small a seed has produced so monstrous a manuscript, on which he gave such kindly judgment; to my friends, Ed Ball, Gerald Bray, Chip Coakley, Paul Hammond and David McKie, who advised or corrected at many points; and finally to Miss Jean Cunningham of the SCM Press for all her devoted attention to tedious detail.

John Robinson

Trinity College
Cambridge

ABBREVIATIONS

AF	*Apostolic Fathers*
Ant.	*Antiquities*
AP	*Apocrypha and Pseudepigrapha*
ASTI	*Annual of the Swedish Theological Institute*
ATR	*Anglican Theological Review*
Bb	*Biblica*
BJ	*Bellum Judaicum*
BR	*Biblical Research*
BZ	*Biblische Zeitschrift*
CBQ	*Catholic Biblical Quarterly*
CH	*Church History*
Chron.	*Chronologie der Altchristlichen Litteratur* (see p. 4 n. 8)
CN	*Conjectanea Neotestamentica*
CQR	*Church Quarterly Review*
DR	*Downside Review*
EB	*Encyclopaedia Biblica*
ed(d).	editor(s), edited by
EGT	*Expositor's Greek Testament*
EQ	*Evangelical Quarterly*
ET	English Translation
ExpT	*Expository Times*
FG	*The Four Gospels*
HBC	*Handbook of Biblical Chronology*
HDB	Hastings' *Dictionary of the Bible*
HE	*Historia Ecclesiastica*
HJ	*Heythrop Journal*
HJP	*History of the Jewish People*
HNT	Handbuch zum Neuen Testament
HTFG	*Historical Tradition in the Fourth Gospel*
HTR	*Harvard Theological Review*
HUCA	*Hebrew Union College Annual*
IB	*Interpreter's Bible*
ICC	International Critical Commentary
IDB	*Interpreter's Dictionary of the Bible*
INT	*Introduction to the New Testament*
JBC	*Jerome Biblical Commentary*

JBL	*Journal of Biblical Literature*
JEA	*Journal of Egyptian Archaeology*
JRS	*Journal of Roman Studies*
JSS	*Journal of Semitic Studies*
JTS	*Journal of Theological Studies*
KEKNT	Kritisch-exegetischer Kommentar über das Neue Testament
NCB	New Century Bible
n.d.	no date
NEB	New English Bible
n.f.	neue Folge
NovTest	*Novum Testamentum*
n.s.	new series
NT	New Testament
NT Apoc.	*New Testament Apocrypha*
NTC	New Testament Commentary
NTI	*New Testament Introduction*
NTS	*New Testament Studies*
OT	Old Testament
par(s).	parallel(s)
PC	*The Primitive Church*
PCB	*Peake's Commentary on the Bible*
PL	*Patrologia Latina*
PP	*Past and Present*
RB	*Revue Biblique*
RBén	*Revue Bénédictine*
RE	*Review and Expositor*
RHPR	*Revue d'Histoire et de Philosophie Religieuses*
RHR	*Revue d'Histoire des Religions*
RSR	*Recherches de Science Religieuse*
RSV	Revised Standard Version
SBT	Studies in Biblical Theology
ST	*Studia Theologica*
TLS	*Times Literary Supplement*
TLZ	*Theologische Literaturzeitung*
TR	*Theologische Rundschau*
tr.	translated
TU	Texte und Untersuchungen
USQR	*Union Seminary Quarterly Review*
VC	*Vigiliae Christianae*
VE	*Vox Evangelica*
v.l.	varia lectio

ZNW *Zeitschrift für die neutestamentliche Wissenschaft*
ZTK *Zeitschrift für Theologie und Kirche*
ZWT *Zeitschrift für wissenschaftliche Theologie*

I

Dates and Data

WHEN WAS THE New Testament written? This is a question that the outsider might be forgiven for thinking that the experts must by now have settled. Yet, as in archaeology, datings that seem agreed in the textbooks can suddenly appear much less secure than the consensus would suggest. For both in archaeology and in New Testament chronology one is dealing with a combination of absolute and relative datings. There are a limited number of more or less fixed points, and between them phenomena to be accounted for are strung along at intervals like beads on a string according to the supposed requirements of dependence, diffusion and development. New absolute dates will force reconsideration of relative dates, and the intervals will contract or expand with the years available. In the process long-held assumptions about the pattern of dependence, diffusion and development may be upset, and patterns that the textbooks have taken for granted become subjected to radical questioning.

The parallel with what of late has been happening in archaeology is interesting. The story can be followed in a recent book by Colin Renfrew.[1] As he presents it, there was in modern times up to about the middle of this century a more or less agreed pattern of the origins and development of European civilization. The time scale was set by cross-dating finds in Crete and Greece with the established chronology of the Egyptian dynasties, and the evidence from Western Europe was then plotted by supposing a gradual diffusion of culture from this nodal point of Aegean civilization, to the remotest, and therefore the most recent, areas of Iberia, France, Britain and

[1] C. Renfrew, *Before Civilization: the Radiocarbon Revolution and Prehistoric Europe*, 1973.

Scandinavia. Then in 1949 came the first radio-carbon revolution, which made possible the absolute dating of prehistoric materials for the first time. The immediate effect was greatly to extend the time span. Renfrew sums up the impact thus:[2]

> The succession of cultures which had previously been squeezed into 500 years now occupied more than 1,500. This implies more than the alteration of a few dates: it changes the entire pace and nature of the cultural development. But . . . it did not greatly affect the relative chronology for the different regions of Europe: the megalithic tombs of Britain, for instance, were still later than those further south. . . . None of the changes . . . challenged in any way the conventional view that the significant advances in the European neolithic and bronze age were brought by influences from the Near East. It simply put these influences much earlier.

There were indeed uncomfortable exceptions, but these could be put down to minor inconsistencies that later work would tidy up. Then in 1966 came a second revolution, the calibration of the radio-carbon datings by dendrochronology, or the evidence of tree-rings, in particular of the incredibly long-lived Californian bristle-cone pine. This showed that the radiocarbon datings had to be corrected in an upward (i.e. older) direction, and that from about 2000 BC backwards the magnitude of the correction rose steeply, necessitating adjustments of up to 1000 years. The effect of this was not merely to shift all the dates back once more: it was to introduce a fundamental change in the pattern of relationships, making it impossible for the supposed diffusion to have taken place. For what should have been dependent turned out to be earlier.

> The basic links of the traditional chronology are snapped and Europe is no longer directly linked, either chronologically or culturally, with the early civilizations of the Near East.[3]

> The whole diffusionist framework collapses, and with it the assumptions which sustained prehistoric archaeology for nearly a century.[4]

This is a greatly oversimplified account, which would doubtless also be challenged by other archaeologists. Nothing so dramatic has happened or is likely to happen on the much smaller scale of New Testament chronology. But it provides an instructive parallel for the way in which the reigning assumptions of scientific scholarship can, and from time to time do, get challenged for the assumptions they are. For, much more than is generally recognized, the chronology of the New Testament rests on presuppositions rather than facts. It is not that in this case new facts have appeared, new absolute datings which cannot be contested – they are still extraordinarily scarce. It is

[2] Ibid., 65f. [3] Ibid., 105. [4] Ibid., 85.

that certain obstinate questionings have led me to ask just what basis there really is for certain assumptions which the prevailing consensus of critical orthodoxy would seem to make it hazardous or even impertinent to question. Yet one takes heart as one watches, in one's own field or in any other, the way in which established positions can suddenly, or subtly, come to be seen as the precarious constructions they are. What seemed to be firm datings based on scientific evidence are revealed to rest on deductions from deductions. The pattern is self-consistent but circular. Question some of the inbuilt assumptions and the entire edifice looks much less secure.

The way in which this can happen, and has happened, in New Testament scholarship may best be seen by taking some sample dips into the story of the subject. I have no intention of inflicting on the reader a history of the chronology of the New Testament, even if I were competent to do so. Let me just cut some cross-sections at fifty-year intervals to show how the *span* of time over which the New Testament is thought to have been written has expanded and contracted with fashion.

We may start at the year 1800. For till then, with isolated exceptions, the historical study of the New Testament as we know it had scarcely begun. Dating was dependent on authorship, and the authorship of the various New Testament books rested on the traditions incorporated in their titles in the Authorized Version – the Gospel according to St Matthew, the Epistle of Paul the Apostle to the Ephesians, the Revelation of St John the Divine, and so on. All were by apostles or followers of the apostles and the period of the New Testament closed with the death of the last apostle, St John, who by tradition survived into the reign of the Emperor Trajan, *c.* 100 AD. At the other end the earliest Christian writing could be calculated roughly to about the year 50. This was done by combining the history of the early church provided in Acts with the information supplied by St Paul in Gal. 1.13–2.1 of an interval of up to seventeen 'silent' years following his conversion, which itself had to be set a few years after the crucifixion of Jesus in *c.* 30. The span of time for the composition of the New Testament was therefore about fifty years – from 50 to 100.

By 1850 the picture looked very different. The scene was dominated by the school of F. C. Baur, Professor of Church History and Dogmatics at Tübingen from 1826 to 1860. He questioned the traditional attribution of all but five of the New Testament books. Romans, I and II Corinthians and Galatians he allowed were by Paul, and Revelation by the apostle John. These he set in the 50s and late 60s respectively. The rest, including Acts and Mark (for him the last of the synoptists, 'reconciling' the Jewish gospel of Matthew and the Gentile gospel of Luke), were composed up to or beyond 150 AD, to effect the mediation of what Baur saw as the fundamental and all-pervasive conflict between the narrow Jewish Christianity of Jesus' original disciples, represented by Peter and John, and the universalistic message preached by Paul. Only a closing of the church's ranks in face of threats from the gnostic and Montanist movements of the second century produced the *via media* of early catholicism. The entire construction was dominated by the Hegelian pattern of thesis, antithesis and synthesis, and the span of time was determined more by the intervals supposedly required for this to work itself out than by any objective chronological criteria. The fact that the gospels and other New Testament books were quoted by Irenaeus and other church fathers towards the end of the second century alone set an upper limit. The end-term of the process was still the gospel of John, which was dated *c.* 160–70. The span of composition was therefore more than doubled to well over a hundred years – from 50+ to 160+.

By 1900 this schema had in turn been fairly drastically modified. The dialectical pattern of development had come to be recognized as the imposition it was.[5] A major factor in the correction of Baur's picture of history was the work of J. B. Lightfoot, who was appointed a professor at Cambridge in 1861, the year following Baur's death.[6] By the most careful historical investigation he succeeded in establishing the authenticity of the first epistle of Clement, which he dated at 95–6, and of the seven genuine epistles of Ignatius, between 110 and 115. In each of these both Peter and Paul are celebrated in the same breath without a trace of rivalry,[7] and he demonstrated how groundless were Baur's second-century datings. This achievement was acknowledged by the great German scholar Adolf von Harnack (1851–1930), who in 1897 published as the second volume of a massive history of early Christian literature[8] his *Chronologie der altchristlichen Litteratur bis Eusebius*. Harnack's survey, which has never been repeated on so comprehensive a scale,[9] gives a good indication

[5] For the story, cf. W. G. Kümmel, *The New Testament: The History of the Investigation of its Problems*, ET 1973, 162–84.

[6] Lightfoot's achievement is particularly well brought out by S. C. Neill, *The Interpretation of the New Testament, 1861–1961*, Oxford 1964, 33–60.

[7] I Clem. 5; Ignatius, Rom. 4.3.

[8] A. Harnack, *Geschichte der altchristlichen Litteratur bis Eusebius*, Leipzig 1893–7, vol. II (cited hereafter as *Chron.*).

[9] For a survey of surveys, cf. O. Stählin in W. Schmid and O. Stählin (edd.), *Geschichte der griechische Literatur*, Munich [6]1961, II.2, esp. 1112–1121.

of where critical opinion stood at the turn of the century. It still carried many of the marks of the Tübingen period and continued to operate with a span of well over a hundred years. Isolating the canonical books of the New Testament (for Harnack covered all the early Christian writings, a number of which he placed before the later parts of the New Testament), we have the following summary[10] (ignoring qualifications and alternative datings at this point as irrelevant to the broad picture):

48–9	I and II Thessalonians
53	I and II Corinthians, Galatians (?)
53–4	Romans
57–9	Colossians, Philemon, Ephesians (if genuine), Philippians
59–64	Pauline fragments of the Pastoral Epistles
65–70	Mark
70–5	Matthew
79–93	Luke–Acts
81–96	('under Domitian') I Peter, Hebrews
80–110	John, I–III John
90–110	I and II Timothy, Titus
93–6	Revelation
100–30	Jude
120–40	James
160–75	II Peter

It is to be observed that the gospel of John has reverted to somewhere around the turn of the first century and no longer represents the *terminus ad quem*. Mark and Acts have been set much further back, and Harnack was subsequently to put them a good deal earlier still.

A similar but slightly more contracted scheme is to be found in the article on New Testament chronology by H. von Soden in the contemporary *Encyclopaedia Biblica*.[11] His summary dates are:

50–60+	the Pauline epistles
70+	Mark
93–6	Hebrews, I Peter, Revelation
—100	Ephesians, Luke, Acts, John, I–III John
100–33	Jude, Matthew, the Pastoral Epistles, James, II Peter

[10] *Cgron.* 717–22. A comparable picture is to be found a few years earlier in A. Jülicher's *Einleitung in das Neue Testament*, Tübingen 1894, though he put Mark after 70 and the Pastoral Epistles (I and II Timothy and Titus) at 125+.

[11] *Encyclopaedia Biblica*, edd. T. K. Cheyne and J. S. Black, 1899–1903, I, 799–819.

The individual articles in the same Encyclopaedia reveal however how volatile opinion was at that time. Acts is still put well into the second century and John shortly before 140. No date for II Peter is given, but even I Peter is put at 130–40. Above all, while I and II Corinthians are set in the mid-50s, Romans and Philippians are put in 120 and 125! But the articles on the latter two were written by the Dutch scholar W. C. van Manen (1842–1905), who regarded *all* the Pauline epistles (and indeed the rest of the New Testament literature) as pseudonymous, or written under false names.

Yet while the radical critics were still oscillating wildly, conservative, yet still critical, opinion of the period was content to settle for a span of composition between 50 and 100+, with the single exception of II Peter at *c.* 150. This was true both of English scholarship reflected in Hastings' *Dictionary of the Bible*[12] and of American represented by B. W. Bacon's *Introduction to the New Testament.*[13] Indeed the most conservative dating of all was by the German Theodore Zahn (1838–1933) whose *Introduction to the New Testament,*[14] a monument of erudition and careful scholarship, set all the books between 50 and 95, *including* II Peter.

By 1950 the gap between radical and conservative had narrowed considerably, and we find a remarkable degree of consensus. There is still marginal variation at the upper limit, but the span of composition has settled down to a period from about 50 to 100 or 110, with the single exception again of II Peter (*c.* 150). This generalization holds of all the major introductions and comparable surveys, English, American and Continental, Protestant and Catholic, published over the twenty years following 1950.[15]

[12] *Dictionary of the Bible,* ed. J. Hastings, Edinburgh 1898–1904.

[13] B. W. Bacon, *Introduction to the New Testament,* New York 1900.

[14] T. Zahn, *Introduction to the New Testament,* originally Leipzig 1897–9, ET Edinburgh 1909.

[15] R. G. Heard, *An Introduction to the New Testament,* 1950; H. F. D. Sparks, *The Formation of the New Testament,* 1952; A. H. McNeile, *An Introduction to the Study of the New Testament,* revised by C. S. C. Williams, Oxford 1953 (cited henceforth as McNeile-Williams); W. Michaelis, *Einleitung in das neue Testament,* Bern 1954; A. Wikenhauser, *New Testament Introduction* (Freiburg [2]1956), ET New York 1958; A. Robert and A. Feuillet, *Introduction to the New Testament* (Tournai 1959), ET New York 1965; D. Guthrie, *New Testament Introduction,* 1961–5, [3]1970; *Peake's Commentary on the Bible,* revised, ed. M. Black, 1962; *The Interpreter's Dictionary of the Bible,* New York 1962; R. M. Grant, *A Historical Introduction to the New Testament,* 1963; W. G. Kümmel, *Introduction to the New Testament* (Heidelberg 1963), ET 1966; [2]1975; W. Marxsen, *Introduction to the New Testament* (Gütersloh 1963), ET Oxford 1968; E. F. Harrison, *Introduction to the New Testament,* 1964; R. H. Fuller, *A Critical Introduction to the New Testament,* 1966; W. D. Davies, *Invitation to the New*

The prevailing position is fairly represented by Kümmel, who tends to be more radical than many Englishmen and more conservative than many Germans. His datings, again omitting alternatives, are:

50–1	I and II Thessalonians
53–6	Galatians, Philippians, I and II Corinthians, Romans
56–8	Colossians, Philemon
*c.*70	Mark
70–90	Luke
80–90	Acts, Hebrews
80–100	Matthew, Ephesians
90–5	I Peter, Revelation
90–100	John
90–110	I–III John
–100	James
c. 100	Jude
100+	I and II Timothy, Titus
125–50	II Peter

In this relatively fixed firmament the only 'wandering stars' are Ephesians, I Peter, Hebrews and James (and occasionally the Pastorals and Jude), which conservatives wish to put earlier, and Colossians and II Thessalonians, which radicals wish to put later. So once more the span (with one exception) is back to little more than fifty years.

But before closing this survey I would draw attention to the latest assessment of all, Norman Perrin's *The New Testament: An Introduction*,[16] since it could suggest a return to a wider spread. His approximate datings are:

50–60	I Thessalonians, Galatians, I and II Corinthians, Philippians, Philemon, Romans
70–90	II Thessalonians, Colossians, Ephesians, Mark, Matthew, Luke–Acts, Hebrews
80–100	John, I–III John
90–100	Revelation
90–140	I Peter, James, Pastoral Epistles, Jude, II Peter[17]

Testament, New York 1966; A. F. J. Klijn, *An Introduction to the New Testament*, ET Leiden 1967; D. J. Selby, *Introduction to the New Testament*, New York 1971.

[16] N. Perrin, *The New Testament: An Introduction*, New York 1974.

[17] The order of this last group is only a guess. No dates are given, except that I Peter is about the end of the first century and II Peter *c.* 140.

Perrin represents the standpoint of redaction criticism, which goes on from source criticism (dealing with documentary origins) and form criticism (analysing the formative processes of the oral tradition) to emphasize the theological contribution of the evangelists as editors. There is no necessary reason why its perspective should lead to later datings. Indeed other representatives of the same viewpoint who have written New Testament introductions, Marxsen and Fuller, have taken over their precursors' datings. Moreover, the gospels, with which the redaction critics have been most concerned, all remain, including the fourth, within what Perrin calls 'the middle period of New Testament Christianity', 'the twenty-five years or so that followed the fall of Jerusalem'. Yet subsequent to this period he sees a further stage, extending into the middle of the second century, in which the New Testament church is 'on the way to becoming an institution'. If we ask why it is only then becoming an institution, the answer is bound up with his 'theological history of New Testament Christianity'.[18] The course of this he traces from 'Palestinian Jewish Christianity', through 'Hellenistic Jewish Mission Christianity', 'Gentile Christianity' and 'the apostle Paul', to 'the middle period', and finally into 'emergent catholicism'. Yet these categories, taken over from Rudolf Bultmann and his successors, have of late come in for some stringent criticism not only from England[19] but from Germany itself,[20] none of which Perrin acknowledges. The entire developmental schema (closely parallel to the 'diffusionist framework' in archaeology), together with the time it is assumed to require, begins to look as if it may be imposed upon the material as arbitrarily as the earlier one of the Tübingen school. It is premature to judge. But certainly it cannot itself be used to *determine* the datings which are inferred from it. It must first be submitted to a more rigorous scrutiny in the light of the independent data.

Indeed what one looks for in vain in much recent scholarship is any serious wrestling with the external or internal evidence for the dating of individual books (such as marked the writings of men like Lightfoot and Harnack and Zahn), rather than an *a priori* pattern of theological

[18] Op. cit., 39–63.

[19] I. H. Marshall, 'Palestinian and Hellenistic Christianity: Some Critical Comments', *NTS* 19, 1972–3, 271–87; 'Early Catholicism' in R. N. Longenecker and M. C. Tenney (edd.), *New Dimensions in New Testament Study*, Grand Rapids, Michigan, 1974, 217–31.

[20] M. Hengel, 'Christologie und neutestamentliche Chronologie' in H. Baltensweiler and B. Reicke (edd.), *Neues Testament und Geschichte: Oscar Cullmann zum 70. Geburtstag*, Zürich and Tübingen 1972, 43–67; *Judaism and Hellenism*, ET 1974.

development into which they are then made to fit.[21] In fact ever since the form critics assumed the basic solutions of the source critics (particularly with regard to the synoptic problem) and the redaction critics assumed the work of the form critics, the chronology of the New Testament documents has scarcely been subjected to fresh examination. No one since Harnack has really gone back to look at it for its own sake or to examine the presuppositions on which the current consensus rests. It is only when one pauses to do this that one realizes how thin is the foundation for some of the textbook answers and how circular the arguments for many of the relative datings. Disturb the position of one major piece and the pattern starts disconcertingly to dissolve.

That major piece was for me the gospel of John. I have long been convinced that John contains primitive and reliable historical tradition, and that conviction has been reinforced by numerous studies in recent years. But in reinforcing it these same studies have the more insistently provoked the question in my mind whether the traditional dating of the gospel, alike by conservatives and (now) by radicals, towards the end of the first century, is either credible or necessary. Need it have been written anything like so late? As the arguments *requiring* it to be set at a considerable distance both in place and time from the events it records began one by one to be knocked away (by growing recognition of its independence of the synoptists and, since 1947, by linguistic parallels from the Dead Sea Scrolls), I have wondered more and more whether it does not belong much nearer to the Palestinian scene prior to the Jewish revolt of 66–70.

But one cannot redate John without raising the whole question of its place in the development of New Testament Christianity. If this is early, what about the other gospels? Is it necessarily the last in time?

[21] Perrin's particular schema is in itself fairly arbitrary. It is hard to see by what criteria of doctrine or discipline I and II Peter are both subsumed under the heading of 'emergent catholicism'; in fact in the analysis of the marks of this phenomenon (op. cit., 268–73) I Peter is scarcely mentioned. Moreover, while he acknowledges his deep indebtedness to E. Käsemann for his estimate of II Peter ('An Apologia for Primitive Christian Eschatology', *Essays on New Testament Themes*, ET (SBT 41) 1964, 169–95), he ignores Käsemann's equally strong contention ('Ketzer und Zeuge', *ZTK* 48, 1951, 292–311) that III John reflects a second-century transition to Ignatian monepiscopacy. (Of the Johannine epistles he merely says, 249: 'We are now in the middle period of New Testament Christianity.') He does not explain why I Clement's concern for apostolic succession and Ignatius' plea for unity around the monarchical bishop (quintessential interests, one would have thought, of 'emergent catholicism') receive no mention in New Testament documents supposedly later than they are.

Indeed does it actually become the first? – or are they earlier too? And, if so, how then do the gospels stand in relation to the epistles? Were all the Pauline letters penned, as has been supposed, before any of the gospels? Moreover, if John no longer belongs to the end of the century, what of the Johannine epistles and the other so-called Catholic Epistles which have tended to be dated with them? And what about the book of Revelation, which, whatever its connection with the other Johannine writings, everyone seems nowadays to set in the same decade as the gospel?

It was at this point that I began to ask myself just why *any* of the books of the New Testament needed to be put after the fall of Jerusalem in 70. As one began to look at them, and in particular the epistle to the Hebrews, Acts and the Apocalypse, was it not strange that this cataclysmic event was never once mentioned or apparently hinted at? And what about those predictions of it in the gospels – were they really the prophecies after the event that our critical education had taught us to believe? So, as little more than a theological joke, I thought I would see how far one could get with the hypothesis that the whole of the New Testament was written before 70. And the only way to try out such a hypothesis was to push it to its limits, and beyond, to discover what these limits were. Naturally, there were bound to be exceptions – II Peter was an obvious starter, and presumably the Pastorals – but it would be an interesting exercise.

But what began as a joke became in the process a serious preoccupation, and I convinced myself that the hypothesis must be tested in greater detail than the seminar-paper with which it started would allow. The result is that I have found myself driven to look again at the evidence for all the accepted New Testament datings. But so far from forcing it to a new Procrustean bed of my own making, I have tried to keep an open mind. I deliberately left the treatment of the fourth gospel to the last (though increasingly persuaded that it should never be treated in isolation from the other three, or they from it) so as not to let my initial judgment on it mould the rest of the pattern to it. Moreover, I have changed my mind many times in the course of the work, and come through to datings which were not at all what I expected when I began. Indeed I would wish to claim nothing fixed or final about the results. Once one starts on an investigation like this one could go on for years. Problems that one supposed in one's own mind were more or less settled (e.g. the synoptic problem) become opened up again; and almost all the books or articles that have been written on the New Testament (and many too on ancient history) threaten to become relevant. But one has to stop somewhere. I am much more aware of what I have *not* read. But this will have to do as a stone to drop into the pond, to see what happens.

Naturally if one presumes to challenge the scientific establishment in any field one must be prepared to substantiate one's case in some detail. So I have tried to give the evidence and provide the references for those who wish to follow them up. However, short of making it one's life's work (and frankly chronology is not mine), one must delimit the task. I have not attempted to go into the theoretical basis of chronology itself or to get involved in astronomical calculations or the complex correlation of ancient dating systems.[22] These things are too high to one who finds himself confused even when changing to summer time or crossing time zones! Nor have I entered the contentious area of the chronology of the birth, ministry and death of Jesus, since it does not seriously affect the dating of the *books* of the New Testament. Nor have I found it necessary to be drawn into the history of the canon of the New Testament, since, unless one has reason to suppose that the books were written very late, how long an interval elapsed before they became collected or acknowledged as scripture is but marginally relevant. Above all, I have not ventured into the vast field of the non-canonical literature of the sub-apostolic age, except to the extent that this is directly relevant to the dating of the New Testament books themselves. Without attempting to survey this literature, both Jewish and Christian, for its own sake (which would have taken me far beyond my competence), I have simply devoted a postscript to it, in so far as by comparison and contrast it can help to check or confirm the conclusions arrived at from the study of the New Testament.

Finally, in a closing chapter I have sketched some of the conclusions and corollaries to be drawn – and not to be drawn – from such a study. My position will probably seem surprisingly conservative – especially to those who judge me radical on other issues. But I trust it will give no comfort to those who would view with suspicion the application of critical tools to biblical study – for it is reached by the application of those tools. I claim no great originality – almost every individual conclusion will be found to have been argued previously by someone, often indeed by great and forgotten men – though

[22] Cf. J. Finegan, *Handbook of Biblical Chronology*, Princeton 1964, for the single most useful survey; also T. Lewin, *Fasti Sacri: A Key to the Chronology of the New Testament*, 1865; J. van Goudoeuver, *Biblical Calendars*, Leiden [2]1961; A. K. Michels, *The Calendar of the Roman Republic*, Princeton, NJ, 1967; E. J. Bickermann, *Chronology of the Ancient World*, 1968; A. E. Samuel, *Greek and Roman Chronology*, Munich 1972; E. Schürer, *The History of the Jewish People in the Age of Jesus Christ*, revised ET, Edinburgh 1973, vol. I, Appendix III ('The Jewish Calendar').

I think the overall pattern is new and I trust coherent. Least of all do I wish to close any discussion. Indeed I am happy to prefix to my work the words with which Niels Bohr is said to have begun his lecture-courses: 'Every sentence I utter should be taken by you not as a statement but as a question.'[23]

[23] Quoted by J. Bronowski, *The Ascent of Man*, 1973, 334.

II

The Significance of 70

ONE OF THE oddest facts about the New Testament is that what on any showing would appear to be the single most datable and climactic event of the period – the fall of Jerusalem in AD 70, and with it the collapse of institutional Judaism based on the temple – is never once mentioned as a past fact. It is, of course, predicted; and these predictions are, in some cases at least, assumed to be written (or written up) after the event. But the silence is nevertheless as significant as the silence for Sherlock Holmes of the dog that did not bark. S. G. F. Brandon made this oddness the key to his entire interpretation of the New Testament:[1] everything from the gospel of Mark onwards was a studied rewriting of history to suppress the truth that Jesus and the earliest Christians were identified with the revolt that failed. But the sympathies of Jesus and the Palestinian church with the Zealot cause are entirely unproven and Brandon's views have won scant scholarly credence.[2] Yet if the silence is not studied it is very remarkable. As James Moffatt said,

[1] S. G. F. Brandon, *The Fall of Jerusalem and the Christian Church*, 1951; [2]1957; 'The Date of the Markan Gospel', *NTS* 7, 1960–1, 126–41; *Jesus and the Zealots*, Manchester 1967; *The Trial of Jesus*, 1968.

[2] Cf. the devastating review of *Jesus and the Zealots* by Hengel, *JSS* 14, 1969, 231–40; and his *Die Zeloten*, Leiden 1961; *Was Jesus a Revolutionist?*, ET Philadelphia 1971; *Victory over Violence*, ET 1975; also W. Wink, 'Jesus and Revolution: Reflection on S. G. F. Brandon's *Jesus and the Zealots*', *USQR* 26, 1969, 37–59; O. Cullmann, *Jesus and the Revolutionaries*, ET New York 1970; and especially the forthcoming symposium edited by C. F. D. Moule and E. Bammel, *Jesus and the Politics of his Day*, Cambridge 1977(?). P. Winter makes the important point that 'nothing that Josephus wrote lends any support to the theory that Jesus was caught up in revolutionary, Zealotic or quasi-Zealotic activities. . . . The relatively friendly

> We should expect . . . that an event like the fall of Jerusalem would have dinted some of the literature of the primitive church, almost as the victory at Salamis has marked the *Persae*. It might be supposed that such an epoch-making crisis would even furnish criteria for determining the dates of some of the NT writings. As a matter of fact, the catastrophe is practically ignored in the extant Christian literature of the first century.[3]

Similarly C. F. D. Moule:

> It is hard to believe that a Judaistic type of Christianity which had itself been closely involved in the cataclysm of the years leading up to AD 70 would not have shown the scars – or, alternatively, would not have made capital out of this signal evidence that they, and not non-Christian Judaism, were the true Israel. But in fact our traditions are silent.[4]

Explanations for this silence have of course been attempted. Yet the simplest explanation of all, that 'perhaps . . . there is extremely little in the New Testament later than AD 70'[5] and that its events are not mentioned because they had not yet occurred, seems to me to demand more attention than it has received in critical circles.

Bo Reicke begins a recent essay[6] with the words:

> An amazing example of uncritical dogmatism in New Testament studies is the belief that the Synoptic Gospels should be dated after the Jewish War of AD 66–70 because they contain prophecies *ex eventu* of the destruction of Jerusalem by the Romans in the year 70.

In fact this is too sweeping a statement, because the dominant consensus of scholarly opinion places Mark's gospel, if not before the beginning of the Jewish war, at any rate before the capture of the city.[7] Indeed one of the arguments to be assessed is that which *distinguishes* between the evidence of Mark on the one hand and that

---

attitude of Josephus towards Jesus contrasts with his severe stricture of the Zealots and kindred activist groups among the Jews responsible for encouraging the people to defy Roman rule' (Excursus II in Schürer, *HJP* I, 441).

[3] J. Moffatt, *Introduction to the Literature of the New Testament*, Edinburgh [3]1918, 3. This is quoted by L. H. Gaston, *No Stone on Another: Studies in the Fall of Jerusalem in the Synoptic Gospels* (*NovTest.* Suppl. 23), Leiden 1970, 5, who continues: 'There is no unambiguous reference to the fall of Jerusalem anyplace outside the gospels.'

[4] C. F. D. Moule, *The Birth of the New Testament*, 1962, 123.

[5] Moule, op. cit., 121.

[6] B. Reicke, 'Synoptic Prophecies on the Destruction of Jerusalem', in D. W. Aune (ed.), *Studies in New Testament and Early Christian Literature: Essays in Honor of Allen P. Wikgren* (*NovTest* Suppl. 33), Leiden 1972, 121–34.

[7] Cf. the summary of opinions in V. Taylor, *St Mark*, [2]1966, 31. He himself opts, with many others, for 65–70. Kümmel, *INT*, 98, hedges his bets: 'Since no overwhelming argument for the years before or after 70 can be adduced, we must content ourselves with saying that Mark was written *ca.* 70.'

of Matthew and Luke on the other. In what follows I shall start from the presumption of most contemporary scholars that Mark's version is the earliest and was used by Matthew and Luke. As will become clear,[8] I am by no means satisfied with this as an overall explanation of the synoptic phenomena. I believe that one must be open to the possibility that at points Matthew or Luke may represent the earliest form of the common tradition, which Mark also alters for editorial reasons. I shall therefore concentrate on the differences between the versions without prejudging their priority or dependence. The relative order of the synoptic gospels is in any case of secondary importance for assessing their absolute relation to the events of 70. Whatever their sequence, all or any could have been written before or after the fall of Jerusalem.

Let us then start by looking again at the discourse of Mark 13. It begins:

> As he was leaving the temple, one of his disciples exclaimed, 'Look, Master, what huge stones! What fine buildings!' Jesus said to him, 'You see these great buildings? Not one stone will be left upon another; all will be thrown down.'
>
> When he was sitting on the Mount of Olives facing the temple he was questioned privately by Peter, James, John, and Andrew. 'Tell us,' they said, 'when will this happen? What will be the sign when the fulfilment of all this is at hand?' (13.1–4).

The first thing to notice is that the question is never answered. In fact no further reference is made in the chapter to the *destruction* of the temple. This supports the judgment of most critics that the discourse is an artificial construction out of diverse teachings of Jesus, with parallels in various parts of the gospel tradition, and linked somewhat arbitrarily by the evangelist to a subsequent question of interest to the church, such as Mark regularly poses by the device of a private enquiry by an inner group of disciples (cf. 4.10; 7.17; 9.28). We need not stop to wrestle with the complex question of how much goes back to Jesus and how much is the creation of the community. That Jesus could have predicted the doom of Jerusalem and its sanctuary is no more inherently improbable than that another Jesus, the son of Ananias, should have done so in the autumn of 62.[9] Even if, as most would suppose,[10] the discourse represents the work of Christian prophecy reflecting upon the Old Testament and remembered sayings

[8] Cf. pp. 92–4 below.

[9] Josephus, *BJ*, 6. 300–9. In citing Josephus I have followed the notation and, unless otherwise indicated, the translation in the Loeb Classical Library.

[10] But cf. D. Hill, 'On the Evidence for the Creative Role of Christian Prophets', *NTS* 20, 1973–4, 262–74.

of Jesus in the light of the church's experiences, hopes and fears, the relevant question is, What experiences, hopes and fears?

The mere fact again that there is no correlation between the initial question and Jesus' answer would suggest that the discourse is not being written retrospectively out of the known events of 70. Indeed the sole subsequent reference to the temple at all, and that only by implication, is in 13.14–16:

> But when you see 'the abomination of desolation' usurping a place which is not his (let the reader understand), then those who are in Judaea must take to the hills. If a man is on the roof, he must not come down into the house to fetch anything out; if in the field, he must not turn back for his cloak.

It is clear at least that 'the abomination of desolation' cannot itself refer to the destruction of the sanctuary in August 70 or to its desecration by Titus' soldiers in sacrificing to their standards.[11] By that time it was far too late for anyone in Judaea to take to the hills, which had been in enemy hands since the end of 67.[12] Moreover, the only tradition we have as to what Christians actually did, or were told to do, is that preserved by Eusebius[13] apparently on the basis of the Memoirs of Hegesippus used also by Epiphanius.[14] This says that they had been commanded by an oracle given 'before the war' to depart from the city,[15] and that so far from taking to the mountains of Judaea, as Mark's instruction implies, they were to make for Pella, a Greek city of the Decapolis, which lay below sea level on the east side of the Jordan valley. It would appear then that this was not prophecy

[11] Josephus, *BJ* 6. 316.

[12] Brandon, who argues for this, *NTS* 7, 133f., merely omits any reference to the injunction to take to the hills.

[13] *HE* 3. 5.3. Quotations from this work are from the translation and edition by H. J. Lawlor and J. E. L. Oulton, 1927–8.

[14] *Adv. haer.* 29.7; 30.2; *de mens. et pond.* 15.2–5. For the case for a common source in the *Hypomnemata* of Hegesippus, cf. H. J. Lawlor, *Eusebiana*, Oxford 1912, 27–34, who prints the full texts (101f.).

[15] According to Epiphanius' version, the flight was made just before the beginning of the siege of Jerusalem itself. At that stage escape was indeed still possible. Speaking of November 66 Josephus says: 'After this catastrophe of Cestius many distinguished Jews abandoned the city as swimmers desert a sinking ship' (*BJ* 2.556). But an earlier reference (*Ant.* 20.256) to the period between the arrival of Gessius Florus as procurator in 64 and the beginning of the war in 66 fits better a popular exodus and the Eusebian dating: 'There was no end in sight. The ill-fated Jews, unable to endure the devastation by brigands that went on, were one and all forced to abandon their own country and flee, for they thought it would be better to settle among gentiles, no matter where'. If the Christian Jews were among them, then the λῃσταί (Josephus' word for the Zealots) would have been the cause for the Christians' dissociation from the revolt rather than, as Brandon thought, their attachment to it. This seems altogether more likely.

shaped by events[16] and cannot therefore be dated to the period immediately before or during the war of 66–70.

What apparently the instruction *is* shaped by (whether in the mind of Jesus or that of a Christian prophet speaking in his name) is, rather, the archetypal Jewish resistance to the desecration of the temple-sanctuary by an idolatrous image under Antiochus Epiphanes in 168–7 BC. This was 'the abomination of desolation . . . set up on the altar' (I Macc. 1.54) referred to by Daniel (9.27 [LXX]; 11.31; 12.11), and it was in consequence of this and of the local enforcement of pagan rites that Mattathias and his sons 'took to the hills, leaving all their belongings in the town' (I Macc. 2.28). It is here that we should seek the clue to the pattern of Mark 13.14–16. Moreover the influence of the book of Daniel is so pervasive in this chapter[17] that it is hard to credit that what is regularly there associated with the abomination of desolation, namely, the cessation of the daily offering in the temple (Dan. 8.13; 9.27; 11.31; 12.11) would not have been alluded to if this had by then occurred, as it did in August 70.[18]

It is more likely that the reference to 'the abomination of desolation standing where *he* ought not' (to stress Mark's deliberate lack of grammatical apposition) is, like Paul's reference to 'the lawless one' or 'the enemy' who 'even takes his seat in the temple of God' (II Thess. 2.1–12),[19] traditional apocalyptic imagery for the incarnation of evil which had to be interpreted ('let the reader understand'; cf. Rev. 13.18) according to whatever shape Satan might currently take. It is indeed highly likely that such speculation was revived, as many have argued,[20] by the proposal of the Emperor Gaius Caligula in 40 to set up his statue in the temple (which was averted only by his death).[21] Paul was evidently still awaiting the fulfilment of such an expectation in 50–1 (to anticipate the date of II Thessalonians), where 'the restrainer' holding it back is probably to be interpreted as the Roman Empire embodied in its emperor (ὁ κατέχων being a

[16] This point is made strongly, perhaps over-strongly, by Reicke, op. cit., 125. For a defence of the Pella tradition, against the criticisms of Brandon, *Fall of Jerusalem*, 168–78, cf. S. S. Sowers, 'The Circumstances and Recollection of the Pella Flight', *TZ* 26, 1970, 305–20.

[17] As well as in this passage, it is echoed in 13.4 (Dan. 12.7); 13.7 (Dan. 2.28); 13.19 (Dan. 12.1); and 13.26 (Dan. 7.13).

[18] Josephus, *BJ* 6.94.

[19] There is here the same transition between neuter and masculine: τὸ κατέχον (v. 6), ὁ κατέχων (v. 7).

[20] E.g. B. W. Bacon, *The Gospel of Mark*, New Haven, Conn., 1925, 53–68.

[21] Josephus, *Ant.* 18. 261–309. For the horror and alarm which this raised among Jews, cf. Philo, *Leg. ad Gaium*, 184–348.

play perhaps on the name Claudius, 'he who shuts'). His expulsion of the Jews from Rome in 49 could be reflected in the phrase of I Thess. 2.16 about retribution having overtaken them εἰς τέλος ('with a view to the end'?).[22] The only other datable incident to which 'the abomination' might conceivably refer in retrospect is the control of the temple not by the Romans but by the Zealots temporarily in 66 and permanently in 68, which Josephus speaks of in terms of its 'pollution'.[23] This would be the very opposite of Brandon's thesis, with the Zealots filling the role of antichrist. But it does not explain the masculine singular (as a *vaticinium ex eventu* should require) and again it is too late for a pre-war flight, and perhaps for any.

One is forced to conclude that the reference in Mark 13.14 to 'the abomination of desolation standing where he ought not' is an extremely uncertain indicator of retrospective dating. G. R. Beasley-Murray[24] ends a note on the history of the interpretation of this verse with the words:

> It would seem a just conclusion that the traditional language of the book of Daniel, the Jewish abhorrence of the idolatrous Roman ensigns, attested in the reaction to Pilate's desecration,[25] and Jesus' insight into the situation resulting from his people's rejection of his message, supply a sufficient background for this saying.

Marxsen, writing from a very different standpoint, regards the phrase as a vague reference to the forthcoming destruction of the temple and is forthright in saying: 'From Mark's point of view, a *vaticinium ex eventu* is an impossibility.'[26]

With regard to Mark 13 as a whole the most obvious inference is that the warnings it contains were relevant to Christians as they were facing duress and persecution, alerting them to watchfulness against false alarms and pretenders' claims, promising them support under trial before Jewish courts and pagan governors, and assuring them of

[22] A suggested interpretation I owe to Dr E. Bammel.

[23] *BJ* 2.422–5; 4.147–92; 5.19. So M.-J. Lagrange, *S. Matthieu*, Paris 1927, 462; R. T. France, *Jesus and the Old Testament*, 1971, 227–39; W. J. Houston, *New Testament Prophecy and Christian Tradition*, unpublished D.Phil. thesis for the University of Oxford, 1973. Cf. F. F. Bruce, 'Josephus and Daniel,' *ASTI* 4, 1965, 153f.

[24] G. R. Beasley-Murray, *A Commentary on Mark Thirteen*, 1957, 72 (cf. 59–72).

[25] The reference is to an incident in Caesarea in 26 (Josephus, *Ant.* 18. 55–9; *BJ* 2.169–74; Philo, *Leg. ad Gaium* 299–305) and therefore well before Jesus' supposed utterance. Cf. P. L. Maier, 'The Episode of the Golden Roman Shields at Jerusalem', *HTR* 62, 1969, 109–21.

[26] W. Marxsen, *Mark the Evangelist*, ET Nashville, Tenn., 1969, 170 (cf. 166–89); similarly E. Trocmé, *The Formation of the Gospel according to Mark*, ET 1975, 104f., 245. He thinks Mark 1–13 was written *c.* 50 (259).

the rewards of steadfastness. Doubtless the phrasing has been influenced and pointed up by what Christians actually experienced, but, as Reicke argues in the second half of his essay,[27] there is nothing that cannot be paralleled from the period of church history covered by Acts (*c.* 30–62). As early as 50 Paul can say to the Thessalonians: 'You have fared like the congregations in Judaea, God's people in Christ Jesus. You have been treated by your countrymen as they are treated by the Jews' (I Thess. 2.14). Unless the flight enjoined upon 'those who are in Judaea' is purely symbolic (of the church dissociating itself from Judaism) – and with the detailed instructions and the prayer that it may not be in winter (Mark 13.18) there is no reason to assume it is figurative any more than the very literal dissolution of Herod's temple – then the directions for it must surely belong to a time when there still *were* Christians in Judaea, free and able to flee. Finally, we are in a period when it could still be said without reserve or qualification on the solemn authority of Jesus: 'I tell you this: the present generation will live to see it all' (13.30).

In fact there is, as we said, wide agreement among scholars that Mark 13 *does* fit better before the destruction of the temple it purports to prophesy. This is relevant as we turn now to Matthew and Luke. What will be significant are differences from Mark: otherwise the same presumption will continue to hold.

We will take Matthew first, since he is closest to the Markan tradition. But the first relevant passage in his gospel is not in fact in Markan material but in that which he has in common with Luke, the parable of the wedding feast (Matt. 22.1–10 = Luke 14.16–24), where Matthew inserts the following:

> The others seized the servants, attacked them brutally and killed them. The king was furious; he sent troops to kill those murderers and set their town on fire (22.6f.).

There can be little doubt that these verses are secondary to the parable.[28] They form part of an allegorical interpretation of the successive servants (Luke has one only) in terms of the prophets and apostles sent to Israel, as in the immediately preceding parable of the wicked husbandmen (Matt. 21.33–45).[29] The introduction of a military expedition while the supper is getting cold is particularly inappropriate. Luke has also allegorized the parable, to match the Jewish and Gentile missions of the church, by introducing two search-

[27] 'Synoptic Prophecies', 130–3.

[28] Matthew has also tacked on the (originally separate) parable of the wedding garment (22.11–14).

[29] Cf. especially 22.4, 6 with 21.35f.

parties, first to the streets and alleys of the city and then to the highways and hedgerows. The secondary character of all these features is now further established by their absence from the same parable in the Gospel of Thomas (64). This version also supports the supposition, which we should independently deduce from his usage elsewhere (Matt.18.23; 25.34, 40), that it is Matthew who has brought in the figure of the king as the subject of the story: Luke and Thomas both simply have 'a man'. It is therefore as certain as anything can be in this field that the crucial verse, 'The king was furious; he sent troops to kill those murderers and set their town on fire', is an addition, probably by the evangelist. The sole question is, When was it added and does it reflect *in retrospect* the destruction of Jerusalem (to which it must obviously allude)?

It has to be admitted that this is the single verse in the New Testament that most looks like a retrospective prophecy of the events of 70, and it has almost universally been so taken. It is the only passage which mentions the destruction of Jerusalem by fire. Yet, as K. H. Rengstorf has argued,[30] the wording of Matt. 22.7 represents a fixed description of ancient expeditions of punishment and is such an established *topos* of Near Eastern, Old Testament and rabbinic literature that it is precarious to infer that it must reflect a particular occurrence. He concludes that it has no relevance for the dating of the first gospel. And this conclusion is borne out in a further study by Sigfred Pedersen,[31] who believes that this and the preceding parable of the wicked husbandmen are fundamentally shaped by material from the Old Testament, especially Jeremiah. The most he will say is that *if* Matthew is writing after 70, then we must see this as a contributory occasion for the addition (which of course no one would deny).

Moreover, if Matt. 22.7 did reflect the happenings of 70 one might expect that it would make a distinction that features in other *post eventum* 'visions', namely, that while the walls of the city were thrown down, it was the temple that perished by fire. Thus the Jewish apocalypse II Baruch clearly reflects the fall of Jerusalem to the Romans, though it purports to be the announcement to the prophet Baruch of a coming Chaldean invasion. It recognizes that the city and the temple suffered separate fates:

[30] K. H. Rengstorf, 'Der Stadt der Mörder (Mt 22.7)' in W. Eltester (ed.), *Judentum-Urchristentum-Kirche: Festschrift für Joachim Jeremias* (*ZNW* Beiheft 26), 1960, 106–29 (especially 125f.).

[31] S. Pedersen, 'Zum Problem der vaticinia ex eventu (eine Analyse von Mt 21.33–46 par; 22.1–10 par)', *ST* 19, 1965, 167–88.

> We have overthrown the wall of Zion and we have burnt the place[32] of the mighty God (7.1).
>
> They delivered . . . to the enemy the overthrown wall, and plundered the house, and burnt the temple (80.3).

If one really wants to see what *ex eventu* prophecy looks like, one should turn to the so-called Sibylline Oracles (4.125–7):

> And a Roman leader shall come to Syria, who shall burn down Solyma's [Jerusalem's] temple with fire, and therewith slay many men, and shall waste the great land of the Jews with its broad way.[33]

It is precisely such detail that one does not get in the New Testament.

Finally, in Matthew's parable the king clearly stands for God. In the war of 66–70 the king who sent the armies to quell the rebels was Nero, followed by Vespasian. Reicke says:

> The picture of God sending his armies to punish all guests not willing to follow his invitation was in no way applicable to the war started by Nero to punish the leaders of rebellion against Roman supremacy.[34]

He argues indeed that there is every reason to assume that the final redactor of the parable would have *altered* the reference if he had been writing after 70. This, I believe, is putting it too strongly, since undoubtedly Christians came to see the destruction of Jerusalem as God's retribution on Israel, whoever the human agent.[35] Yet the correspondence does not seem close enough to *require* composition in the light of the event.

Nevertheless, the conclusion must, I think, stand that on the basis of Matt. 22.7 alone it is impossible to make a firm judgment. It could reflect 70.[36] On the other hand, it need not. One must decide on the evidence of the distinctive features in Matthew's apocalypse in chapter 24.

[32] I.e. the temple. For this sense, cf. II Macc. 5.17–20; John 11.48; Acts 6.14; 21.28; etc.

[33] Tr. R. H. Charles, *The Apocrypha and Pseudepigrapha of the Old Testament* II, Oxford 1913, 395.

[34] Op. cit., 123.

[35] Cf. later (*c.* 300) Eusebius, *HE* 3.5.3: 'The justice of God then visited upon them [the Jews] all their acts of violence to Christ and his apostles, by destroying that generation of wicked persons root and branch from among men'; also (*c.* 400) Sulpicius Severus, *Chron.* 2.30. But evidence for this is remarkably absent from earlier writings where one might expect it, e.g. the Epistle of Barnabas or Justin's *Dialogue with Trypho*.

[36] R. V. G. Tasker, *St Matthew* (Tyndale NTC), 1961, 206, suggests that the verses may have been marginal comment (subsequently embodied in the text) added after 70 to draw attention to the judgment on Israel for persecuting the Christians. The weakness in this suggestion is of course the lack of any textual evidence.

The first observation to be made is how few these are. As K. Stendahl says, 'He does not have any more explicit references than Mark to the Jewish War or the withdrawing of the Christians from Jerusalem'.[37] Apart from minor verbal variations he follows the tradition common to Mark, with only the following differences of any significance:

1. In 24.3, the purpose of the discourse is broadened to answer the disciples not merely on the date of the destruction of the temple ('Tell us, when will this happen?') but on the theme to which the chapter (and the one following) is really addressed: 'And what will be the signal for your coming and the end of the age?' It is significant, however, that the former question does not drop out, as might be expected (especially since Matthew has no more answer to it than Mark) if at the time of writing it now related to the past whilst the *parousia* was still awaited.

2. In 24.9–14, the prophecies of persecutions ahead found in Mark 13.9–12 are omitted, being placed by Matthew in Jesus' mission charge to the disciples during the Galilean ministry (10.17–21). Whatever the motives for this, the effect is to see the predictions fulfilled earlier rather than later, and evidently they are not intended by Matthew to have any reference to the sufferings of the Jewish war. In their place Matthew has warnings against division and defection within the church, which are presumably relevant to the state of his own community but have no bearing on the question of date.

3. In 24.15, the cryptic reference to 'the abomination of desolation' is specifically attributed to the prophet Daniel (which was obvious anyhow), and Matthew has the neuter participle ἑστός for the masculine ἑστηκότα (as the grammar demands), and ἐν τόπῳ ἁγίῳ for the vague ὅπου οὐ δεῖ. Despite the lack of article, '(the) holy place' must mean the temple (evidently intended by Mark's allusion), and the choice of phrase may again reflect the scriptural background already referred to:

> How long will impiety cause desolation, and both the holy place and the fairest of all lands be given over to be trodden down? (Dan. 8.13)

> They sat idly by when it [Jerusalem] was surrendered, when the holy place was given up to the alien (I Macc. 2.7).

[37] *PCB*, 793. Cf. Marxsen, *Mark the Evangelist*, 198, who himself has no doubt that Matthew is later than 70: 'If we begin by inquiring into the time of Matthew's composition, we encounter the startling fact that chap. 24 is scarcely ever used in evidence. It is rather on the basis of 22.7 that the Gospel is assumed to have originated after AD 70.'

Yet none of Matthew's changes affects the sense or makes the application more specific (in fact the neuter participle does the opposite). Again he does not mention the reference in Daniel to the cessation of the daily sacrifices. If Matthew intended the reader to 'understand' in the prediction events lying by then in the past he has certainly given him no help. Moreover, as Zahn said long ago,[38] in view of Matthew's appeal to conditions in Jerusalem 'to this day' (27.8; cf. 28.15), one would have expected him of all people to draw attention to the present devastation of the site.

4. In 24.20, there occurs the only other change in the decisive paragraph about Judaea, with the addition of the words in italics:

> Pray that it may not be winter *when you have to make your escape, or Sabbath.*

'When you have to make your escape' merely specifies what must be meant in Mark. The reference to the sabbath could again contain an allusion back to the fact that when the faithful of Judaea took to the hills after the original 'abomination of desolation' their first encounter with the enemy was on the sabbath and because of scruples which they later abandoned they were massacred without resistance (I Macc. 2.29–41). But it is more likely to refer to the obstacles to movement on the sabbath for Jewish Christians who were strict observers of the law. In any case it bespeaks a primitive Palestinian milieu and a community-discipline stricter than that recommended in Matthew's own church (cf. Matt. 12.1–14). It is certainly not an addition that argues for a situation after 70. Indeed it is one of those points of difference where, unless one is committed to over-all Markan priority, it looks as though Mark has omitted an element in the tradition no longer relevant for the Gentile church.

5. Matthew's material without parallel in the Markan tradition (24.26–8; 24.37–25.46) has no reference to the fall of Jerusalem but, like the additional signs of the *parousia* in 24.30f., solely to 'the consummation of the age'. Yet his version of the 'Q' material in 24.26, 'If they tell you, "He is there in the wilderness", do not go out', clearly shows that in his mind the scene is still in Judaea (in the Lukan parallel in 17.23 it could be anywhere). It is significant therefore that in 24.29, 'the distress of those days' (i.e., on the assumption of *ex eventu* prophecy, the Judaean war) is to be followed 'immediately' (εὐθέως) by the coming of the Son of Man, whereas in Mark 13.24 it is promised vaguely 'in those days, after that distress'. Normally Matthew edits out (if this is the relationship between them) Mark's

[38] *INT* II, 571.

incessant use of εὐθύς. Never elsewhere does he alter a Markan phrase to εὐθέως.[39] This makes it extraordinarily difficult to believe that Matthew could deliberately be writing for the *interval* between the Jewish war and the *parousia*. So conscious was Harnack[40] of this difficulty that he insisted that the interval could not be extended more than five years (or ten at the very most), thus dating Matthew *c*. 70–5. He would rather believe that Matthew wrote before the fall of Jerusalem than stretch the meaning of εὐθέως further. It seems a curious exercise to stretch it at all! Even E. J. Goodspeed,[41] who put Luke at 90, said of Matthew, 'A book containing such a statement can hardly have been written very long after AD 70' (though his elastic was prepared to extend to 80). The only other way of taking this verse retrospectively is to say that 'the coming of the Son of Man', though *not* 'the consummation of the age', *did* occur with the fall of Jerusalem.[42] But it is a fairly desperate expedient to seek to distinguish these two (joined by Matthew by a single article in 24.3) in face of the usage of the rest of the New Testament.

Finally, Matthew retains unaltered Jesus' solemn pronouncement, 'The present generation will live to see it all' (24.34), preserving also (as the equivalent of Mark 9.1) the saying, 'There are some standing here who will not taste of death before they have seen the Son of Man coming in his kingdom' (16.28). Most notoriously of all, he has, alongside the apocalyptic material from the Markan tradition which he sets in his mission charge, the promise, 'Before you have gone through all the towns of Israel the Son of Man will have come' (10.23).[43] If, on the usual reckoning, the evangelist is writing some 50–60 years after the death of Jesus, it is surely incredible that there are no traces of attempts to explain away or cover up such obviously

39 Though he adds the word, without significant change of sense, in 27.48. B. W. Bacon, 'The Apocalyptic Chapter of the Synoptic Gospels', *JBL* 28, 1909, 2, argued (without a shred of evidence) that εὐθύς could 'easily' have been in the original text of Mark 13.24 – though this would still not explain why Matthew *retained* it.

40 *Chron*., 653f.

41 E. J. Goodspeed, *An Introduction to the New Testament*, Chicago 1937, 176.

42 Cf. A. Feuillet, 'La synthèse eschatologique de saint Matthieu', *RB* 55–6, 1949–50, 340–64, 62–91, 180–211 (especially 351–6); 'Le sens du mot parousie dans l'évangile de Matthieu' in W. D. Davies and D. Daube (edd.), *The Background of the New Testament and its Eschatology: In Honour of C. H. Dodd*, Cambridge 1956, 261–80; Gaston, *No Stone on Another*, 484; also (somewhat differently) France, *Jesus and the OT*, 227–39; and G. B. Caird, *Jesus and the Jewish Nation* (Ethel M. Wood Lecture), 1965.

43 This again could well be a saying which Mark has *omitted* from the common tradition as irrelevant to his Gentile readers.

by then unfulfillable predictions. One would equally expect modifications to prophecies after the non-event.

Indeed, I think that it needs to be asked much more pressingly than it is why warnings and predictions relating to the crisis in Judaea should have been produced or reproduced in such profusion *after* the events to which they referred. Just as Jesus' parables were reapplied to the life of the church and to the *parousia* when their original setting in the crisis of his ministry was no longer relevant,[44] so one might suppose that instructions given, or pointed up, for earlier situations would, if remembered at all afterwards, have become related more timelessly to the End. Alternatively, if subsequent occasion required, they might have been brought out and subjected to recalculation (the way that Jeremiah's unfulfilled prediction of the seventy years' duration of the exile is reapplied 'on reflection' in Dan.9.1–27). But the period of composition commonly assigned to both Matthew and Luke (80–90) was, as far as we know, marked by no crisis for the church that would reawaken the relevance of apocalyptic.[45] I fail to see any motive for preserving, let alone inventing, prophecies long after the dust had settled in Judaea, unless it be to present Jesus as a prognosticator of uncanny accuracy (in which case the evangelists have defeated the exercise by including palpably unfulfilled predictions). It would seem much more likely, as the form critics have taught us to expect, that these sayings, like the rest, were adapted to the use of the church when and as they were relevant to its immediate needs.

There is one other passage common to Matthew and Luke which it will be convenient to mention briefly before turning to Luke. This refers to the murder of Zechariah 'between the sanctuary and the altar'. In Matthew (23.35), but not Luke (11.51), he is called 'son of Berachiah', and this has been held[46] to contain an allusion to the murder by two Zealots 'in the midst of the temple' of a certain Zacharias, son of Baris (v.l., Beriscaeus) in 67–8.[47] But the identification rests on a rather remote resemblance of names, and this Zacharias,

[44] Cf. C. H. Dodd, *The Parables of the Kingdom*, 1935, and J. Jeremias, *The Parables of Jesus*, ET ³1972.

[45] B. H. Streeter, *The Four Gospels*, 1924, 516–23, associated it with the rumours of the return of Nero *redivivus*. But there is no other evidence connecting this myth with the gospel tradition, even if we could date it with certainty (see pp. 245f. below). Moreover Streeter's argument depends on his omission (with the Sinaitic Syriac) of 'standing in the holy place' from Matt.24.15.

[46] E.g. by J. Wellhausen, *Einleitung in die drei ersten Evangelien*, Berlin ²1911, 118–23. To the contrary, Zahn, *INT* II, 589f.

[47] Josephus, *BJ* 4, 334–44.

not being a priest, would have been unlikely to have been 'between the sanctuary and the altar.' On Jesus' lips it makes entirely good sense to interpret the reference, with the Gospel according to the Hebrews,[48] as being to the murder of Zechariah son of Jehoiada the priest (II Chron. 24.20–2), whom Matthew, like some of the rabbis, has evidently confused with Zechariah son of Berechiah, the prophet (Zech. 1.1).[49] In any case it is far too uncertain a piece of evidence to carry any weight by itself.

Finally, then, we turn to Luke. His parallel to the Markan apocalypse must be taken closely with another earlier passage relating to Jerusalem and it will be convenient to set them out together.

> When he came in sight of the city, he wept over it and said, 'If only you had known, on this great day, the way that leads to peace! But no; it is hidden from your sight. For a time will come upon you, when your enemies will set up siege-works against you; they will encircle you and hem you in at every point; they will bring you to the ground, you and your children within your walls, and not leave you one stone standing on another, because you did not recognize God's moment when it came' (19.41–4).

> But when you see Jerusalem encircled by armies, then you may be sure that her destruction is near. Then those who are in Judaea must take to the hills; those who are in the city itself must leave it, and those who are out in the country must not enter; because this is the time of retribution, when all that stands written is to be fulfilled. Alas for women who are with child in those days, or have children at the breast! For there will be great distress in the land and a terrible judgment upon this people. They will fall at the sword's point; they will be carried captive into all countries; and Jerusalem will be trampled down by foreigners until their day has run its course (21.20–4).

The latter passage replaces, and at some points echoes, that in Mark 13.14–20 beginning, 'But when you see "the abomination of desolation" . . .'. Its relation to it must be considered shortly. But first let us look at what Luke himself actually says.

At first sight it seems clearly to be composed (or at any rate pointed up) in the light of the siege of 68–70. For here indeed is the greater specification we expect but fail to find in Matthew. The details, says Kümmel, 'correspond exactly to the descriptions which contemporary accounts offer of the action of Titus against Jerusalem'.[50]

[48] According to Jerome, *in Matt.* 23.35.

[49] So e.g. A. H. McNeile, *St Matthew*, 1915; J. M. Creed, *St Luke*, 1930; H. St J. Thackeray, *Josephus*, Loeb Classical Library, 1928, *ad locc.*

[50] *INT*, 150. Similarly, among many others, R. Bultmann, *The History of the Synoptic Tradition*, ET Oxford 1963, 123.

Yet this is far from indisputable. In an article[51] written now thirty years ago but strangely neglected, Dodd argued strongly and circumstantially that no such inference could be drawn.

> These operations are no more than the regular commonplaces of ancient warfare. In Josephus's account of the Roman capture of Jerusalem there are some features which are more distinctive; such as the fantastic faction-fighting which continued all through the siege, the horrors of pestilence and famine (including cannibalism), and finally the conflagration in which the Temple and a large part of the city perished. It is these that caught the imagination of Josephus, and, we may suppose, of any other witness of these events. Nothing is said of them here. On the other hand, among all the barbarities which Josephus reports, he does not say that the conquerors dashed children to the ground.[52] The expression *ἐδαφιοῦσίν σε καὶ τὰ τέκνα σοῦ ἐν σοί* is in any case not based on anything that happened in 66–70: it is a commonplace of Hebrew prophecy.[53]

Dodd then proceeds to show in detail how all the language used by Luke or his source is drawn not from recent events but from a mind soaked in the Septuagint.

> So far as any historical event has coloured the picture, it is not Titus's capture of Jerusalem in AD 70, but Nebuchadrezzar's capture in 586 BC. There is no single trait of the forecast which cannot be documented directly out of the Old Testament.[54]

It has justly been said that if this article had appeared in the *Journal of Theological Studies* rather than the *Journal of Roman Studies* New Testament scholars would have taken more notice of it. It is still ignored in Kümmel's extensive bibliography, and no recognition is given to the case it argues. Interestingly, it had no influence on Reicke's article cited above,[55] which independently reaches much the same position.

But the absence of any clear reference to 70 does not settle the question of what Luke is doing in relation to the Markan material. Indeed on this Dodd and Reicke come to opposite conclusions. Reicke, with the majority of critics, thinks that Luke 21.20–4 is an editing of Mark: Dodd holds that it is independent tradition into

[51] C. H. Dodd, 'The Fall of Jerusalem and the "Abomination of Desolation" ', *JRS* 37, 1947, 47–54; reprinted in his *More New Testament Studies*, Manchester 1968, 69–83.

[52] The youths under the age of seventeen were sold into slavery (*BJ* 6.418).

[53] Op. cit., 49f. (74f.).

[54] Ibid., 52 (79). Cf. earlier (though Dodd does not refer to it) C. C. Torrey, *The Composition and Date of Acts* (Harvard Theological Studies, I), Cambridge, Mass., 1916, 69f., who concludes: 'Every particle of Luke's prediction not provided by Mark was furnished by familiar and oft-quoted Old Testament passages.'

[55] Though it is cited with approval by Pedersen, *ST* 19, 168.

which the evangelist has simply inserted *verbatim* two phrases from Mark: 'Then those who are in Judaea must take to the hills' (21.21a) and 'Alas for women who are with child in those days, or who have children at the breast!' (21.23a).[56] The latter alternative seems to me the more probable,[57] if only because the introduction of 'Judaea' in 21.21a upsets the reference of ἐν μέσῳ αὐτῆς in 21b, which must be to Jerusalem (the αὐτῆς of 21.20). But, whether or not this was material which Luke had prior to his use of the Markan tradition, he has clearly now united the two. Is the effect of their combination to suggest or to require a later date?

Luke has preferred to concentrate on the destruction of the city rather than the temple, the last reference, veiled or unveiled, to the sanctuary having disappeared, *despite* his retention of the opening question about the fate of the temple buildings (21.5–7).[58] The answer therefore is even less precise, though there is now a definite reference to devastation and not simply to desecration. Reicke indeed argues that by replacing Mark's 'abomination of desolation standing where he ought not' with 'Jerusalem surrounded by armies' Luke actually makes it more certain that he is *not* writing after the event. For

> if the Gospel of Luke is supposed to have been composed after the historical siege of Jerusalem in AD 70, the evangelist must be accused of incredible confusion when he spoke of flight during that siege, although the Christians were known to have left Judaea some time before the war even began in AD 66.[59]

The last clause goes beyond the evidence, for Luke may not have known it. Nevertheless the point stands against a *vaticinium ex eventu.* Things did not in fact turn out like that. Indeed they could not, for there was no escaping once the city had been encircled.

But the saying about getting out and not going back in, which in Luke 21.21 is applied to the *city*, has probably nothing in origin to do with a siege. In Mark and Matthew it relates to a man's house, as in the closely parallel saying which Luke himself preserves in 17.31:

[56] In 21.20 the reference to the 'desolation' of Jerusalem derives, Dodd argues, not from Mark (and Daniel) but from the frequent use of the word in this context by Jeremiah.

[57] Cf. my *Jesus and His Coming*, 1957, 122–4. Similarly T. W. Manson, *The Sayings of Jesus*, 1949, 328–37; Taylor, *Mark*, 512; Gaston, op. cit., 358.

[58] Luke broadens the audience ('some people were saying') but not, like Matthew, the question.

[59] 'Synoptic Prophecies', 127.

On that day the man who is on the roof and his belongings in the house must not come down to pick them up; he, too, who is in the fields must not go back.

As when Mattathias and his sons 'took to the hills, leaving all their belongings behind in the town', the context seems more likely to be local harassment than a military siege. If, as is entirely possible, Jesus himself did utter some such urgent exhortations to vigilance and rapid response,[60] they were almost certainly independent of any programme of future events. If subsequently they were incorporated by the church into instructions for Christians in Judaea and combined with other words of his about the desolation of the city,[61] this does not mean that they were edited after or even during the war. In fact there is nothing that requires them to be restricted to the events of the latter 60s. The 'wars and rumours of wars' between nations (ἔθνος ἐπ' ἔθνος) and kingdoms (Mark 13.7f. and pars) have no obvious reference to Vespasian's campaign against the Jewish extremists.[62] In Luke this is 'wars and insurrections' (ἀκαταστασίας) (21.9). The latter word appears here to have the same meaning as στάσις, which is used by Luke (23.19, 25), as by Mark (15.7), of the Barabbas incident, and in the context (cf. Luke 21.8) seems to refer to risings led by messianic pretenders, such as he also records from the 40s and 50s in Acts (5.36f.; 21.38).[63] There is no ground for assuming that he is alluding specifically to *the* Jewish revolt of 66–70, let alone writing after it.

None of this in itself decides the issue of when the synoptic gospels were written. In fact, despite the arguments he puts forward, Dodd (followed by Gaston and Houston) thinks that Luke and Matthew were composed after 70. Reicke, although regarding Luke 21 as secondary to Mark, concludes that 'Matthew, Mark and Luke wrote their Gospels before the war began'.[64] That issue must be considered in due course on its own merits. The one conclusion we can draw so far is to agree with Reicke's opening statement that it is indeed 'an amazing example of uncritical dogmatism' that 'the synoptic gospels should be dated after the Jewish War of AD 66–70 *because* they contain prophecies *ex eventu* of the destruction of Jerusalem'. Indeed

[60] Cf. the whole of Luke 17.20–37; also 12.35–13.9; Mark 13.33–6; Matt. 24.37–25.30.

[61] Cf. Matt. 23.37–9 = Luke 13.34f. Without Mark's story of the widow's mite, Matthew makes this saying lead directly into the programme of ch. 24.

[62] Cf. Reicke, op. cit., 130f., who instances rather the wars of Rome against the Parthians in 36 and 55 which inspired the Jewish nationalists to violent activities.

[63] στάσις refers also, of course, to purely civil disturbances (Acts 19.40; 23.10; 24.5), as presumably do the ἀκαταστασίαι of II Cor. 6.5.

[64] Op. cit., 133.

on these grounds alone one might reverse the burden of proof, and re-issue Torrey's challenge, which he contended was never taken up:[65]

> It is perhaps conceivable that *one* evangelist writing after the year 70 might fail to allude to the *destruction of the temple* by the Roman armies (every reader of the Hebrew Bible knew that the Prophets had definitely predicted that foreign armies would surround the city and destroy it), but that *three* (or four) should thus fail is quite incredible.[66] On the contrary, what is shown is that all four Gospels were written *before* the year 70. And indeed, there is no evidence of any sort that will bear examination tending to show that any of the Gospels were written later than about the middle of the century. The challenge to scholars to produce such evidence is hereby presented.

But before we can even consider that piece of bravado it is necessary to establish some sort of scale of measurement by which the progress of affairs in the Christian church 'about the middle of the century' can be assessed. And the best, indeed the only, way of discovering any fixed points is to turn to the evidence provided by the life and writings of Paul.

[65] C. C. Torrey, *The Apocalypse of John*, New Haven, Conn., 1958, 86, quoting his earlier book, *The Four Gospels*, New York [2]1947.

[66] Wink, *USQR* 26, 48, poses a similar question to Brandon who wishes to put Mark after 70: 'Is it really conceivable that Mark should fail to mention, even by allusion in a single instance, an event so traumatic that it is alleged to be the sole motification for his undertaking to write his gospel?'

III

The Pauline Epistles

'ON THE SUBJECT of the chronology of St Paul's life originality is out of the question.' So Lightfoot began his lectures at Cambridge in 1863.[1] It might seem a discouraging start to any re-examination. In fact it is not strictly true. Since then there has been at least one find of major importance for fixing the chronology of St Paul, the discovery of an inscription at Delphi, published in 1905, which enables us to date fairly accurately Gallio's proconsulship of Achaia (Acts 18.12). It has had the effect of shifting Lightfoot's dates a couple of years or so earlier. Moreover, there has been at least one highly original reconstruction of the sequence of events, John Knox's *Chapters in a Life of Paul*[2] – which, ironically, brushes aside the new

[1] J. B. Lightfoot, 'The Chronology of St Paul's Life and Epistles', *Biblical Essays*, 1893, 215–33. It is remarkable that of the more than 700 pages of Harnack's *Chronologie* only 7 (233–9) are devoted to the life and letters of Paul, most of which are spent in trying (unsuccessfully I believe) to fix the date of Festus' accession. Other surveys include: Zahn, *INT* III, 450–80; C. H. Turner, 'Chronology of the New Testament: II. The Apostolic Age', *HDB* I, 415–25; M. Goguel, 'Essai sur la chronologie Paulinienne', *RHR* 65, 1912, 285–359; D. Plooij, *De chronologie van het leven van Paulus*, Leiden 1918; K. Lake, 'The Chronology of Acts' in F. J. Foakes Jackson and K. Lake (edd.), *The Beginnings of Christianity*, 1920–33 (hereafter *Beginnings*), V, 445–74; G. B. Caird, 'The Chronology of the New Testament: B. The Apostolic Age', *IDB* I, 603–7; G. Ogg, *The Chronology of the Life of Paul*, 1968 (with a bibliography to date); J. J. Gunther, *Paul: Messenger and Exile: A Study in the Chronology of his Life and Letters*, Valley Forge, Pa., 1972.

[2] John Knox, *Chapters in a Life of Paul*, New York 1950. Knox's work has been followed up by J. C. Hurd, 'Pauline Chronology and Pauline Theology' in W. R. Farmer, C. F. D. Moule, R. R. Niebuhr (edd.), *Christian History and Interpretation: Studies Presented to John Knox*, Cambridge 1967, 225–48; and C. Buck and G. Taylor, *St Paul: A Study of the Development of his Thought*, New York 1969.

piece of evidence.[3] Yet the relative fixity of the Pauline datings remains. If we ignore eccentric solutions and the penumbra of disputed epistles, one can say that there is a very general consensus on the dating of the central section of St Paul's ministry and literary career, with a margin of difference of scarcely more than two years either way. This is nowhere near the case with any other part of the New Testament – the gospels, the Acts, the other epistles, the Apocalypse. The Pauline epistles constitute therefore an important fixed point and yardstick, not only of absolute chronology but of relative span, against which to measure other developments.

Having said this, however, it is important to remember Lightfoot's other preliminary warning: 'It may be as well to premise at the outset that as regards the exact dates in St Paul's life absolute certainty is unattainable.'[4] There is not only a margin of disagreement but a margin of error to be allowed for. I shall be giving a number of fairly precise-sounding dates, which on balance seem to me the most probable. But the reader should be warned that they are always more specific than the evidence warrants. A shift of a year or two in either direction – and sometimes more – is entirely possible, without the over-all position being affected. Mention may be made in advance of a number of factors[5] which cause uncertainty and allow room for genuine difference of judgment even when (as is rarely the case) the evidence itself is fairly hard.

1. The sources, Roman, Jewish and Christian, are largely uncoordinated and share no common canon of chronology such as is presupposed by any modern historian. The evidence, for instance, from Tacitus, Josephus and Acts has to be set together from different systems of time measurement and then reduced to our (quite arbitrary) BC and AD.

2. The actual calendar years begin at a bewilderingly different number of points – e.g. (ignoring internal changes with periods and places) the Jewish in the spring, the Macedonian (which was spread to the Greek-speaking world by the conquests of Alexander the Great) in the autumn, the Julian (the official calendar of the Roman empire and still ours today) in midwinter. (The same applies to the time the day was reckoned to begin, but this is not so relevant to the epistles as to the gospels.)

[3] Or rather he locates it in Paul's last visit to Corinth, not (as Acts says) his first. Buck and Taylor do the same.

[4] Ibid.

[5] For further discussion of these factors, which of course affect much more than this chapter, cf. Finegan, *HBC*.

3. Dates are designated not by the calendar but by the year of office of some king or official. This does not, of course, usually commence neatly with the calendar year. There is the additional uncertainty whether the 'first' year of, say a particular emperor is the residue of that year from the day of his accession (assuming, too, that that follows immediately on the demise of his predecessor) or whether it is counted from the next new year's day. For instance, is what we call AD 55 the second or the first year of Nero, who was proclaimed emperor on 13 October 54?

4. When we are dealing with intervals, there is the uncertainty whether the reckoning is inclusive (with parts of the day or year being counted as wholes) or exclusive. For instance, 'on the third day' (Matt. 16.21; Luke 9.22; I Cor. 15.4) in all probability means the *same* as 'after three days' (Mark 8.31), whereas we should say it was 'after two days'. The question arises which usage a particular New Testament writer (e.g. Paul or Luke) is following.

With such latitude it is obviously possible, by taking all the doubtful decisions one way, to interpret the same piece of evidence to yield a rather different date from that which would be obtained by taking them all the other way. And when the evidence itself is doubtful or patient of more than one meaning, the divergence can be still greater. Thus it is fairly easy to expand or contract intervals to suit the requirements of a particular theory. Ultimately dating is almost always a matter of assessing the balance of probabilities.

There is one further methodological decision which is of great importance in this area, namely, the credence to be given to the evidence of Acts in relation to that of Paul. There can be no dispute that Paul writing in his own name is the primary witness, and the author of Acts, whom for convenience we shall call Luke (the date and authorship of Acts will occupy us in the next chapter), a secondary witness. When they conflict we are bound to prefer Paul. But most of the time they do not conflict. Indeed Kümmel, who does not think Acts could have been written by a companion of Paul,[6] says nevertheless that

> the sequence of Paul's missionary activities that can be inferred from his letters is so remarkably compatible with the information from Acts that we have good grounds for deriving the relative chronology of Paul's activity from a critical combination of the information from Paul's letters with the account in Acts.[7]

So we shall follow the procedure of trusting Acts until proved other-

[6] *INT*, 184.

[7] *INT*, 254, supporting what he calls the convincing proof of T. H. Campbell, 'Paul's "Missionary Journeys" as reflected in his Letters', *JBL* 74, 1955, 80–7.

wise and allow this procedure to be tested by the results it yields.[8]

We must however recognize that Acts itself is very uneven in the chronological details it supplies – and it is not of course primarily interested in being a chronicle but an account of the Spirit in action. Thus there are some stages of Paul's life that are treated very summarily. The longest stay of his career in one place, in Ephesus, which Acts itself says lasted three years (20.31), occupies but a single chapter (19.2–20.1), whereas the period from Paul's final arrival in Jerusalem to the end of his first court-hearing, which lasted just over a fortnight and where the passage of time is detailed very precisely,[9] occupies three and a half chapters (21.17–24.23). We should have no idea from Acts that Paul visited Corinth three times (II Cor. 13.1), the second visit having to be fitted somewhere into the thinly covered Ephesian period. This must make arguments from the silence of Acts very precarious, particularly since Acts never mentions Paul writing a single letter and omits all reference to Titus, one of his most constant emissaries. Furthermore, Luke intersperses detailed datings with vague statements such as 'in those days', 'about that period', 'after some (or many)[10] days' or 'for a time'. At least when he generalizes we know it and may treat the indications of time freely; when he does not we may have the more confidence in him. If he discriminates, so can we.

With these preliminary observations, let us first try to get an outline framework of Paul's life into which we can then fit his letters – though naturally the letters also provide primary evidence for the framework.

[8] For the general relation of Acts to history, cf., among others, W. M. Ramsay, *St Paul the Traveller and the Roman Citizen*, 1920; H. J. Cadbury, *The Book of Acts in History*, New York 1955; E. Trocmé, *Le 'livre des Actes' et l'histoire*, Paris 1957; R. R. Williams, 'Church History in Acts: Is it reliable?' in D. E. Nineham (ed.), *Historicity and Chronology in the New Testament*, 1965, 145–60; R. P. C. Hanson, *Acts* (New Clarendon Bible), Oxford 1967, 2–21; W. W. Gasque, 'The Historical Value of the Book of Acts: An Essay in the History of New Testament Criticism', *EQ* 41, 1969, 68–88; E. Haenchen, *Acts*, ET Oxford 1971, 90–103. For a classical historian's assessment, cf. A. N. Sherwin-White, *Roman Society and Roman Law in the New Testament*, Oxford 1963, 189: 'For Acts the confirmation of historicity is overwhelming. Yet Acts is, in simple terms and judged externally, no less of a propaganda narrative than the Gospels, liable to similar distortions. But any attempt to reject its basic historicity even in matters of detail must now appear absurd. Roman historians have long taken it for granted.'

[9] Acts 21.18 ('next day'); 21.26 ('next day'); 21.27 ('before the period of seven days was up'); 22.30 ('the following day'); 23.11 ('the following night'); 23.12 ('when day broke'); 23.32 ('next day'); 24.1 ('five days later').

[10] The vague and untranslatable ἱκανός is one of his favourite words.

The most reliable fixed point from which we can work both backwards and forwards is supplied by the inscription to which I have already referred. This enables us to date the proconsulship of Gallio in Achaia, before whom, according to Acts 18.12–17, Paul was summoned towards the end of his first visit to Corinth. With increasing certainty we may say that Gallio entered upon his office in the early summer of 51[11] and that Paul appeared before him soon afterwards, probably in May or June.[12] By that time Paul had been in Corinth for at least eighteen months (Acts 18.11) and probably longer – for this period appears to be reckoned from the time of Paul's full-time preaching (18.5) and his residence with Titus Justus (18.7). Prior to that he had lodged and earned a living with Aquila and Priscilla (18.1–4). So his arrival in Corinth is probably to be dated in the autumn of 49. This would fit well with the statement of 18.2 that Aquila 'had recently arrived from Italy because Claudius had issued an edict that all Jews should leave Rome', which is usually dated in 49.[13] To allow for the visits of Acts 15.36–17.34, Paul and Barnabas must have set out from Antioch at least in the early spring of 49. This in turn probably puts the Council of Jerusalem late in 48, allowing for the vaguely defined but apparently quite extensive interval of 15.30–6.

Working backwards from this we find the chronology of Acts, as we might expect, increasingly uncertain. The incidents of 11.27–12.25, introduced by such nebulous time-references as 'during this period' (11.27) and 'about this time' (12.1), appear to be arranged topically rather than chronologically. The famine of 11.27–30 seems to correspond with that recorded by Josephus[14] as coming to its

[11] For the text of the inscription, which reproduces a letter from Claudius to the city of Delphi mentioning Gallio, cf. E. M. Smallwood, *Documents illustrating the Principates of Gaius, Claudius and Nero* (no. 376), Cambridge 1967, 105; or briefly C. K. Barrett, *The New Testament Background: Selected Documents*, 1956, 48f. For the dating, cf. A. Deissmann, *Paul: A Study in Social and Religious History*, ET ²1926, 261–86; Lake, *Beginnings* V, 460–4; Finegan, *HBC*, 316–19; Ogg, op. cit., 104–11; and, for the most recent discussion, A. Plessart, *Fouilles de Delphes* (École Française d'Athènes) III. 4 (nos. 276–350), Paris 1970, 26–32 (especially 31); B. Schwank, 'Der sogenannte Brief an Gallio und die Datierung des 1 Thess.', *BZ* n.f. 15, 1971, 265f.

[12] That the Jews 'tried their luck' (Deissmann, op. cit., 264) with the new proconsul by bringing Paul before him when Gallio had but recently arrived is, however, only a presumption.

[13] On the authority of Orosius, *Hist. adv. pagan.* 7.6.15. For the evidence, which is not as firm as one could wish, cf. Lake, *Beginnings* V, 459f.; Finegan, *HBC*, 319; Ogg, op. cit., 99–103; Bruce, 'Christianity under Claudius', *BJRL* 44, 1961–2, 313–18.

[14] *Ant.* 20.101.

climax in 46 (or perhaps a year earlier or later),[15] whereas the death of Herod Agrippa I, which Luke relates after it (though he does not make Barnabas and Paul return to Antioch till after Herod's death), occurred in 44.[16] If then the famine-relief visit of Paul and Barnabas to Jerusalem in Acts 11.30–12.25 is to be dated *c.* 46, then the first missionary journey described in Acts 13–14 would occupy 47–8,[17] with the controversy and council-meeting of Acts 15 coming later in 48. So far there are no serious problems.

It is when we come to tie up the Acts story with Paul's own statements in Gal. 1–2 that the difficulties begin. There Paul relates two visits to Jerusalem – and two only – to make contact with the apostles. At this point we must give absolute priority to Paul's own account, not merely because he is writing in the first person, whereas Luke is at this stage clearly dependent on sources (and can be shown to be chronologically unreliable), but because Paul is speaking on oath (Gal. 1.20) and any slip or dissimulation on his part would have played into the hands of his opponents. Indeed we may say that the statements of Gal. 1–2 are the most trustworthy historical statements in the entire New Testament.

After first describing his conversion, Paul goes on:

> When that happened, without consulting any human being, without going up to Jerusalem to see those who were apostles before me, I went off at once to Arabia, and afterwards returned to Damascus.
>
> Three years later (ἔπειτα μετὰ τρία ἔτη) I did go up to Jerusalem to get to know Cephas. I stayed with him a fortnight, without seeing any of the other apostles, except James the Lord's brother. What I write is plain truth; before God I am not lying.
>
> Next (ἔπειτα) I went to the regions of Syria and Cilicia, and remained unknown by sight to Christ's congregations in Judaea. . . .
>
> Next, fourteen years later (ἔπειτα διὰ δεκατεσσάρων ἐτῶν), I went again to Jerusalem with Barnabas, taking Titus with us (Gal. 1.17–2.1).

The first question is whether the fourteen years are to be counted

[15] Cf. K. S. Gapp, 'The Universal Famine under Claudius', *HTR* 28, 1935, 258–65; Lake, *Beginnings* V, 454f.; Ogg, op. cit., 49–55; Gunther, op. cit., 36–40. K. F. Nickle, *The Collection: A Study of Paul's Strategy* (SBT 48), 1966, 29–32, puts it as late as 48.

[16] Josephus, *Ant.* 19.350f. We shall have occasion later (p. 113 below) to suggest that Luke may also have run together the arrest of Peter and the death of Herod, the former occurring perhaps two years earlier in 42.

[17] Ogg, op. cit., 58–71, estimates this as lasting *c.* 18 months; but the estimates vary – and are in the last resort only calculated guesses.

from the first visit or from his conversion. There is no way of being certain, but the natural presumption[18] is that Paul is detailing a sequence (ἔπειτα . . . ἔπειτα . . . ἔπειτα – exactly as in I Cor. 15.5–8) and that the two intervals of three years and fourteen years are intended to follow on each other. Moreover, the 'again' of 2.1, if part of the true text (as it surely is), would naturally refer the reader back to the former visit, not to the conversion. No one, I believe, would begin by supposing otherwise, though once the other way of taking it is suggested there is no way of disproving it.

The second question is whether the reckoning is to be regarded as inclusive or exclusive. Again we cannot be sure, but Jewish usage would indicate the former. 'After eight days' in John 20.26 is evidently intended to refer to the following Sunday (not Monday), and is rightly rendered in the NEB 'a week later'. When Paul says he stayed with Peter for fifteen days (Gal. 1.18) the NEB is again surely correct in rendering it 'a fortnight'. So we may begin by assuming that 'after three years' means in the third year following, or what we would call after two years. Similarly, 'with the lapse of (διά, cf. Acts 24.17) fourteen years' probably means thirteen years later.

The third question (and much the most difficult) is which visit of Acts it is to which the visit of Gal. 2.1 corresponds. If it is the second (that of Acts 11), then it must have occurred *c.* 46; if it is the third (that of Acts 15), then it would on our calculation have been in 48. On the assumption that the two intervals are sequential and the reckoning is inclusive, then 13 + 2 from 46 would bring us back to 31 for Paul's conversion; if from 48, then to 33. Though we cannot be absolutely certain, it looks as if the most likely date for the crucifixion is 30[19] – the only serious alternative astronomically and calendrically being 33. Even on the former dating, 31 would be almost impossibly early for Paul's conversion if all the developments of Acts 1–8 are to be accounted for.[20] If then the equation of Gal. 2.1 with Acts 11.30 is preferred, the two intervals *have* to be run concurrently, bringing the date for the conversion to 33. This is the same date as is reached by equating the visits of Gal. 2.1 and Acts 15 if the intervals are non-concurrent. (Of course if the time-reckoning is not inclusive, or the famine was really before the death of Herod in 44, or the crucifixion was in 33, then the equation with the earlier visit is out of the

[18] So Zahn, *INT* III, 452, strongly.

[19] The case is argued in detail and I believe convincingly by A. Strobel, 'Der Termin des Todes Jesu', *ZNW* 51, 1960, 69–101; and independently by Finegan, *HBC*, 285–301. Gunther, op. cit., 19–24, comes to the same conclusion.

[20] Despite Gunther, op. cit., 168f., who however provides no solid grounds for it.

question.) The initial chronological probability must therefore favour identifying the visit of Gal. 2 with the subsequent council visit of Acts 15.

However, before examining the points for and against this, we may pause to look at the equation of the first visits of all recorded in Gal. 1.18–24 and Acts 9.26–30. There is no serious dispute that these must refer to the same occasion, yet it is worth bearing in mind how divergent the accounts are. Luke suggests that Paul went to Jerusalem direct from Damascus after no great interval (Acts 9.20–6), and indeed from Paul's subsequent account of the matter in Acts 22.17 we could gather that he returned to Jerusalem at once. There is no hint of his going off to Arabia or of a two- to three-year gap. Moreover in Gal. 1 he is insistent that he saw *only* Peter and James and remained unknown by sight to the congregations in Judaea. In Acts 9 he is introduced by Barnabas (who is not mentioned in Gal. 1) to the apostles, moves freely about Jerusalem, debating 'openly' with the Greek-speaking Jews; while in 26.20 he says that he turned 'first to the inhabitants of Damascus, and then to Jerusalem and all the country of Judaea' (though Paul himself agrees in Rom. 15.19 that he started his preaching 'from Jerusalem'). Subsequently, according to Acts 9.30 he went to Caesarea and thence direct to Tarsus. According to Gal. 1.21 he went to 'the regions of Syria' – presumably including Antioch – 'and Cilicia'.[21] Acts however says that it was much later (11.25f.) – we should gather a year before the famine visit in 46 – that he was fetched by Barnabas from Tarsus to Antioch. None of these discrepancies is fatal or sufficient ground for not identifying the first visit of Galatians with the first of Acts.[22] As Kirsopp Lake,[23] who holds no particular brief for the reliability of Acts, remarks, 'Their disagreement in descriptions is not really any proof that they do not refer to the same things.' But it is a warning against expecting too much coincidence in the accounts of the later visits or dismissing their equation if we do not find it.

Comparing then the details of Gal. 2 with Acts 11 and 15, what do we find? With Acts 11 the correspondences are not in fact great.[24]

[21] According to Knox, *Chapters*, 85, he also visited Galatia, Macedonia, Greece and Asia (and possibly elsewhere) before going up to Jerusalem – but somehow omitted to mention them!

[22] P. Parker, 'Once More, Acts and Galatians', *JBL* 86, 1967, 179–82, equates the first visit of Galatians with the second of Acts, and D. R. de Lacey, 'Paul in Jerusalem', *NTS* 20, 1973–4, 82–6, the second visit of Galatians with the first of Acts. But neither is convincing.

[23] K. Lake, *The Earlier Epistles of St Paul*, 1911, 273.

[24] For presentations of this case, cf. Ramsay, *St Paul*, 48–60; Lake, *Earlier*

There Paul and Barnabas go up from Antioch to Jerusalem, but they are alone, they meet none of the apostles, only the elders (Acts 11.30; contrast the repeated 'apostles and elders' of 15.2, 4, 6, 22f.), and they are not recorded as having conversations or debate with anyone. Other possible points of convergence are (*a*) that Paul describes himself as having gone up by 'revelation' (Gal. 2.2) and, on the assumption that this means by an inspired utterance (as in I Cor. 14.6, 26), it could be a reference to the prophecy of Agabus (Acts 11.28) which gave rise to the visit; and (*b*) that Gal. 2.10 could refer to the famine relief that occasioned it, *if* Paul's comment on the charge 'remember the poor' is interpreted to mean 'which was the very thing I had made, or was making, it my business to do'. But neither is the obvious translation of the aorist ἐσπούδασα,[25] which would naturally refer to a resolve from that moment on. Moreover, the only other reference to 'the poor' at Jerusalem in Paul's epistles is to the collection towards the close of his ministry (Rom. 15.26). Since we know he wrote to the Galatians about that (I Cor. 16.1), it is natural to take the reference to point forward to it.

With Acts 15 on the other hand, as Lightfoot observed in his extended note on the subject,[26] the correspondences are considerable. There is the same tension between Judaizing Christians and the church at Antioch over the same issue (the requirement of circumcision), with the same persons (Paul, Barnabas, and Titus in Galatians; Paul, Barnabas and 'some others'[27] in Acts) going up from Antioch to Jerusalem, and back, to meet the same people (James, Peter and John in Galatians; James, Peter with the apostles and elders in Acts) with the same essential result (recognition of the non-necessity of circumcision, with corollaries for mutual respect and support). The actual meetings described are indeed different; the one

---

Epistles, 274–97; A. W. F. Blunt, *Galatians*, Oxford 1925, 77–84; Bruce, 'Galatian Problems: 1. Autobiographical Data', *BJRL* 51, 1969, 302–7; Gunther, op. cit., 30–6. For a conspectus of the debate, cf. C. S. C. Williams, *Acts* (Black's NTC), 1957, 24–30; D. Guthrie, *Galatians* (NCB), 1969, 29–37. C. H. Talbert, 'Again: Paul's Visits to Jerusalem', *NovTest* 9, 1967, 26, tabulates seven different possible positions. Though I have come down firmly for one in the text, I am aware of the strength of other alternatives.

[25] E. de W. Burton, *Galatians* (ICC), Edinburgh 1921, 115, argues that it positively excludes this interpretation; but cf. to the contrary D. R. Hall, 'St Paul and Famine Relief: A Study in Galatians 2.10', *ExpT* 82, 1970–71, 309–11.

[26] J. B. Lightfoot, *Galatians*, 1865; [4]1874, 122–7; cf. H. Schlier, *Galater* (KEKNT 7), Göttingen [11]1951, 66–78; Ogg, op. cit., 72–8; Parker, *JBL* 86, 175–9.

[27] As we have seen, for whatever reason, Titus is never mentioned by name in Acts.

is a private consultation, the other a public council, and no attempt should be made to identify the two. Indeed, as Lightfoot pointed out, Paul's own form of expression in Gal. 2.2, 'I laid it before them (αὐτοῖς), but privately to the men of repute', 'implies something beside the private conference'. It is simply that the occasion provided by the gathering of so many church leaders gives the opportunity for confirming previous missionary policy toward Gentiles[28] and planning future division of labour. The differences of emphasis between the two accounts, from inside and outside, are certainly no greater than the divergences between Paul's and Luke's accounts of the first, post-conversion visit, which have not prevented the vast majority of scholars from equating them. Indeed, as Knox,[29] who is certainly not biased towards harmonizing Acts and the epistles, points out, there can be 'little doubt' that Acts 15 and Gal. 2 describe the same occasion, and 'it seems fair to say that no one would have thought of the possible identification' of the visit of Gal. 2 with that of Acts 11 were it not for other difficulties.

For Knox these other difficulties are with 'the usual Pauline chronology' – such as we are following. I am not in fact persuaded of them; but the greatest difficulty for Knox, and therefore the strongest argument for resorting to his reconstruction, turns on another point (the date of Festus' accession) to which we shall come later. Meanwhile there are, of course, very real difficulties for those who (unlike Knox but like myself) wish to fit the visits of Gal. 1–2 into the framework of Acts.

The first is why Paul passes over in apparently damaging silence the second visit described by Acts 11.30–12.25. This has led many to excise this visit as unhistorical or as a doublet in Luke's sources of the visit of Acts 15. But this is an arbitrary way of cutting the knot, for which there is no evidence nor indeed other probability (the two visits are, as we have seen, very different in purpose and detail). The most likely reason for Paul's silence is surely that there was no occasion for him to mention this visit. As Lightfoot succinctly stated it years ago,

> His object is not to enumerate his journeys to Jerusalem, but to define his relations with the Twelve; and on these relations it had no bearing.

Secondly, it is said, Why does not Galatians refer to the decrees of

[28] One of the difficulties in equating Acts 11.30 with Gal. 2.2 is that Paul is not recorded as having begun his preaching to Gentiles until Acts 13. But this could be put down to the silence of Acts; and a combination of 11.20 and 25f. might suggest such activity earlier.

[29] Op. cit., 63.

Acts 15.28f.? One of the corollaries of equating Gal. 2 with Acts 11 is that it is possible to date Galatians *before* the council-visit of 48 and therefore to explain Paul's lack of reference to it. Yet this is not a necessary corollary, and the date of Galatians must be determined, in due course, on its own merits. Indeed, Caird goes so far as to say, 'This rider has done more to discredit than to commend the theory to which it has been attached.'[30] For Paul had no reason to quote the decrees. The decrees presupposed in what they did *not* say (cf. Acts 15.19: 'no irksome restrictions . . . but') the non-necessity of circumcision, on which Paul affirms the concurrence of the Jerusalem apostles (Gal. 2.3). What the decrees *did* say was that when Gentiles and Jews eat together the former must be prepared to make certain concessions to the conscience of the latter. But this is not at issue in Galatians. As Lightfoot put it again,

> The object of the decree was to *relieve* the Gentile Christians from the burden of Jewish observances. It said, 'Concede so much and we will protect you from any further exactions.' The Galatians sought no such protection. They were willing recipients of Judaic rights; and St Paul's object was to show them, not that they need not submit to these burdens against their will, but that they were wrong and sinful in submitting to them.

More explanation indeed is needed for why he does not mention the decrees in I Corinthians and Romans, where he not merely passes them over in silence but actually sets aside the prohibition of eating meat offered to idols (I Cor. 10.25–29; Rom. 14). The answer of course is that the decrees were devised for a local, predominantly Jewish-Christian church situation 'in Antioch, Syria and Cilicia' (Acts 15.23) – not even for Galatia. In a cosmopolitan city like Corinth or Rome, where the conditions in the markets were very different, they were simply no longer practicable. In Galatians the only reference to meals is not to conditions to be observed when Jews and Gentiles eat together, but to their refusal to do so (Gal. 2.11–14). And *that* for Paul was a matter not of concession but of principle, to which the decrees were irrelevant – quite apart from the fact that, as Lightfoot says again,

> by appealing to a decree of a Council held at Jerusalem for sanction on a point on which his own decision as an Apostle was final, he would have made the very concession which his enemies insisted upon.

To sum up, whatever the differences in the accounts – and there is no need to deny or minimize them – I find the case for equating the visits of Gal. 2 and Acts 15 more compelling than any alternative. It

[30] *IDB* I, 606.

also enables us to take the two intervals, 'after three years' and 'after fourteen years', in sequence rather than concurrently. For 33 is certainly a possible date for Paul's conversion – though we are still free to run the intervals together and to put the date later if we wish.[31]

We have now sketched what is at least a credible and coherent chronology of Paul's life up to the time of his appearance before Gallio in 51. After that point it is impossible to tell how long a period Luke intended by the 'some (or many) days' (Acts 18.18) that Paul stayed on in Corinth. But there seems no good reason to stretch it to months.[32] It looks likely that he was back in Antioch by winter, before setting out once more for Asia Minor – after an unspecified delay (18.23) – when travelling again became possible in the spring.

At this point the Acts narrative enters a thin patch. As we have seen, it is not much help for filling in the three years in Ephesus that it itself requires, quite apart from placing the mass of experiences which Paul relates as having occurred to him by the time of writing II Cor. 11.23–27 (though these of course are not to be placed exclusively in the Ephesus period):

> Are they servants of Christ? I am mad to speak like this, but I can outdo them. More overworked than they, scourged more severely, more often imprisoned, many a time face to face with death. Five times the Jews have given me the thirty-nine strokes; three times I have been beaten with rods; once I was stoned; three times I have been shipwrecked, and for twenty-four hours I was adrift on the open sea. I have been constantly on the road, I have met dangers from rivers, dangers from robbers, dangers from my fellow-countrymen, dangers from foreigners, dangers in towns, dangers in the country, dangers at sea, dangers from false friends. I have toiled and drudged, I have often gone without sleep; hungry and thirsty, I have often gone fasting; and I have suffered from cold and exposure.

Then there is the evidence of an additional visit to Corinth and probably to southern Illyricum (or Dalmatia, our Jugoslavia) (Rom. 15.19) before Paul returns to Jerusalem for the last time. Since a chronological sequence of events is lacking, it will be best to see if we can set a *terminus ad quem* for this period and then work backwards.

[31] The upper limit is *c.* 37, if the incident in Acts 9.25 of Paul's escaping from Damascus in a basket is equated, as it must be, with his description of the same thing in II Cor. 11.32f. under 'the commissioner of king Aretas' and *if* this occurred just before his going to Jerusalem two (or three) years after his conversion. For Aretas' reign ended in 39 or 40. But the incident could have come earlier.

[32] With Ramsay, op. cit., xxxiii–iv, and F. F. Bruce, *Acts*, 1954, 377; *New Testament History*, 1969, 301. They make Paul winter in Corinth. But the addition in the Western and Antiochene texts of Acts 18.21 ('I must at all costs keep the approaching feast in Jerusalem'), which makes Paul wish to hasten back in time for Passover (?), is almost certainly secondary.

Unfortunately the evidence is nowhere near so firm for the end of it as it is for the beginning.

The crucial date is when Porcius Festus succeeded Felix as procurator of Judaea (Acts 24.27). This is a fact of Roman history which one might think could be securely established. But unfortunately there is (as yet) no inscription to settle the matter and the testimony of the historians is conflicting and inconclusive. Since, however, much turns on it, it is necessary to examine it in some detail.

There is general agreement that Felix himself had succeeded Cumanus in 52, but Tacitus[33] differs from Josephus[34] in saying that by then Felix had already shared the title of procurator with Cumanus for some time. It is not impossible to harmonize the accounts; but it is agreed that in this matter Josephus is more likely to be right,[35] and this throws our first doubt on the accuracy of Tacitus. Josephus is also clear that Felix was recalled under Nero, who had confirmed him in office on his accession as emperor in 54. Later he records that the Jews of Caesarea sent complaints to Nero about him, and 'he would undoubtedly have paid the penalty for his misdeeds against the Jews had not Nero yielded to the urgent entreaty of Felix's brother Pallas, whom at that time he held in the highest honour'.[36] Now according to Tacitus[37] Pallas fell from office as chief of the imperial treasury at a date that it is possible to calculate as late 55 – though this depends on juggling with discrepancies between Tacitus and Suetonius and is very far from certain.[38] So, it is argued, 55 would be the latest date for the recall of Felix if Pallas was to protect him.

Eusebius, in the Latin version of his *Chronicle* (the Greek original is lost) gives the date of Festus' succession as the second year of Nero, i.e., 56[39] – though in the Armenian version it is put in the last year of Claudius (54), which is impossible if, as Eusebius himself agrees in his *History*,[40] he also served under Nero.

Now, *if* Festus arrived as early as 55, then the phrase in Acts 24.27, 'when two years had passed' (διετίας δὲ πληρωθείσης), must be referred not to Paul's time in prison but to Felix's term of office. For it is agreed

33 *Ann.* 12.54. 34 *Ant.* 20.137; *BJ* 2.247.

35 So Zahn, *INT* III, 470; Lake, *Beginnings* V, 464f.; Ogg. op. cit., 149; Haenchen, *Acts*, 68–70.

36 *Ant.* 20.182. 37 *Ann.* 13.14.

38 Cf. Lake, *Beginnings* V, 466; Ogg, op. cit., 155–8.

39 Ed. A. Schoene, *Eusebii Chronicorum Libri Duo* II, Berlin 1866, 152–5. Harnack, *Chron.*, 238, supporting the date of 56, had to admit 'a little error' of one year on Tacitus' part. For whether Harnack changed his mind on this in favour of a later dating, see below p. 91.

40 *HE* 2.22.1.

that Paul could not possibly have arrived in Jerusalem as early as the summer of 53,[41] having only set out on his third journey, which included two to three years in Ephesus alone, in the spring of 52. But there are difficulties in taking it this way. Assuming the phrase to mean 'when his two years were up', we have to argue, with Haenchen, that Felix had only two years in office, and that therefore, though appointed in 52, he did not arrive till 53 and left again in 55. Certainly we should not get this impression from Josephus, who records a long list of events, which must have occupied a considerable time, while Felix was procurator, not only before but also after Nero's accession in 54.[42] They include (and that not at the beginning of Nero's reign) the rising of the Egyptian, which according to Acts 21.38 already lay in the past (πρὸ τούτων τῶν ἡμέρων) when Paul was first arrested under Felix. Moreover, though the phrase in Acts 24.27 *could* refer to Felix's time in office, it is virtually certain that *Luke* did not intend it to do so, for he has already made Paul congratulate Felix on having administered justice in the province 'for many years' (24.10). In its context too it is much more natural to take it of Paul's stay in prison ('He had high hopes of a bribe from Paul, and for this reason he sent for him very often and talked with him. When two years had passed, Felix was succeeded by Porcius Festus'). Indeed those who want to interpret it the other way have to say that, while Luke thought it applied to Paul, 'this does not exclude the possibility that a source spoke of a two-year term of office for Felix.'[43] Yet here we are in the midst of a very detailed section of Acts where Luke shows no sign of relying on second-hand material. The only other recourse, if one is committed to 55, is to say with Knox[44] that Paul after all *did* arrive two years earlier in 53, and with that abandon the entire chronological framework of Acts (and the Gallio date) and start again without it. It is however somewhat ironical that the pressure to do this should be occasioned by a moment in Paul's career which is mentioned solely by Acts and whose dating is far less certain than the fixed point which Knox discards.[45]

In fact the date 55 rests upon two fairly weak supports. The first is

[41] Harnack had no such problem, as, prior to the discovery of the Gallio inscription, he could simply push all the dates two years earlier.

[42] *Ant.* 20. 148–81; *BJ* 2. 248–70.

[43] Haenchen, *Acts*, 661. It is to be observed how totally hypothetical and insubstantial this statement is.

[44] *Chapters*, 66, 84f.

[45] Cf. the review of Knox by Ogg, 'A New Chronology of Saint Paul's Life', *ExpT* 64, 1952–3, 120–3.

the conclusion that *if* Felix was saved by the intercession of Pallas[46] it must have been before the latter was dismissed from the treasury, assuming that this *was* in 55. But it is far from certain that this was the decisive turning-point. As Caird says,

> It is plain that Nero had always disliked Pallas and intended to dismiss him from the moment he became emperor, so that it is hard to see why Pallas' influence with Nero should have been greater before his dismissal than after it. For Pallas was not disgraced; he was able to make his own terms with Nero, was exempt from the scrutiny normally undergone by retiring Roman officials, and was allowed to keep the vast fortune he had accumulated as secretary of the treasury under Claudius.[47]

Secondly there is the self-conflicting evidence of Eusebius, though it is highly doubtful if he had anything to go on at this point apart from his reading of Josephus.[48] Caird also adopts an ingenious way of accounting for this. In the Armenian version of the *Chronicle* Eusebius puts Festus' arrival in the fourteenth year of Claudius and the tenth of Agrippa II. The former, as we have seen, must be wrong, since Eusebius himself was well aware that Felix was recalled by Nero. But, says Caird,

> It is a mistake which becomes intelligible if we assume that the second figure was the only one that stood in Eusebius' source. Knowing that Agrippa I had died in 44, Eusebius assumed that 45 was the first year of his son, Agrippa II, and therefore identified the tenth year of Agrippa II with 54, the fourteenth of Claudius. Actually, as we know from Josephus (*BJ* 2.284), the beginning of Agrippa's reign was reckoned from Nisan 1, AD 50, so that his tenth year began on Nisan 1, AD 59. There is thus good reason for believing that, according to Eusebius' source, Festus became procurator in the summer of 59.[49]

This would allow him three years in office (59–62), which would match the relatively small space which Josephus devotes to him compared with Felix.[50] The older writers gave him still less, opting for 60, though allowing 59 as entirely possible.[51] 59 is also the date

[46] Schürer, *HJP* I, 466; Zahn, *INT* III, 473; and Ogg, *Chronology*, 158f., are convinced that Josephus is simply mistaken on Pallas.

[47] *IDB* I, 604.

[48] Cf. especially Schürer, 'Zur Chronologie des Lebens Pauli', *ZWT* 41, n.f. 6, 1898, 21–42; *HJP* I, 466.

[49] *IDB* I, 604f. Yet this argument, which goes back to Plooij, *Chronologie*, 60f., and behind him to K. Erbes, 'Die Todestage der Apostel Paulus und Petrus und ihre römischen Denkmäler', TU 19. 1, Leipzig 1899, 27, was already criticized by Lake, *Beginnings* V, 472, on the ground that the shift in years should apply not only to the date of Festus' appointment but also to that of Felix. But this would bring forward the latter into the reign of Nero, which is impossible.

[50] *Ant.* 20.182–96; *BJ* 2.271.

[51] Lightfoot, *Biblical Essays*, 217–20; Schürer, *HJP* I, 466; Zahn, *INT* III, 469–78. Ogg, op. cit., 160–70, indeed puts it as late as 61.

favoured by a number of scholars[52] on the grounds that a new issue of provincial coinage for Judaea in the fifth year of Nero may point to a change of procuratorship before October 59.[53] Yet this inference is very far from certain.[54]

From the external evidence the conclusion must be that no firm date can be given.[55] 59 seems as likely as any other, putting Paul's arrival in Jerusalem at 57. But the actual date must be decided, if we can, from what the New Testament story itself requires. What is methodologically unsound on the evidence before us is to fix an upper limit (as we can fix the lower with a reasonable degree of confidence) and then adjust the material to this Procrustean bed. So, with the ends open, let us then return to the longest and most important stretch of Paul's work represented by what Acts depicts as the third missionary journey.

We left him setting out again for Asia Minor in all probability in the spring of 52 (18.23).[56] Confining ourselves first to the Acts outline, we should conclude that he arrived at Ephesus (19.1), say, in the late summer of 52. He based his teaching on the synagogue there for three months (19.8) before withdrawing his converts and starting daily discussions in the lecture-hall of Tyrannus, which went on for the next two years (19.10). This would bring us, on our chronology, nearly to the end of 54. There is then an undated incident (19.13–20), followed by a typically vague Lukan time-reference:

> When things had reached this stage (ὡς δὲ ἐπληρώθη ταῦτα) Paul made up his mind to visit Macedonia and Achaia and then go on to Jerusalem; and he said, 'After I have been there, I must see Rome also'. So he sent two of his assistants, Timothy and Erastus, to Macedonia, while he himself stayed some time longer (χρόνον) in the province of Asia (19.21f.).

[52] A. R. S. Kennedy, 'Palestinian Numismatics', *Palestine Exploration Fund Quarterly*, 1914, 198; Ramsay, *St Paul*, xiv–xx; Cadbury, *Acts in History*, 10; Bruce, *NT History*, 327; Gunther, *Paul*, 140f. Goguel and Plooij also opt for 59.

[53] Cf. F. W. Madden, *History of Jewish Coinage*, 1864, 153. A. Reifenberg, *Ancient Jewish Coins*, Jerusalem ²1947, 27, supports this.

[54] Pilate became procurator in 26 and as far as we know issued no new coins till 29/30 (Madden, op. cit., 147–9). This point is made by Haenchen, *Acts*, 71, and Ogg, op. cit., 170.

[55] This was also the outcome of Turner's very careful investigation (*HDB* I, 417–20). He opted for 58. But he wrote before the Gallio date was fixed.

[56] Ogg, op. cit., 132–4, 'assumes' (!) that Paul was ill for the whole of 52 and did not set out till June 53. He then has him spend more than a year in Galatia, reaching Ephesus only in the autumn of 54. But Ogg has an interest in stretching the chronology, as we shall see later that Barrett has an interest in contracting it. There is no objective evidence from Acts – or the epistles – for such a long-drawn-out progress.

This is followed by the story of the silversmiths' riot (19.23–41), introduced by the words 'about that time'. This is the same formula used in 12.1 of Herod's action against James and Peter, which we have already had reason to think is misplaced in relation to the famine visit. All we can say therefore is that the riot probably took place towards the end of Paul's stay in Ephesus, perhaps in the first half of 55. In any case further time must be allowed for the dispatch (with the coming of spring?) of Timothy and Erastus to Macedonia and for Paul's continued stay in Asia, which would bring us naturally to the early summer of 55. This would fit very well with Paul's assertion to the Ephesian elders at Miletus (20.31) that 'for three years, night and day' he had not ceased to have the most intimate contact with them.

Then, to round off the Acts story as far as Jerusalem, we will follow him from Ephesus:

> When the disturbance had ceased, Paul sent for the disciples and, after encouraging them, said good-bye, and set out on his journey to Macedonia. He travelled through those parts of the country, often speaking words of encouragement to the Christians there, and so came into Greece. When he had spent three months there and was on the point of embarking for Syria, a plot was laid against him by the Jews, so he decided to return by way of Macedonia (20.1–4).

He set sail from Philippi after the Passover season (20.6), making all speed so as 'to be in Jerusalem, if he possibly could, on the day of Pentecost' (20.16) – and there is no reason to suppose that he did not achieve his object.

For the journey from Philippi onwards we are in a narrative recounted by Luke in the first person plural (20.6–21.18) and the notes of time are characteristically precise. But prior to that there is no indication of time apart from the three months' stay in Greece (i.e., Achaia). From Acts alone there would be nothing to suggest that if Paul left Ephesus for Macedonia in the summer of 55 he should not have reached Corinth by the end of that same year, left the following March, and arrived in Jerusalem in May 56.

But at this point we must turn to the evidence of Paul himself, and in particular that of the Corinthian correspondence which covers much of this period.

First it is important to notice how it confirms as well as supplements (and stretches) the Acts framework. In II Cor. 1.19 Paul speaks to the Corinthians of the gospel which he had originally proclaimed to them, adding 'by Silvanus and Timothy, I mean, as well as myself'. This strikingly confirms Acts 18.5 when Silas (Silvanus) and Timothy join Paul in preaching at Corinth for eighteen months on his first visit to the city. It is significant too that Paul does not mention Apollos in this connection, who according to Acts 18.20–19.1 arrived in Corinth only after Paul's first visit. II Cor. 11.7–9 taken with I Thess. 2.2; II Thess. 3.1, 6; and Phil. 4.15f. also confirm the sequence of Acts 16.12–18, viz. Philippi, Thessalonica, Athens, Corinth.[57]

Paul himself also speaks of his intention to revisit Corinth *via* Macedonia, having already sent Timothy ahead to prepare the way; and the details and timing again fit well with the plan outlined in Acts 19.21f. In I Cor. 16.5–11 he says:

> I shall come to Corinth after passing through Macedonia – for I am travelling by way of Macedonia – and I may stay with you, perhaps even for the whole winter, and then you can help me on my way wherever I go next. I do not want this to be a flying visit; I hope to spend some time with you, if the Lord permits. But I shall remain at Ephesus until Whitsuntide, for a great opportunity has opened for effective work, and there is much opposition.
>
> If Timothy comes, see that you put him at his ease; for it is the Lord's work that he is engaged upon, as I am myself; so no one must slight him. Send him happily on his way to join me, since I am waiting for him with our friends.

Earlier Paul had made it clear that he had planned for Timothy to go as far as Corinth, and he promised: 'I shall come very soon, if the Lord will' (4.17–19). At this stage he had evidently not finally decided whether to accompany the bearers of the collection to Jerusalem himself: 'If it should seem worth while for me to go as well, they shall go with me' (16.3f.); and he leaves his further destination open: 'You can help me on my way wherever I go next' (16.6). Indeed there is a tentativeness about his plans ('If the Lord permits', 'if the Lord will') which suggests that in Acts 19.21f. Luke is summarizing in the light of subsequent events. Nevertheless there can be little doubt that I Corinthians was written in the spring of Paul's last year in Ephesus, round about Easter-time, which the references to Passover in 5.7f. would support:

> The old leaven of corruption is working among you. Purge it out, and then you will be bread of a new baking, as it were unleavened Passover bread. For indeed our Passover has begun; the sacrifice is offered – Christ himself. So we who observe the festival must not use the old leaven, the leaven of corruption and wickedness, but only the unleavened bread which is sincerity and truth.

Paul plans to stay on in Ephesus till Pentecost in the early summer, by which time Timothy should be back to report on the situation he has found. So far all is straightforward.

Then the upsets begin. For some reason or other (perhaps because of Timothy's report) Paul apparently changed his original plan, and

[57] Cf. Campbell, *JBL* 74, 82f.

then later went back on the second – though the details are far from certain.[58] In II Cor. 1.15f. he says,

> I had intended to come first of all to you[59] and give you the benefit of a double visit. I meant to visit you on my way to Macedonia, and after leaving Macedonia, to return to you, and you would then send me on my way to Judaea.

In other words, instead of going to Corinth *via* Macedonia (as proposed in I Cor. 16.5) he had decided to go to Corinth direct (by sea), then do his work in Macedonia, and return to Corinth (by land) *en route* for Jerusalem, which was by that stage fixed in his mind as his next destination. It is fairly clear that he did pay the first of these two visits (his second in all), since in II Cor. 12.14 and 13.1f. he speaks of his second visit and says that his next will be his third. It is also clear that he abandoned the plan to come straight back to Corinth after his work in Macedonia. 'It was out of consideration to you', he says in II Cor. 1.23, 'that I did not come again[60] to Corinth'; for, he explains later, 'I made up my mind that my next visit to you must not be another painful one' (2.1). In place of the visit he wrote them a letter, 'out of great distress and anxiety' (II Cor. 2.3), which, he says, he does not now regret, even though he may have done so (7.8).[61] It is not clear from where he wrote the letter, but evidently it had been sent *via* Titus, whose report on its effect Paul awaited anxiously (2.13). By that time he was in the Troad (*τὴν Τρῳάδα*, not simply Troas), in north-west Asia minor (2.12). How he got there – *via* Macedonia, as planned, or from Ephesus – we do not know. He went there to preach the gospel, and a considerable opening beckoned him, but because he could find no relief of mind he 'took leave of the people there and went off to Macedonia' (2.13). This appears to be the departure, however spun out, that Acts refers to in 20.1, though of course Acts records no intermediate visit to Corinth. By that time it must have been autumn at least, and it has been convincingly

[58] The best recent discussion is by C. K. Barrett, *II Corinthians* (Black's NTC), 1973, introduction and *ad locc.* I find his general solution convincing, though his time-table intolerably constricted.

[59] It could mean 'I had originally intended to come to you' (NEB margin), but this would not explain the double visit.

[60] *οὐκέτι*. The NEB's 'after all' suggests that he never paid the visit at all, which is contradicted by II Cor. 13.2.

[61] Lightfoot and earlier commentators identified this letter with I Corinthians, but it is almost universally agreed that it does not fit its tone. Lightfoot indeed put the second visit to Corinth in Paul's first year at Ephesus, prior even to the 'previous letter' mentioned in I Cor. 5.9 (*Biblical Essays*, 222). But then it is surely incredible that this visit should have left no trace in I Corinthians.

suggested[62] that Paul waited at Troas for as long as there was hope that Titus might still arrive there by boat from Corinth. When winter put an end to shipping across the Aegean it was clear that he would be coming by land. So Paul set out to meet him. Yet, he says,

> Even when we reached Macedonia there was still no relief for this poor body of ours: instead, there was trouble at every turn, quarrels all round us, forebodings in our heart (7.5).

Eventually, however, Titus did arrive, and with joyful news (7.6f.), which made Paul write off to Corinth again from Macedonia (9.2). He sent Titus back (8.6, 17), presumably with the letter and certainly with two other 'brothers' (8.18–24), to complete the collection which earlier he had initiated (8.6) and which Paul had told the Macedonians was ready (as it should have been) 'last year' (8.10; 9.2). Clearly by now we are in the year following the instructions which Paul had given concerning this in I Cor. 16.1–3 – and there seems little point in seeking to argue (with Barrett) that, since the new year (in all probability on Paul's calendar) began in the autumn, II Corinthians could have been written in the October of what to us is the same year (55). Rather, Paul appears to be writing in the first part of 56. And he promises to come again himself when time has been given for the collection to be prepared (9.4f.).

It remains to ask whether he fulfilled this promise at once or after yet further delay. This depends on the relation we believe II Cor. 10–13 to bear to II Cor. 1–9. Many have felt that its tone is so different that the two sections cannot form continuous parts of the same letter. It has often indeed been suggested with much plausibility that chs. 10–13 are a part of the severe or sorrowful letter which Paul sent earlier. Yet in 12.14 and 13.1 he says in no uncertain terms that he is intending to visit the Corinthians, whereas the earlier letter had explained why he was not coming (2.3). Moreover, it looks as if the reference in 12.17, 'I begged Titus to visit you and I sent our brother with him', must be to the same mission mentioned in 8.17–24. The only question is whether in each case the aorist is an epistolatory aorist (meaning 'I am sending') or whether (as the NEB takes it) in the second passage Paul is now looking back, in a separate and subsequent letter, on this previous mission. In this case we have to assume, with Barrett,[63] that there was further trouble and that Paul writes yet again, threatening this time to come and deal with the situation unsparingly (13.2, 10). There is no need for us here to

[62] W. L. Knox, *St Paul and the Church of the Gentiles*, Cambridge 1939, 144; Bruce, *NT History*, 315.

[63] So too, Bruce, *I and II Corinthians* (NCB), 1971, 166–70.

decide this question. But if we do posit an interval between the two sections of II Corinthians, then the second part must come from yet later in 56. It becomes the more incredible that everything can be fitted into the previous year, if Paul is to have three months in Achaia before leaving for Jerusalem in March. It appears far more likely that most of 56 was spent in Macedonia and 'those parts' (Acts 20.1) and that this was also the occasion when, as he reports in Romans, Paul 'completed the preaching of the gospel . . . as far round as Illyricum' (Rom. 15.19). For 'now', he says, he has no further scope in these parts (Rom. 15.23) and can thus press on beyond, as previously he had hoped to do (II Cor. 10.15f.). But first he must go to Corinth to 'finish the business' of the collection before delivering it under his own seal to Jerusalem (Rom. 15.28). Even then he was prevented by a plot of his Jewish opponents from sailing direct (Acts 20.3), but accompanied by the delegates of the congregations (Acts 20.4; cf. II Cor. 8.18–24) he set off once more through Macedonia.

It looks therefore as if we should allow a further year for Paul's final preparations than the bare summary of Acts 20.2 would suggest.[64] He writes to the Romans in 15.22 that he has been 'prevented all this time' from coming to them, and certainly he would appear to have run up against frustrating delays and changes of plan of which Acts gives no hint. Only when the Acts narrative once again supplies a detailed time-table, as it does from 20.6 to the end, may we safely assume that there are no substantial gaps.

If then we may conclude that Paul probably arrived in Jerusalem for the last time at the end of May 57, the next period of his career is fairly certain. Matters came rapidly to a head. Within twelve days (Acts 24.11), or a little longer,[65] he had been arrested, tried, and remanded in jail at Caesarea, where he was to stay for two years (24.23–27) till the arrival of the new procurator provided occasion for his case to be reopened. As we saw earlier, the date of this cannot be fixed with certainty from the external sources, but the possible, if not probable, date of 59 fits precisely. Within a fortnight of Festus taking up his appointment (25.1, 6) Paul is in court again and, threatened with being returned to Jerusalem, makes his dramatic appeal to Caesar (25.9–12). A further appearance before Agrippa and Bernice follows, after an interval of 'some days' (25.13f., 23). There is no precise indication of when Paul was finally put on board for Italy (27.1), but evidently it was (as we should expect) in the late

[64] Plooij, Ogg and Bruce agree.

[65] See n. 9 above.

summer. 'Much time' had already been lost by the time they were in Crete (27.9) and with the equinoctial gales the 'danger season' for sailing had begun (September 14–November 11).[66] Indeed 'even (*kai*) the Fast' (i.e. the Day of Atonement) had passed – or the Fast 'as well' as the equinox (September 23 or 24), which was reckoned to be the last safe day for shipping.[67] It has convincingly been argued that this may also afford some confirmation of the year.[68] For there would have been no point in this further time-reference if the Day of Atonement was not late that year or at any rate later than the equinox. Of the years in question only 59 really fits, when it fell on October 5.[69] Moreover unless they did not leave Crete till well into October, taking something over a fortnight (27.13–28.1) to reach Malta in November, a three months' stay in Malta (?November, December, January) would not have been sufficient to see the winter out. Even so it is difficult to stretch it to March 10, when Vegetius says the seas opened,[70] though Pliny allows that sailing could start from February 8.[71] In any case 'after three months' (28.11) must be taken to mean what it means for us and not 'after two months' – and this may provide a key to Luke's usage in similar statements of interval when we are in no position to check him (e.g. 24.1; 25.1; 28.13, 17). A further two to three weeks were to see them in Rome. There, from the spring of 60 to the spring of 62, Paul spent two full years (28.30) under open arrest. Beyond that we cannot go with any certainty, though we shall return to the discussion later.[72]

At this point we may summarize our conclusions about the outline of Paul's career, remembering that the absolute datings cannot be more than approximate:

33	Conversion
35	First visit to Jerusalem
46	Second (famine-relief) visit to Jerusalem
47–8	First missionary journey
48	Council of Jerusalem
49–51	Second missionary journey

[66] Vegetius, *De rei milit.* 4. 39.

[67] Caesar, *Bell. Gall.* 4.36; 5.23.

[68] W. P. Workman, 'A New Date-Indication in Acts', *ExpT* 11, 1899–1900, 316–19. Plooij, op. cit., 86–8; Bruce, *Acts*, 506; and Gunther, op. cit., 141, support this.

[69] The only other possible year is 57, when it fell on September 27. In 61, which Ogg favours, it was as early as September 12, when the danger season had not even begun. He admits this, but slurs over it.

[70] *De rei milit.* 4. 39. [71] *Nat. hist.* 2.47. [72] Pp. 140–150 below.

52–7 Third missionary journey
57 Arrival in Jerusalem
57–9 Imprisonment in Caesarea
60–2 Imprisonment in Rome.

Within this framework let us now try to fit his letters.

I Thessalonians. According to I Thess. 3.6 Paul is writing just after Timothy arrived from Thessalonica, whither Paul had sent him when he was in Athens (3.1f.). According to Acts 18.5 Timothy and Silas rejoined Paul in Corinth. The presumption therefore is that the letter was written by Paul, with the other two (1.1), from Corinth towards the beginning of the eighteen-month period that ended in the summer of 51 (Acts 18.11). Acts however elides two journeys of Timothy. He and Silas had been left behind in Beroea with instructions to join Paul with all speed at Athens, where he waited for them (17.15f.). Evidently they (or Timothy at least) did do this, but were then sent back to Thessalonica. By the time they returned Paul had moved on to Corinth and set up with Aquila. Once again Acts appears to summarize more complex travels, but the over-all situation is not in doubt. Precisely how long an interval is required after Paul's original visit to Thessalonica in the summer of 49 is disputed; but neither Kümmel,[73] nor Ernest Best,[74] who take into account all the most recent scholarship on the matter, sees reason to question the traditional placing. We may therefore accept early 50 as the most probable date for the Epistle.

II Thessalonians. To go into the challenges that have been made to the authenticity and integrity of this epistle and to its order in relation to I Thessalonians would take us far afield. The arguments are set out in all the commentaries. Suffice it here to say again that, after full examination of all the theories, both Kümmel[75] and Best[76] come down decisively in favour of the traditional view that Paul wrote II Thessalonians, with Silas and Timothy (1.1), from Corinth within a short time of I Thessalonians, either late in 50 or early in 51. The hypothesis of pseudonymity, *despite* the authentication of the personal signature in 3.17, would require a date at the end of the first century. Yet, as Kümmel says, 2.4 ('he . . . even takes his seat in the temple of

[73] *INT*, 257–60.
[74] E. Best, *I and II Thessalonians* (Black's NTC), 1972, 7–13.
[75] *INT*, 263–9.
[76] Op. cit., 37–59.

God') 'was obviously written while the temple was still standing'.[77] There is no sound reason for not accepting the usual dating.[78]

I Corinthians. We have already argued that this was written from Ephesus about Passover-time (March–April) when Paul had been nearly three years in Ephesus and was beginning to make plans to move on. There is wide agreement that this must, as we have reckoned, have been in 55.[79] It is surprising therefore that Barrett makes it 54 or even 53.[80] The reason becomes clear when we realize that he is one of those who is convinced that everything must be adjusted to allow Paul to appear before Festus in 55. (He cannot of course have arrived in Jerusalem by 53, so the 'two years' of Acts 24.27 have, as we have seen, on this view to be referred to Felix.) Barrett agrees that Paul came to Ephesus in the late summer of 52, but he has to make him leave again by the early summer of 54. He argues that the 'three years' of Acts 20.31 is notin consistent with the two years and three months of 19.8 and 10. But it is difficult to see how it can be consistent with *less* than two years – quite apart from the fact that the two dated spells in Acts do not claim to cover all Paul's time at Ephesus (cf. 19.22). It seems much easier to take the space of 'three years, night and day' to mean what it says and put I Corinthians in the spring of 55. Barrett has subsequently to compress all the further journeys and letters of Titus and Paul to Corinth and the work in the Troad and Macedonia (let alone Illyricum) into the remaining months of the same year – and this despite the fact that he believes that II Cor. 10–13 reflects yet further trouble and a fifth letter in all. It is more natural to reckon that his dealings with the church there dragged on well into 56 and the early part of 57.

II Corinthians. The first part of this epistle at any rate (i.e. chs. 1–9) is written from Macedonia, in all probability in the early part of 56. If chs. 10–13 belong to a subsequent letter, then they must come from

[77] The authenticity of II Thessalonians is defended by F. W. Beare, *IDB* IV, 626, even though he would question both Ephesians and I Peter and is doubtful about Colossians.

[78] The attempt by Buck and Taylor, *St Paul*, 146–62, to establish absolute dates for Pauline chronology, not from Gallio, but from placing II Thess. 2.1–12 three and a half years (as in Dan. 12.11–13) after Caligula's frustrated attempt to set up his statue in the temple, i.e. in 44 (with I Thessalonians in 46) is so subjective as to be almost unanswerable.

[79] Thus, summarizing other scholarship, C. S. C. Williams, *PCB*, 954; S. M. Gilmour, *IDB* I, 692.

[80] C. K. Barrett, *I Corinthians* (Black's NTC), 1968, 5; *II Corinthians*, 4f.

later that same year, shortly before Paul descends upon Corinth for the last time to winter there (13.1–10). In any case we can safely place the whole of II Corinthians in 56.

Romans. Paul is writing shortly before setting off for Jerusalem (15.25), while staying with Gaius in Corinth (16.23; cf. I Cor. 1.14) and completing the work on the collection (15.26–8). It can confidently be dated during the three months spent in Achaia (Acts 20.3), early in 57.[81] The only issue is whether the final ch. 16 is part of the letter sent to Rome or, as many have argued,[82] a covering letter for dispatching a version of it at the same time to Ephesus. As this does not affect the date, it is not directly our concern. But since the destination of the chapter determines the use of its material elsewhere, I simply register my conviction, with that of most recent commentators,[83] that, despite the evidence of textual dislocation, it belongs to Rome with the rest of the Epistle.

Galatians presents much more uncertainty. The view that we have taken that the visit to Jerusalem in Gal. 2 corresponds to the council visit of 48 means that it cannot be written before that date. There would in any case be no initial reason to think that it was, since the closest contacts of the epistle are with II Corinthians and still more with Romans. It is however difficult to be more precise. We do not even know for certain the location of the recipients, whether in the Roman province of Galatia, which included the churches in Pisidia and Lycaonia founded on Paul's first missionary journey (Acts 13–14) and revisited on the second (16.1–5), or the territory of Galatia further north (which *could* be referred to in 16.6 and 18.23.)[84] The weight of scholarly opinion appears to favour the former,[85] with which on balance I would side, though Kümmel[86] and J. A. Fitzmyer[87] still argue for the latter view, championed by Lightfoot.[88]

[81] Notwithstanding J. R. Richards, 'Romans and I Corinthians: Their Chronological Relationship and Comparative Dates', *NTS* 13, 1966–7, 14–30.

[82] E.g. T. W. Manson, 'The Letter to the Romans', *Studies in the Gospels and Epistles*, Manchester 1962, 225–41.

[83] E.g. C. H. Dodd, *Romans* (Moffat NTC), 1932; C. K. Barrett, *Romans* (Black's NTC), 1937; and even J. C. O'Neill, *Romans* (Pelican NTC), Harmondsworth 1975, who believes that remarkably little else is an original part of the epistle. So too, Kümmel, *INT*, 314–20.

[84] For a balanced survey of the arguments, cf. Guthrie, *NTI*, 450–7.

[85] Cf. F. F. Bruce, 'Galatian Problems: North or South Galatians?', *BJRL* 52, 1970, 243–66.

[86] *INT*, 296–8.

[87] J. A. Fitzmyer, *Jerome Biblical Commentary*, 1968, 236f.

[88] *Galatians*, 18–31. Similarly, strongly, Moffatt, *ILNT*, 90–101.

Fortunately we do not have to decide this issue for the purposes of dating, since both options remain open *unless* we wish to put Galatians before the council of Jerusalem and therefore before the second missionary journey. If in Gal. 4.13, as is probably the contrast intended in II Cor. 1.15, τὸ πρότερον means 'on the first of my two visits' (rather than simply 'formerly' or 'originally', as it certainly could mean), then the epistle must be written at least after the visit of Acts 16.6[89] (in 49), if not after that of 18.23 (in 52). The reference in Gal. 1.6 to the Galatians having turned 'so quickly' (ταχέως) from the true gospel is sometimes taken as an argument in favour of an earlier rather than a later date. But such an expression, even if it has a temporal sense and does not mean 'hastily' or 'suddenly' (cf. II Peter 2.1), is highly relative.

The undoubted affinities with II Corinthians and Romans,[90] though certainly not decisive for dating, have inclined the majority of scholars who do not wish for other reasons to put Galatians back in 48 to place it either during Paul's time in Ephesus[91] (52–5) or between II Corinthians and Romans, perhaps on his travels in northern Greece, in 56. The greeting in 1.2, 'I and the group of friends now with me', perhaps suggests that Paul is not writing from an established Christian congregation like Ephesus or Corinth, and there are no personal messages at the end (contrast I Cor. 16.19f. and Rom. 16). It is more like what we find in II Corinthians (written in Macedonia), where he simply sends greetings from 'all God's people' (13.13). Again, though he longs to be with the Galatians (Gal. 4.20), he appears to be in no position even to propose a visit – and this would, on balance, count against a place so accessible as Ephesus. A further possible pointer may be found in I Cor. 16.1: 'About the collection in aid of God's people: you should follow my directions to our congregations in Galatia.' Clearly our epistle to the Galatians contains no such directions and it must either have been written before the project (i.e., well prior to I Corinthians) or later on. In favour of the latter there is one of the parallels between Galatians and II Corinthians. In II Cor. 9.6 Paul says, in relation to the collection, 'Remember, sparse sowing, sparse reaping; sow bountifully, and you will reap bountifully'. In Gal. 6.7–10 he writes:

Make no mistake about this: God is not to be fooled; a man reaps what he

[89] To refer the second visit to the return journey in 14.21–23 is possible, though forced.

[90] Cf. Lightfoot, *Galatians*, 44–50; C. H. Buck, 'The Date of Galatians', *JBL* 70, 1951, 113–22; Buck and Taylor, op. cit., 82–102.

[91] So e.g. Moffatt, *ILNT*, 102; Sanders, *PCB*, 973; Fitzmyer, *JBC*, 237.

> sows. . . . So let us never tire of doing good, for if we do not slacken our efforts we shall in due time reap our harvest. Therefore, as opportunity offers, let us work for the good of all, especially members of the household of the faith.

It is possible (though no more than possible) that Paul is here reproving the Galatians for their lack of liberality in the same cause.

I would conclude therefore, with Lightfoot and others,[92] that Galatians most probably comes from the period between II Corinthians and Romans, which we have already argued covers most of 56. But this conclusion is much less sure than that for the other epistles so far discussed. Indeed Knox has suggested that, so far from being the first of Paul's writings, it may have been among the last,[93] written from prison. However, the absence of the slightest reference to his 'bonds' (particularly in a letter which has so much to say about freedom) makes this very arbitrary. Yet it is a salutary warning. For Philippians, which carries the same greeting, 'the brothers who are now with me' (Phil. 4.21; cf. Gal. 1.2), and which many have put last of all, has equally forcibly been argued to come from the period of Paul's Ephesian ministry (where indeed Knox puts it) because of its common themes with Galatians, Corinthians and Romans.

This brings us to the so-called captivity epistles, and we may start with *Philippians*, which, it is generally agreed, stands apart from the other three, Colossians, Philemon and (assuming its authenticity) Ephesians. The dating of all these is almost entirely dependent on the judgment made about their place of writing. Three locations have been canvassed, Ephesus (52–5), Caesarea (57–9) and Rome (60–2), and none has finally prevailed over the others. Rome has been the traditional one for all four, but many scholars have wished to discriminate and allocate different letters to different places. It will be well to say at the beginning of the discussion that complete certainty cannot be established on the evidence available and that it is a matter of assessing probabilities. Whatever conclusions we finally reach, other alternatives cannot be ruled out.

With regard, then, to Philippians, we may note that of all the captivity epistles this is the one for which the hypothesis of an

[92] *Galatians*, 36–56; E. H. Askwith, *The Epistle to the Galatians: An Essay on its Destination and Date*, 1899, a valuable and forgotten book which combines this dating (as I would) with a south Galatian destination and an identification of the visits of Gal. 2 and Acts 15; Buck, *JBL* 70, 113–22; C. E. Faw, 'The Anomaly of Galatians', *BR* 4, 1960, 25–38.

[93] *IDB* II, 342f.; cf. Hurd in Farmer, Moule and Niebuhr, *Christian History*, 241–3.

Ephesian origin has won greatest support.[94] Indeed it can at first sight be fitted neatly into the Acts narrative at this point. In Phil. 2.19–24 Paul says that he hopes to send Timothy soon, confident that he himself will come before long. In Acts 19.22 he sends Timothy and Erastus ahead of him to Macedonia, of which Philippi was 'a city of the first rank' (Acts 16.12), while he stays on for a time in Asia. Referring apparently to the same situation, Paul speaks in I Cor. 16.5–11 of Timothy having gone before him to Corinth. And he will wait in Ephesus for his return, just as in Phil. 2.19 he hopes that Timothy will bring him news of the church at Philippi.[95] On the other hand, there is not the slightest hint in Acts or I Corinthians that Paul is or has been in prison. On the contrary, he is a free agent planning his future travels (Acts 19.21; I Cor. 16.6–8) and fully stretched by his evangelistic opportunities (I Cor. 16.9). He sends greetings from the churches of Asia and from Aquila and Prisca and the congregation at their house (I Cor. 16.19). The *cri de coeur* of Phil. 2.20, that, apart from Timothy,

> there is no one else here who sees things as I do and takes a genuine interest in your concerns; they are all bent on their own ends, not on the cause of Christ Jesus,

fits neither Acts 19.22, 'he sent two of his assistants, Timothy and Erastus, to Macedonia', nor I Cor. 16.11f., 'I am waiting for him with our friends' (who include Apollos).

Of course, it is always possible to say that the imprisonment of Paul and the sending of Timothy occurred independently, before or after the events of which we have record. But this merely exposes the main weakness of the hypothesis of an Ephesian captivity, that it rests on no direct evidence whatsoever – merely unspecified references to *φυλακαί* in II Cor. 6.5; 11.23 and Rom. 16.7 (cf. I Clem. 5.6, which mentions seven imprisonments of Paul). No description of Paul's

[94] Cf. e.g. the survey by Bruce, 'The Epistles of Paul', *PCB*, 932f.; and Guthrie, *NTI*, 149: 'There is a much greater inclination to attribute Philippians than the other Captivity Epistles to Ephesus.' For the Ephesian hypothesis in general, cf. especially W. Michaelis, *Die Gefangenschaft des Paulus in Ephesus und der Itinerar des Timotheus*, Gütersloh 1925; *Die Datierung des Philipperbriefs*, Gütersloh 1933; G. S. Duncan, *St Paul's Ephesian Ministry*, 1929. On the other side, C. H. Dodd, 'The Mind of Paul: II', *New Testament Studies*, Manchester 1953, 85–108; Guthrie, *NTI*, 472–8. It is notable that Dodd does not even consider the alternative of Caesarea.

[95] Kümmel correctly points out, *INT*, 330f., that Paul himself does not say that he is sending Timothy to Corinth *via* Macedonia (only that he is planning to come that way himself) and that Acts 19.22 does not indicate that Paul expects Timothy back before his own departure. But these would be negligible differences if everything else fitted.

many troubles and dangers in Ephesus or Asia (Acts 19.23–20.1; I Cor. 15.32; 16.9; II Cor. 1.8f.; and [perhaps] Rom. 16.3f.) includes imprisonment. Moreover, the imprisonment referred to in Philippians must have been an extended one (1.13f.) (and based on a capital charge, 2.17) – having lasted long enough even by the time of writing for the Christians in Philippi to have heard about it and sent Epaphroditus with relief, and then for Epaphroditus to have recovered from a near fatal illness, of which they had also had time to get news (2.25–30).

Another difficulty is that in Philippians there is no reference whatever to the collection for the poor, in which Macedonia was so prominent (II Cor. 8.1–5; 9.1–4; Rom. 15.26f.). On the contrary, stress is laid upon the Philippians' collection for Paul's personal needs (Phil. 2.25, 30; 4.10–19), which he is especially sensitive to dissociate from the other collection (II Cor. 8.16–24; 12.13–18; Acts 20.33–35). It looks then as if Philippians must come from a period well before or well after the project that occupied so much of Paul's time and thought in the two years (at least) prior to 57. And if it came before it must be well prior to the spring of 55, when the Corinthians are already assumed to know about the collection (I Cor. 16.1–4). This scarcely fits the impression which we get from Philippians that Paul's relations with that church have by then extended over many years (1.5; 4.10f., 15f.). Nor does it comport with his expressed desire for death (1.20–26), which is very different from what he is looking forward to even in Romans. It seems altogether easier to place it later.

The only advantages indeed of an Ephesian locale for Philippians would seem to be: (*a*) the affinity of language with the other epistles in the central section of Paul's ministry. But the parallels are spread amongst all the Pauline epistles;[96] and, as with Galatians, this is a fairly uncertain criterion. (*b*) The shorter distance required for the journeys described to and from Philippi (Phil. 2.19–30). But it is generally conceded that this latter cannot be decisive. For the rest, the references to the praetorium in 1.13 and the servants of the imperial establishment ('Caesar's household') in 4.22, though not impossible in Ephesus, point more obviously to Rome or Caesarea.

Certainly these latter two references would seem to favour Rome, though again it is agreed even by the advocates of this hypothesis that they cannot be decisive. Indeed, if it is in Rome, then the phrase ἐν ὅλῳ τῷ πραιτωρίῳ must be taken, with Lightfoot,[97] to refer to the

[96] Cf. C. L. Mitton, *The Epistle to the Ephesians*, Oxford 1951, 322–32.

[97] J. B. Lightfoot, *Philippians*, [3]1873, 97–102.

members of the Praetorian guard, whom Paul it is supposed influenced by rota, and not a building – since according to Acts 28.30 he is in his own hired lodging. This is not however how it is used anywhere else in the New Testament (Matt. 27.27; Mark 15.16; John 18.28, 33; 19.9; Acts 23.35). An alternative is to say that it refers to a later stage in Paul's Roman captivity when he has been moved into the praetorium to stand trial – though Lightfoot insisted that 'in Rome itself a "praetorium" would not have been tolerated'. But then we lose all contact with the evidence and can invent any circumstance that suits us (as at Ephesus).

In Caesarea,[98] on the other hand, Paul is specifically said to be in the praetorium of Herod's palace, the headquarters of the procurator of Judaea (Acts 23.55). Moreover, the sense of Phil. 1.16f. is correctly rendered in the NEB by 'as I lie in prison'. He is in jail. And yet, according to Acts 24.23, Felix 'gave orders to the centurion to keep Paul under open arrest[99] and not to prevent any of his friends from making themselves useful to him' – a statement which fully fits the description of his conditions in Phil. 2.25–30; 4.10–19. Furthermore a hearing has already taken place (1.7), which suits the situation at Caesarea following the appearance before Felix; but by the time Acts ends there has been no hearing in Rome. It has been objected that at Caesarea Paul was not facing the possibility of death, since he could always appeal to Caesar. Yet it is constantly made clear that his life is in danger from the Jews (Acts 21.31, 36; 22.22; 23.30; 25.3, 24; 26.21), a fate from which he is protected only by Roman custody. If he had really brought a Greek into the temple, then, even as a Roman citizen, he would under Jewish law have been liable to death. In fact he says to Festus, 'If I am guilty of any capital crime, I do not ask to escape the death penalty' (25.11). Yet he knows, like the authorities, that he is innocent of this (23.29; 25.10, 25; 26.31; 28.18) and therefore has every ground for expecting discharge (26.32) – which, it is suggested, he could have bought at any time (24.26). His appeal to the emperor is only a last desperate recourse when it looks as if Festus is going to hand him back as a sop to the Jews (25.11). At the time of writing to the Philippians his confidence was that he would be alive and free to visit them once more (Phil. 1.24–26; 2.24) on his projected journey back west (Rom. 1.13; 15.23–29; Acts 19.21;

[98] For this case, cf. E. Lohmeyer, *Philipper* (KEKNT 9), Göttingen [8]1930, 3f., 14f., 41; L. Johnson, 'The Pauline Letters from Caesarea', *ExpT* 68, 1956–7, 24–6; Gunther, op. cit., 98–107.

[99] ἄνεσις (cf. Josephus, *Ant.* 18.235) 'apparently means leave to communicate with friends and receive food' (Lake and Cadbury, *Beginnings* IV, 304).

23.11). That he had any plans for returning east from Rome is entirely hypothetical – though of course we can never prove that he did not change his mind. The only evidence is for journeys further west still, whether planned or accomplished.

Further support for Caesarea as the place of writing is the bitter polemic in Phil. 3.1–11 against the Jews, who are much more fiercely attacked even than fellow-Christians who betray the gospel (1.15–18; 3.18f.). This fits the fanatical and unrelenting Jewish opposition Paul encountered in Jerusalem and Caesarea (Acts 21.37–26.32; cf. 28.19). There *may* have been such bitterness later in Rome, but the only evidence we have is of Jews who are conspicuously fair to Paul, even if sceptical and obtuse (28.21–28).

I would agree therefore with Kümmel[100] in thinking that Caesarea as the place of origin for Philippians has been too quickly abandoned, and it is certainly preferable to Ephesus. Rome has little to be said against it, precisely because the evidence is so thin. Reicke, who argues, as we shall see, strongly for the Caesarean locale of the other captivity epistles, still places Philippians in Rome.[101] He urges, rightly, that on grounds of personalia it does not belong with the rest. Yet I believe the best hypothesis may turn out to be that all these epistles come from the same place but at different times. But before deciding on a date for Philippians, we should turn to the other letters.

Colossians, Philemon and Ephesians. At once we are up against the problem of authenticity, not for the last time. There is virtually no one now who denies the genuineness of Philemon.[102] There are those, especially in Germany,[103] who question Colossians on stylistic and theological grounds. But the close and complex interrelationship of names with Philemon points strongly to the fact that the two epistles were dictated by the same man at the same time and sent to Colossae by Tychicus, in company with Onesimus (Col. 4.7–9; Philem. 12). Reicke summarizes the connections thus:

> Greetings were conveyed from and to nearly the same persons in both letters, but their names were by no means given in the same order so that any hypothesis

[100] *INT*, 329.

[101] B. Reicke, 'Caesarea, Rome and the Captivity Epistles', in W. W. Gasque and R. P. Martin (edd.), *Apostolic History and the Gospel: Biblical and Historical Essays Presented to F. F. Bruce*, 1970, 277–86; 'The Historical Setting of Colossians', *RE* 70, 1973, 429–38.

[102] John Knox, *Philemon among the Letters of Paul*, Nashville, Tenn., ²1959, makes its genuineness a corner-stone of his case against Ephesians. Cf. also Bruce, 'St Paul in Rome: 2.The Epistle to Philemon', *BJRL* 48, 1965, 81–97.

[103] For names, cf. Kümmel, *INT*, 340.

> of dependence can‹not› be plausible (Philem. 1f., 23f.; Col. 1.7; 4.7–19). In particular, the fact that Epaphras of Colossae appears in both writings, though in different contexts (Philem. 23; Col. 1.7; 4.9), is a remarkable evidence of a common background. . . . This complex of relations cannot be understood as the result of artificial imitation.[104]

After a careful weighing of the pros and cons Kümmel ends by saying 'all the evidence points to the conclusion that Colossians . . . is to be regarded as Pauline',[105] and I would agree.

Ephesians presents a difficult problem to handle here. To argue in any detail the question of Pauline authorship would take us far from our primary purpose, which is to establish a chronology. If it is not Pauline, then there are two alternatives: either it is by an amanuensis or agent writing on the apostle's behalf at the same date; or it is strictly pseudonymous, claiming to be Pauline but coming (probably) from towards the end of the first century. The former alternative has commanded little support (though it has recently been argued by Gunther, who believes that the author was Timothy)[106] and it does not affect the date anyway. It is really a straight issue between attributing it to Paul[107] and to a second-generation Paulinist imitating and expounding his theology.[108] The pros and cons are summarily set out by Sanders and Nineham[109] and assessed by Guthrie[110] (who comes down in favour of Paul), Kümmel[111] (who comes down against), and H. Chadwick[112] (who regards the issue as evenly balanced).

Short of going over the whole evidence afresh, I can only express my own considered conviction. In contrast with most of the other judgments in this book, which have been modified, often radically, in

[104] *RE* 70, 434. Cf. also the different way Archippus comes into Philem. 2 and Col. 4.18.

[105] *INT*, 340–6; similarly Goodspeed, *INT*, 102–4; C. F. D. Moule, *Colossians and Philemon* (Cambridge Greek Testament), 1957, 13f.

[106] Op. cit., 130–8. The absence of Timothy's name from the address (in contrast with Colossians, Philemon and Philippians) has to be put down to self-effacing modesty! M. Goguel, *Introduction au Nouveau Testament*, Paris 1923–6, IV.2, 474f., suggested an original homily by Tychicus, with subsequent additions attributing it to Paul. From the point of view of dating, these theories are interesting as testimony to the difficulties felt in regarding Ephesians simply as a late pseudepigraph.

[107] Cf. most recently and massively, A. van Roon, *The Authenticity of Ephesians*, Leiden 1974, and M. Barth, *Ephesians*, New York 1974.

[108] Major presentations of this thesis are: E. J. Goodspeed, *The Meaning of Ephesians*, Chicago 1933; *INT*, 222–39; *The Key to Ephesians*, Chicago 1956; and Mitton, *Ephesians*.

[109] In F. L. Cross (ed.), *Studies in Ephesians*, 1956, 9–35.

[110] *NTI*, 479–508. [111] *INT*, 357–63. [112] *PCB*, 980f.

the process of writing it, I have never really doubted the Pauline authorship of Ephesians.[113] It has always struck me as noteworthy that in what has remained a classic English commentary on Ephesians,[114] Armitage Robinson, who was in close touch with Harnack and contemporary German scholarship[115] and certainly not conservative for his day (and whose very late dating of the Didache I shall subsequently disagree with completely),[116] never even raised the question of authorship. Features of style and theology which have struck others as impossible for Paul[117] apparently to him, with as extensive a knowledge of the early Christian literature as any Englishman since Lightfoot, seemed entirely at home. In a nicely balanced article Cadbury asks the question:[118]

> Which is more likely, that an imitator of Paul in the first century composed a writing ninety or ninety-five per cent in accordance with Paul's style or that Paul himself wrote a letter diverging five or ten per cent from his usual style?

Moreover there is the question of what sort of imitator. If he were a scissors-and-paste copyist and conflator, it would be relatively simple. Yet everyone agrees that his relationship to the genuine Paul is more subtle than that. He is so near (especially to Colossians) and yet apparently so far. The only thing he does reproduce virtually *verbatim* from Colossians is the note in 6.21f. (= Col. 4.7f.) about the sending of Tychicus to convey Paul's news. Why this, and no other personalia, should have been inserted to add verisimilitude is inexplicable. Moreover, as Dodd says, 'Does one find such faithful dependence and such daring originality in one and the same person?'[119] For he is a spiritual and theological giant, and these men do not appear and disappear without leaving any other trace, especially in that singularly flat sub-apostolic age from which the Epistle of Barnabas and the Shepherd of Hermas are typical samples. Even if, with the

[113] Cf. my study *The Body* (SBT 5), 1952, 10.

[114] J. Armitage Robinson, *St Paul's Epistle to the Ephesians*, 1903. Note the title.

[115] Harnack left the matter open in his *Chron.*, 239, but in his later 'Die Addresse des Epheserbriefs des Paulus', *Sitzungsberichte der königlich preussischen Akademie der Wissenschaften*, Berlin 1910, 696–709, argued that it represented Paul's letter to the Laodiceans mentioned in Col. 4.16. Jülicher, *Einleitung*, [1]124–8, declared a verdict of 'non liquet' (though the edition revised by E. Fascher, [7]1931, 138–42, subsequently came down against). Zahn, *INT* I, 491–522, vigorously defended Pauline authorship.

[116] See ch. x below.

[117] Thus Nineham, *Historicity and Chronology*, 27, holds that key words in Colossians and Ephesians are used '*to convey completely different ideas*' (italics his). This at any rate is an exaggeration.

[118] H. J. Cadbury, 'The Dilemma of Ephesians', *NTS* 5, 1958–9, 91–102 (101).

[119] In the *Abingdon Bible Commentary*, 1929, 1225, favouring Pauline authorship.

majority of scholars, we regard the Pastoral Epistles and II Peter as pseudonymous, we are not in these cases dealing with original and creative productions. The only comparable unknown author is the writer to the Hebrews. But he is not imitating anyone, and in any case, I believe,[120] belongs firmly within the apostolic age. Here as so often the case is cumulative and to some extent circular. If on other grounds half the literature of the New Testament is to be located in the last quarter of the first century, then the epistle to the Ephesians will seem to stand in good company. If on the other hand it is isolated there, it will look very exposed.

I propose therefore to proceed as though Ephesians comes from Paul, and to see how it fits in if it does. There is not in fact much that turns on it for chronology, since its dating (if genuine) is derivative from Colossians and Philemon rather than *vice versa*. If, therefore, anyone prefers to regard it as an exception and set it outside the series altogether, the consequences for the rest are not decisive.

If then all three epistles are by Paul, there can be no doubt that they were written closely together and sent by Tychicus on the same journey, with Ephesians being composed in all probability shortly after Philemon and Colossians, almost certainly as a general homily to the Asian churches. This is strongly supported by the absence of 'in Ephesus' from the best manuscripts of Eph. 1.1 and the lack of local details or personal messages. Where, and therefore when, may we say that they were written?

Again the same three options are open. Only, of course, if Ephesians was *not* sent to Ephesus (and the inclusion of that church in the general circulation is difficult to deny) is Ephesus itself a credible source of origin. Indeed all the previous objections and more arise to this hypothesis. Mark and Luke are with Paul (Col. 4.10, 15; Philem. 24). Yet according to Acts (15.37–39) Mark had not accompanied Paul to Ephesus, and the absence of any 'we' passage for the Ephesus period, let alone any account of an imprisonment, tells strongly against Luke's presence there (assuming for the moment the Lukan authorship of Acts). Indeed the only real argument for Ephesus[121] is again its geographical proximity, which considerably eases Paul's request to Philemon to have a room ready for him should he be released (Philem. 22) and, according to some, the arrival there of the runaway slave Onesimus. But that Onesimus would have been most

[120] See ch. VII below.

[121] Colossians is indeed assigned to Ephesus by the Marcionite Prologue, but the value of this statement is negatived by its assignation of Philemon (which clearly belongs with it) to Rome.

likely to flee to Ephesus, a mere hundred miles away, to escape detection seems to others less credible. As Dodd says, 'If we are to *surmise*, then it is as likely that the fugitive slave, his pockets lined at his master's expense, made for Rome *because* it was distant, as that he went to Ephesus because it was near.'[122] We cannot tell. Moreover, though arguments from theological development are notoriously dangerous, there are strong grounds for thinking that the elaboration of the doctrine of the church as the body of Christ, with Christ as its head, found in Colossians and Ephesians follows rather than precedes its much more tentative formulation in I Corinthians and Romans (written on or after Paul's departure from Ephesus). It has not seemed to anyone to come earlier: the only question is whether it is so much later as to require an author other than Paul.

We are back then with Caesarea or Rome. The latter has been the traditional location, and the only argument has been whether these epistles precede or follow the somewhat different situation presupposed by Philippians. There is nothing finally against Rome, and from the 'we' passages Luke can certainly be presumed to have been there. But the lack of obstacles again is largely due to the fact that we know so little about Paul's prospects there that we can create what conditions we like – for instance, that he is expecting release and plans to travel east (though the idea of asking from Rome for a guest-room to be prepared in Colossae has always stretched credibility).

The case for Caesarea has recently been stated again by Reicke with much persuasiveness.[123] Of the people with Paul, Timothy (Col. 1.1; Philem. 1), Tychicus (Col. 4.7; Eph. 6.21), Aristarchus (Col. 4.10; Philem. 24) and Luke (Col. 4.14; Philem. 24) all travelled with the collection (Acts 20.4; cf. 20.6 for the 'we') and may be presumed, like Trophimus (20.4; 21.29), to have reached Jerusalem together (21.17f.) and to have stayed with Paul at any rate for a time to see him through the troubles which their presence brought him (21.27–29). Aristarchus, described as a fellow-prisoner in Col. 4.10, indeed is still with Paul (as is Luke) as he sets out for Italy (Acts 27.2).[124]

122 *New Testament Studies*, 95.

123 Opp. cit. (n. 101 above). I am much indebted to him also for valuable suggestions in conversation and correspondence. Johnson and Gunther (opp. cit., n. 98) also argue that these epistles come from Caesarea.

124 Lightfoot, *Philippians*, 34, argued that Aristarchus did not go all the way to Rome but was put off at Myra for his home in Thessalonica. But the case is highly speculative. Dodd, *New Testament Studies*, 91, goes so far as to call it an 'irresponsible conjecture'. It is to be noted that Lightfoot then has to make Aristarchus come later to Rome (on no evidence whatever) if Colossians is to be written from there.

Meanwhile Epaphras has joined Paul from Colossae (Col. 1.7; 4.12) and has apparently also been arrested (Philem. 23).[125] Reicke argues that there is no reason why he should have been arrested in the mild conditions of the Roman detention but that in Caesarea he could well have shared the danger to the other Hellenistic companions of Paul, who once more laments how little support or comfort he has had from the Jewish Christians (Col. 4.11).[126] The fact that Tychicus rather than Epaphras is taking the letters and news (Col. 4.7; Eph. 6.21) may reflect the fact that the latter was not free to leave. Yet it would be natural by then for Tychicus to go back, since he came from those parts (Acts 20.4).[127] Onesimus would also return with him (Col. 4.9), far less of an undertaking in either direction than the journey from Rome. Paul, too, as we have seen, could reasonably have been expecting release from Caesarea and would naturally hope to revisit Colossae, as well as Philippi, on his way west.

Reicke also makes the interesting suggestion[128] that the political situation at that time in Jerusalem and Caesarea throws light on the language of Ephesians. According to Acts 21.28f. Paul had been unjustly accused of bringing Greeks into the inner sanctuary (τὸ ἱερόν) of the temple. On the wall which marked it off from the court of the Gentiles were inscriptions, fragments of which survive to this day, giving warning of the death-penalty for any foreigner transgressing this line.[129] Reicke draws attention to the particularly virulent animosity at this time between Jews and Gentiles in Caesarea, leading later to an appeal to the emperor, with each party denying the other the right of citizenship (ἰσοπολιτεία);[130] and he observes how closely these themes are reflected in the language of Ephesians:

> Paul speaks of (*a*) the ethnic dividing wall (Eph. 2.14b), which has been removed in Christ, and the new temple (2.20); (*b*) the animosity between Jews

[125] Unless συναιχμάλωτος is purely figurative (so Moule, *Colossians*, 136f.). But cf. E. Lohmeyer, *Kolosser* (KEKNT 9), Göttingen [8]1930, ad loc., to the contrary.

[126] Kümmel, *INT*, 347, takes this to mean that there *were* only a few Jewish Christians and therefore as an argument against Caesarea (a location, however, which he does not reject). But, as in Phil. 2.15–18, all that Paul implies is that the Jewish Christians were very doubtful fellow-workers.

[127] Gunther, op. cit., 102, makes the point that Col. 4.7 implies that the Colossians would receive Tychicus before the Laodiceans did (4.15f.): 'Since Colossae is south-east of Laodicea it is legitimate to assume that Tychicus was coming from that direction. Such would be the case if he were proceeding from Caesarea *via* Attalia, but hardly from Rome or Ephesus.'

[128] 'Caesarea, Rome and the Captivity Epistles', 281f.

[129] Josephus, *BJ* 5. 193f.; *Ant.* 15. 417.

[130] Josephus, *Ant.* 20. 173f.

and Gentiles (2.14c; 16b; cf. Col. 1.21), which has been changed into peace through Christ (2.15b, 17); (*c*) the divine citizenship (2.19), which in Christ belongs also to the Gentiles (3.6), as well as the fact that every nationality (πατριά) on earth has its origin in God the Father (3.15; cf. Col. 3.11).

No one of course is to say that such language could not have been written in Rome, but in the Caesarean context its appropriateness is striking. As Reicke says, 'If the epistle is a forgery, then the author had unusually accurate information to hand.' It is also a strong argument, as with the epistle to the Hebrews, against a date after 70. For by then the situation had been obliterated by events, and Paul's spiritual point could scarcely have been made without reflecting the fact that the infamous dividing wall had quite literally been 'broken down'.

In his second article, 'The Historical Setting of Colossians', Reicke has extended his argument by drawing attention to the links of personalia not only between Colossians, Philemon and Ephesians but with *II Timothy*, venturing the conclusion that this also was written (whether by Paul or on his behalf) about the same time from Caesarea.[131] I confess that when I first read this I thought it incredible. For, unlike Ephesians, I had never believed the Pastoral Epistles to be Pauline, nor contemplated that if they did fall within his lifetime (as I was prepared to accept) they could be fitted into any other period but a presumed further stage of missionary activity after the close of the Acts story. Until half-way through the writing of this book I had planned to deal with them in a separate and subsequent chapter. I am persuaded however that here as elsewhere one must be prepared to suspend previous assumptions and be open to the evidence wherever it may point.

The issue of authorship is relevant for our purposes only in relation to chronology; and with regard to dating two questions may be isolated:

(*a*) Is there anything that requires, or makes probable, a date for the Pastoral Epistles outside the lifetime of the Apostle, whether or not genuine fragments from an earlier period are incorporated in them?

(*b*) If there is not, how may they be fitted into his career, whether he composed them personally or not?

(*a*) For the former it would have to be established that the vocabulary, the church organization and the theology presupposed by the

[131] Johnson and Gunther make the same suggestion (though Gunther, op. cit., 107–14, argues that only the fragment II Tim. 4.9–22a comes from Caesarea). The three appear to have written independently of each other.

epistles could not come from the 50s or 60s of the first century but only from the end of the first century or the beginning of the second – if not later. Without going into the detail needed to determine this, I can only say that I do not regard the case as proven. There is nothing decisive to require us to say that the distinctive vocabulary of the Pastorals could only have come from the second century. On the contrary, it has been shown that nearly all the words in question are to be found in Greek literature by the middle of the first century and that half of them occur in the Septuagint, with which Paul was well acquainted.[132]

With regard to the organization of the church, the Pastorals do not presuppose monarchical episcopacy (on the second-century Ignatian model), but rather the equivalence of bishop and presbyter (cf. I Tim. 3.1f.; 5.17; Titus 1.5–7), and they demand nothing more elaborate than the local ministry of 'bishops and deacons' of Phil. 1.1.[133] Timothy and Titus themselves are travelling delegates of Paul, not residential archbishops with fixed territorial assignments. While therefore concern for orderly ministry and appointments in the church *could* argue a later date, there is nothing that requires a second-century setting – or indeed anything subsequent to the pastoral solicitude already shown by Paul, according to Luke, in his speech to the Ephesian elders at Miletus (Acts 20.28–31). Parry[134] concludes an extensive examination with the words:

> There is no substantial reason in the character of the organisation implied in the Pastoral Epistles for assigning them to a date later than the lifetime of S. Paul.

With regard to doctrine too, the type of gnosticizing Judaism attacked in the Pastorals betrays no more elaboration than that refuted in Colossians (if anything less) and certainly bears no comparison with the fully-blown gnostic systems of the second century, which we now know so much better at first hand. Indeed Kümmel,[135]

[132] Cf. R. F. M. Hitchcock, 'Tests for the Pastorals', *JTS* 30, 1928–9, 278f.; W. Michaelis, 'Pastoralbriefe und Wortstatistik', *ZNW* 28, 1929, 69–76; F. J. Badcock, *The Pauline Epistles and the Epistle to the Hebrews in their Historical Setting*, 1937, 115–27; D. Guthrie, *The Pastoral Epistles and the Mind of Paul*, 1956, 39f.; B. Metzger, 'A Reconsideration of Certain Arguments against the Pauline Authorship of the Pastoral Epistles', *ExpT* 70, 1958–9, 91–4.

[133] Cf. Jeremias, 'Zur Datierung der Pastoralbriefe', *ZNW* 52, 1961, 101–4; and earlier Zahn, *INT* II, 89–99, and R. St J. Parry, *The Pastoral Epistles*, Cambridge 1920, lix–lxxx. Even Goodspeed, *INT*, 337, who puts the Pastorals as late as 150, has to admit that they do not show the 'fully developed polity' of later catholicism already present in Ignatius.

[134] Op. cit., lxxviii.

[135] *INT*, 379; cf. earlier Zahn, *INT* II, 99–121.

who believes that the way in which this false teaching is *countered* is uncharacteristic of Paul, is nevertheless emphatic that there is

> not the slightest occasion, just because the false teachers who are being opposed are Gnostics, to link them up with the great Gnostic systems of the second century. . . . The Jewish-Christian-Gnostic false teaching which is being combated in the Pastorals is . . . thoroughly comprehensible in the life span of Paul.

The preoccupation with purity of doctrine, the quotation of hymns and teaching formulae, and the stress on 'the faith' rather than 'faith', though certainly more marked in these epistles, represent but shifts in emphases already present in other parts of Paul and the New Testament.[136] None of them rules out a first-century date; and unless a date well after the death not only of Paul but of Timothy and Titus is presupposed it is hard to imagine a situation in which the fiction would either have deceived or have been taken for granted. We may contrast the situation presupposed by II Thessalonians, where Paul warns of the effect of 'some letter purporting to come from us' (2.2) and is most insistent to add the authentication of his personal signature: 'In my own hand, signed in my name, PAUL; this authenticates all my letters; this is how I write' (3.17; cf. I Cor. 16.21; Gal. 6.11; Col. 4.18).

The inherent difficulties of the alternative theories, whether of total fabrication – with purely fictional messages, like 'I am hoping to come to you before long' (I Tim. 3.14) – or the incorporation of genuine (but highly-fragmented) fragments,[137] do not directly concern us. All one can say is that the case which makes a second-century composition necessary or even probable has very far from established itself. Indeed Reicke has pointedly argued that the call for 'petitions, prayers, intercessions and thanksgivings' for 'sovereigns and all in high office, that we may lead a tranquil and quiet life in full observance of religion and high standards of morality' (I Tim. 2.1f.; cf. Titus 3.1) betokens an attitude towards authority and its beneficent effects which would be inconceivable after the Neronian persecution (we may contrast the Apocalypse). Among the recent commentators it is interesting that J. N. D. Kelly,[138] the patristic scholar, should judge that the Pastorals could not come from the second century,

[136] Cf. Guthrie, *NTI*, 604–6; Parry, op. cit., xc–cx.

[137] The major statement of this latter theory is P. N. Harrison's, *The Problem of the Pastoral Epistles*, Oxford 1921, whose second thoughts are to be found in *Paulines and Pastorals*, 1964. There are many other fragment theories, but no two agree on all the same passages (cf. Guthrie, *NTI*, 590f.).

[138] J. N. D. Kelly, *The Pastoral Epistles* (Black's NTC), 1963.

while, writing in the same year, Barrett,[139] the Pauline scholar, should judge that they could not come from Paul. Perhaps both may be right. At any rate there would seem to be a detectable swing back,[140] if not to apostolic authorship, at any rate to taking seriously the second set of questions relating to dating.

(*b*) The presupposition here is that Timothy and Titus are the same real persons who meet us in the rest of the New Testament and that they are being addressed by Paul in genuine pastoral situations, whether directly at his dictation or through someone writing on his behalf or by a combination of the two. It is not necessary for our present purpose to come to a decision on the purely literary issue. But, whether the style is Paul's own or not, this is the position taken by such scholars as Jeremias,[141] Kelly, Moule[142] and Reicke, as well as by the more conservative Guthrie[143] and by the majority of Roman Catholics.[144] I believe it to be open to fewer difficulties than any theory that requires the letters to be pseudonymous, whether in whole or part. Whether Paul penned them himself must remain questionable. There are very real differences from his usual style and theology (though also many more similarities); but I am not persuaded that there is anything he *could* not have written.[145] Yet the Pastorals were after all composed for a very distinctive purpose. Paul would not be the last church leader whose style (and indeed subject-matter) in an *ad clerum* differed markedly from his already highly diverse and

[139] C. K. Barrett, *The Pastoral Epistles* (New Clarendon Bible), Oxford 1963.

[140] Cf. E. E. Ellis, 'The Authorship of the Pastorals: A Résumé and Assessment of Current Trends', *EQ* 32, 1960, 151–61; and Kelly, op. cit., 30: 'The strength of the anti-Pauline case has surely been greatly exaggerated.'

[141] J. Jeremias, *Die Briefe an Timotheus und Titus*, Göttingen [6]1953, 7f.

[142] C. F. D. Moule, 'The Problem of the Pastoral Epistles', *BJRL* 47, 1965, 430–52. He suggests that Paul used Luke as his agent. For the same thesis, cf. A. Strobel, 'Schreiben des Lukas? Zum sprachlichen Problem der Pastoralbriefe', *NTS* 15, 1968–9, 191–210.

[143] D. Guthrie, *The Pastoral Epistles and the Mind of Paul; The Pastoral Epistles* (Tyndale NTC), 1957; and *NTI*, 584–622, 632–4.

[144] E.g. C. Spicq, *Les Épîtres Pastorales* (Études Bibliques), Paris 1947, cxix; P. Benoit in the *Jerusalem Bible*, 1966, 264; G. A. Denzer, 'The Pastoral Letters', *JBC*, 351f., and the literature there cited.

[145] Moule, *BJRL*, 432, instances I Tim. 1.8: 'We all know that the law is an excellent thing [Paul may well be quoting his opponents here; cf. the οἴδαμεν of I Cor. 8.1, 4] provided we treat it as law.' But this is surely his position elsewhere. If we treat the law as a means of salvation, it is worse than useless; but as a dyke against the lawless and sinful (I Tim. 1.9f.) it is admirable (cf. Rom. 7.12, 14; 13.1–6). Zahn, *INT* II, 121, ironically quotes I Tim. 1.9 in *support* of Pauline authorship and comments, 'Nowhere in these Epistles do we find sentences that sound so "un-Pauline" as I Cor. 7.19'!

adaptable manner of speaking and writing for wider audiences. He himself claims to 'have become everything in turn to men of every sort' (I Cor. 9.22). But the issue of authorship for its own sake may here be left on one side. Our concern is with the occasions and circumstances which the letters might fit if they do belong to his period.

The consensus among those who wish to place the Pastorals within Paul's lifetime is that they cannot be made to fit any part of his career covered by Acts. They are therefore located in the gap between his (inferred) release from custody in Rome in 62+ and his execution there some years later. This view was first propounded, as far as we know, by Eusebius[146] and is based by him on nothing else than deductions from II Timothy. But the complexity of Paul's itinerary and the divergence between the proposed schemes vividly illustrate how totally hypothetical this construction is.[147]

[146] *HE* 2.22.2–8.

[147] E.g. Lightfoot, *Biblical Essays*, 223: *First journey eastward*: He revisits Macedonia (Philippi) (Phil. 2.24), Asia and Phrygia (Colossae) (Philem. 22). *Journey westward*: He founds the church of Crete. Visits Spain, Gaul (?) (II Tim. 4.10 *v.l.*), and Dalmatia (?) (II Tim. 4.10). *Second journey eastward*: He revisits Asia and Phrygia (II Tim. 1.15f.), visits Ephesus (I Tim. 1.3); here probably he encounters Alexander the coppersmith (I Tim. 1.20; II Tim. 4.14). Leaves Timothy in charge of the Ephesian church. Revisits Macedonia (Philippi) (I Tim. 1.3) and Achaia (?) (Athens and Corinth). Writes I Timothy. Visits (perhaps revisits) Crete, and leaves Titus in charge of the church there (Titus 1.5). Returns to Asia. Writes Epistle to Titus. Visits Miletus (II Tim. 4.20), sails to Troas (II Tim. 4.13), is at Corinth (II Tim. 4.20) on his way to Nicopolis to winter (Titus 3.12). Arrested (probably at Corinth) and carried to Rome. Titus joins him there. Writes II Timothy. Timothy shares his imprisonment (Heb. 13.23). Martyrdom of Paul.

Guthrie, *NTI*, 598f.: 'The Pastorals tell us that Paul again visited Asia (Troas, II Tim. 4.13, and Miletus, II Tim. 4.20) although it is not necessary to suppose that he visited Ephesus on the strength of I Tim. 1.3. But he urged Timothy to stay there when he was *en route* for Macedonia. At some time he paid a visit to Crete, where he left Titus, but his main activity appears to have been in Macedonia and Greece. From the Captivity Epistles we may surmise that he visited the Lycus valley, no doubt on the same occasion as he urged Timothy to remain at Ephesus, and that he paid his promised visit to Philippi. . . . He may have been rearrested in the western districts of Macedonia or Epirus (which is mentioned in Titus 3.12) and taken to Rome.'

Denzer, *JBC*, 351: 'He might have gone to Crete first. When he left Crete, Titus might have remained there as his legate (Titus 1.5). From Crete, Paul might have gone to Asia Minor. When he left Ephesus for Macedonia, Timothy remained as his legate (I Tim. 1.3). Possibly, Paul passed through Troas on his way to Macedonia (II Tim. 4.13), and there wrote I Timothy and Titus. Paul then perhaps spent the winter at Nicopolis in Epirus (Titus 3.12). The following spring he might have returned to Ephesus, according to his plan (I Tim. 3.14; 4.13). It would seem that he was then arrested in the region of Ephesus (II Tim. 1.4). In the

Since there are no controls, we can make Paul do anything, go anywhere, and the sole evidence for any of the journeys (let alone for their dating) is that surmised from the documents themselves – on the odd assumption, judging from his previous experience, that all Paul's hopes and plans were fulfilled. It is interesting that those who suppose that the fragments represent genuine travel-plans do not think of placing them here, but, by dint of judicious selection and drastic dissection, slot them into the Acts framework – though even so they do not agree together.[148] But this is testimony to the fact that some external control is felt to be necessary for any plausibility. Those who believe that the travel plans are all part of the fiction do not explain why the inventor of them should not have aimed at greater verisimilitude. One would have expected him to quarry the details from existing sources (as the author of Ephesians is supposed to have drawn on Colossians for the journey of Tychicus), or at any rate to have seen that they matched. The very difficulty of squaring them with any itinerary deducible from Acts or the other Pauline epistles is a strong argument for their authenticity.

An attempt was indeed made some time ago by Vernon Bartlet[149] to fit them, with the rest of the captivity epistles, into the first imprisonment of Paul in Rome between 60 and 62. But quite apart from the hypothetical nature of *any* journeys back east from Rome, Bartlet's reconstruction is open to at least three weaknesses: (1) He does not attempt to explain why, if I Timothy and Titus were written from prison, they contain no references to Paul's 'bonds', like all the other prison epistles. (2) He is hard put to it to account for Paul's

---

course of Paul's voyage to Rome as a prisoner, the ship might have stopped at Miletus and Corinth (II Tim.4.20). During his imprisonment in Rome, Paul wrote II Timothy. In this letter, Paul is without hope of being released; he expects to be condemned and to suffer martyrdom in the near future (II Tim.4.6–8).'

[148] In his *Problem of the Pastoral Epistles*, 115–27, Harrison isolated five fragments and placed them as follows: (1) Titus 3.12–15 in western Macedonia; (2) II Tim.4.13–15, 20, 21a in Macedonia; (3) II Tim.4.16–18a (18b?) in Caesarea; (4) II Tim.4.9–12, 22b, and (5) II Tim.1.16–18; 3.10f.; 4.1, 2a, 5b, 6–8, 18b, 19, 21b, 22a in Rome (before the end of Acts). Duncan, op. cit. (n. 94), 184–225, scattered all his fragments among or between different imprisonments in or near Ephesus. Subsequently Harrison, *Paulines and Pastorals*, 106–28, converted to an Ephesian origin for Colossians and Philemon, reduced his fragments to three and located them as follows: (1) Titus 3.12–15, in western Macedonia; (2) II Tim.4.9–15, 20, 21a, 21b in Ephesus; (3) II Tim.1.16–18; 3.10f.; 4.1, 2a, 5b–8, 16–19, 21b, 22a in Rome.

[149] Vernon Bartlet, 'The Historic Setting of the Pastoral Epistles', *The Expositor*, 8th series, 5, 1913, 28–36, 161–7, 256–63, 325–47, especially 326–39.

referring back after some five years to his instruction to Timothy to stay on in Ephesus (I Tim. 1.3 = Acts 20.1) when so much else has happened to both of them in the interval. (3) He can do nothing with II Tim. 4.20 ('Erastus stayed behind at Corinth, and I left Trophimus ill at Miletus'), which he has to explain, rather tamely, as a misplaced fragment of a much earlier, and entirely hypothetical, letter.

With the other alternatives so unsatisfactory, it is at least worth exploring one more, and I do so by taking up the suggestive hint dropped by Reicke in the second of the two articles to which I referred (n. 101 above).

He draws attention to the names in common between Colossians and Philemon (which he has already argued were written from Caesarea) and II Timothy.[150] Demas, Luke and Mark reappear in different contexts (Col. 4.10, 14; Philem. 24; II Tim. 4.10f.). Moreover, in II Tim. 4.12 the sending of Tychicus to Ephesus (Eph. 6.21f.; cf. Col. 4.7–9) is again mentioned, but this time in the past tense. Timothy, associated with the writing of Colossians and Philemon, but not of Ephesians, is by now away on Paul's behalf apparently somewhere near Troas in Mysia, north-west of Ephesus (II Tim. 4.13). Mark, for a possible visit from whom Paul had previously prepared the Colossians (Col. 4.10), is to be collected from the same parts (II Tim. 4.11). Reicke's suggestion is that it is Mark who is to take II Timothy, which, he argues, is an open pastoral letter for reading aloud in the various churches visited. The names and places mentioned in it reflect his itinerary:

> A reference to the belief found in Timothy's mother and grandmother was inserted (II Tim. 1.5), for they lived in the city of Derbe (Acts 16.1), through which Mark had to pass on his way from Caesarea to Colossae (Col. 4.10). For the same reason the Christians, to whom Mark would come in other cities of Lycaonia, were reminded of Paul's earlier troubles in Antioch, Iconium and Lystra (II Tim. 3.11). After the visit to Colossae (Col. 4.10), Mark was expected to make the Christians of Ephesus familiar with the epistle of Timothy. He should especially let the house of Onesiphorus know about Paul's appreciation of this man (II Tim. 1.16–18; 4.19) and make sure that people in Asia realised the danger of the new heresy (1.15; 2.16–3.9).[151] After this it was planned that

[150] Though the personalia in Philippians are different, both Johnson, *ExpT* 68, 25, and Gunther, op. cit., 97, suggest that 'those who belong to the imperial establishment' in Phil. 4.22 could well be represented in the predominantly Latin names of Eubulus, Pudens, Linus, and Claudia, unique to II Tim. 4.21.

[151] We might add 4.14f., if (as Reicke subsequently agrees) Alexander the coppersmith is the same Alexander put forward in Acts 19.33f. by the silversmiths and workers in allied trades (19.25) of Ephesus. He is mentioned, in conjunction with Hymenaeus (who also appears in II Tim. 2.18), in I Tim. 1.20, which we shall argue comes from shortly after that incident.

> Mark should meet Timothy in Mysia (4.11) and go back with him *via* Troas (4.13). Paul needed their help since his only collaborator was presently Luke (4.11).[152]

Reicke adds, 'It is questionable whether any member of the early church would have found it worthwhile to restore or construct such antiquities in a later situation.'

Obviously such a reconstruction is hypothetical (and I shall question its detail), but at least it is not grounded on air. And once we make it, other connections open up. Above all, 'my first defence' (τῇ πρώτῃ μου ἀπολογίᾳ) in II Tim.4.16 will now refer not to some entirely undocumented court appearance in Rome but, like the ἀπολογία mentioned in Phil. 1. 7 and 16, to the hearings in Jerusalem and Caesarea, which in Acts 22.1 Paul specifically introduces as μου τῆς νυνὶ ἀπολογίας and which Felix adjourns in 24.22. As soon as this identification is made, other correspondences are recognizable. II Tim.4.17a, 'But the Lord stood by me and lent me strength, so that I might be his instrument in making the full proclamation of the Gospel[153] for the whole pagan world to hear,' reflects with considerable precision Acts 23.11, 'The following night the Lord appeared to him and said, "Keep up your courage: you have affirmed the truth about me in Jerusalem, and you must do the same in Rome"', while II Tim.4.17b, 'And thus I was rescued out of the lion's jaw', will refer to Paul's narrow escape from ambush the following day (Acts 23.12–35).[154] Even the phrase in II Tim.1.3, 'God, whom I, like my forefathers, worship with a pure conscience' echoes the speech Paul made before Felix in Acts 24.14 and 16: 'I worship the God of our fathers . . . and keep at all times a clear conscience.' Either the correspondences arise from the facts, or the author of the Pastorals is using Acts. But in that case why did he not draw on Acts for the travel-notes – or at least not make them so hard to harmonize?

If then we equate the captivity in II Timothy with that at Caesarea, Onesiphorus' services on Paul's behalf (II Tim.1.16f.) will fall into line with those of Epaphroditus (Phil.2.25–30) and of Onesimus (Philem.11–13), who were among the friends permitted to 'make

[152] *RE* 70, 438.

[153] Cf. earlier Rom.15.19: 'I have completed the preaching of the gospel of Christ from Jerusalem as far round as Illyricum.'

[154] Cf. M. Dibelius, *Die Pastoralbriefe* (HNT 13), Tübingen [8]1966, 95 who saw the strength of the case for Caesarea. Harrison, *The Problem of the Pastoral Epistles*, 121f., also recognized these parallels in his earlier placing of II Tim.4.16–18 in Caesarea – though he confused the issue by supposing, apparently, that only the speech of Acts 22.1–29 represented the 'first defence'. But later he put the fragment in Rome, where no hearing is recorded at all.

themselves useful to him' (Acts 24.23). But here we meet the first of two objections to the whole reconstruction. For apparently, according to II Tim. 1.17, Paul was not in Caesarea but in Rome, where Onesiphorus 'took pains to search me out when he came to Rome'. So fatal to his theory of an Ephesian imprisonment did Duncan find this verse that he was reduced to the desperate expedient of emending the text to *ἐν Πριήνῃ* or *ἐν Λαοδικίᾳ*.[155] But though it has regularly been taken to mean that Paul was in Rome when Onesiphorus came to see him, I am indebted to Reicke for an interpretation[156] which I believe in the context makes better (though admittedly less obvious) sense.

Onesiphorus was evidently a man of some substance, whose household in Ephesus was the centre of notable church work (II Tim. 1.16, 18; 4.19). In the last of these passages his name is linked with those of Prisca and Aquila, who, as we know, were in business (Acts 18.3) and are to be found at short intervals in a succession of places. Though hailing originally from Pontus, Aquila with his wife were, prior to 49, living in Rome (18.2). From 49 to 51 they were in Corinth (18.2–11), in 52 (18.26) and again in 55 (I Cor. 16.19) in Ephesus, in 57 in Rome, where they had a house (Rom. 16.3–5), and finally back once more in Ephesus (II Tim. 4.19). It is not unreasonable to suppose that Onesiphorus was also an itinerant Jewish business-man, of the sort so vividly described by James, who say to themselves: 'Today or tomorrow we will go off to such and such a town and spend a year there trading and making money' (James 4.13). It was on some such business trip that we may guess that Onesiphorus found himself in Rome (*γενόμενος ἐν Ῥώμῃ*). As was his wont, for Paul said he had 'often' relieved his needs (II Tim. 1.16), he looked out for Paul, expecting him to be there, since the apostle had made no secret of his

155 *Paul's Ephesian Ministry*, 189. Here Harrison could not follow him (*Paulines and Pastorals*, 93–5). Badcock, *Pauline Epistles and Hebrews*, 115–27, who also wished to put II Timothy in Caesarea (with Ephesians – though not Colossians and Philemon, which he located in Ephesus) was reduced in 1.17 to emending 'Rome' to 'Antioch' (of Pisidia), as well as placing 4.20 much earlier. Unfortunately his book is spoilt throughout by a tissue of speculation. E. G. Selwyn, *I Peter*, 1946, 392, referring to it with approval, says: 'I hesitate to express any opinion either as to the date or the genuineness of the Pastoral Epistles as they stand; but the view that the greater part of 2 Timothy was written during St Paul's imprisonment in Caesarea seems to me to merit careful consideration'. Gunther, op. cit., 95, 177, though placing II Tim. 4.9–22a in Caesarea, is compelled, without any supporting evidence, to see 1.15–18 (and 4.6f.) as a fragment of a later letter to Timothy from Rome.

156 To be included in his forthcoming article in *TLZ*, 'Chronologie der Pastoralbriefe'.

intention to go on to Rome after visiting Jerusalem (Acts 19.21; Rom. 1.15; 16.22–9). He failed to find him; but hearing he was in prison, he determined to search him out. He was 'not ashamed', says Paul, (though his business interests might have prompted otherwise?) to visit one who was 'shut up like a common criminal' (II Tim. 1. 16; 2.9). He made strenuous efforts to track him down (σπουδαίως ἐζήτησεν), and eventually found him. If Paul had been in a Roman jail, it is hard to believe that with his well-placed Christian contacts Onesiphorus would have had difficulty in being directed to him. Paul's extravagant gratitude (II Tim. 1.16, 18) seems to demand something more, and this would indeed be explained if Onesiphorus had made it his business to go out of his way to Caesarea to visit him before returning to Ephesus. At any rate the reference to Onesiphorus being in Rome cannot of itself be allowed to settle the question of *Paul's* being there, if the evidence points in another direction. We must judge the location of the epistle on its own merits.

The second difficulty is occasioned by II Tim. 4.20, 'I left Trophimus ill at Miletus'. For if this refers to Paul's brief stay at Miletus on the way to Jerusalem (Acts 20.15–38), Trophimus had not been left behind, for he was subsequently seen with Paul in the city (21.29). The easiest (perhaps too easy) solution would be to say that in a highly confused situation, of which there were garbled reports and rumours (21.27–40), Luke has simply mixed up the twin delegates from Asia (20.4) and confused Tychicus with Trophimus. It would be a pardonable error.

But Paul may not be referring to the journey up to Jerusalem. It is assumed both here and in Titus 1.5 that 'I left' (ἀπέλιπον) must imply that Paul himself was present. In Titus, as we shall see, there is no reason to suppose this to be implied. When speaking of his own personal possessions, as in II Tim. 4.13 ('the cloak I left with Carpus at Troas'), this of course is so. But Paul is also speaking in these letters very much as the director of operations, with 'the responsibility', as he puts it in II Cor. 11.28, 'that weighs on me every day, my anxious concern for all our congregations'. He is like a general reporting on the movements of his commanders in the field (cf. the metaphor of II Tim. 2.4: 'A soldier on active service . . . must be wholly at his commanding officer's disposal') or the head of a missionary society giving news of his staff. 'Demas has deserted and gone to Thessalonica: Crescens to Galatia, Titus to Dalmatia. Only Luke is here with me. Tychicus I have sent to Ephesus. Erastus has stayed in Corinth.[157]

[157] Perhaps because he now has a permanent post there, if Rom. 16.23 (written at Corinth) refers to the same man (cf. also Acts 19.22). Harrison argues persuasi-

Trophimus I have had to leave ill at Miletus.' Perhaps Trophimus was on his way back to Ephesus with his fellow-delegate Tychicus: we do not know.[158] Reicke suggests that Timothy is notified so that he may call in on him at Miletus, after Troas and Ephesus, on his way home (cf. the sequence in 4.13, 19, 20).

The one thing of which we can be reasonably sure is that Paul is reporting on recent events, not only for Timothy's benefit (who would have known of the first hearing of Paul's case from being at Jerusalem and Caesarea),[159] but for the leaders of the congregations, to whom the letter would be read out – for all the Pastoral Epistles end with greetings to the church as well as to the individual (I Tim. 6.21; II Tim. 4.22; Titus 3.15). This brings us back to our main question, the date of II Timothy, which, if our hypothesis is right, must be considered in close conjunction with that of the other letters from the Caesarean jail.

We may begin again with Philippians, which as we saw stands apart from the rest not only in style and content but in personalia. If it comes from the same place, it must be either before or after the rest. I had originally thought it came last, and indeed most scholars who see them written from the same imprisonment (Lightfoot was an exception)[160] have put it after Colossians and Ephesians, because it

---

vely for this in 'Erastus and his Pavement', *Paulines and Pastorals*, 100–5. He believes that οἰκονόμος means something more like 'clerk of works' than the NEB's 'city treasurer'. H. J. Cadbury, 'Erastus of Corinth', *JBL* 50, 1931, 42–58, comes down on the whole against the identification.

158 A *possible* alternative would be to take ἀπέλιπον in 4.19f. to mean 'they left' (for the history of this interpretation, cf. Zahn, *INT* II, 26) and refer it, with Johnson, *ExpT* 68, 25, to Onesiphorus and his family, who after visiting Paul (1.17) were taking Trophimus back home with them to Ephesus, while Tychicus was sent independently on Paul's work. Yet there is no reason to think that Onesiphorus' family was with him at the time and the subject for the plural verb is both remote and difficult.

159 This is a genuine diffculty, but not so hard surely as positing, with Johnson, op. cit., 26, another defence before Felix (why then is it called the first?) unrecorded by Acts, or referring it, with Gunther, op. cit., 109f., to the first defence under Festus (Acts 25.6–12). The latter solution would confine the writing of II Timothy to the few days (25.13) between that and the second ἀπολογία (26.1, 24) before Festus and Agrippa. Moreover it totally fails to explain why Paul does not inform Timothy of the major new turn in events – namely, his appeal to Caesar and the transfer of his case to Rome (25.11f.).

160 *Philippians*, 29–45. He rested his case, somewhat dubiously, on the resemblances with earlier epistles, especially Romans.

speaks of Paul looking forward to death.[161] Yet it is not at all natural to put it after II Timothy (as Reicke has to, since he locates Philippians in Rome), which reads if anything does like a last will and testament.

I am now persuaded, especially after reading Johnson's article already quoted,[162] that it is the first of the letters from Caesarea. He argued that the Philippians, who saw Paul and his party off on their journey to Jerusalem (Acts 20.6), would with their characteristic forwardness (Phil. 4.15–18) have lost no time in collecting for Paul's needs once they had heard of his imprisonment. The journey from Philippi to Caesarea in Acts 20.6–21.8 did not require longer, even with stopovers, than the six weeks between Passover and Pentecost, and there is no reason why, once the news had got back, Epaphroditus should not have arrived with their supplies by the autumn of 57. He then fell dangerously ill, for long enough for the Philippians to get news of it and for Epaphroditus to hear that they had done so. By the time Paul feels he must send him back (Phil. 2.25–30), with the letter, we may judge that winter has passed and that we are in the spring of 58. Timothy is associated with the writing of it (1.1) and Paul hopes shortly to send him too, so soon as ever he can see how things are going with him (2.19, 23). Timothy is still with Paul when he writes Colossians and Philemon but not, apparently, Ephesians (even though the three letters are taken together by Tychicus). However he writes to Timothy to inform him of Tychicus' dispatch to Ephesus (II Tim. 4.12) and asks him to collect the cloak which he had left with Carpus at Troas, together with his books and note-books (4.13), and to bring them before winter (4.21). Paul had doubtless deliberately deposited them there as he set out on foot for Assos in the warmth of late spring (Acts 20.13f.), fully expecting to pick them up on his way back after delivering the collection. Now he faces the prospect of a second winter without them in prison and is understandably pressing to have them in time. Reicke assumes that Timothy is in Mysia near Troas, but there is nothing actually to suggest this, nor anything to say that Mark should meet him there. It seems more natural to suppose that Paul writes to Timothy in Philippi (where he has sent him) and asks him to call in at Troas, and later at Miletus and Ephesus, on the route

[161] So Lohmeyer, *Kolosser*, 14f., who sets Colossians and Philemon as well as Philippians in Caesarea. But he does not reckon with II Timothy.

[162] *ExpT* 68, 24–6. His argument is unhappily mixed up with highly speculative theories that stichometrical analysis shows the 'two years' in Rome of Acts 28.30f. to be misplaced from the two years at Caesarea in 24.26 and *γενόμενος ἐν Ῥώμῃ* in II Tim. 1.17 to be an interpolation.

back to Caesarea that both of them had followed before (Acts 20.6–21.8). He is to pick up Mark, perhaps from Colossae, where Timothy, as joint-author of the letter to that church, would not need to be told he was due to be (Col. 4.10).[163]

If so, we may reconstruct the following time-table for the year 58:

Spring: Philippians written and dispatched *via* Epaphroditus to Philippi.
Summer: Philemon and Colossians written.
Timothy sent to Philippi.
Ephesians written and dispatched with the other two letters *via* Tychicus to Asia Minor.
Mark sent to Colossae.
Autumn: II Timothy written and dispatched to Philippi.

Reicke argues that Paul's appeal in Philem. 9 as 'an ambassador[164] of Christ Jesus and *now* his prisoner' indicates that this betokens a new situation and that Paul had therefore 'quite recently' been arrested. But this is surely to read a great deal into one word.[165] For Onesimus has already had time to become Paul's spiritual child in prison (Philem. 10f.) and indeed to begin, like Timothy, to 'be at his side in the service of the Gospel like a son working under his father' (Phil. 2.22; cf. I Tim. 1.2; II Tim. 1.2). Moreover time must be allowed for Epaphras to have come from Colossae bringing news of the state of that church, to which, after some thought and prayer, Paul responds (Col. 1.7–9). I believe that 58 is the earliest likely date. It is also probably the latest. For, like the rest of the news in II Timothy, the sending of Tychicus would appear to be quite recent. Anyhow by the following year Paul was already in late summer awaiting shipment to Rome: the request to have his cloak before winter would have been too late.

The only good reason for putting II Timothy later in Paul's career (unless we judge from 1.17 that it *must* come from Rome) is the sense it conveys that, as he sees it, the end is at hand – combined with *our* knowledge that it was not yet so. Yet already, according to Acts 20.24, he had said at Miletus in the spring of 57: 'I set no store by life; I only want to finish the race and complete the task which the Lord Jesus has assigned to me, of bearing testimony to the Gospel of God's grace.' But things dragged on for him. At first he had every reason to assume that his case would last no longer than it took Lysias to come down

[163] This involves abandoning Reicke's assumption that Mark is the carrier of II Timothy, but that is only a guess.

[164] More likely than 'old man', especially if Eph. 6.20, 'an ambassador in chains', is Pauline. Anyhow no inference for dating can safely be drawn from Paul's age.

[165] So too when he argues, *RE* 70, 435, that it could 'only' fit Caesarea.

from Jerusalem to Caesarea (Acts 24.22) and that he could expect early release. Until then he had had, as far as we know, no experience of more extended detention than being locked up on the order of local magistrates, which (if the incident at Philippi in Acts 16.19–40 is any sample) would not have lasted more than a night or so (16.35), even without the intervention of the earthquake. The word describing these experiences, *φυλακαί*, custody (II Cor.6.5; 11.23), is never used in the captivity epistles, where it is always *δέσμοι*; and the situation thus reflected is indeed different. As the weeks and months pass at the imperial headquarters, Paul's confidence ebbs. In Philippians, though he cannot yet see the outcome, he is sure that he will live to be with them again before long (1.25f.; 2.24). In Philemon he hopes, in answer to their prayers, to be granted to them (22). In Colossians and Ephesians he says merely that Tychicus will tell them all the news, and prays that he may be given the right words when the time comes (Col.4.7–9; Eph.6.19–22). By the time of II Timothy only the prospect of death appears to await him, hope of release having faded: he is deserted, and men must come to him (1.12; 4.6–13). As he was to explain later (Acts 28.19), he had 'no option' left – except his last card, appeal to the emperor.

To bear out the interconnections – and the mutual order – of Philippians and II Timothy, it is interesting to observe how he takes up the language of 'finishing the race' (*τελειώσω τὸν δρόμον*) which, according to Luke's report (Acts 20.24), had come into his speech at Miletus. (Earlier he had used the same metaphor but spoke of running rather than finishing: I Cor.9.24–6; I Tim.6.12.) We may set the phrases out in parallel columns:

Philippians	*II Timothy*
What I should like is to depart (*ἀναλῦσαι*) (1.23)	The hour for my departure (*ἀναλύσεως*) is upon me (4.6).
If my life-blood is to crown the sacrifice (*εἰ καὶ σπένδομαι*) (2.17).	Already my life-blood is being poured out on the altar (*ἤδη σπένδομαι*) (4.6).
I have not yet reached perfection (*οὐκ . . . ἤδη τετελείωμαι*) but I press on (3.12).	I have run the great race, I have finished the course (*τὸν δρόμον τετέλεκα*) (4.7).
I press toward the goal to win the prize (3.14).	Now the prize awaits me (4.8).

It is hard to resist the conclusion that both epistles reflect the mind of the same man, at not too great an interval and in that sequence.

So we may put Philippians in the spring of 58, Philemon, Colossians and (a little later) Ephesians in the summer of 58, and II Timothy in the autumn of 58.

But what finally of the other Pastoral Epistles, I Timothy and Titus? Working backwards from II Timothy, let us take *Titus* first.

We last heard of Titus in Corinth, whither he had been sent from Macedonia to reorganize the collection (II Cor. 8; 12.17f.). By the time Paul writes Romans early the next year, he is evidently no longer there – or he would certainly have featured, like Timothy, in the greetings of Rom. 16.21–3. Paul is finishing off the business of the collection himself (15.28). It could well have been at this stage that he had sent Titus to Crete, for which Cenchreae, the port of Corinth (cf. 16.1f.), was the natural point of embarkation. He was sent, as Paul reminds him in Titus 1.5, to set right the shortcomings of the church there (τὰ λείποντα:[166] *not* what remained to be done after some hypothetical visit of Paul's) and to appoint local presbyters. Paul explains that he had deliberately left him behind, instead of taking him with the rest (as Titus of all people had surely earned the right to expect) as one of the delegates to Jerusalem. This is just the opposite of what he had done earlier when, he explains to the Thessalonians, 'we decided to be left in Athens alone and sent Timothy' (I Thess. 3.1). So he writes Titus a charge, for public recitation, to reinforce his original instructions (1.5) and promises him a replacement (3.12).

When is Paul writing? There is no hint that he is in prison.[167] Any time in the first half of 57 would fit. Reicke has made the plausible suggestion that Paul writes to Titus *en route* to Jerusalem, perhaps from Miletus, whence a boat could easily go to Crete and where we know his mind was occupied with similar matters. Indeed he may well have used material prepared for his charge to the Ephesian elders. Themes common to the speech and the epistle are the warnings to elders, who are also ἐπίσκοποι (Acts 20.18, 28; Titus 1.5–9), against those who like wild beasts will ravage the flock from within and by distortion of the truth break up the family of God (Acts 20.29f.; Titus 1.10–12) and an insistence on the example of honest work (Acts 20.33f.; Titus 3.8, 14). Paul has with him Artemas as well as Tychicus (Titus 3.12), one of whom (and the uncertainty argues strongly for authenticity) he promises to post to Crete. Presumably it was Artemas, of whom we hear nothing more, since Tychicus was sent subsequently to Ephesus. When the replacement arrives, Titus is to hasten to join Paul in Nicopolis, where, he says, he has decided to spend the winter. This would be the same winter of 57, for Paul was fully intending at this point, having delivered the collection, to come back west to Italy and

166 Cf. Titus 3.13, 'See that they are not short (λείπῃ) of anything'.

167 Failure to recognize this vitiates Gunther's reconstruction of the epistle (op. cit., 114–20) as coming from the same time as II Timothy.

Spain (Rom. 15.28). And there is no suggestion that he planned to go by sea, as eventually he was forced to. On the contrary, he would follow his usual practice of going over the ground he had covered. Naturally he would go *via* Asia Minor (Philem. 22), stopping at Troas to pick up his cloak and other valuables (II Tim. 4.12f.). Then he would call in at Philippi (Phil. 2.24), before taking the *Via Egnatia* to consolidate the work in Illyricum and the north-west begun the previous year. He would winter with Titus on the coast at Nicopolis in Epirus, and thence cross the Adriatic, when the spring weather allowed, for southern Italy and Rome. But, alas, as it turned out, Titus had to go to Dalmatia alone (II Tim. 4.10) and Paul was to spend the winter languishing in a Palestinian jail.

What finally of *I Timothy?* With far fewer personal details than the other two, it is correspondingly difficult to locate. There is no more suggestion than in Titus that Paul is or has been in prison. The only clear clue is in 1.3, where he says to Timothy, 'When I was starting for Macedonia, I urged you to stay on at Ephesus.' It is natural to look to Acts 20.1, where Paul sets out for Macedonia from Ephesus after the silversmiths' riot, and natural, too, as we have said, to surmise that the Alexander mentioned in 1.20 recalls the same incident. Unfortunately, as we have seen, Luke's notice in Acts 20.1f. condenses a considerable amount of time and activity which it is impossible to reconstruct accurately. During the interval Paul probably went to Corinth and back and certainly spent some time in the neighbourhood of Troas. From where he would have written to Timothy we cannot know. Perhaps it was from Corinth, if he *did* travel there *via* Macedonia, as he originally planned (I Cor. 16.5) – though probably he went direct (II Cor. 1.16). More likely it was from the Troad, where he had gone for missionary work, which turned out to present many openings (II Cor. 2.12). At the time of writing he is still hoping to come to Timothy before long, though he recognizes the possibility of delay (I Tim. 3.14f.). The next time in fact they meet, owing to Paul's restless determination to push on (instead of returning to Ephesus?) in order to make contact with Titus (II Cor. 2.13), is evidently in Macedonia, where Timothy joins Paul in the sending of II Corinthians (1.1). It looks therefore as if the autumn of 55 is the most likely space for I Timothy. Indeed the farewell exhortation for which Paul assembled the disciples in Acts 20.1 may be the occasion mentioned in I Tim. 1.3, where the same word is used (παρακαλέσας, παρεκάλεσα). The letter will then reinforce on paper as a pastoral charge the gist of this address, whose substance could indeed be incorporated in I Tim.2.1–3.13 (beginning παρακαλῶ οὖν). I Timothy more than any other epistle stresses the aspect of παραγγελία or pastoral 'order' (1.3, 5, 18; 4.11; 5.7; 6.13, 17), which had been a distinctive feature of Paul's apostolic method from the beginning (I Thess.4.11; II Thess.3.4, 6, 10, 12; I Cor.7.10; 11.17). We should not therefore see anything un-Pauline or indeed novel here. If the dating seems surprisingly early we must not forget that at this stage Timothy is evidently still quite junior and is working closely under Paul's supervision. Earlier the same year he had felt it necessary to say to the Corinthians:

> If Timothy comes, see that you put him at his ease; for it is the Lord's work that he is engaged upon, as I am myself; so no one must slight him. Send him happily on his way to join me, since I am waiting for him with our friends (I Cor. 16.10f.).

Now he writes to his protégé in very similar terms:

> Let no one slight you because you are young, but make yourself an example to believers in speech and behaviour, in love, fidelity, and purity. Until I arrive . . . make these matters your business and your absorbing interest, so that your progress may be plain to all (I Tim.4.11–15).

It is not difficult to believe that these words were written six months apart.

Each of these three epistles appears to embody directions for an immediate pastoral occasion. We tend to assume that Paul is appointing Timothy and Titus to extended supervision over designated areas. But in fact the instructions relate to specific short-term tours. In II Timothy Timothy is to do his best to come back as soon as possible (II Tim.4.9); Titus is to be relieved whenever Paul can arrange for a replacement (Titus 3.12); and I Timothy is written only for the brief interval during which Timothy is to stay on[168] at Ephesus until Paul himself can come (I Tim.3.14; 4.13). They do not presuppose, nor do they require, long gaps. They are more like the charges composed by a modern missionary bishop for an archidiaconal visitation lasting weeks or months rather than years. It is not unknown for a busy bishop to have these written for him. But in any case their style is determined much more by their form and content than by their date. If Paul had need for such specialized and formal communications there is no reason why he should not have put them together, or had them put together, probably out of material prepared (as Acts would suggest) for spoken exhortations to church leaders, in amongst, rather than after, his other correspondence. So it should not surprise us if they

[168] The same word that is used in Acts 18.18 for Paul staying on 'for some days' at Corinth.

were not composed, as is usually assumed, in a bloc by themselves. Nor is there valid recourse to explain the change of style by the passage of years. For if our conclusions are right, the whole of Paul's extant correspondence (not forgetting that as early as II Thess. 3.17 he spoke of 'all my letters') appears to fall within a period of nine years – indeed apart from his early letters to the Thessalonians within the astonishingly short span of four and a half years.

To clarify this we may end with a summary of the resultant dates:

50 (early)	I Thessalonians
50 (or early 51)	II Thessalonians
55 (spring)	I Corinthians
55 (autumn)	I Timothy
56 (early)	II Corinthians
56 (late)	Galatians
57 (early)	Romans
57 (late spring)	Titus
58 (spring)	Philippians
58 (summer)	Philemon
	Colossians
	Ephesians
58 (autumn)	II Timothy

It must be stressed again that the absolute datings could be a year or so out either way and that the schema is more tentative than it looks. But the importance of these conclusions, which, except for the Pastoral Epistles, are not particularly controversial, is threefold:

(*a*) They provide a reasonably fixed yardstick or time scale against which to set other evidence.

(*b*) If in fact the whole of Paul's extremely diverse literary career occupied so brief a span, this gives us some objective criterion of how much time needs to be allowed for developments in theology and practice. Though it may at first sight appear extraordinarily short, we should not forget two other canons of measurement. The whole of Jesus' teaching and ministry (which I believe to have involved at least three fundamental shifts in the way he saw his person and work)[169] occupied at most three or four years. And the whole development of early Christian thought and practice up to the death of Stephen and the conversion of Paul, including the first Hellenistic statement of the gospel, took place within something like the same period.[170] Indeed Hengel, in his important article 'Christologie und neutestamentliche

[169] Cf. my book *The Human Face of God*, 1973, 80–4.
[170] Cf. R. B. Rackham, *Acts*, [6]1912, lxix.

Chronologie',[171] argues strongly that the crucial stage in the church's basic understanding of Christ and his significance was represented by the four to five 'explosive' years between 30 and 35. These years included the tension between the groups in Jerusalem (*c.* 31–2), the murder of Stephen and the dispersion of the church apart from the apostles (*c.* 32–3), the conversion of Paul (*c.* 32–4), and the first missionary work in Judaea and Samaria, Phoenicia, Damascus and Antioch (*c.* 33–5). By the time of his first extant epistle (I Thessalonians) Paul's Christology, Hengel maintains, is in all fundamentals complete, having reached its essential shape in the years prior to any of his missionary journeys. Speaking of the period up to the council of Jerusalem in 48 (and his dates agree with ours), he says: 'Fundamentally more happened christologically in these few years than in the following 700 years of church history.'[172] *A priori* arguments from Christology to chronology, and indeed from any 'development' to the time required for it, are almost wholly unreliable.

(*c*) The working assumption we made to trust Acts until proved otherwise has been very substantially vindicated. There is practically nothing in Luke's account that clashes with the Pauline evidence, and in the latter half of Acts the correspondences are remarkably close. Even in the speeches attributed to Paul, and especially those at which Luke can be presumed to have been present (Acts 20 and 22–5), there are parallels to suggest that they are far from purely free compositions. This conclusion must also be relevant as we turn now to consider how close in date Acts stands to the events which it records.

[171] In Baltensweiler and Reicke, *Neues Testament und Geschichte*, 43–67.
[172] Hengel, op. cit., 58; cf. his *Son of God*, ET 1976, 2.

IV

Acts and the Synoptic Gospels

WITH THE PAULINE chronology is bound up the question of Acts, and so of Luke and the other synoptists. Whether, according to the unanimous external tradition, Luke is the author of the third gospel and the Acts of the Apostles is not directly our problem. Though a second-century date clearly rules out a companion of Paul, the middle ground of 80–90 for which most recent critics opt need not. In fact Goodspeed[1] argues for the authorship of Luke only *if* Acts is put late (*c.* 90). On the other hand, the earlier the joint work is dated the less reason there is for questioning the ascription. For if it is not by Luke, then it is by some other unknown figure who stood as close to the events and for whom Paul was equally clearly the hero. It is possible to deny, on theological grounds, that the author could have been a close associate of Paul's and yet to come to exactly the same dating as those who think that he was.[2] I do not propose therefore to go into the question of authorship, but simply record that with the majority of English scholars I see no decisive reason against accepting the traditional ascription.[3]

If an author for the Gospel, in particular, were being invented or guessed at there would have been the strongest possible reason for fastening on an apostle or at any rate a disciple of the Lord. Moreover, the style of the 'we' sections of Acts (16.10–17; 20.5–15; 21.1–18;

[1] *INT*, 197–204.

[2] Kümmel, *INT*, 147–9, 179–87, and G. W. H. Lampe, *PCB*, 820f., 882f.

[3] For a balanced assessment of the points at issue, cf. C. S. C. Williams, *Acts*, introduction. In favour of Lukan authorship: Streeter, *FG*, 540–62; E. E. Ellis, *Luke* (NCB), 1966, 40–52. Against: Haenchen, *Acts*, 112–16; Kümmel, *INT*, 147–50, 174–85.

27.1–28.16) is, as Harnack showed,[4] the style *par excellence* of the writer of the whole when freely composing in his own hand. There is no real ground for arguing that he is here using a source or travel-diary other than his own. The discrepancies with Pauline teaching[5] have in my judgment been much exaggerated, and room must be allowed for two facts. (*a*) Acts is presenting Paul for the most part addressing those outside the church, in contrast with the epistles which deal with concerns between Christians. The only speech in Acts addressed by Paul to Christians is that to the elders at Miletus in 20.17–38, which we have already seen contains some remarkable parallels with the later Pauline writings.[6] In Rom. 1.18–2.16 Paul shows how far he is prepared to go in accepting pagan presuppositions in addressing those outside the law; there is no fundamental contrast with the speech put into his mouth at Athens in Acts 17.22–31.[7] (*b*) The author of Acts is an independent lay mind of Gentile upbringing who presents himself (Luke 1.1–4) *primarily* as an historian,[8] not a professional theologian. Thus, Acts 13.39 ('It is through him that everyone who has faith is acquitted of everything for which there was no acquittal under the Law of Moses') is a typical 'lay' summary of a theologian's position: inadequate in precision of statement (for it could be taken to imply that for some things justification by the law was possible), but sufficient in general intention. The recent tendency to turn Luke into a 'theologian's theologian',[9] is, I believe, a misguided exercise and detracts from appreciation of his stated purpose and, within his own terms, still profoundly theological understanding of events. Absence of reference to the epistles of Paul cannot be regarded as a decisive objection. For Luke is not writing his 'life and letters' any more than he is writing a biography of Jesus, and Paul himself sees his letters as stopgaps or preparations for the visits, and these are what Acts records. On the other hand, silence on the very existence of the epistles is, as Kümmel says,[10] a formidable objection,

[4] A. Harnack, *Date of Acts and the Synoptic Gospels*, ET 1911, ch. 1; cf. his earlier *Luke the Physician*, ET 1907, ch. 2. Goodspeed and Williams here concur.

[5] Emphasized by Haenchen, *Acts*, 112–16. [6] Pp. 80f. above.

[7] For the historical setting of this, cf. T. D. Barnes, 'An Apostle on Trial', *JTS* n.s. 20, 1969, 407–19.

[8] For the most recent assessment of Luke's intention, in the light of the Hellenistic parallels, cf. W. C. van Unnik, 'Once more St Luke's Prologue', *Neotestamentica* 7, 1973, 7–26, and the literature there cited.

[9] E.g. H. Conzelmann, *The Theology of St Luke*, ET 1960. For a balanced corrective, cf. I. H. Marshall, *Luke: Historian and Theologian*, Exeter 1970. For a survey of recent views, cf. C. K. Barrett, *Luke the Historian in Recent Study*, 1961; [2]Philadelphia 1970.

[10] *INT*, 186; cf. Zahn, *INT* III, 125f.

amongst many others,[11] to a second-century date. It is unbelievable that a later writer should not have made use of them for his reconstruction or at least alluded to them.

When we come to the issue of dating proper, we may note in passing that one argument, namely, the supposed dependence of Acts on Josephus' *Antiquities*,[12] which would require a date after 93, seems to have been almost totally abandoned.[13] Apart from general considerations of the time required for the development of the theological and historical perspective of Luke–Acts, which are notoriously subjective, and in turn depend on other datings, the three 'hard' pieces of evidence are: (*a*) the prophecies of the fall of Jerusalem in Luke; (*b*) the dependence (according to the most widely held solution of the synoptic problem) of the gospel of Luke upon that of Mark; and (*c*) the fact that Acts ends where it does.

The first, (*a*), we have already examined and concluded that these prophecies afford no ground for supposing that they were composed or even written up after the event. Rather, the contrary. This does not of course mean that they could not have been incorporated, without change (though this in itself would need explanation), into a gospel written later. But in themselves they provide no evidence for a later dating. Indeed they afford a presumption (from *unfulfilled* prophecy) of a dating not simply before the fall of the city in 70 but before the flight of Christians to Pella prior to the beginning of the war in 66.

The second, (*b*), depends for its force on the fact (if it is a fact) that Luke is subsequent to Mark and, of course, on the dating of Mark. The main reason for supposing Luke to have been written after 70 even by those (like Dodd) who agree that the prophecies do not

[11] Cf. Harnack, whose knowledge of the field of early Christian literature was second to none: 'It is a perfect mystery to me how men like Overbeck and now again P. W. Schmidt can set the Acts of the Apostles in a line with the works of Justin Martyr! St Luke's Christology simply cries out in protest against such procedure; nor is the case different with other characteristics of this writer' (*Date of Acts*, 109). He might now have added John Knox, *Marcion and the New Testament*, Chicago 1942, ch. 5, who argues for a date of Acts *c.* 140, and J. C. O'Neill, *The Theology of Acts*, 1961, ch. 1, who dates it between *c.* 115 and 130.

[12] Stressed, for instance, by F. C. Burkitt, *The Gospel History and its Transmission*, Edinburgh 1906, 109f.

[13] Cf. F. J. Foakes Jackson, *Acts* (Moffatt NTC), 1931, xivf.; Kümmel, *INT*, 186; Lampe, *PCB*, 883; Manson, *Studies in the Gospels and Epistles*, 64f. Writing in 1910, Harnack regarded this point as having been 'settled thirty-four years ago by Schürer'. Quoting the latter's summary, 'Either St Luke had not read Josephus, or, if he had read him, he had forgotten what he had read', Harnack said: 'Schürer here exactly hits the mark' (*Date of Acts*, 114f.).

demand it is that the dating of Mark forces Luke later. This, however, must be considered on its own merits in conjunction with the wider synoptic problem. It will be convenient then to look first at the third piece of evidence, relating to the ending of Acts.

(*c*) The closing words of Acts are:

> He [Paul] stayed there [in his own lodging in Rome] two full years at his own expense, with a welcome for all who came to him, proclaiming the kingdom of God and teaching the facts about the Lord Jesus Christ quite openly and without hindrance (28.30f.).

The question is: why does the account stop at this point? As Harnack said,[14]

> Throughout eight whole chapters St Luke keeps his readers intensely interested in the progress of the trial of St Paul, simply that he may in the end completely disappoint them – they learn nothing of the final result of the trial! Such a procedure is scarcely less indefensible than that of one who might relate the history of our Lord and close the narrative with his delivery to Pilate, because Jesus had now been brought up to Jerusalem and had made his appearance before the chief magistrate in the capital city!

Various reasons have been advanced to explain this ending.[15] It is said that it suits Luke's apologetic purpose to close with Paul preaching 'openly and without hindrance' to the Roman public. But this must surely have been rendered less than cogent for Theophilus by glossing over in silence the common knowledge that he and Peter and 'a vast multitude' of other Christians in the city had within a few years been mercilessly butchered. There is no hint of the Neronian persecution, which because of its excesses won considerable sympathy for the Christians, as Tacitus says.[16] Nor for that matter is there any hint of the death of James the Lord's brother in 62, which took place at the hands of the Sanhedrin *against* the authority of Rome. The high priest Ananus seized the opportunity of an interregnum in the procuratorship after the death of Festus to exercise capital jurisdiction for which the Sanhedrin had no authority. Agrippa took immediate steps to put himself and the Jewish people in the right with Rome by removing Ananus from office before the new procurator arrived.[17] No incident could have served Luke's apologetic purpose better, that it was the Jews not the Romans who were the real enemies of the gospel.

[14] *Date of Acts*, 95f.

[15] For a summary of suggested solutions, cf. Lake and Cadbury in *Beginnings* IV, 349f.; for Lake's own proposals, V, 326–32. R. P. C. Hanson, 'Interpolations in the "Western" Text of Acts', *NTS* 12, 1965–6, 224–30, suggests merely that Luke did not need to go on because his (Roman) readers knew the rest. But presumably they also knew about the two previous years.

[16] *Ann.* 15.44. [17] Josephus, *Ant.* 20.200–3.

Yet there is not a hint of James ever falling foul of the Jewish authorities, unlike his namesake, James the brother of John (Acts 12.1f.). Nor is there any shadow in Acts of the impending Jewish revolt, let alone of the destruction of Jerusalem to bear out the earlier prophecies of the Gospel. When last we hear of them, the representatives of Judaism, alike of church (24.2f.; 25.1–5) and state (25.13–26.32), are living in a condition of courteous, if suspicious, detente with Rome. One could never guess from Acts what was to break within a few years.

Other explanations, that Acts was left unfinished (yet never supplied with an ending such as was deemed necessary for Mark) or that Luke intended a third volume[18] (for which there is no evidence whatever – and in any case why break *there?*), are recourses of desperation. Harnack wrote again:[19]

> For many years I was content to soothe my intellectual conscience with such expedients; but in truth they altogether transgress against inward probability and all the psychological laws of historical composition. The more clearly we see that the trial of St Paul, and above all his appeal to Caesar, is the chief subject of the last quarter of Acts, the more hopeless does it appear that we can explain why the narrative breaks off as it does, otherwise than by assuming that the trial had actually not yet reached its close. It is no use to struggle against this conclusion.[20]

Harnack is still worth quoting, not merely because he is one of the great ones in the field, whose massive scholarship and objectivity of judgment contrast with so many who have come after him, but because on this subject he was forced slowly and painfully to change his mind. In his *Chronologie*, itself, as he says in his preface,[21] the product of fifteen years' study, he dated Luke–Acts with some confidence between 78 and 93.[22] By the time he wrote his *Acts of the Apostles*[23] he personally felt that an earlier date was far more probable but cautiously deferred to the weight of contrary opinion:

> Therefore for the present we must be content to say: St Luke wrote at the time of Titus [79–81] or in the earlier years of Domitian [81–96], *but perhaps even so early as the beginning of the seventh decade of the first century.*[24]

[18] So Zahn, *INT* III, 58–61. [19] *Date of Acts*, 96f.

[20] Even Manson, op. cit., 67, who thinks Mark early enough to accommodate such a date for Acts (see below, p. 111), struggles aganist this conclusion to the extent of saying that Luke perhaps did not himself know the outcome of Paul's trial, or, granted that he *must* have heard of his martyrdom if it had occurred 'anywhere near the dates usually given for it', is ready to appeal to Luke's silence as evidence that it did not!

[21] *Chron.*, vi, dated 31 May 1896. [22] *Chron.*, 250.

[23] A. Harnack, *The Acts of the Apostles*, originally Leipzig 1908; ET 1909.

[24] Op. cit., 297. Italics his when quoted in his subsequent *Date of Acts*, 91.

But three years later in his *Date of Acts and the Synoptic Gospels*[25] he concluded without reservation that it is 'in the highest degree probable' that Acts was written at the stage at which the narrative terminates, i.e., on our reckoning, if not his,[26] in 62. He argues that in 28.30 the aorist ἐνέμεινεν, rather than an imperfect, suggests that the period of Paul's relative freedom was now closed, but that if he had left Rome Luke could hardly have failed to mention it. He therefore thinks that Acts was written very soon after this time of unhindered evangelism was over and Paul was removed to the praetorium to begin the process of his trial.[27]

If the outcome of that trial (or a subsequent one) was already known, it is surely incredible, as Harnack says, that no foreshadowing or prophecy of it after the event is allowed to appear in the narrative. For earlier Agabus, besides foretelling a famine (Acts 11.28), prophesies that Paul would be bound by the Jews in Jerusalem and handed over to the Gentiles (21.11); and Paul himself is represented as knowing in advance that he was destined to appear safe before the emperor, with the lives of all that were sailing with him (27.24). Yet the only hint he gives of his ultimate fate is that 'imprisonment and hardships' await him and that his friends at Miletus would 'never see his face again' (20.24f., 38). What we should expect, but do not get, are such clear predictions (whether genuine or not) as we find of the death of Peter in John 21.18f. and II Peter 1.14.

Harnack goes on to adduce numerous positive indications of an early dating of Acts derived from the primitive character of its terminology.[28] But none of these is proof against the argument that Luke is using the language of his sources or consciously archaizing.

[25] Originally *Neue Untersüchungen zur Apostelgeschichte*, Leipzig 1911; ET, 90–135.

[26] I raise the question, without having been able to document the answer, whether Harnack may not have changed his mind on this too. According to his *Chronologie*, Paul left Jerusalem in 56, arrived in Rome in 57, and the two years' detention there would have ended in 59. Yet in *The Date of Acts* he argues for a date in the early 60s and quotes (92) with approval a fellow German scholar who, on the basis of his own previous statement in *The Acts of the Apostles*, dated it in 62. Despite the English title of his second book, he never actually dates Acts. But it certainly looks as though, without mentioning it, he had moved away from his previous (unsatisfactory) argument for an early dating for Festus' accession. Bammel agrees and tells me it was probably due to Schürer's article, *ZWT* 41, 21–42, replying to his *Chronologie* a year later.

[27] Parry, *The Pastoral Epistles*, xvf., while agreeing with Harnack's conclusion on the date, argues that the implication of the aorist is that Paul left *Rome* after two years. But neither inference can be more than a guess, and indeed even to press the implications of the tense at all is hazardous. See below p. 141.

[28] *Date of Acts*, 103–14.

Nor may we draw any certain conclusion from the notable absence from Acts of subsequent changes in Roman administration and law.[29] Nevertheless, the burden of proof would seem to be heavily upon those who would argue that it *does* come from later, and there is nothing, as far as I can see, in the theology or history of the Gospel or Acts that *requires* a later date if the prophecies of the fall of Jerusalem do not.[30] From the internal evidence of the two books we should therefore conclude (as did Eusebius)[31] that Acts was completed in 62 or soon after, with the Gospel of Luke some time earlier.[32] But what of the repercussions of this for the dating of the other synoptists, and in particular of Mark, which, on the prevailing hypothesis of the priority of Mark, Luke was using? It is the difficulty of squaring this conclusion with the dominant view that Mark comes from the latter 60s (if not later) that has weighed most heavily against its acceptance.

At this point one comes up against the synoptic problem and its solution. In some circles there has of late been a vigorous revival, led by W. R. Farmer,[33] of the hypothesis first formulated by J. J. Griesbach in 1783 that Mark represents a conflation of Matthew and Luke, Luke himself being dependent on Matthew. In this case there is no problem as far as the dating of Mark is concerned, since it can be put as late after Luke as desired. But a similar question then arises with the dating of Matthew which on this hypothesis Luke used, and this for most scholars would present even greater difficulties. It has even been argued that Luke was written first of all,[34] though this has not

[29] Cf. Sherwin-White, *Roman Society and Roman Law*, especially 85, 120–2, 172–93.

[30] Cf. Reicke, 'Synoptic Prophecies', 134: 'The only reasonable explanation for the abrupt ending of Acts is the assumption that Luke did not know anything of events later than 62 when he wrote his two books.' J. Munck, *Acts* (Anchor Bible), New York 1967, xlvi–liv, added the weight of his authority to a dating at the beginning of the 60s, concluding: 'It is simply not possible to use relative chronologies based on internal comparison among the gospels as arguments against an early date for Luke-Acts, until the datings proposed either by source critics or members of other schools can be demonstrated beyond cavil to have a firmer foundation than is at present the case' (liv). Cf. earlier Rackham, *Acts*, l–lv; Torrey, *Composition and Date of Acts*, 66–8; Bruce, *Acts*, 10–14.

[31] *HE* 2.22.6.

[32] C. S. C. Williams, 'The Date of Luke-Acts', *ExpT* 64, 1952–3, 283f., and *Acts*, 12f., argues that Acts is early but Luke late. But this is an unnecessary expedient, which reverses the author's clear indication that the first volume of his work was already with Theophilus by the time that he undertook the sequel (Acts 1.1). There is no reason to believe that 'Proto-Luke' (as Williams argues) was ever a sufficiently finished product to leave its author's hands.

[33] W. R. Farmer, *The Synoptic Problem*, New York and London 1964.

[34] R. L. Lindsay, *A Hebrew Translation of the Gospel of Mark*, Jerusalem n.d. [1969], and *A New Approach to the Synoptic Gospels*, Jerusalem 1971.

commended itself widely. In any case, the question of relative order is secondary to that of absolute dating. Reicke, working with the hypothesis of Markan priority, is prepared to date all three synoptists before 60, whereas the great majority of its other representatives put all of them later. On the other hand Farmer thinks them all to be late (with Mark possibly even in the second century),[35] while another exponent of the Griesbach hypothesis, J. B. Orchard,[36] would see Matthew as composed in the 40s with Luke and Mark in the early 60s.

This is not the place to become involved in the synoptic problem for its own sake. It is also a time when the state of opinion with regard to it is more fluid than it has been for fifty years. The consensus frozen by the success of the 'fundamental solution' propounded by Streeter[37] has begun to show signs of cracking. Though this is still the dominant hypothesis, incapsulated in the textbooks, its conclusions can no longer be taken for granted as among the 'assured results' of biblical criticism. It is far too early yet to say what new patterns or modifications of older patterns will establish themselves. The main thing required is a suspension of former dogmatisms and an admission that none of the various hypotheses so confidently advanced as overall solutions may satisfy all the facts. As E. P. Sanders concludes in his careful study, *The Tendencies of the Synoptic Tradition*,

> The evidence does not seem to warrant the degree of certainty with which many scholars hold the two-document hypothesis. It would also seem to forbid that a similar degree of certainty should be accorded to any other hypothesis. . . . I believe our entire study of the Synoptic Gospels would profit from a period of withholding judgments on the Synoptic problem while the evidence is resifted. . . . I rather suspect that when and if a new view of the Synoptic problem becomes accepted, it will be more flexible and complicated than the tidy two-document hypothesis.[38]

With that judgment I should fully concur, and it has been borne out for me by a test-study I have recently made on a small but representative sample, the parable of the wicked husbandmen in Mark 12.1–12 and pars.[39] Though its conclusions do not depend upon any particular dating nor is the dating dependent on them, I would refer the reader to it to indicate at one point how the fresh openness for which I am pleading is not simply based on a vague impression but demanded by a detailed analysis of the evidence. My conclusion

[35] Op. cit., 227. [36] J. B. Orchard, *Why Three Synoptic Gospels?*, 1975.

[37] *FG*, chapter 7.

[38] E. P. Sanders, *The Tendencies of the Synoptic Tradition*, Cambridge 1969, 278f. In the context of his argument the author italicized the first sentence.

[39] See my article, 'The Parable of the Wicked Husbandmen: A Test of Synoptic Relationships', *NTS* 21, 1974–5, 443–61.

is that we must be open to seeing that the most primitive state of the triple, or 'Markan', tradition (as indeed most scholars would agree in relation to the double, or 'Q', tradition) is not consistently or exclusively to be found in any one gospel, to which we must then assign over-all temporal priority. Rather I believe that there was written (as well as oral) tradition underlying each of them, which is sometimes preserved in its most original form by Matthew, sometimes by Luke, though most often, I would judge, by Mark. Hence the strength of the case for the priority of Mark, which is nevertheless overstated when this gospel is itself regarded as the foundation-document of the other two. The gospels as we have them are to be seen as parallel, though by no means isolated, developments of common material for different spheres of the Christian mission, rather than a series of documents standing in simple chronological sequence. This still allows the possibility that Matthew, say, may have been affected by Mark in the course of the redactional process, or indeed Luke by Matthew, without requiring us to believe that one is simply to be dated after the other.

We have been accustomed for so long to what might be called linear solutions to the synoptic problem, where one gospel simply 'used' another and must therefore be set later, that it is difficult to urge a more fluid and complex interrelation between them and their traditions without being accused of introducing unnecessary hypotheses and modifications. But if we have learnt anything over the past fifty years it is surely that whereas epistles were written for specific occasions (though they might be added to or adapted later), gospels were essentially for continuous use in the preaching, teaching, apologetic and liturgical life of the Christian communities. They grew out of *and with* the needs. One can only put approximate dates to certain states or stages and set a certain *terminus ad quem* for them, according to what they do or do not reflect. And at any stage in this development one must be prepared to allow for cross-fertilization between the ongoing traditions. This does not at all mean that all interrelationships are equally probable or that rigorous sifting of various hypotheses to explain them is not required. But in dealing with the dating of the gospels one is dealing not so much with a succession of points in time as with potentially overlapping spans of development in which oral and literary processes went on together and in which the creative hand of the individual evangelist is not to be isolated from the continuing pressures of community use. And one has always to make allowance for the fact that the external evidence which speaks of the 'writing' or 'putting out' of the gospels, even if it reflects good tradition, cannot with confidence be assigned to any one stage or state of this process.

With these general observations, which can only be ratified by specific studies, I would venture to sketch what would appear to be a plausible account of how and when the gospel traditions took shape.

We may begin with the earliest external testimony which we have, the well-known words of Papias, Bishop of Hierapolis in the early part of the second century, whom Irenaeus described as 'a hearer of John and a companion of Polycarp, a man of primitive times'.[40] Papias is quoted by Eusebius,[41] first of all, with regard to Mark:

> This also the elder used to say. Mark, indeed, having become[42] the interpreter of Peter, wrote accurately, howbeit not in order, all that he recalled of what was either said or done by the Lord. For he neither heard the Lord, nor was a follower of his, but, at a later date (as I said), of Peter; who used to adapt his instructions to the needs [of the moment],[43] but not with a view to putting together the dominical oracles in orderly fashion: so that Mark did no wrong in thus writing some things as he recalled them. For he kept a single aim in view: not to omit anything of what he heard, nor to state anything therein falsely.

And, then, immediately afterwards,[44] concerning Matthew:

> So then, Matthew compiled the oracles in the Hebrew language; but everyone interpreted them as he was able.

Papias here distinguishes the *ad hoc* instructions (διδασκαλίας) used for preaching and teaching, which were adapted to the requirements of the occasion, and the more orderly collection (σύνταξιν) of the sayings of the Lord (τῶν κυριακῶν λογίων). The former were reflected, so he believed, in the recollections of Mark, the latter in the compilation (συνετάξατο) of Matthew. The former were, we may suppose, judging from the content of St Mark's gospel, primarily *stories* ('of what was either said or done by the Lord') culminating in the passion story, the latter primarily *sayings*. These two elements are recognizably the building bricks of all the matter represented in different proportions in our synoptic gospels. Without pressing any hard and fast distinction,

[40] *Adv. haer.* 5. 33.4; cited Eusebius, *HE* 3. 39.1.

[41] *HE* 3.39.15. For recent discussions of this, cf. H. E. W. Turner, 'The Tradition of Mark's Dependence upon Peter', *ExpT* 71, 1959–60, 260–3; Martin, *Mark: Evangelist and Theologian*, 52f., 80–3.

[42] Lawlor and Oulton here translate γενόμενος 'having *been*', implying that he was the 'late' interpreter of Peter, who was by then dead. But it is best not to prejudge this.

[43] For an attractive alternative interpretation of χρείαι (adopted by Farmer, op. cit., 266–70, and Orchard) to mean brief biographical apophthegms for instructional purposes, cf. R. O. P. Taylor, *The Groundwork of the Gospels*, Oxford 1946, 29f., 75–90. He takes Papias to mean: 'Peter drew up his lessons with a view to supplying maxims and anecdotes to be learnt in order to be quoted' (30).

[44] *HE* 3. 39.16.

we may judge that the dominant context in the life of the church for the preservation of the first was *kerygma* or preaching, that for the second *didachē* or teaching. The needs of the former are reflected in such summaries as that in Acts 10.37–41:

> I need not tell you what happened lately all over the land of the Jews, starting from Galilee after the baptism proclaimed by John. You know about Jesus of Nazareth, how God anointed him with the Holy Spirit and with power. He went about doing good and healing all who were oppressed by the devil, for God was with him. And we can bear witness to all that he did in the Jewish country-side and in Jerusalem. He was put to death by hanging on a gibbet; but God raised him to life on the third day, and allowed him to appear, not to the whole people, but to witnesses whom God had chosen in advance – to us, who ate and drank with him after he rose from the dead.

The needs of the latter will have led to such collections of sayings[45] (and how far and when they were written down is quite secondary) as we have learnt to label for convenience 'Q' and (to the extent that they are sayings rather than stories) 'M' and 'L'. This first stage must have gone back to the earliest days of the Christian mission and the instruction of converts in the 30s and 40s, and was doubtless perpetuated after the demand for more complex formulations arose.

Secondly, out of these stories and sayings (under the influence of a variety of motives, evangelistic, apologetic, catechetical, disciplinary and liturgical) one may see emerging for the first time documents which could in a proper sense be described, not indeed as 'gospels' in the plural, a use not to be found until the last quarter of the second century,[46] but as 'the gospel' in writing. This is the usage that appears to be reflected in the Didache:[47]

> As the Lord commanded in his Gospel, thus pray ye: Our Father . . . (8.2).
>
> But concerning the apostles and prophets, so do ye according to the ordinance of the Gospel. Let every apostle, when he cometh to you, be received as the Lord . . . (11.3).
>
> Reprove one another, not in anger but in peace, as ye find in the Gospel (15.3).
>
> But your prayers and your almsgivings and all your deeds so do ye as ye find it in the Gospel of the Lord (15.4).

[45] For this category of sayings-collections within and beyond our canonical gospels, cf. J. M. Robinson, '*Logoi Sophōn:* On the Gattung of Q', in J. M. Robinson and H. Koester, *Trajectories through Early Christianity*, Philadelphia 1971, 71–113.

[46] For the evidence cf. G. W. H. Lampe (ed.), *A Patristic Greek Lexicon*, Oxford 1961–8, *εὐαγγέλιον*.

[47] All translations of the Apostolic Fathers are from J. B. Lightfoot, *The Apostolic Fathers*, 1891. His five-volume edition of the same title, ²1889–90, will be distinguished by inclusion of the volume number.

The reference is evidently to some document familiar and accessible to the readers. Though closest to the Matthean tradition, the quotations cannot be demonstrated to depend on the canonical gospel of Matthew. The dating of the Didache is notoriously uncertain and we shall return to it in ch. x. Here I shall anticipate the findings of J.-P. Audet's massive and detailed investigation[48] that though these passages come in his judgment from the second stage of its composition they still reflect a period before our gospels were completed and throw valuable light on their prehistory. We may for the sake of argument call this document proto-Matthew. Its milieu is clearly Palestinian or Syrian and many have seen the most probable locale both of the Didache and of Matthew to be Antioch. It is likely to have represented the first formulated statement of 'the gospel' used by the apostles, teachers and prophets to whom the Didache refers (10.7–15.2), and whom Acts also mentions in connection with Antioch and its missionary work (13.1–3; 14.14). Inasmuch as Paul went out in the first instance as the delegate of this church, we may suppose that this was primarily the tradition of the 'words of the Lord' which he took with him, and it would explain the otherwise rather unexpected affinity alike in doctrine and in discipline between Paul and Matthew,[49] especially in early writings like the Thessalonian epistles.[50] (To the implications of this for the dating of Matthew I shall return.)

If this is the case, it would go a long way to explain the external tradition that Matthew was the first gospel. It has been widely recognized, even by advocates of the priority of Matthew, that this cannot be true of our canonical Matthew, which quite apart from its possible (indeed probable) dependence on Mark, shows every sign of incorporating some of the latest developments in the synoptic tradition. It is scarcely sufficient, either, to make it refer to the λόγια mentioned by Papias as collected by Matthew in the Hebrew tongue, which are much more likely to relate to a pre-gospel stratum like 'Q'.[51] But it might reflect the composition which for the sake of a label we have called proto-Matthew. This *could* have some relationship to what is referred to by Irenaeus (assuming he had any tradition independent of Papias) when he reports that 'Matthew published a

[48] J.-P. Audet, *La Didachè: Instructions des Apôtres* (Études Bibliques), Paris 1958.

[49] Cf. B. C. Butler, 'St Paul's Knowledge and Use of St Matthew', *DR* 60, 1948, 363–83; Dodd, 'Matthew and Paul', *NT Studies*, 53–66; D. L. Dungan, *The Sayings of Jesus in the Churches of Paul*, Oxford 1971.

[50] Cf. J. B. Orchard, 'Thessalonians and the Synoptic Gospels', *Bb* 19, 1938, 19–42; J. A. T. Robinson, *Jesus and His Coming*, 1957, 105–11.

[51] For a strong statement of this, cf. Manson, *Studies in the Gospels*, 75–82.

gospel in writing (γραφὴν ἐξήνεγκεν εὐαγγελίου) among the Hebrews in their own language',[52] though clearly what is being quoted by the Didache and used at Antioch is in Greek. This stage may coincide with the needs of the missionary expansion from Antioch in the second half of the 40s, described in Acts 13 and 14.

What such a document contained it is, of course, impossible to be sure. All that the Didache, as its name implies, is interested in citing is material relating to liturgical, ethical and disciplinary instruction. But the Didache, or 'the Teaching of the Twelve Apostles', refers to it, with deference, as 'the Gospel of the Lord' (or 'his Gospel'), as though it were clearly different from teaching and nothing else. Dogmatism about what a gospel 'must' have included at this stage is clearly out of place. The 'Gospel of Thomas' is indeed no more than a collection of sayings, but this title (confined to its colophon: at the beginning it describes itself as 'the secret words'), like that of 'The Gospel of Truth', may reflect the polemical usage of heretical circles in the second century. It could represent 'a flag under which various kinds of writings circulated at a time when the canonical gospels and hence the title "gospel" had gained wide acceptance in the orthodox church'.[53] Indeed this is what Irenaeus suggests.[54] Within the main stream of the church's tradition there is no suggestion that 'the gospel' centred on anything but what was 'proclaimed', the *kerygma* – and that found its focus in the death and resurrection of Christ.[55] This is true of 'the gospel' that Paul himself received in the earliest days (I Cor. 15.1–4), and it is still true when 'the gospel' comes to have the overtones of a written book set alongside the Old Testament: 'Give heed to the Prophets, and especially to the Gospel, wherein the passion is shown to us and the resurrection is accomplished'.[56] It is a fair assumption

[52] *Adv. haer.* 3.1.1. The Greek is cited in Eusebius, *HE* 5.8.2. For further discussion of this passage, see below p. 110.

[53] J. M. Robinson in Robinson and Koester, op. cit., 76.

[54] 'For indeed they go on to such great audacity as to entitle what they themselves only recently wrote as "The Gospel of Truth", although it agrees at no point with the gospels by the apostles, so that not even the gospel can be among them without blasphemy. For if what they publish as of truth is the gospel, but is dissimilar to those handed down to us by the apostles, persons who so wish can learn (as is shown from the writings themselves), that what was handed down from the apostles is not the gospel of truth' (*Adv. haer.* 3.11.9; quoted by J. M. Robinson, op. cit., 77).

[55] Cf. F. F. Bruce, 'When is a Gospel not a Gospel?', *BJRL* 45, 1962–3, 319–39: 'A Gospel without a passion narrative is a contradiction in terms' (324).

[56] Ignatius, Smyrn. 7.2; cf. Philad. 8.2 (cf. 9.2). Koester, *Synoptische Überlieferung bei den apostolischen Vätern*, Berlin 1957, 6–12, argues that in Ignatius the reference of 'the gospel' is still oral, though he agrees that there is a transition to

then that what the Didachist deferred to as 'the Gospel' contained, as well as the matter which he was interested in citing, the story of Jesus up to and including his death and resurrection.

Now there is no evidence to suggest that the Matthean tradition, unlike the Lukan and the Johannine, ever contained passion material (except of a suspiciously secondary strain)[57] independent of that which it shares with Mark. Whatever the relationship between our Matthew and our Mark, it is clear that there was common material (evidently, from the degree of verbal agreement, in written form) which, as I read the evidence, goes back behind them both and which Matthew on some occasions at least still preserves in its most primitive state.[58] And this passion material is of a piece with other material in a common order of which the same is true. We normally call this 'the Markan tradition', since it is represented most distinctly and usually, I would judge, most originally in our second gospel. But I am persuaded that it goes back behind both our first two gospels (and indeed the third). It may well be that it bears, as Papias believed, through Peter a special relationship to Mark, just as the sayings collection bore a special relationship to Matthew, without this 'P' tradition (if we may so call it)[59] any more than the 'Q' material being exclusively identified with the gospels of Mark and Matthew as we now have them. All we can say with reasonable confidence is that it was these two streams that united, with other distinctively Palestinian matter, to produce (in Greek) what I have called proto-Matthew and what the Dida-

---

written form in Did. 15.3f. It is remarkable that neither these passages nor those in the Didache are mentioned by Koester in his discussion of the origins of the 'Gattung' gospel in Robinson and Koester, op. cit., 158–66, nor again by W. Schneemelcher in his survey of the history of the term 'Gospel' in E. Hennecke (ed.), *New Testament Apocrypha*, ET 1963–5, I, 71–84.

[57] E.g. stories like that of Pilate's wife's dream (Matt. 27.19), his hand-washing (27.24f.), and the guards at the tomb (27.62–6; 28.11–15).

[58] I have argued this of Matt. 26.64 = Mark 14.62 = Luke 20.69 in my *Jesus and His Coming*, 43–50. I contended there, on the assumption of the priority of Mark, for subsequent alterations to the Markan *text*. But the evidence for this is not strong, and I would prefer now to attribute the secondary features in Mark to editorial activity.

[59] In this I venture to follow my uncle J. Armitage Robinson, who, according to R. H. Lightfoot, *History and Interpretation in the Gospels*, 1935, 27, used this symbol in his lectures at Cambridge, with 'Q' simply as the next letter in the alphabet for the sayings-collection. (This is without prejudice to whether this was the *origin* of the symbol 'Q', which appears improbable; cf. Moule, *Birth of the NT*, 84.) 'P' may carry the overtones of 'preaching' or 'Petrine' if desired, but I would not wish to identify it *simpliciter* either with Peter's preaching or with Mark's gospel.

chist speaks of as 'the Gospel' in his area. This in itself carries no implications for the priority either of our Matthew or of our Mark, though it suggests, as Papias implies, that the 'P' material was both apostolic and early. Indeed in his version of the tradition there is no tying of it to Peter's preaching mission in Rome, but rather to Peter's general evangelistic practice (ἐποιεῖτο), such as Paul must certainly have intended to include in his reference to the common apostolic proclamation: 'whether it be I or *they*' (I Cor. 15.11).[60]

Elsewhere there were doubtless other attempts to set down in writing presentations of the gospel in a form that lay between preachers' notes and collections of sayings on the one hand and finished gospels on the other. Luke in his preface refers indeed, no doubt with some exaggeration, to a quantity of such:

> Many writers have undertaken to draw up an account (διήγησιν) of the events that have happened among us, following the traditions (καθὼς παρέδοσαν) handed down to us by the original eyewitnesses and servants of the Gospel. And so I in my turn, your Excellency, as one who has gone over the whole course of these events in detail, have decided to write a connected narrative (καθεξῆς γράψαι) for you (1.1–3).

The fact that he contrasts these attempts at an 'account', alike with the traditions that lie behind them and with his own connected narrative, may suggest that we are here dealing with the stage of what we have labelled proto-gospels, written statements of the gospel for local use which, in retrospect, were 'accurate' but were felt to lack 'ordered presentation'. Indeed it may well be that the production to which the Elder gave this description was not Mark's gospel as we now have it (which does not strike *us* as lacking order) but a summary of Peter's mission-preaching, which was to become later a proto-gospel for the Roman church. But it is Luke himself who has provided occasion, in what Streeter called 'proto-Luke', for the supposition of a stage in the construction of the gospels which would correspond in a modern work to a first draft. What, again, this consisted of, if it was ever a self-subsistent document, will never be known; but it certainly fits much of the evidence (as Streeter argued) to suppose that Luke used the 'P' material as a secondary source to supplement the 'account' he in his turn had begun to put together 'following the traditions handed down' to him ('Q' and 'L') as a tentative statement of the gospel for the Gentile mission.

Whatever these precursors, the next stage is the formulation, in response to the changing and growing needs of the church, of the

[60] Cf. Gal. 2.9 ('we and they'); I Cor. 1.2 ('theirs and ours'); and Manson, op. cit., 192–4.

gospels as we know them, basically in their present form, though not necessarily in their final state.

Matthew represents the gospel for the Jewish-Christian church, equipping it to define and defend its position over against the arguments and institutions of the main body of Judaism. But, in contrast with the Judaizers, it is a Jewish-Christian community open to the Gentile mission and its tensions. For while Matthew contains some of the most Judaistic (5.18f.; 10.5; 15.26; 18.17; 23.2f.) texts in the gospels, it also contains the most universalistic (21.43; 24.14; 28.19). Antioch again seems a likely locale (cf. e.g. the tension there described in Gal. 2.11–14), though the tradition behind it is surely Palestinian.

Luke (followed by Acts) is, in contrast, essentially the gospel for that imperial world evangelized by Paul 'from Jerusalem to Rome' (Rom. 15.19–24), though not repudiating any more than Paul did its deep roots in Judaism and the Septuagint.

Mark (in whatever order it comes) is the gospel for the 'Petrine centre', serving a mixed community like the church in Rome which owes its origin and ethos exclusively to neither wing but which has its own problems and pressures.

The gospel of John must also, I believe, be seen as an integral part of the same interconnected scene, being fashioned, out of a similar process, for the church's mission among Greek-speaking Jews first in Palestine and then in the *diaspora*. But I shall be deferring consideration of it to a later chapter.

All these gospels will doubtless have continued to go through different states (what we might anachronistically call editions) as the needs grew and changed. This is probably least true of *Luke*, whose gospel is the nearest equivalent to a modern book written and published for a single individual and at a particular moment in time: 'I have decided (ἔδοξε) to write . . . for you', he says to Theophilus (1.3). As the Muratorian Canon puts it, Luke 'composed [the Gospel] in his own name on the basis of report'.[61] Unlike the others it does not seem to have been put together at the request, or for the purposes, of a group. Yet the evidence for an original beginning with the formal dating at 3.1 suggests an earlier state, and the whole work – with the collecting of the material for Acts – may have occupied Luke for many years (cf. 1.3: 'as one who has gone over the whole course of events in detail'). *Mark* may have gone through more than one recension. Thus I have suggested[62] there are grounds for supposing

[61] Cadbury's translation, *Beginnings* II, 211. Cf. Manson, op. cit., 52f.

[62] *Jesus and His Coming*, 128–36; cf. Trocmé, *Formation of Mark*, ch. 4; he argues that chapters 14–16 belong to the 'second edition' (*c.* 85).

that its present eschatology (represented in ch. 13) developed from one which originally viewed the *parousia* as an exaltation scene in Galilee (prefigured at the transfiguration), such as we still find in Matt. 28.16–18. Indeed I am happy to discover that Goodspeed[63] also thought that this passage incorporated the 'lost ending' of Mark – or rather, let us say, the 'P' material missing, for whatever reason, from the end of the second gospel. Later I shall be arguing that there were at least two 'editions' of *John* (the second with the prologue and epilogue added), and most scholars have detected more. But it is *Matthew* that gives evidence of the longest formation history. It has often been observed that Matthew is a 'collector', accumulating diverse layers of tradition (e.g. of eschatology in 10.23; 24.29–31; 26.64; 28.20), which may reflect different states or stages of composition. *If* (as those who abandon the 'two-document' hypothesis have to assert) Luke knew and used Matthew, and there was not merely a relationship through 'P' and 'Q', then it could be easier to explain the absence from Luke, or the lack of influence upon Luke, of some of the more secondary features of the special Matthean material and editorial additions on the hypothesis of an earlier 'edition' of Matthew than by Luke's deliberate omission of Jewish features that did not interest him. These would include such things as the quotation-formulae, the ecclesiastical and Petrine additions, some quasi-legendary stories, the allegorization and embellishment of many of the parables, the apocalyptization of the eschatology, and the 'prologue' of the first two chapters answering the questions, for apologetic with Judaism, of the genealogical and geographical origins of the Messiah. The 'school of Matthew', to use K. Stendahl's phrase,[64] may well have continued for some time the process of bringing forth things old and new (13.52). Matthew could therefore in a real sense turn out to be both the earliest and the latest of the synoptists. This is interestingly reflected in a judgment of Harnack's, who was certainly no advocate of the priority of Matthew in the usual sense:

> That the synoptic gospel which was most read should have received the most numerous accretions, and should be the latest in date, is nothing remarkable, but only natural. Moreover, it remains, in regard to *form*, the oldest 'book of the Gospel'; the others have obtained the rank and dignity of such a title because they have been set by the side of St Matthew's gospel, which from the first, unlike the others, claims to be an ecclesiastical book.[65]

[63] *INT*, 156. [64] K. Stendahl, *The School of St Matthew*, Uppsala 1954.

[65] *Date of Acts*, 134f. He goes on: 'As the place of origin of the first gospel, Palestine alone can come into consideration.' I would agree as far as the material is concerned, though the concern for the Gentile mission perhaps suggests a more cosmopolitan place of redaction.

The process of what Harnack calls 'accretions' continued for a long time in the textual tradition.[66] But can we say when Matthew reached its present canonical form?

We have looked at the arguments for dating it after 70 on the ground of its possible references to the Jewish war and the fall of Jerusalem. The addition to the parable of the great supper in 22.7 ('The king was furious, he sent troops to kill those murderers and set their town on fire') we agreed *could*, but by no means necessarily must, have been supplied *ex eventu*. But from the examination of the apocalyptic discourse in ch. 24 we concluded that there was no case for thinking that it was written for the interval between the fall of Jerusalem and the *parousia*: rather the opposite. Indeed there was no reason for supposing that it reflected even the beginning of the war: the flight to Pella prior to its outbreak is actually contradicted by the instructions to take to the hills of Judaea. Is this conclusion borne out or overturned by the evidence of the rest of the gospel?

Matthew's gospel shows all the signs of being produced for a community (and by a community) that needed to formulate, over against the main body of Pharisaic and Sadducaic Judaism, its own line on such issues as the interpretation of scripture and the place of the law, its attitude toward the temple and its sacrifices, the sabbath, fasting, prayer, food laws and purification rites, its rules for admission to the community and the discipline of offenders, for marriage, divorce and celibacy, its policy toward Samaritans and Gentiles in a predominantly Jewish milieu, and so on. These problems reflect a period when the needs of co-existence force a clarification of what is the distinctively Christian line on a number of practical issues which previously could be taken for granted. It corresponds to the period when the early Methodists were compelled by events to cease to regard themselves as methodical Anglicans, loyal to the parish church and its structures as well as to their own class meetings. At this stage all kinds of questions of organization, ministry and liturgy, doctrine and discipline, law and finance, present themselves afresh, as a 'society' or 'synagogue' takes on the burden of becoming a 'church'. But uneasy co-existence does not necessarily imply an irrevocable break: indeed John Wesley claimed that he lived and died a priest of the Church of England. It is in some such interval that the gospel of Matthew seems most naturally to fit. Its are not the problems of the first careless, expansionist years. Yet for all the tension there is not the altercation of two estranged and separated camps, such as followed the defeat of Judaism and is reflected in the

[66] The doxology to the Lord's Prayer (Matt. 6.13) is an obvious example.

Epistle of Barnabas,[67] the consolidation of rabbinic Judaism at Jamnia, and the formal ban on Christians from the synagogue.[68] One may agree with Reicke when he says:[69] 'The situation presupposed by Matthew corresponds to what is known about Christianity in Palestine between AD 50 and *ca.* 64.'

Two illustrations will indicate that the old *status quo* is still in operation.

Matthew is more concerned than any other evangelist with the relationship of Christianity to the temple, the priesthood and the sacrifices. Typical is a passage peculiar to this gospel in the middle of a discussion, common to the other synoptists, on the sabbath law:

> Or have you not read in the Law that on the Sabbath the priests in the temple break the Sabbath and it is not held against them? I tell you, there is something greater than the temple here. If you had known what that text means, 'I require mercy, not sacrifice', you would not have condemned the innocent (12.5–7).

Matthew alone has the same quotation from Hos. 6.6, 'I require mercy, *not* sacrifice' also in 9.13, while it may perhaps be significant that he does not have that from I Sam. 15.22 cited in Mark 12.33, where love of God and neighbour is declared to be '*far more* than any burnt offerings or sacrifices'. Matthew's concern, like that of the author to the Hebrews, is evidently to present Jesus as the *substitute* for Christians of all that the temple stands for. Yet there is no more suggestion in the one than the other that the levitical system is not still in active operation. Indeed Matthew has seven references to the Sadducees (compared with one each by Mark and Luke), warning against their influence.[70] Since this was a group whose power disappeared with the destruction of the temple, preoccupation with them argues strongly for an earlier period.

The same applies to Matthew's characteristic interest in the Christian community's attitude to the half-shekel tax for the upkeep of the temple (17.24–7). The teaching of Jesus is taken to be that even though Christians may rightly consider themselves free of any obligation to the system, the tax should be paid, 'as we do not want to cause difficulty for these people'. This certainly does not argue a situation of open breach, but rather a concern not to provoke one. In any case, it clearly points to a pre-70 milieu. For after that date this tax had to be paid to the temple treasury of Jupiter Capitolinus

[67] For the dating of this, see below, ch. x.

[68] For a discussion of this, cf. pp. 272–4 below.

[69] 'Synoptic Prophecies', 133.

[70] See especially Matt. 16.1–12. In the other gospels (Mark 8.11–15; Luke 12.1) it is the Pharisees (and in Mark also Herod) who are singled out for warning.

in Rome[71] and would have had no bearing on the *Jewish* question Jesus is represented as settling.[72] As H. W. Montefiore has said,[73]

> The difference between Jesus' voluntary payment of the upkeep of the Jewish Temple and the Christians' payment under duress for the upkeep of a pagan shrine is very great indeed. It is almost impossible to see how a story about the former could have been constructed in order to give a precedent about the latter. . . . It is easier to suppose that an earlier saying had been adapted to meet the need of Christians in the period after AD 70.

It is surely easier still, unless we start, as he does, by saying 'it may be assumed that St Matthew's Gospel was written sometime between AD 70 and AD 96', to suppose that this 'adaptation' (which he describes as 'far too inappropriate' for invention) did not need to be made at all. The saying (which basically, he argues, goes back to Jesus) was very relevant to the pre-70 situation of the Jewish-Christian church: it was quite irrelevant afterwards. As the Mishnah specifically says,[74] '[The laws concerning] the Shekel dues . . . apply only such time as the Temple stands.'

Finally, there are two arguments which carry no weight in themselves but which may confirm an early date for Matthew if this is on other grounds probable.

In a study of the parallels between the apocalyptic material in Thessalonians and the synoptic gospels,[75] I recorded what then seemed to me the bizarre conclusion that the closest connections were between what appeared to be the earliest material in the epistles and the latest developments in the synoptic tradition, the editorial matter in Matthew. Of these developments, characteristic of the distinctively Matthean treatment both of 'P' and 'Q' material, I wrote:

> The tendencies which produced them set in much earlier than the Gospels by themselves would lead us to expect. Already, it appears, by the year 50, the Church was thinking in a manner reflected in the Synoptic material only in its latest strands.[76]

Dating Matthew, as I then did, well after the fall of Jerusalem, I attributed this to an (unexplained) time lag. But what if these tendencies *were* already those of the Matthean community and its

[71] Josephus, *BJ* 7. 218.

[72] To be distinguished from the very different issue of the payment of tribute to Caesar (Mark 12.13–17 and pars).

[73] H. W. Montefiore, 'Jesus and the Temple Tax', *NTS* 11, 1964–5, 65.

[74] *Shek.* 8.8. All translations of the Mishnah are from H. Danby, *The Mishnah*, Oxford 1933.

[75] *Jesus and His Coming*, 105–11. [76] Op. cit., 105.

version of the gospel by the time Paul left Antioch after the council of Jerusalem in 49?[77] For the same connections are to be found with the apocalypse in the Didache (16), which we have already had occasion to associate with this period and place. Obviously these arguments for dating are circular, and we shall have to return to the dating of the Didache in particular. But the evidence of Thessalonians at any rate shows that this way of thinking was rife in the year 50. The marks of it in Matthew 24 cannot therefore be used to *require* any later date for that gospel.

Secondly, there is an argument from silence to which no importance can be attached on its own but which is perhaps just worth including since it supports the same conclusion. After the martyrdom of James the Lord's brother in 62, which itself has left no echo in the New Testament (as we might have expected if so much of it had been written later),[78] Eusebius records,[79] on the authority of Hegesippus, that he was succeeded as bishop of Jerusalem by Symeon, the son of Clopas, Joseph's brother. There is much in this tradition that is evidently hagiographical. But it seems likely that the succession would be kept within the family, the lineage necessarily for a Jew being traced through the father's side. Moreover, if a name was being invented later, one would have expected one to be supplied from among those mentioned in scripture. But the 'Mary wife of Clopas' mentioned in John 19.25, and referred to in this connection by Eusebius,[80] who is probably (though not certainly) to be identified with 'the other Mary' (Matt. 27.61)[81] at the cross and tomb, is described as the mother of James and Joseph (Mark 15.40; Matt. 27.56), or of the one (Mark 16.1; Luke 24.10), or the other (Mark 15.47), but never of Symeon. If Symeon was the son who after 62 achieved leadership of the mother church one might at least have expected his mention, especially in the Palestinian tradition. For Mark goes to the trouble of naming the sons of Simon of Cyrene, Alexander and Rufus (Mark 15.21), perhaps because, like their mother, Rufus was a member of the Christian congregation in Rome (Rom. 16.13), and Matthew alone identifies Salome with the mother of the sons of Zebedee

[77] Orchard, *Bb* 19, 39, draws the conclusion that Paul knew Matt. 23.31–25.46 and that 'this passage is something absolutely primordial and must be dated somewhere between 40 and 50 AD'. But this goes with his belief in the priority of Matthew in its present form and seems to me to be pushing the evidence much too far.

[78] It rates a long chapter in Eusebius, *HE* 2.23, who gives an extensive quotation from Hegesippus, as well as being recorded by Josephus, *Ant.* 20. 200–3.

[79] *HE* 3.11; 3.32.1–6; 4.22.4.

[80] *HE* 3.11.

[81] Cf. A. Meyer and W. Bauer in Hennecke, *NT Apoc.* I, 425f.

(Matt. 27.56, as well as introducing her in 20.20). For what little it is worth, it suggests again that the first gospel is prior to this date.

In this case we have pushed Matthew back at any rate before 62, which is exactly the date to which we were driven for Acts, with Luke a little earlier This would mean that the final stage of the formation of the synoptic gospels roughly coincided with the end of the 50s. Our argument so far would therefore yield the following provisional schema:

1. Formation of stories- and sayings-collections
   ('P', 'Q', 'L', 'M'): 30s and 40s +
2. Formation of 'proto-gospels': 40s and 50s +
3. Formation of our synoptic gospels: 50–60 +

But how, finally, does Mark fit into this, from the question of whose dating we started?

It is a curious phenomenon that for the gospel that was least read or esteemed in the early church there is more tradition relating to its date of composition than any other. For the rest there are statements about the sequence in which they were written, which for the most part merely reflect or rationalize the canonical order. The only exception is that of Clement of Alexandria, who is reported by Eusebius[82] to have inserted into his *Hypotyposeis* 'a tradition of the primitive elders' that 'those gospels were first written which include the genealogies' (i.e. Matthew and Luke). As Mark was honoured as the first bishop of Alexandria there would seem to be no motive there in deliberately putting his gospel last of the synoptists. But this tradition can scarcely be used, as it is by Farmer,[83] in support of his hypothesis that Mark represents a literary conflation of Matthew and Luke, since the same tradition went on to say of the origin of the gospel of Mark:[84]

> When Peter had publicly preached the word at Rome, and by the Spirit had proclaimed the Gospel, that those present, who were many, exhorted Mark, as one who had followed him for a long time and remembered what had been spoken, to make a record of what was said; and that he did this, and distributed the Gospel among those that asked him. And that when the matter came to Peter's knowledge he neither strongly forbade it nor urged it forward.[85]

It is natural to regard this tradition as being the same as that

[82] *HE* 6. 14.5. [83] Op. cit., 226. [84] *HE* 6.14.6f.

[85] The text here is probably corrupt. The Greek reads *ὅπερ ἐπιγνόντα τὸν Πέτρον προτρεπτικῶς μήτε κωλῦσαι μήτε προτρέψασθαι*. The repetition *προτρεπτικῶς . . . προτρέψασθαι* is odd to say the least. An amendment *πνευματικῶς* has been suggested, in line with the similar statement ('by revelation of the Spirit') in *HE* 2.15.2 (cited p. 108 below). The Latin version has 'postmodum' ('later').

quoted from Papias earlier:[86] indeed elsewhere[87] Eusebius says that Papias 'corroborates' the testimony. Yet the matter common to both is actually limited to the bare fact of Mark being a follower of Peter who wrote down what he recalled of his teaching. It is Clement who links it to a particular preaching mission in Rome, and to the production and distribution of a book to which Peter's reaction is recorded – clearly implying that Peter was still alive (though absent) at the time of its writing.[88] Both passages however tend to damn Mark's efforts with faint praise, and Peter's neutral attitude towards it may reflect no more than the church's doubts about the value of St Mark's gospel for the canon. In his other account of it[89] Eusebius relates a more enthusiastic response, which suggests a desire to reinforce the apostolic authority of the second gospel:

> So brilliant was the light of piety that shone upon the minds of Peter's hearers [in Rome], that they were not content to be satisfied with hearing him once and no more, nor with the unwritten teaching of the divine message; but besought with all kinds of entreaties Mark, whose Gospel is extant, a follower of Peter, that he would leave them in writing also a memoir of the teaching they had received by word of mouth; nor did they relax their efforts until they had prevailed upon the man; and thus they became the originators of the book of the Gospel according to Mark, as it is called. Now it is said that when the apostle learnt, by revelation of the Spirit, what was done, he was pleased with the men's zeal, and authorized the book to be read in the churches.

Jerome also mentions the authorization of the gospel by Peter,[90] citing Clement and Papias, but he is evidently merely copying Eusebius without checking his references. For the two passages conflict. Moreover the affirmative response of the apostle is introduced by the words, 'now it is said' (φασί), suggesting that Eusebius is at this point reporting popular tradition rather than Clement's words. The passages, particularly the second, tell us nothing reliable about Peter's attitude to the gospel of Mark, but they both presuppose, if there is anything in them at all, that Peter was alive, though no longer present in Rome, when it was first committed to writing.

Moreover there are two further passages extant from Clement himself which describe Mark as writing while Peter was still in Rome. The first is preserved only in Latin translation:

[86] Pp. 95 above. [87] *HE* 2. 15.2.

[88] Thus contradicting the implication Lawlor and Oulton find in Papias' statement that Mark's link with Peter lay in the past.

[89] *HE* 2.15.1f.; quoting Clement, *Hypotyp*. 6.

[90] *De vir. ill*. 8. Indeed elsewhere (*Ep*. 120 *ad Hedib*. 11) he has Peter narrating as Mark writes! Origen (apud Euseb. *HE* 6.25.5) says that Mark wrote 'in accordance with Peter's instructions'.

> Mark, the follower of Peter, while Peter was preaching (praedicante) publicly the gospel at Rome in the presence of certain of Caesar's knights and was putting forward many testimonies concerning Christ, being requested by them that they might be able to commit to memory the things which were being spoken, wrote from the things which were spoken by Peter the Gospel which is called according to Mark.[91]

The other passage (whose genuineness has yet to be established, though it seems to be coming to be accepted as Clement's) is from a letter of Clement recently published:[92]

> As for Mark, then, during Peter's stay in Rome (*κατὰ τὴν τοῦ Πέτρου ἐν Ῥώμῃ διατριβήν*) he wrote an account of the Lord's doings, not, however, declaring all of them, nor yet hinting at the secret ones, but selecting what he thought most useful for increasing the faith of those who were being instructed. But when Peter died a martyr, Mark came over to Alexandria,[93] bringing both his own notes (*ὑπομνήματα*) and those of Peter, from which he transferred to his former book the things suitable to whatever makes for progress towards knowledge (*γνῶσιν*). Thus he composed a more spiritual Gospel for the use of those who were being perfected.[94]

[91] *Adumbr.*, on I Peter 5.13.

[92] Text and translation from Morton Smith, *Clement of Alexandria and a Secret Gospel of Mark*, Cambridge, Mass., 1973, 446–53. Reviewing the book, R. M. Grant, *ATR* 56, 1974, 58, writes: 'Smith definitely proves that the incomplete letter... was written by Clement.'

[93] According to Eusebius, *HE* 2.16.1, 'It is said that this Mark journeyed to Egypt and was the first to preach [there] the Gospel, which also he had written; and that he was the first to form churches at Alexandria itself.' Eusebius, evidently relying on hearsay tradition, places this immediately after his account of the writing of the gospel in Rome during the reign of Claudius. In 2.24 he says 'Now when Nero was in the eighth year of his reign [i.e. 62], Annianus succeeded, first after Mark the evangelist, to the ministry of the community at Alexandria.' He does not actually say that the change was due to Mark's death. But Jerome (*De vir. ill.* 8) takes it so: 'Taking the gospel which he had completed, he came to Egypt, and proclaiming Christ first in Alexandria, established the church in such doctrine and continence of life that he induced all the followers of Christ to follow his example.' After describing Mark as a teacher ('doctor') there, he concludes: 'But he died in the eight year of Nero and was buried at Alexandria, Annianus succeeding him.' This dating is clearly incompatible, not only with what Clement says about Mark's going to Alexandria after Peter's martyrdom, but with Irenaeus' tradition (also preserved by Eusebius, *HE* 5.8.3) that Mark outlived Peter and Paul (see below p. 110). More importantly, it is irreconcilable with I Peter 5.13 (also adduced by Eusebius, *HE* 2.15.2, as evidence of Mark's stay with Peter in Rome), if, as in all probability (see ch. VI below), this epistle comes from 65. Whatever the truth about Mark's association with Alexandria, Eusebius' dating is evidently unreliable.

[94] Clement goes on: 'Nevertheless, he yet did not divulge the things not to be uttered, nor did he write down the hierophantic teaching of the Lord, but to the stories already written he added yet others and, moreover, brought in certain sayings (*λόγια*) of which he knew the interpretation would, as a mystagogue, lead

The gospel for catechumens of which Clement speaks is evidently our canonical Mark, for he refers subsequently to a passage inserted into its text between 10.34 and 35, which he quotes *verbatim*. So this new fragment supports the dating of Mark during Peter's lifetime, though it could also help to explain other traditions now to be examined which seem to put it after the death of Peter.

There is first the so-called Anti-Marcionite Prologue (dated by D. de Bruyne[95] and Harnack[96] in 160–80, but perhaps much later)[97] which says of Mark:

> He was the interpreter of Peter. After the death (post excessionem) of Peter himself he wrote down this same Gospel in the regions of Italy.

Then there is the statement of Irenaeus:[98]

> Matthew published a Gospel in writing also, among the Hebrews in their own language, while Peter and Paul were preaching the Gospel and founding the church in Rome.[99] But after their decease (ἔξοδον) Mark, the disciple and interpreter of Peter – he also transmitted to us in writing the things which Peter used to preach. And Luke too, the attendant of Paul, set down in a book the Gospel which Paul used to preach. Afterwards John, the disciple of the Lord, the same who leant back on his breast – he too set forth the Gospel, while residing at Ephesus in Asia.

It is very doubtful if Irenaeus had access to any independent

---

the hearers into the innermost sanctuary of that truth hidden by seven veils. Thus, in sum he prepared matters, neither grudgingly nor incautiously, in my opinion, and, dying, he left his composition to the church in Alexandria, where it even yet is most carefully guarded, being read only to those who are being initiated into the great mysteries.'

[95] D. de Bruyne, 'Les plus anciens prologues latins des Évangiles', *RBén* 40, 1928, 193–214.

[96] A. Harnack, 'Die ältesten Evangelien-Prologe und die Bildung des Neuen Testaments', *Sitzungsberichte der preussischen Akademie der Wissenschaften*, Phil-hist. Klasse, 1928, 322–41; cf. Bacon, 'The Anti-Marcionite Prologue to John', *JBL* 49, 1930, 43–54; W. T. Howard, 'The Anti-Marcionite Prologues to the Gospels', *ExpT* 47, 1935–6, 534–8; Manson, *Studies in the Gospels and Epistles*, 48–51.

[97] R. G. Heard, 'The Old Gospel Prologues', *JTS* n.s. 6, 1955, 1–16; Haenchen, *Acts*, 10f.

[98] *Adv. haer.* 3.1.1; as quoted in Eusebius, *HE* 5. 8.2–4, who supplies the Greek.

[99] Cf. Harnack: 'The genitive absolute is not temporal; it does not imply that the gospel of St Matthew was written at that time; it simply contrasts the ministry of the two great Apostles with that of St Matthew'. He argues (*Date of Acts*, 130f.), following Dom John Chapman ('St Irenaeus on the Dates of the Gospels', *JTS* 6, 1905, 563–9), that the purpose of this passage in the context of Irenaeus' argument was not to provide chronology but 'to prove that the teaching of the four chief apostles did not perish with their death, but that it has come down to us in writing'.

tradition[100] and his chronology merely reflects the canonical order. He evidently meant ἔξοδον to refer to the death of Peter and Paul (as must be its primary meaning in II Peter 1.15). Yet neither this nor the 'excessionem' of the Anti-Marcionite Prologue need originally have meant more than 'departure'. Manson, after examining the matter carefully, concluded:

> If Peter had paid a visit to Rome some time between 55 and 60; if Mark had been his interpreter then; if after Peter's departure from the city Mark had taken in hand – at the request of the Roman hearers – a written record of what Peter had said; then the essential points in the evidence would all be satisfied.[101]

He added:

> If there is anything in this, it suggests that the date of Mark may be a few years earlier than is usually thought likely. A date before 60 would be quite possible.[102]

But what of the date of Peter's visit to Rome? Manson's estimate seems merely to be a guess. For if we are to take any of this tradition seriously we must also take into account Eusebius' clear statements that the preaching visit from which all this followed occurred in the reign of Claudius (41–54).[103] Peter is said to have come to Rome on the heels of Simon Magus, whom Justin (himself from Samaria and a resident of Rome) twice tells us arrived in Rome in the days of Claudius Caesar[104] – though he does not mention Peter. There is obviously much legend here,[105] fully exploited later in the Pseudo-Clementines.[106] But that Simon met Peter in Rome is attested by Hippolytus[107] (also from the same city), and there would seem no good ground for denying that Peter could have gone to Rome during Claudius' reign.[108] We know that he had in all probability been in Corinth during the early 50s for long enough for some there to

[100] Harnack regarded the testimony of Irenaeus as having been derived from Papias and the Anti-Marcionite Prologue. Dependence on the former is certain.

[101] Op. cit., 40. He is quoted and supported by Bruce, *NT History*, 375, and Martin, *Mark*, 53.

[102] Cf. his concluding words, 45: 'The composition of the Gospel may be put several years earlier than the date commonly accepted.'

[103] *HE* 2.14.6; 17.1. There is no indication that he derived this part of the tradition from Clement, who mentions no date for the visit.

[104] *Apol.* 1.26 and 56.

[105] Eusebius repeats (*HE* 2.13.3) what has been demonstrated to be Justin's error in supposing that the inscription in Rome '*Simone deo sancto*' was evidence of his presence there. In fact it evidently referred to an altar to Semo Sanctus, a Sabine god. Cf. Lawlor and Oulton, ad loc., op. cit., II, 65.

[106] *Recog.* 3.63. [107] *Refut.* 6.15.

[108] Cf. Harnack, *Chron.*, 244: 'Whether the old tradition that brings Peter to Rome already under Claudius is completely unusable is to me questionable.'

regard him as their leader (I Cor. 1.12; 3.22; cf. 9.4)[109] – though we should never have guessed this from Acts. It is possible too that Paul's reluctance to go to Rome earlier because he did not wish to build on another's foundation (Rom. 15.20) may reflect a knowledge of Peter's work there[110] – though it is inconceivable that Peter could still have been in the city at the time of the writing of Romans (in 57) without being mentioned in the letter or its greetings.

In the Latin version of his *Chronicle*,[111] followed by Jerome,[112] Eusebius indeed dates Peter's arrival in Rome in the *second* year of Claudius (42), making him 'bishop' of Rome for 25 years. Clearly this does not imply continuous residence – not even Eusebius can have thought that – but it might be compatible with general apostolic oversight, in the same sense that he is said to have been 'bishop' of Antioch at an earlier stage.[113] The natural reaction of scholars has been to dismiss the dating of this visit as groundless.[114] But there is a sizable body of evidence, both in inscriptions and literary tradition, to suggest an association of Peter with Rome a good deal longer than the brief stay at the end of his life[115] (for which last the case is agreed to be very strong).[116] It is assembled by G. Edmundson in his Bampton Lectures for 1913, *The Church in Rome in the First Century*,[117] a scholarly study which has been almost completely ignored, having had the bad luck to be swamped by the first world war.[118] He pro-

[109] Cf. later Dionysius, bishop of Corinth, apud Euseb. *HE* 2.25.8, who says that Peter and Paul both taught at Corinth.

[110] Cf. Lake, *Earlier Epistles*, 378f.

[111] The Armenian version dates it in the third year of Caligula (39), which is quite impossible.

[112] *De vir. ill.* 1.

[113] Origen, *In Luc.* 6; Eusebius, *HE* 3.36.2; Jerome, *De vir. ill.* 1. The *Liber Pontificalis* and Gregory, *Epp.* 7.40, have this lasting seven years. G. Edmundson, *The Church in Rome in the First Century*, 1913, 77, argues that these were the seven years 47–54 (prior to Peter's second visit to Rome) during which he made Antioch the centre of his work (cf. Gal. 2.11).

[114] E.g. B. H. Streeter, *The Primitive Church*, 1929, 10–14.

[115] At the earliest this could not have begun till after the last year covered by Acts (62), and the very latest date for Peter's martyrdom is 68. But it was probably a good deal less. Cf. pp. 140–50 below.

[116] Cf. e.g. H. Lietzmann, *Petrus und Paulus in Rom*, Berlin [2]1927; O. Cullmann, *Peter: Disciple, Apostle, Martyr*, ET [2]1962, ch. 3; E. Dinkler, 'Die Petrus-Rom-Frage', *TR* 25, 1959, 189–230.

[117] Op. cit., 47–56.

[118] It was not even reviewed in the *Journal of Theological Studies* (uniquely for Bampton Lectures?) or in the *Journal of Roman Studies*. It received a brief notice of contents only in *ExpT* 25, 1913–14, 242f., and but little more in *TLZ* 40, 1915, 9–11, where W. Bauer dismissed it as showing 'more learning than critical sense'.

ceeds to sift the various traditions[119] and by careful historical methods reaches surprisingly conservative conclusions. He believes, and his position has a good deal of support from Harnack,[120] that there are in fact sound reasons for accepting a visit by Peter and Mark to Rome after Peter's disappearance from Jerusalem in 42.[121] This visit could have lasted a couple of years,[122] till Herod's death in 44 made Judaea safe again. Peter was back in Jerusalem in any case by the time of the council in 48: Edmundson thinks by 46, but he identifies Gal. 2.1–10 with the famine visit. He then goes on to argue ingeniously but I believe persuasively that Peter and Barnabas went on to Rome for a second time in 55 from Corinth[123] after the death of Claudius in October 54 (when Jews, expelled by him from Rome in 49, were once

[119] Op. cit., 59–86. He has the great merit of citing his sources, with references, in the original.

[120] *Chron.*, 243f. For a recent statement of the same case, cf. J. W. Wenham, 'Did Peter go to Rome in AD 42?', *Tyndale Bulletin* 23, 1972, 94–102.

[121] This date would fit with what Harnack took seriously as the 'very old and well attested' tradition (Clement, *Strom.* 6.5.43, quoting the lost *Kerygma Petri*; Apollonius [*c.* 200], 'relying on tradition', apud Euseb. *HE* 5.18.14; *Acta Petri* 5; etc.) that the apostles were to stay in Jerusalem for twelve years after the crucifixion. The narrative of Acts would indeed suggest that the death of James and the flight of Peter took place just before the death of Herod Agrippa I, i.e. in 44. But there is nothing to indicate that what was seen by the church as a judgment of God for his attack on the apostles followed immediately upon it. (The argument *propter hoc ergo instanter post hoc* is a familiar one. Cf. Hegesippus, on the death of James the Lord's brother, apud Euseb. *HE* 2.23.18: 'He has become a true witness both to Jew and Greeks that Jesus is the Christ. And immediately Vespasian attacked them.' Josephus sets a five-year gap between the two events.) The time links in this section of Acts are, as we have seen, very vague. The 'about this time' of Acts 12.1 is almost certainly referring to a moment *before* the 'during this period' of 11.27, since the famine did not take place till *c.* 46, after the death of Herod. There is ground therefore for thinking that Edmundson may be right in dating the death of James and the imprisonment of Peter in the spring of 42 as part of Herod's attempt to ingratiate himself with the Jews (cf. Josephus, *Ant.* 19.293f.) on his return to Jerusalem from Rome late in 41, where he had been instrumental in promoting the peaceful accession of Claudius and been rewarded with a large extension to his kingdom (*Ant.* 19.265–77; *BJ* 2.206–17). His residence at Caesarea and death there (Acts 12.19–23) did not occur till 44, 'after the completion of the third year of his reign over the whole of Judaea' (*Ant.* 19.343–51; *BJ* 2.219). It looks as if Luke may have elided the two in the transitional *καί* of Acts 12.19. Peter's departure to 'another place' in 12.17 is of course entirely vague, but if he was to put himself beyond Herod's new jurisdiction he would have had to have left Palestine.

[122] Eusebius' *Chronicle* makes Peter go to Rome in the second year of Claudius and to Antioch two years later.

[123] Cf. I Cor. 9.6 for the Corinthians' acquaintance with Barnabas. He was also, of course, a cousin of Mark's (Col. 4.10), which makes a further connection.

more free to return) for a supplementary visit to strengthen the church there and to appoint elders.[124] By 57 Paul felt himself at liberty to propose a passing visit to Rome (Rom. 15.23f.), put off many times (Rom. 1.13; 15.22), because by then again there was no danger of interfering with 'another's work'. Edmundson's argument is scrupulously documented, and if he gives more credence to what lies at the bottom of the traditions than most it is certainly not without judicious weighing of the evidence.

One must therefore, I believe, be prepared to take seriously the tradition that Mark, at whose home in Jerusalem Peter sought refuge before making his hurried escape (Acts 12.12–17) and whom later in Rome he was to refer to with affection as his 'son' (I Peter 5.13), accompanied Peter to Rome in 42 as his interpreter[125] and catechist, and that after Peter's departure from the capital he acceded to the reiterated request for a record of the apostle's preaching, perhaps about 45.[126] Mark himself was certainly back in Jerusalem by the end of the famine visit, in 46 or 47 (Acts 12.25). We have no record of his being in Rome again till the mid-60s (to anticipate the date and place of I Peter),[127] though this silence proves nothing, since from ch. 15 onwards Acts is solely concerned with Paul's companions, among whom it is made clear at that time Mark was not (Acts 15.37–9).

Where then does this leave us? The 'unordered' transcripts of Peter's preaching to which Papias refers (perhaps, as Edmundson said,[128] anticipating the form critics, as 'a set of separate lections intended for public exposition and for instruction') could well correspond to what earlier we called 'P'.[129] This record certainly cannot

[124] Such as are mentioned later in I Peter 5.1–4, where the apostle (1.1) addresses them fraternally as a 'fellow-elder'. For a discussion of this epistle and its Roman location, see ch. VI below.

[125] For a wider sense of 'interpreter' than 'translator' cf. Zahn, *INT* II, 454–6; R. O. P. Taylor, *Groundwork of the Gospels*, 20–30, 36–45. Coming from a family of some standing in Jerusalem (cf. Acts 12.12f.), John Mark had both a Jewish and a Roman name, suggesting a foot in both cultures. Cf. Silas, alias Silvanus, who was a leading Jerusalem disciple (Acts 15.22) and a Roman citizen (16.37f.) and, like Mark, served both Paul (Acts 15.40; I Thess. 1.1; II Thess. 1.1; II Cor. 1.19; etc.) and Peter (I Peter 5.12).

[126] For a similar date, though not place of origin, for the gospel, cf. W. C. Allen, *St Mark*, 1915, 5f.

[127] In 58, according to our chronology, he was in Asia Minor (Col. 4.10; II Tim 4.11).

[128] Op. cit., 67.

[129] For evidence of Petrine reminiscences embodied in the Markan tradition, cf. Manson, *Studies in the Gospels*, 40–3, who took seriously and elaborated the suggestions of C. H. Turner in C. Gore, H. L. Goudge and A. Guillaume (edd.),

simply be equated with our present gospel of Mark, which reflects wider and more developed church tradition. But the earlier document could well, as Clement said, have been 'distributed' by Mark 'among those who asked him'. It is not at all improbable that it should have been among the 'traditions' which Luke lists in his prologue as having been 'handed down to us by the original eyewitnesses and servants (ὑπηρέται) of the Gospel' (1.2), the two categories by which in Acts he describes, respectively, Peter (1.21f.) and Mark (13.5).[130] At what stage or stages Mark wrote up these notes into *his* statement of 'the Gospel of Jesus Christ the Son of God', to use his own title (1.1), we shall never know. Luke could well have seen and used this too in some stage of its development as one of the earlier 'accounts' to which he refers. If our argument in the last chapter was correct, there would have been no need for him to have waited to find the gospel till he reached Rome in 60; he had direct access to Mark at Caesarea (Col. 4.10, 14; Philem. 24). It is possible indeed that the final form of the Markan gospel may not have taken shape till after the Lukan and could reflect the needs of the Roman church as it faced the threat of the Neronian persecution[131] – though there is certainly nothing specific enough to require this. Or it could be, *if* Farmer should turn out to be right, that Mark represents the first harmony of the gospels, conflating Matthew and Luke. In this case it would be the last of the synoptists – though there is still nothing to suggest that it reflects the fall of Jerusalem or even the flight to Pella before the war.[132]

Perhaps we shall conclude that the evidence for Mark's association

---

A New Commentary on Holy Scripture, 1928, 47–50. D. E. Nineham, *St Mark* (Pelican NTC), [2]1968, 26f., while conceding 'the fact that much of the information in the Gospel is of a kind that seems unlikely to have come from anyone but Peter', stresses that 'St Mark's material *bears all the signs of having been community tradition* and cannot therefore be derived *directly* from St Peter or any other eyewitness' (italics his). But these two statements are not incompatible.

[130] Cf. Edmundson, op. cit., 68: 'He would find the Marcan lections, embodying as they did the teaching of St Peter, almost certainly in the possession of such a leader among the Hellenist teachers as Philip the Evangelist, who was residing at Caesarea at the same time as Luke' (cf. Acts 21.8: 'We went to the home of Philip the Evangelist, who was one of the Seven, and stayed with him'). It looks too as if Luke may have got from him the traditions in Acts 8.5–40 (which also link Philip both with Caesarea [8.40] and with Peter and Simon Magus [8.9–24]) and possibly 6.1–8.3 and 10.1–11.18 (so Zahn, *INT* III, 128).

[131] So e.g. Martin, *Mark*, 65–70.

[132] For trenchant criticism of the theory of Marxsen, *Mark the Evangelist*, 102–16, that it comes from Galilee (so 'fluidly' interpreted as to include Pella!) in the period 66–70, cf. Martin, *Mark*, 70–5.

with Peter or with Rome is altogether too tenuous to be trusted. In this case we shall simply be thrown back on guess-work and have to fit Mark into whatever chronology we are led to for Matthew and Luke. But this I am persuaded would represent excessive scepticism. For if we trust, however critically, the clues that have been left (and, as I said, there are a surprising number of them for Mark), then I believe that they point independently to the same span of development at which we arrived provisionally for Matthew and Luke. It may well be (as Papias' imperfect tense would suggest) that Peter's preaching material was committed to writing by Mark independently of any specific visit to Rome (by which time Clement says he had already 'followed him for a long time'),[133] and it could have been combined with the sayings collections and the independent Matthean and Lukan traditions at almost any stage. But on the assumption that Mark initially put pen to paper after the first preaching mission of Peter in Rome (*c.* 45), gave it limited circulation as what we called 'P', and subsequently put it out in more ordered form as 'proto-Mark', this would fit well with the dates already suggested for the first drafts of the Matthean and Lukan gospels. The final stages of the three synoptic gospels as we have them would then have occupied the latter 50s or early 60s.[134] In any case, whatever precise pattern of synoptic interdependence will prove to be required or suggested by the evidence, all could quite easily be fitted in to comport with the writing of Acts in 62+.

The objection will doubtless still be raised that all this allows too little time for the development in the theology and practice of the church presupposed by the gospels and Acts. But this judgment is precariously subjective. It is impossible to say *a priori* how long is required for any development, or for the processes, communal and redactional, to which scholarly study has rightly drawn attention. We have noted how much could happen within three years of the crucifixion – and we are allowing a further thirty for the full flowering of the synoptic tradition. There is nothing, I believe, in the theology of the gospels or Acts or in the organization of the church there depicted that requires a longer span, which was already long enough, if we are right, for the creation of the whole Pauline corpus, including the Pastoral Epistles. Of course, if Acts is held to reflect a long look back

[133] Eusebius, *HE* 6. 14.6.

[134] C. F. Nolloth, *The Rise of the Christian Religion*, 1917, 12–24, also put all the synoptic gospels between 50 and 60, arguing for the same basic dependence on the 'two ancient documents' that we called 'P' and 'Q'. He is one of the few scholars to refer, *en passant*, to Edmundson's work.

on church history and the distant perspective of another century, then the development of the rest of the New Testament can and will be stretched to fit in. But if the production of the synoptic gospels and Acts does in fact cover the years 30 to 60+ which the latter records (the gradual committal to writing occupying perhaps the period 40 to 60+), then this in turn provides a valuable yardstick by which to assess the chronology of the documents that remain for us still to consider.

V

The Epistle of James

THE WRITINGS REVIEWED so far, those of Paul, Acts and the synoptic gospels, all of which are linked through the person of Luke, constitute virtually three-quarters of the New Testament. Yet, apart from the possibility of a Petrine background to St Mark, none is associated with any of the so-styled 'pillars' of the early church whom Paul met in Jerusalem – James, Cephas and John. The literature attributed to these figures is a good deal more problematic, both in regard to date and authorship, than anything we have hitherto considered. The literary problem, in the narrow sense of who precisely penned the documents we now have, is not our direct concern. Authorship is relevant only as attribution, whether genuine or fictional, is a factor in assessing the probability of a particular dating. In practice the two issues are intimately connected. Yet methodologically we shall start from the question of chronology and ask how the traditional ascription of the writings relates to this. We may take the three names mentioned – James, Cephas and John – in the order Paul lists them, including others on the way, like Jude and the author to the Hebrews, as they become relevant.

The epistle of James is one of those apparently timeless documents that could be dated almost anywhere[1] and which has indeed been placed at practically every point in the list of New Testament writings. Thus Zahn[2] and Harnack,[3] writing in the same year, 1897, put

[1] Cf. K. and S. Lake, *An Introduction to the New Testament*, 1938, 164: 'As far as its contents go, it might, as has been said, have been written any time from the second century BC to the eighteenth century AD'!

[2] Zahn boldly gives it pride of place as the first book to be treated in his *INT* (I, 73–151). His dating (*c.* 50) would be earlier still on our chronology since he does not put the council of Jerusalem till 52.

[3] *Chron.*, 485–9. He dates it 120–140.

it first and last but one – at an interval of nearly a hundred years! It contains reference to no public events, movements or catastrophes. The 'conflicts and quarrels' it speaks of are the perennial ones of personal aggressiveness (4.1f.), not the datable wars and rumours of wars between nations or groups. Its calendar is determined by the natural cycle of peace-time agriculture (5.7) and the social round of petit-bourgeois society (4.11–5.6). There are no place names, and no indication of destination or dispatch, whether in address or greetings. In fact there are no proper names of any kind except that of James himself in the opening verse and stock Old Testament characters like Abraham and Isaac, Rahab, Job and Elijah. As a form of literature too it stands in that almost undatable tradition of Judaeo–Christian practical wisdom which includes Proverbs, Ecclesiasticus, the Wisdom of Solomon, the Testaments of the Twelve Patriarchs, the Qumran Manual of Discipline, the Epistle of Barnabas, the Shepherd of Hermas, and the Didache. Yet though the links, backwards and forwards, are evident,[4] there is no decisive evidence for literary dependence in either direction that could fix the epistle of James in time or space. The only clear frontier which this stream of tradition crosses is that between Judaism and Christianity – and even this boundary is less marked here than in any other genre of literature. Indeed there is general agreement that James is only just across the line, and some have argued that originally it belonged on the Jewish side of it.[5] There are only two explicit references to Jesus Christ (1.1; 2.1), and it has been held – without the support of any textual evidence – that these are interpolations. However scholars from very different standpoints agree in thinking that the Christian character of the epistle is much more pervasive of the whole than anything that could be added or subtracted by isolated phrases.[6] It is manifestly Christian, yet the

[4] For the fullest list of (possible) literary connections, see J. B. Mayor, *The Epistle of James*, 1892, [3]1910, lxx–cxxvii. Cf. more briefly, the introductions to R. J. Knowling, *St James*, 1904; J. H. Ropes, *St James* (ICC), Edinburgh 1916; Reicke, *James, Peter and Jude* (Anchor Bible), New York 1963; E. M. Sidebottom, *James, Jude and 2 Peter* (NCB), 1967.

[5] So F. Spitta, *Zur Geschichte und Litteratur des Urchristentums* II, Göttingen 1896, 1–239; L. Massebieau, 'L'Épître de Jacques, est-elle l'oeuvre d'un Chrétien?', *RHR* 32, 1895, 249–83. Cf. A. Meyer, *Das Ratsel des Jakobusbriefes*, Giessen 1930, who argued that it is a Christian adaptation of an allegory on Jacob's farewell address to his twelve sons!

[6] So Harnack, *Chron.*, 489f.; Mayor, *James*, cxciii–ccv; Zahn, *INT* I, 141–6; Knowling, *James*, xv–xxiv; H. Windisch, *Die katholischen Briefen* (HNT 15), Tübingen [2]1930, 3; Reicke, *James, Peter and Jude*, 9f.; Kümmel, *INT*, 407–10; Guthrie, *NTI*, 756f.; Moule, *Birth of the NT*, 166.

marks of difference are not emphasized nor the lines of demarcation clearly drawn.

This absence of any clear-cut frontier between Christianity and Judaism introduces the first of many points at which the epistle is primarily significant for what it does *not* mention or contain. And these have chronological implications as important as the specific references that we look for and lack. Arguments from silence are notoriously suspect, but cumulatively they can be impressive as pointers. One or two things not referred to may be insignificant and explicable. But when none of the indicators are present which we should expect from a particular period we may be reasonably confident that we should be looking elsewhere.

The lack of opposition, or indeed distinction, between Christianity and Judaism is in marked contrast, for instance, to the gospel of Matthew, with which it has so much else in common. There are no signs such as we noted in that gospel of the church having to formulate or justify its own stand *over against* the main body of non-Christian Judaism. There is no polemic or even apologetic directed towards Judaism – merely attacks on the exploiting classes in the manner of the Old Testament prophets or of Jesus himself. There is no sense of 'we' and 'they' such as we find, say, on the subject of sacrifice in Heb. 13.10 ('our altar is one from which the priests of the sacred tent have no right to eat') or fasting in Did. 8.1 (where 'the hypocrites' keep the second and fifth days of the week, Christians the fourth and sixth). Still less is there any indication of a permanent breach with a Judaism desolated by national defeat, such as marks the Epistle of Barnabas. Not only does the fall of Jerusalem receive no mention (for which arguably there would be no occasion), but the reference to rich landowners withholding the wage of their reapers (5.1–6) is noted by many commentators as reflecting a situation in Palestine which disappeared for good with the war of 66–70. And it is Palestine which such climatic and social conditions as are mentioned would suggest is the background of the writer, whatever the location of his readers. Though many of the allusions would be relevant throughout the Mediterranean, some have been seen to apply more peculiarly to Palestine (e.g., 1.11; 3.11f.; 5.7, 17f.). Thus, the reference to 'the former and the latter rains' (5.7), so familiar from the Old Testament (Deut. 11.4; Jer. 5.24; Joel 2.23; Zech. 10.1), would seem to point specifically to the climate of Palestine and southern Syria.[7]

The author appears to be a Christian voice addressing Israel, like

[7] Cf. especially, Ropes, *James*, 295–7; and D. Y. Hadidian, 'Palestinian Pictures in the Epistle of James', *ExpT* 63, 1951–2, 227f.

one of its own prophets or teachers, from within. Indeed it has seriously, but not I think convincingly, been argued[8] that he is writing for both Christians and Jews and is deliberately ambiguous in his choice of phrases. For he is still conscious of being of one body with his unbelieving compatriots. The local Christian gathering is spoken of as a 'synagogue' within Judaism (2.2; cf. Acts 6.9). The basis of everything he says is the fundamental Jewish doctrine of the unity of God (2.19), who is invoked as 'the Lord of Sabaoth' (5.4). Abraham is 'our father' (2.21) – and there is no need to add, as Paul must, 'according to the flesh' (Rom. 4.1), for no such distinction arises. The appeal is to the Jewish law and its giver (2.9–11; 4.11f.), and there is not a hint that the Christian message represents anything but its fulfilment. Social justice, prayer, alms-giving and sick-visiting are the (characteristically Jewish) scope of Christian good works. Hell is represented by Gehenna – only here in the New Testament outside the teaching of Jesus. There is indeed nothing that conflicts with or goes beyond the best of main-stream Judaism.[9] Even when the inspiration of James' message is clearly the teaching of Jesus, there is no suggestion of its being offered or defended on *his* authority. In fact never once – in contrast with Paul's usage – is a 'word of the Lord' appealed to or cited.

Even the source of the opposition that Christians have to face is not apparently organized Judaism (as in Paul), let alone the civic authorities (as in I Peter) or the state machine (as in Revelation). Those who 'drag you into court and pour contempt on the honoured name by which God has claimed you' (2.6f.) are doubtless Jews; but they are attacked not because they are Jews (as already in I Thess. 2.14), but because they are rich. The readers of the epistle are harassed and oppressed, facing 'trials of many kinds' (1.2), yet in the same way that the righteous poor always are, and the reassurance given is that of the psalmist that 'the rich man shall wither away as he goes about his business' (1.11). Christians indeed are particularly subject to such treatment because of 'the name' (2.7; cf. Acts 5.41) – yet apparently, as in Acts (24.5, 14; 28.22), as a sect or party within Judaism comparable with *αἱρέσεις* of the Sadducees (5.17) or Pharisees (15.5; 26.5). In fact there is nothing in James that goes outside what is described in the first half of Acts. There too it is the Jewish aristocracy that opposes this new lower-class movement (Acts 4–5) and it is 'the women

[8] McNeile-Williams, *INT*, 206–8.

[9] For the strong Jewish colouring of the whole epistle, cf. especially W. O. E. Oesterley, *James* in W. R. Nicoll (ed.), *The Expositor's Greek Testament*, 1897–1910, IV, 393–7, 405f., 408–13.

of standing who were worshippers' together with 'the leading men of the city' who are incited to persecute it (13.50). The court actions against Christians (James 2.6) do not go further than anything described in Acts 8.1, 3; 9.2 (cf. 26.10f.); 11.19 – in fact, not as far. For the *πειρασμοί* in James seem to come, not from any wave of terror or organized persecution, but from the regular opposition which any Christian must be prepared to expect and accept with patience and joy, as part of that faithful belonging to the true Israel of God to which the epistle is addressed.

The wording of the address, to 'the Twelve Tribes dispersed throughout the world' (1.1), has been variously interpreted. It recalls the phrase in Acts 26.7, 'our twelve tribes', for whose hope Paul, as a Christian and a Jew, saw himself on trial, and of which Jesus had appointed his apostles 'judges' (Matt. 19.28). The *διασπορά* does not appear here, as in John 7.35, to be *contrasted* with metropolitan Judaism, nor, as in I Peter 1.1, to stand for scattered *Christians*, many if not most of whom had never been Jews (cf. I Peter 2.10). Like 'the twelve tribes that inhabit the whole world' in the Shepherd of Hermas (Sim. 9.17.1f.), it is a way rather of describing 'the whole Israel of God', for whose peace Paul prayed (Gal. 6.16). James is addressing all who form the true, spiritual Israel, wherever they are. And he can address them in such completely Jewish terms not because he is singling them out from Gentile Christians but because, as far as his purview is concerned, *there are no other Christians*. In Zahn's words, 'the believing Israel constituted the entire Church'[10] – and that was true only for a very limited period of Christian history.

There is no suggestion throughout the epistle of a Gentile presence. Even the peripatetic businessmen who say, 'Today or tomorrow we will go off to such and such a town and spend a year there trading and making money', are evidently Jews (like Aquila and Priscilla) who, as pious Israelites, should preface their plans with the phrase, 'If it be the Lord's will' (4.13–17). There is no discussion of the Christian's relation to heathen masters, such as concerns Paul (Col. 3.22–5; Eph. 6.5–8) and Peter (I Peter 2.18–20). Even within the church there is no sign of a Gentile mission, no mention of its claims, no evidence of the conflicts and tensions arising from it. Above all there is no hint of Judaizing, as opposed to Jewish, attitudes. For these become relevant only in the context of a demand that Gentile Christians shall 'live like Jews' (Gal. 2.14). There is not a mention in the epistle of the issues that formed the heart of this controversy – of circumcision, dietary rules and ritual law. There is no discussion of

[10] *INT* I, 77.

the Christian's attitude to the temple, the sacrifices, or 'the customs handed down . . . by Moses' (contrast the altercation in Acts 6.13f.). Equally there is no reference to the characteristic dangers of a Gentile environment such as fornication and the pollution of idols (Acts 15.20).[11] We are dealing with Jewish abuses and temptations. As Knowling says,[12]

> The sins and weaknesses which the writer describes are exactly those faults which our Lord blames in his countrymen . . . the excessive zeal for the outward observance of religious duties, the fondness for the office of teacher, the false wisdom, the overflowing of malice, the pride, the hypocrisy, the respect of persons.

They are the faults which John the Baptist and Paul also found characteristic of the Jew, the fatal trust in religious privilege and the gap between profession and practice (Matt. 3.7–10 and par; Rom. 2.17–24). The sins attacked are not particularly sophisticated, nor such as could have arisen only in second-generation Christians. There are no warnings against relapse or loss of early love, which feature so markedly in Hebrews and the Apocalypse and even in Galatians. There are no signs of heresy or schism, as are inveighed against in the later Paul and the Johannine epistles; no marks of incipient gnosticism,[13] whether speculative or even, as we might expect in this epistle, moral (with the tell-tale swing between asceticism and licence), such as is characteristic of Jewish Christianity in the latter half of the New Testament (Colossians, the Pastorals, the epistles of John, Jude and II Peter).

On the doctrinal side, there is equally no sign of christological sophistication or controversy. 'Our Lord Jesus Christ of glory' (2.1) is the epistle's most theologically advanced statement. There is no reference to the death or resurrection of Christ, and one is left with what one commentator describes as 'the impression of an almost pre-crucifixion discipleship'.[14] A 'patient and stout-hearted' trust is urged in the speedy coming of the Lord (5.7–11), but there is no elaborated

[11] Contrast the early compromise of Did. 6.3 (reflecting the situation in the mixed society of Antioch?): 'Concerning eating, bear that which thou art able; yet abstain by all means from meat sacrificed to idols; for it is the worship of dead gods.'

[12] *James*, xiii. So, in further detail, Zahn, *INT* I, 90f.

[13] Allusions to gnostic tendencies have been seen e.g. in the antithesis between the true and false wisdom (3.13–18), in the word ψυχική (3.18), and in the use of τέλειος (1.4, 17, 25; 3.2). But none of these need imply anything more than can be found in the Jewish wisdom literature or in Philo or, for example, in I Cor. 2.12–14; 15.44–6. Cf. particularly Ropes, ad locc.

[14] Sidebottom, *James, Jude and 2 Peter*, 14.

eschatology nor any hint of reappraisal prompted by the delay of the *parousia*. Equally there is no preoccupation with doctrinal orthodoxy – rather its depreciation (2.19) – and no defence of 'the faith once delivered', such as marks the Pastorals and Jude. Indeed, as Ropes points out,[15]

> The post-apostolic notion sometimes ascribed to James, of Christianity as a body of doctrine to be believed ('the faith', '*fides quae creditur*'), and correspondingly of faith as an 'intellectualistic' acceptance of propositions, is not at all the 'dead' faith of which James speaks.[16] The demons' faith in one God stands, in fact, at the opposite pole from this 'intellectualism'; for as a faith in God's existence and power it is sincere and real, its fault lies in its complete divorce from love or an obedient will.
>
> When we make a comparison with the Apostolic Fathers the positive traits which give definite character to the thinking of every one of them are all lacking in James.

The same applies if we put to the epistle another test of later development, namely, the state of concern for liturgy and the ministry. In contrast again with the Didache, there are no instructions about worship or the sacraments, and James' 'manual of discipline', to use Reicke's designation of its brief finale in 5.12–20,[17] contents itself with simple injunctions on swearing, ministry to the sick, mutual confession, prayer, and the reclamation of erring brothers. There is no reference to orders of Christian ministry like bishops and deacons (contrast Phil. 1.1, the Pastorals and again the Didache), merely to elders (5.14), which were evidently taken over direct from Judaism (cf. Acts 4.5, 8, 23; 6.12; etc. of Judaism; 11.30; 14.23; 15.2; etc. of the church), and to teachers (3.1; cf. Acts 13.1; Heb. 5.12). But the last do not seem to be part of a hierarchy of ministries (as e.g. in I Cor. 12.28; Eph. 4.11; Did. 13.2; 15.1f.; Hermas, Vis. 3.5.1 et passim). Rather James' injunction against wanting to become teachers seems to be more in line with Jesus' quashing of the desire to be called 'rabbi' and 'teacher' and thus win honour from men (Matt. 23.6–11). 'The greatest among you', Jesus goes on, 'must be your servant' (23.12); and it is simply as 'a servant of God and the Lord Jesus Christ' (James 1.1) that James, even though he does stand in the relationship to them of teacher (3.1), chooses to address his readers. The simplicity of the address suggests no crisis of authority or need to resort to credentials, such as Paul was driven to at Corinth. Its unaffected spiritual directness is all part of the uncomplicated but

[15] *James*, 37.

[16] He adds in a footnote at this point: 'This error is common and has led to many unwise inferences about relative dates.'

[17] *James, Peter and Jude*, 8.

decisive message he conveys. Like his master, he speaks with authority: he does not cite authorities – not even that of his master.

Yet there is no doubt that it is Jesus' teaching, particularly as found in the Sermon on the Mount and the Matthean tradition, that lies behind everything James says.[18] But he appears to be quoting from or referring his readers to no written book (in contrast, again with Did. 15.3f., 'as you find in the Gospel'). No case can be demonstrated for literary dependence on our gospel of Matthew[19] (or indeed on Luke and John).[20] His contacts rather are with the pre-Matthean Palestinian tradition.[21] As Ropes says with some perceptiveness, 'James was in religious ideas nearer to the men who collected the sayings of Jesus than to the authors of the Gospels': what is conspicuous, for all the common matter, is the 'omission of some of the chief motives which have produced the Synoptic Gospels'.[22]

> Indeed, James exhibits not one distinctly marked individual theological tendency which would set him in positive relation to any of the strong forces either of the apostolic or of the post-apostolic period.[23]

These words have still greater significance today than when Ropes was writing at Harvard during the first world war. For almost all the 'motives' and 'tendencies' subsequently fastened on by the form critics and redaction critics appear to have bypassed James. The influences – kerygmatic, apologetic, polemical, liturgical and the rest – which have rightly been seen as selecting and shaping the traditions about Jesus to the uses of the church can scarcely be illustrated by any convincing examples from this epistle. Factors such as Jeremias isolates as moulding the parabolic teaching of Jesus, like allegorization,[24] or the changed situation of the church in the Hellenistic world, or the Gentile mission, or the delay of the *parousia*, do not feature in James. Even the evidence for common catechetical patterns, which should above all be relevant to his subject-matter, is far weaker than in the

[18] The parallels are set out by Mayor, *James*, lxiif., with the comment: 'Close as is the connection of sentiment and even of language in many of these passages, it never amounts to an actual quotation.' For simple comparison, cf. Sidebottom, *James, Jude and 2 Peter*, 8–11.

[19] M. H. Shepherd, 'The Epistle of James and the Gospel of Matthew', *JBL* 75, 1956, 40–51, argues the case for dependence, putting James into the second century, but admits that there is no proof.

[20] For the parallels here, cf. Knowling, *James*, xxi–iv.

[21] So Sidebottom, *James, Jude and 2 Peter*, 14f.

[22] *James*, 39. [23] Ibid., 37.

[24] Ropes, ibid., 37, also drew attention to 'the entire absence of allegory' as one of the most notable contrasts between James and the sub-apostolic literature – particularly the Shepherd of Hermas, to which in other respects it stands closest.

other New Testament epistles. In the essay of over a hundred pages which Selwyn devotes to this in his commentary on I Peter,[25] the material he can garner from James is extraordinarily meagre. In his central section on the General Catechumen Virtues he admits that 'James is difficult to bring into the picture'[26] and the common citation in I Peter 5.5f. and in James 4.6, 10 of Prov. 3.34 ('God opposes the arrogant and gives grace to the humble') and the conclusions drawn from it 'can be accounted for without reference to any underlying code'.[27] The remaining scattered verses containing topics in some way common to other New Testament epistles (James 1.3, 12, 18, 21, 27; 3.13–18; 4.7f.; 5.7–11) provide no evidence for the teaching patterns to be found, for example in I Thess. 5, Col. 3, Eph. 5–6, and I Peter 5.

The one issue of controversy which could, on the face of it, be used to place the epistle within the developing life of the church is the debate between faith and works in 2.14–26. But the reference of this is far from self-evident, as the divergence between the commentators has shown. Some have seen it as a direct reply to Paul's teaching on justification by faith; others, since it so crudely misinterprets him, as a riposte from a later age when the controversy was no longer understood. On the other hand, others have viewed the relationship just the other way round, with what Paul says in Galatians and particularly in Romans as a rebuttal of James; while yet others have seen no direct connection between them at all.

We may begin with the truth in the last position. It is natural, in view of later controversy, to assume that what we are overhearing is an internal Christian debate. But in the first instance James, here as elsewhere, is evidently taking up an attack, begun by Jesus and the Baptist before him, on the inadequacies of contemporary Judaism. Being a hearer of the word without doing the works, or claiming the heritage of Abraham without the fruits to show for it, or merely *saying* 'I go' or 'Lord, Lord' – these are the failings constantly condemned in the gospels (Matt. 3.8–10; 7.16–27; 12.33–5; 21.28–31; 25.31–46; etc.). The debate about what 'justified' a man before God was already being argued within Judaism, and Jesus' words about this (Matt. 12.37; Luke 16.15; 18.14) precede the controversy within the church.[28] Was it works (as in Prov. 24.12 and Jer. 32.19) or was it faith (as in Gen. 15.6 and Hab. 2.4) that would see a man through at the last? The inseparability of the two for salvation is stressed in I

[25] Op. cit., 363–466. [26] Ibid., 407. [27] Ibid., 426.

[28] For a defence of this last statement, cf. Jeremias, 'Paul and James', *ExpT* 66, 1954–5, 368–71, who however takes a different view of the relation of James to Paul from that argued below.

Macc. 2.51f. (where first among 'the works' of the fathers is cited, as in James, Abraham's faithfulness in temptation) and later in II Esd. 7.34; 9.7; 13.23.[29] We now know that the Qumran community interpreted Hab. 2.4 ('the righteous man will live by being faithful') to include *both* deeds *and* faith in the teacher of righteousness as the interpreter of the law (1Q pHab. 8.1–3). The discussion in James takes its place within the ongoing Jewish and Christian debate as to how to combine the conviction, on which Paul was equally insistent, that while a man might be justified through faith he would be judged by works. And the faith from which James, like Jesus (cf. Mark 5.34; 9.23; 11.22–4; etc.), takes his departure is the common Jewish faith in *God* (2.19, 23). He is not, like Paul, contrasting the works of the *law* with faith in *Christ* (Gal. 2.16). He is saying, with Paul, to his fellow-Jews that 'it is not by hearing the law, but by doing it, that men will be justified before God' (Rom. 2.13); that being a Jew has value 'provided you keep the law; but if you break the law, then circumcision is as if it had never been' (2.25); and that 'the true Jew is the one who is such inwardly, and the true circumcision is of the heart' (2.29). He is also insisting, as Paul does, to Christians that 'the only thing that counts is faith active in love' (Gal. 5.6), 'faith that has shown itself in action' (I Thess. 1.3; cf. I Cor. 13.2); for 'faith divorced from deeds is barren . . ., lifeless as a corpse' (James 2.20, 26).

Yet though the starting-point of the debate is Jewish and the common ground is indisputable, it is difficult to believe that there is *no* connection with the Christian battle Paul is waging in Galatians and Romans. This is especially true when in Rom. 4.2f. and James 2.23f. Paul and James cite precisely the same scripture, 'Abraham put his faith in God and that faith was counted to him as righteousness' (Gen. 15.6), and draw from it diametrically different conclusions. The question arises, Who is answering whom? – though the degree of correspondence (let alone of mutual understanding) is not such as requires one to have read the other or be quoting from his epistle. It is impossible to be dogmatic on this (and the interrelationship will obviously depend on wider judgments about dating and authorship). But I am impressed by Mayor's contention that Paul's reasoned argument in Rom. 4.2–5 (that 'if Abraham was justified by anything he had done, then he has ground for pride', whereas the very word 'counted' excludes any notion of credit) reads more intelligibly as an answer to James rather than *vice versa*. As a reply to Paul's position James' argument totally misses the point; for Paul never contended

[29] For the Jewish rather than the Christian background to this debate, cf. Knowling, *James*, xli–v, and Oesterley, *EGT* IV, 411–13 and *ad loc.*

for faith *without* works. But as a reply, not indeed to James, but to the use made of him by the Judaizers in a subtly different context (that of the basis of salvation for *Gentiles*), the argument of Rom. 4 is very effective. If, as Mayor says, James is writing after Paul,

> How inconceivable is it that he should have made no attempt to guard his position against such an extremely formidable attack! Again if St James was really opposed to St Paul and desired to maintain that man was saved, not by grace, but by obedience to the law of Moses, which was incumbent alike on Gentile and on Jew, why has he never uttered a syllable on the subject, but confined himself to the task of proving that a faith which bears no fruit is a dead faith?[30]

The answer to this last question, as the whole of the rest of the epistle bears out, is that James is not concerned with the controversy between Jews and Gentiles in the church. Yet, whatever its original intention or context, what he had to say clearly was brought into and applied to that controversy. In fact it has plausibly been suggested that, when 'certain persons who had come down from Judaea began to teach the brotherhood that those who were not circumcised in accordance with Mosaic practice could not be saved' (Acts 15.1), what they were doing, 'without' indeed, as James and the apostles say, 'any instructions from us' (15.24), was pushing to its logical conclusion teaching like that in James 2.10: 'If a man keeps the whole law apart from one single point, he is guilty of breaking all of it.' At any rate it is certainly in reaction to 'certain persons come from James' (Gal. 2.12) that Paul has later to insist that 'no man is ever justified by doing what the law demands, but only through faith in Christ Jesus' (2.16). But this argument depends on the assumption that the epistle *is* by the same James and is as early as its primitive features have suggested. The issue of authorship can be postponed no longer.

The sole indication of who the writer was is the bald greeting in 1.1: 'From James the servant of God and the Lord Jesus Christ'. It is also this alone that turns what is otherwise a pastoral homily into a letter; for there are no greetings or even a grace at the end. There have been those, including Harnack,[31] who have regarded the opening verse as a later addition.[32] But there is no textual evidence for this, and, as many have pointed out, the play on words χαίρειν and χαράν connecting

[30] *James*, xcviii. Zahn, *INT* I, 124–8, sees the dependence lying in the same direction.

[31] *Chron.*, 489f.

[32] So too L. E. Elliott-Binns, *Galilean Christianity* (SBT 16), 1956, 47f.; unlike Harnack, he regards the work itself as very primitive. There seems no positive evidence for his association of it with Galilee, though admittedly it breathes a rural rather than a metropolitan air.

vv. 1 and 2 speaks against it. It has found little support either amongst those who would defend the authorship of James or amongst those who would not. There is general agreement too that whether the ascription is genuine or not the James intended must be James the Lord's brother, who alone of the five men of that name in the New Testament is regularly referred to without further specification. As Kümmel says,

> Without doubt James claims to be written by him, and even if the letter is not authentic, it appeals to this famous James and the weight of his person as authority for its content.[33]

There is no one else who could so speak without need of introduction or explanation. Similarly, when the writer of the epistle of Jude introduces himself as 'brother of James' (1.1), nothing more requires to be said. The very simplicity of the address speaks forcibly against pseudonymity. For if this device was felt to be necessary to give the epistle 'apostolic'[34] aegis it is incredible that he was not described as 'the brother of the Lord' or 'bishop of Jerusalem'[35] or even, as later in the address of the pseudo-Clementine Letter to James, 'bishop of bishops'. If it is reasonable to ask why, if he stood in this special relationship to Jesus, he mentions nothing of his life, death or resurrection, it is still more difficult to explain why such details were not inserted later, to add credence and verisimilitude. For the Gospel of the Hebrews[36] elaborates the personal appearance to James, mentioned casually in I Cor. 15.7, and the legendary description of James 'the Just' given by Hegesippus[37] shows the lengths that hagiography had reached by the second century. Yet, as Zahn says,[38] the epistle 'does not bring out a single one of those characteristics by which James is distinguished in history and legend.' In fact the argument for pseudonymity is weaker here than with any other of the New Testament epistles. At least the Pastorals and the Petrines are claiming to be written by men calling themselves apostles, and a case can be

[33] Kümmel, *INT*, 412.

[34] I use the term without prejudice to whether James was actually regarded as an apostle or not. Gal. 1.19, 'without seeing any other of the apostles, except (*or* but only) James the Lord's brother', is notoriously ambiguous. Certainly by the Pauline test (I Cor. 9.1) James had 'seen the Lord' (cf. I Cor. 15.7: 'Then he appeared to James, and afterwards to all the apostles'). In I Cor. 9.5 'the rest of the apostles' are distinguished from 'the Lord's brother' – but also from Cephas.

[35] As in a spurious letter of James, translated from the Armenian by P. Vetter, *Literarische Rundschau*, 1896, 259; cf. *Ep. Petr.* 1.1: 'Peter to James, the lord and bishop of the holy church' (Hennecke, *NT Apoc.* II, 111).

[36] Hennecke, *NT Apoc.* I, 165.

[37] Quoted by Eusebius, *HE* 2. 23. 4–18. [38] *INT* I, 140.

made for their being put out in the name of authorities from the past to say things that require to be said in the conflicts or controversies of a later age. But why produce a non-polemical Jewish–Christian epistle that is not even taking the position of the Judaizers but simply giving a call, as the NEB heads it, to 'practical religion'? And if it was to oppose Paul and all his works, why is he not more specifically attacked and why is there no stress on the unique and unrepeatable status of the writer as the brother of the Lord himself? It would seem easier to believe that it was the work of another completely unknown James.[39]

Before considering the very real objections to the attribution of the epistle to a brother of Jesus, there are the parallels to be taken into account with the Acts story and in particular with the speech of James and the apostolic letter in Acts 15. Much has been made of these and indeed on purely statistical grounds the number of verbal parallels between these brief passages and the short epistle of James is remarkable.[40] The initial salutation (James 1.1; Acts 15.34) is used by no other apostolic writer, the only other occurrence in the New Testament being in the address of Lysias to Felix in Acts 23.26. The phrase 'listen, my brothers' (James 2.5) is paralleled in Acts 15.13, 'men and brothers, listen'. The expression 'the . . . name which was called upon you' (James 2.7) occurs nowhere else in the New Testament except in the quotation from Amos 9.12 in Acts 15.17. In James 1.27 there is the exhortation to the Christian to 'keep himself untarnished by the world' and in Acts 15.29 the closing injunction, 'If you keep yourselves free from these things you will be doing right.' There are also a number of isolated words in common: ἐπισκέπτεσθαι (James 1.27; Acts 15.14), ἐπιστρέφειν (James 5.19f.; Acts 15.19), and ἀγαπητός (James 1.16, 19, 25; Acts 15.25).

None of these parallels is however particularly impressive in itself. χαίρειν is a stock epistolatory greeting in Hellenistic practice. It is used frequently in letters in Maccabees, including those by Jews (I Macc. 12.6; II Macc. 1.10), and in verbal greetings by Christians in II John 10f. 'Men and brothers, listen' (Acts 15.13) is again a fixed formula and in fact is more exactly paralleled in Stephen's speech in Acts 7.2 and Paul's in Acts 22.1 than in James 2.5. The calling of the name of God upon his people is so regular an Old Testament usage (e.g.,

[39] Moffatt, *ILNT*, 472–5, sees the objections to pseudonymity and indeed to *every* other alternative so forcibly that he is reduced to concluding: 'The phenomena of criticism upon the Jacobean homily are perplexing, but they are not to be taken as discrediting the science of New Testament literary research' (475)!

[40] All possible connections with Acts 15, and with James' words in Acts 21.24, are set out by Mayor, *James*, iiif.

Deut. 28.10; Isa. 63.19; etc.) as to be quite unremarkable in a Jewish writer (cf. II Macc. 8.15: 'called by his holy and glorious name'). The idea of keeping oneself holy or unspotted finds closer parallels in I Tim. 5.22 and 6.14 than in James. Both ἐπισκέπτεσθαι and ἐπιστρέφειν are used in markedly different contexts in Acts and James and represent in fact characteristic Lukan usage rather than anything distinctive of James; while ἀγαπητός is overwhelmingly common in all the New Testament epistles (Paul, John, I and II Peter, Jude). Nothing therefore can be built on such parallels. All that can be said is that they certainly do not stand against the writing of James by someone in the main stream of apostolic Christianity.

But what of the objections to James' authorship, which to many modern commentators have seemed decisive? They may be considered under three headings.

1. The attitude to the law in the epistle is not, it is said, that which fits the position of James. If by this position is meant the legalistic attitude adopted by Paul's Judaizing opponents, then even at the height of the controversy there is nothing in Paul or Acts to identify James with it. In Galatians Paul distinguishes the attitude of James himself (2.9) from that of 'certain persons . . . from James' (2.12). In Acts too it is made clear that James is no Judaizer (15.13–21), and he decisively dissociates himself from 'some of our number' who speak 'without any instructions from us' (15.24). Later also James welcomes the news of Paul's missionary activity and seeks to disarm the misrepresentation of him by his own more zealous adherents (21.18–26).

If, on the other hand, the point of the critics is that 'keeping the law' means for James observing its ritual requirements (as in Acts 21.24), then, to be sure, the emphasis in the epistle is very different. For there the stress is entirely on moral righteousness. If the epistle is set in the context of the controversy described in Acts and Galatians and its crucial passage, 2.18–26, is viewed as James' answer to Paul, then indeed we are dealing not only with quite a different concept of faith but with quite a different understanding of law and works. However, if we set it not against the debate over the admission of Gentiles to the church but against the kind of Jewish formalism condemned by Jesus, then James' understanding of the law is entirely consistent. So far from its being, as Harnack supposed, a notion of law 'which he has distilled for himself',[41] his is that inner delight in the perfect law of liberty which inspired Ps. 119 (cf. especially vv. 7, 32, 45) and which Paul himself would have been the first to say was the mark of

[41] *Chron.*, 486.

'the true Jew' (Rom. 2.25–29). Even subsequently circumcision and ritualism were not the heart of the matter for James. When that issue arose, circumcision was waived as a condition of church membership (Acts 15.19, 28), and ritual observance was urged as a matter not of principle but of tact, in a way that Paul himself was perfectly prepared to fall in with (21.21–26). The attitude to the law in the epistle can scarcely therefore be urged as an objection to Jacobean authorship, though it is certainly an argument against placing it in the context of the Judaizing controversy.

2. There is the relatively weak external evidence for the epistle's acceptance in the early church. Yet this cannot, it would be agreed, be decisive against arguments from the internal evidence, since citation and attestation are so fortuitous a matter. Even those like Origen and Eusebius who refer to the doubts about the epistle in parts of the church themselves accept it and use it as scripture.[42] Moreover, the reasons for questioning or neglecting it, whether in the early church or later by Luther, are by no means simply to be identified with the issue of authorship. As Sparks puts it,[43]

> The fact that the Epistle is a Jewish–Christian document, whoever wrote it, may have been in itself sufficient to discredit it in the eyes of Gentile Christians; while its essentially practical attitude would inevitably make it seem of little consequence to those whose main interests were theological. Accordingly, its neglect by the early Church is by no means an insuperable barrier to accepting the Lord's brother as the author.

The conclusion must be that this evidence does not point decisively in either direction: it cannot be used to establish or to discredit apostolic authorship.

3. Much the most serious objection is the language in which the epistle is written. For it combines being one of the most Jewish books in the New Testament with what has been described as a 'high *koine*' Greek style. At any stage, indeed, this is a conjunction that requires explanation, and the difficulties do not disappear by relegating them to the second century or an unknown author. But the combination would certainly appear to be made more difficult by the supposition that the author was a first-century 'Galilean peasant'.

This is an issue that will present itself again in the cases of Peter and John, but there it *may* be softened by putting down the style of I Peter to Silvanus (I Peter 5.12) and the Greek of the fourth gospel (which in any case is not that idiomatic) to a writer other than his apostolic

[42] For a summary of this evidence, cf. Kümmel, *INT*, 405f.; Guthrie, *NTI*, 736–9.

[43] *Formation of the NT*, 129.

source. These possibilities we shall examine in due course. But in James there is no suggestion of another hand at work. The epistle presents a test case of whether a non-literary lower-class Palestinian in the period before 70 could or would have spoken or written such good (though still limited and Semitic) Greek.[44] It is so seen in the most extensive study of this issue to date, J. N. Sevenster's *Do You Know Greek? How Much Greek Could the First Jewish Christians have Known?* He devotes virtually his entire introduction[45] to the question posed by the epistle of James.

He dismisses recourse to the hypothesis of a secretary (to whom there is no allusion in any form) as highly improbable. He thinks pseudonymity (in the absence of any deliberate pose) or attribution to an otherwise unknown writer equally unlikely. So he is left with the question, Could James have written such Greek? He assembles and sifts the now considerable evidence from literary and archaeological sources, outside and inside Palestine, at different cultural levels. His conclusion is that there is in fact no reason why Jesus or the first apostles or James should not have spoken Greek as well as their native Aramaic.

> It is no longer possible to refute such a possibility by recalling that these were usually people of modest origins. It has now been clearly demonstrated that a knowledge of Greek was in no way restricted to the upper circles, which were permeated with Hellenistic culture, but was to be found in all circles of Jewish society, and certainly in places bordering on regions where Greek was much spoken, e.g. Galilee.[46]

[44] For the limitations of James' Greek, cf. Zahn, *INT* I, 117f. He certainly does not have the facility of a genuinely bilingual man like Paul.

[45] J. N. Sevenster, *Do you Know Greek?* (*NovTest* Suppl. 19), Leiden 1968, 3–21.

[46] Op. cit., 190. Cf. among others all coming to much the same conclusion: G. Dalman, *Jesus–Joshua*, ET 1929, 1–7; J. Weiss, *The History of Primitive Christianity*, ET 1937, 165f.; he makes the point that 'the crowd on the temple square expected that Paul would address them in Greek (Acts 22.2) and were agreeably surprised when he spoke to them in Aramaic'; S. Lieberman, *Greek in Jewish Palestine*, New York 1942; R. O. P. Taylor, *Groundwork of the Gospels*, 91–105; R. H. Gundry, 'The Language Milieu of First Century Palestine', *JBL* 83, 1964, 404–8; and *The Use of the Old Testament in St Matthew's Gospel*, Leiden 1967, 174–8; N. Turner, *Grammatical Insights into the New Testament*, Edinburgh 1965, 174–88; J. A. Fitzmyer, 'The Languages of Palestine in the First Century AD', *CBQ* 32, 1970, 501–31; J. Barr, 'Which Language did Jesus Speak?', *BJRL* 53, 1970–1, 9–29 (especially 9f.); Hengel, *Judaism and Hellenism*, especially I, 58–65, 103–6 (he speaks of 'the Judaism of Palestine as "Hellenistic Judaism" '); A. W. Argyle, 'Greek among the Jews of Palestine in New Testament Times', *NTS* 20, 1973–4, 87–9; he draws the analogy: 'To suggest that a Jewish boy growing up in Galilee would not know Greek would be rather like suggesting that a Welsh boy brought up in Cardiff would not know English.'

He argues that *Christian* Jews often probably had a better knowledge of Greek (certainly they were from the start more cosmopolitan than the Qumran covenanters) and that there is no reason why a church-leader like James (or Peter) could not have taken the trouble, like Josephus, to acquire a reasonable command of literary Greek. Indeed Zahn, who long ago argued strongly in the same direction,[47] made the point that Greek-speaking Christians were probably in the *majority* in the earliest period.

> According to the notices of Acts, which are the only sources we have, the membership of the Church from the start consisted predominantly of Hellenists. The first three thousand converts (Acts 2.41) to gather about the personal disciples of Jesus, who were mainly Galileans, were not natives of Jerusalem and Palestine. From the names of their home countries one must infer that the language 'in which most of them were born' was Greek.[48]

And these 'devout Jews drawn from every nation' were permanent residents (*κατοικοῦντες*; Acts 2.5, 14) in Jerusalem, not temporary visitors up for the feast (contrast the *παροικεῖς Ἰερουσαλήμ*; of Luke 24.18). Of their seven leaders appointed subsequently (Acts 6.5) only Nicolas of Antioch is described as a foreigner or as a proselyte: they were indigenized, born Jews who spoke Greek. It was only with the growing accession of 'Hebrews' or Aramaic-speaking converts that the 'Hellenists' or Greek-speaking majority felt their position in the church threatened (Acts 6.1). Zahn maintained that it would have been impossible for the early Christian leaders to have fulfilled the immediate duties of their office, such as are described in Acts 8.14–25 or 9.32–11.18, let alone done anything beyond Palestine, 'without a good deal of readiness in speaking Greek'.[49] Certainly James' position, as we see it later in Acts 21.18–29, as head of the church in a city visited by thousands of Greek-speaking Jewish pilgrims would have made this highly desirable, if not essential.

Sevenster's cautious conclusion[50] with regard to the epistle of James is that:

> Even though absolute certainty cannot be attained on this point, in view of all the data made available in the past decades the possibility can no longer be precluded that a Palestinian Jewish Christian of the first century AD wrote an epistle in good Greek.

Or, as the most recent writer puts it:[51]

> There may be valid arguments against the ascription of apostolic authorship to I Peter and James, but the linguistic argument can no longer be used with any confidence among them.

[47] *INT* I, 34–72. [48] Ibid., 43. [49] Ibid., 45. [50] Op. cit. 191.
[51] Argyle, *NTS* 20, 89.

Clearly this is as far as the evidence from language can take us. It can prove nothing, but equally it holds open the possibility of apostolic authorship, and with it of early dating.

So finally we come back to the question of chronology from which we started. There are three main possibilities.

1. The epistle comes from an unknown Christian (whether or not he is claiming to be James the brother of the Lord) from the first half of the second century or the end of the first. Harnack[52] argued, as we have seen, for a date as late as 120–140 on the ground that the degeneracy of the church implies a state of affairs comparable only with that envisaged in the Shepherd of Hermas.[53] Quite apart from when *that* document should be dated,[54] I agree with Mayor, in his very astringent analysis of Harnack's position,[55] that what he calls this hangover of 'the old Tübingen tradition, from which he has receded in regard to many of the other documents of the New Testament' is incredible. There is no situation in the reign of Hadrian, whether before or after the final Jewish revolt under Bar-Cochba in 132, that begins to fit the many signs of primitiveness noted earlier. Yet a date of 125–50 is still favoured by A. E. Barnett in the article on James in *The Interpreter's Dictionary of the Bible*, on the ground that the author of the epistle knew Romans, I Corinthians, Galatians and Ephesians ('which means that he knew them as members of a published collection') as well as Matthew, Luke, Hebrews, I Peter, Hermas and Clement! There seems to be no limit to the circularity of arguments from literary dependence.[56]

More soberly, Reicke[57] agrees that there is no polemic against Paul in the epistle, which must, he argues, have come into existence 'before Paul's ministry, or a considerable time after'. He goes on, 'It is practically impossible, however, that the work is pre-Pauline', and he concludes that it comes from the reign of Domitian, *c.*90.[58] The

[52] *Chron.*, 485–91.

[53] He takes James 2.6f., 'Are not the rich your oppressors? Is it not they who drag you into court and pour contempt on the honoured name by which God has claimed you?', to refer to internecine quarrels between *churchmen*. But it is not implied that these oppressors are Christian: it is 'you' over whom 'the name' has been called, not 'they'. *Contrast* Hermas, Sim. 8.6.4: 'These are the renegades and traitors to the Church, that blasphemed the Lord in their sins, and still further were ashamed of the Name of the Lord, which was invoked upon them.' For the differences between James and Hermas, cf. Mayor, *James*, cxcf.

[54] See pp. 319–22 below. [55] *James*, clxxviii–cxcii.

[56] Contrast Kümmel, *INT*, 410: 'No clearly perceptible literary connection with other early Christian writings exists.'

[57] *James, Peter and Jude*, 5f.

[58] Kümmel, *INT*, 414, will be no more specific than 'toward the end of the

absence of any reference to the defeat of Judaism or to the final break between the church and the synagogue (the supposed evidence for which in the fourth gospel is also said to point to the reign of Domitian!)[59] seems to me to make this supposition highly improbable. But what are the reasons he gives for an early date being 'practically impossible'? The first is that 'the persecutions mentioned in 1.2f., 12f.; 2.6; 4.6; 5.10f. refer to Christians outside Palestine, but none are known prior to Paul's time'. But this presupposes that the address to 'the twelve tribes dispersed throughout the world' applies only to Christians living outside Palestine. On the contrary, as we have argued, it would appear to be a designation for 'the whole Israel of God', and the conditions referred to point time and again to those of Palestine. Moreover, the violent persecution that followed the death of Stephen had 'scattered' Christians not only throughout Judaea and Samaria (Acts 8.1, 4) but to Phoenicia, Cyprus and Antioch (11.19). It is to such 'scattered' Christians facing trials of many kinds that the epistle of James is addressed (1.1f.). The other details in the epistle adduced by Reicke as indicating a stage of development 'a considerable time after' Paul's ministry would seem to prove nothing. Denunciations of the rich (1.2–7; 4.13–5.6) are as old as Jesus and as the prophets before him. The need to distinguish between the true wisdom from above and that which is 'earth-bound, sensual and demonic' (3.15) could come from any time in the period of late Judaism. The need to be patient 'for the coming of the Lord is near' (5.8) can scarcely be said to require an advanced date (especially from a scholar who would now put all the synoptic gospels, with their much more specific injunctions, before the Jewish war!), while the instructions about bringing back 'those who stray from the truth' (5.19f.) might have come straight out of the teaching of Qumran or of Jesus.

If therefore the arguments for a later date are not compelling there are two further positions, both of which are compatible with apostolic authorship, though naturally they do not require it.

2. Since there is no reference to the fall of Jerusalem or the Jewish revolt and since James was put to death in 62,[60] this latter date pro-

---

first century' – arguing from 'the conceptual distance from Paul'. But how long is that? Earlier critics were for the same reason putting it in the middle of the second century. Conceptual distance is hardly amenable to quantitative measurement.

[59] See below pp. 272–4.

[60] Josephus, *Ant.* 20. 200f. Hegesippus (*apud* Euseb. *HE* 2.23.18) says that Vespasian's attack on the Jews (in 67) followed 'immediately' upon it, but this, as we have seen, is probably a case of translating sureness of judgment into temporal

vides a natural *terminus ad quem*. If the passage about faith and works reflects argument with Paul, then it would seem to come from about the same time as Romans or a little after. This was the position of F. J. A. Hort[61] and Parry,[62] who dated James *c.* 60.[63] It has been the mediating position taken by a number of English scholars[64] and also by P. Feine, whose work[65] Kümmel revised and at this point reversed, and by Klijn.[66] It was also the view that I originally accepted. One advantage of it is that it enables us, if we wish to, to think of James as already having been in the Greek *diaspora*. For in I Cor. 9.5 Paul asks, with reference to missionary travel, 'Have I no right to take a Christian wife about with me, like the rest of the apostles and the Lord's brothers, and Cephas?', and it seems he would hardly have put the Lord's brothers before Cephas unless, as in Gal. 2.9, they included James.[67] But there is no evidence that James was married, unlike Jude,[68] and it is in any case highly speculative. The real difficulty of this dating is that it presupposes that James was written at a time (on our reckoning, about that of Ephesians) when the issue of Jew and Gentile in the church and the resulting antagonism between Jews and Christians very much dominated the scene and when Paul, as a direct result of it, lay imprisoned in Caesarea. Yet the epistle makes absolutely no reference even to the existence of the Gentile mission, let alone to the tensions it occasioned for both Jews and Christians. I agree with Reicke in finding this impossible. I am therefore driven, against my initial expectation, to take seriously the third and still more conservative position.

3. This places the epistle of James, as its 'primitive' character at so many points would suggest, very early indeed, before the controversy

---

immediacy – or of running together sources. Josephus' circumstantial account of the opportunity afforded by the interregnum between Festus and Albinus is certainly to be preferred. In his *Chronicle* Eusebius himself dates it in 62.

[61] F. J. A. Hort, *Judaistic Christianity*, Cambridge and London 1894, 148f.; *St James*, 1909, xxivf.

[62] R. St J. Parry, *A Discussion of the General Epistle of St James*, 1903, 99f.

[63] G. H. Rendall, *The Epistle of St James and Judaic Christianity*, Cambridge 1927, 87, argued that it comes just *before* Romans, between 49 and 55.

[64] E.g. A. T. Cadoux, *The Thought of St James*, 1944; C. L. Mitton, *The Epistle of James*, 1966, who interestingly believes James wrote James, but not Paul Ephesians nor Peter I Peter; and Sidebottom, *James, Jude and 2 Peter*, 19f.

[65] P. Feine, *Einleitung in das neue Testament*, Leipzig [5]1930, 200.

[66] *INT*, 151.

[67] Kümmel, *INT*, 290, allows the force of this as a conjecture.

[68] Cf. Hegesippus (apud Euseb. *HE* 3.20.1), who however gives a very different impression of James as an extreme ascetic (*HE* 2.23.5f.). In all the references to the dominical family (*HE* 3.11f., 19, 20.1–8, 32.6; 4.22.4) no mention is made of any progeny of James.

about circumcision and the terms of Gentile admission. This does not mean that there was by then no Gentile mission, only that it had not as yet become divisive. For there was doubtless a period, as both Paul (Gal. 2.2) and Luke (Acts 13–14) indicate, when missionary work went on among Gentiles on a scale that provoked no crisis of principle. It was only when 'certain persons who had come down from Judaea began to teach the brotherhood that those who were not circumcised in accordance with Mosaic practice could not be saved' (Acts 15.1) that conflict broke out. This can be dated fairly exactly to *c.* 48. Now James seems to have occupied some position of leadership in Jerusalem, if not from *c.* 35 (cf. Gal. 1.19), at least since 42 (or at the latest 44) when Peter went into hiding (cf. Acts 12.17, 'report this to James'). But the indications are that the epistle is more likely to belong to the end of this period than to its beginning. To address a pastoral homily to the whole church (such as it then was) presupposes that James had already established the spiritual authority to do so, without having, apparently, any need to assert it. The argument too whether justification is by faith or works, even if conducted still within a Jewish frame of reference, could very well reflect garbled reports (cf. Gal. 2.4) of 'the gospel' that Paul 'preached to the Gentiles' during his first mission of 47–48, which he subsequently felt it desirable to clear, privately, with James and the others in Jerusalem (Gal. 2.2). Moreover, if anything in James' letter (e.g., as we have suggested, 2.10) had been taken to mean that Christians must observe the whole law or nothing – and the need for an official denial (Acts 15.24) makes this more than possible – then it is likely to have been written not long before the incident of Acts 15.1. Perhaps therefore we should date the epistle of James early in 48 – not later, and possibly a year or so earlier: let us say 47–8. In this case the similarities of language with James' speech and the apostolic letter in Acts 15, though not probative, are certainly interesting.

This early dating has had surprisingly persistent support. Mayor argues for it strongly, citing many earlier writers, including B. Weiss and Zahn.[69] Knowling also supported it, adding other names.[70] More recently it has been favoured in a notable series of articles by G. Kittel,[71] and also by Heard,[72] Michaelis[73] and Guthrie.[74] The

[69] For a list of the others, see Mayor, *James*, cl. [70] *James*, lxviii–lxxii.

[71] G. Kittel, 'Die Stellung des Jakobus zu Judentum und Heidenchristentum', *ZNW* 30, 1931, 145–57; 'Der geschichtliche Ort des Jakobusbriefes', *ZNW* 41, 1942, 71–105; 'Die Jakobusbrief und die apostolischen Väter', *ZNW* 43, 1950–1, 54–112.

[72] *INT*, 167. [73] *Einleitung*, 282. [74] *NTI*, 761–4.

problem of a letter written in Greek to an audience inside as well as outside Palestine remains. But it is no more difficult then than ten years later, and we shall return to this question in connection with the fourth gospel.[75] If, as we argued in the previous chapter, the gospel of Matthew, whose tradition is closest to that of this epistle, was also beginning to take shape, in Greek, in a similar milieu at the same time, then the epistle of James will no longer be an anomalous exception. It can take its natural place, alongside other literature in the process of formation in the second decade of the Christian mission, as the first surviving finished document of the church.

[75] Pp. 293–301 below.

VI

The Petrine Epistles and Jude

WHETHER EITHER OF the epistles ascribed to Peter or that attributed to Jude are by the apostle or the Lord's brother respectively is again not our primary concern. While the issues of chronology and authorship are, here more than ever, inextricably connected, it is the former that must continue to have priority in determining our approach. The best way therefore will be to adopt the same procedure as with the Pauline epistles. This is to attempt to construct a chronological framework, into which the epistles of Peter can be fitted if they are genuine or into which they will purport to fit if they are not. The epistle of Jude comes into this picture because of its manifest interdependence – one way or the other – with II Peter.

The reconstruction of the chronological framework may be begun where that for Paul left off, with the point at which Acts ends. But mention of Acts merely underlines our previous reliance on it. When it stops, we find ourselves almost wholly lost. Whatever framework is reconstructed, it must be said at once that it is bound to be extremely hypothetical and sketchy, for the evidence is simply insufficient. What we miss in particular are the *intervals*, which it is Luke's particular contribution to supply. In fact the situation is now reversed. Whereas before we were strong on relative dates but very weak on absolute dates (the pro-consulship of Gallio being about the only really secure one, and that by a fortuitous discovery), we now are strong on absolute dates, but extremely weak on relative ones. Thus we have quite precise datings for two cardinal events, the fire of Rome, which broke out on 19 July 64, and the suicide of Nero, which occurred on 9 June 68. But how, within or around that period, happenings or writings of relevance to the Christian church are to be placed in relation either to each other or to these fixed points is highly problematic.

Let us begin by trying to round off the life of Paul. On the basis of the aorist ἐνέμεινεν rather than the imperfect in Acts 28.30 it will be recalled that Harnack argued that at the end of two years Paul's situation changed: it was not simply that the narrative ceased, for whatever reason.[1] This could well be true; but the inference is precarious, since the aorist would in any case have been a natural choice of tense: for two years he stayed (ἐνέμεινεν) and during that period he used to receive (ἀπεδέχετο). Nor of course does it tell us how Paul's situation changed – whether, as Harnack guessed, it was because he was then transferred to stand trial (whatever the outcome) or whether, as Lake and Cadbury argued,[2] the case lapsed because the statutory two-year period expired within which the accusers had to appear. Sherwin-White[3] criticizes the latter theory on the ground that there is no real evidence for such a limit. Paul may have been released by an act of clemency, or simply to clear the lists, but there is no reason to construe Acts to mean that he was released at all. All theories which reconstruct this period either from hopes expressed in the Captivity Epistles or from plans in the Pastorals presuppose that the former come from his Roman imprisonment and the latter (genuinely or supposedly) from the period subsequent to it. If our previous argument was sound, neither of these presuppositions holds. In particular, the decisive reference in II Tim.4.16 to his 'first hearing' refers not to anything in Rome but to the first trial under Felix in Caesarea. It is difficult to be certain whether any of the later tradition reflects more than deductions from a combination of Paul's hope to visit Spain (Rom. 15.23, 28) and the Pastoral Epistles interpreted as Roman in origin. Certainly it is the latter that supply the basis for everything that Eusebius has to say on the subject.[4] The fragment of the Muratorian Canon (coming from Rome at the end of the second century?) simply says that 'from the city he proceeded to Spain',[5] but this could merely be part of the presumption we

[1] Cf. L. P. Pherigo, 'Paul's Life after the Close of Acts', *JBL* 70, 1951, 277–84: 'Since the author of Acts seems to have known the *duration* of the imprisonment, it certainly seems to follow that he knew also of its *termination*' (277; italics his).

[2] *Beginnings* V, 325–36.

[3] *Roman Society and Roman Law*, 108–19; cf. F. F. Bruce, 'St Paul in Rome', *BJRL* 46, 1964, 343–5; Ogg, *Chronology of the Life of Paul*, 180f.

[4] *HE* 2.22.

[5] Zahn, *INT* II, 62f., 73–5, and F. F. Bruce, 'St Paul in Rome: 5. Concluding Observations', *BJRL* 50, 1968, 272f., argue that its remark that Luke omits 'the passion of Peter, as well as Paul's journey when he set out from Rome for Spain'

observed before that (despite the evidence of II Corinthians!) Paul's plans were always fulfilled. Much the most important piece of evidence is that of I Clem. 5.6f., which asserts that, after he had preached both in the east and the west, he reached the 'extreme west' (*τὸ τέρμα τῆς δύσεως*). I would agree with Lightfoot[6] and Zahn[7] that to interpret this in a writer living in Rome to mean Rome itself is incredible. We must assume it means Spain, and depending on the date and weight we attach to the evidence of I Clement,[8] it speaks in favour of a release from Rome and further travel (though only to the west).

Beyond that we are in the dark. Clement clearly refers to Paul having perished in the same persecution as Peter and a 'great multitude of the elect',[9] which cannot be other than that under Nero.[10] But Paul appears to have stood alone as he 'gave witness before rulers', and the subsequent tradition, that, whereas Peter was crucified,[11] Paul (as a Roman citizen) was executed, strongly suggests that this was as a result of a separate judicial action, not of mass violence such as Tacitus describes. Again, in the first-century Ascension of Isaiah 4.2f.[12] it is only 'one of the Twelve' who 'will be delivered into his [viz. Nero's] hands': there is no mention of Paul. Dionysius, Bishop of Corinth, says in *c.* 170 that Peter and Paul 'having taught together in Italy, suffered martyrdom at (or about) the same time' (*κατὰ τὸν αὐτὸν καιρόν*).[13] This comes to be interpreted, first in the Liberian Catalogue of 354,[14] to mean 'on the same day',

---

suggests that it is here dependent on the *Acts of Peter* which includes both of these (Hennecke, *NT Apoc.*, II, 279–82, 314–22).

[6] *AF* I.2, 30f.

[7] *INT* II, 72. Similarly Pherigo, *JBL* 70, 279–82.

[8] It has often been argued that Clement's details may be explained entirely from Acts But Zahn, *INT* II, 68–73, is still convincing to the contrary, as is Lightfoot. For a recent defence of Clement's tradition, cf. Dinkler, *TR* 25, 207–14.

[9] I Clem. 5f.; cf. the similar phrase in Tacitus, *Ann.* 15. 44 of the Neronian persecution.

[10] So Tertullian, *Scorp.* 15.

[11] Cf. John 21.18f.; Tertullian, *Scorp.* 15; *Praescript.* 36; *Adv. Marc.* 4.5. This is independent of the elaboration of the tradition that he was crucified upside down (*Acta Petr.* 37f.; Origen apud Euseb. *HE* 3.1.2).

[12] For the dating of this passage, cf. pp. 239f. below. It could come from not long after the event.

[13] Quoted by Eusebius, *HE* 2.25.8. *If*, as Munck argued (*Petrus und Paulus in der Offenbarung Johannis*, Copenhagen 1950), the vision of the two witnesses in Rev. 11.3–12 alludes to the deaths of Peter and Paul, this would be early evidence for their simultaneous martyrdom. But this theory is at best extremely hypothetical. Cf. p. 241 below.

[14] For the evidence, cf. Edmundson, *The Church in Rome*, 149f.

namely, 29 June. But this day is almost certainly the one which in the year 258 saw some veneration of their joint memories, possibly the translation of their relics from the Vatican and the Ostian Way to a catacomb on the Appian Way for safety during the Valerian persecution.[15] Indeed, despite the great influence of Jerome (*c.* 342–420), who said that they suffered in the same year,[16] the tradition still survived in Prudentius (348–*c.* 410)[17] and Augustine (354–430)[18] that Paul died exactly a year after Peter[19] – evidence which is worthless as a positive indicator but useful as a corrective.

When we come to the question of the date, or dates, of their deaths, we are equally in the dark. There are two separate issues: (*a*) Did the Neronian persecution follow immediately upon the fire of Rome?; and (*b*) Did Peter and/or Paul perish in that first assault? If we could answer 'Yes' to both these questions, our chronological problems would be over and everything could be dated in 64. Unfortunately, however, it is not so simple. Indeed if it had been as simple as the textbooks tend to make it, it is difficult to explain how the divergences could have arisen. The presumption must be that there was a tendency to conflate not only the day but the year, and that, other things being equal, preference should be given to the less tidy solution. But let us first look at what evidence there is for answering the two questions.

(*a*) So indelibly etched upon the common memory is the association between the fire of Rome and the persecution of Christians that it comes as a surprise to realize that the entire connection rests upon one unsupported piece of evidence – a single chapter in Tacitus' *Annals* (15.44). To this important, and excellent, source we must return in detail. But first it is worth stressing the point that it stands alone not only in classical but in Christian literature – until it itself is quoted.[20] In classical literature the only other reference to the persecution of Christians is in Suetonius' *Lives of the Twelve Caesars*, which because it rests so obviously on independent tradition is important corroborative testimony. But the persecution is brought into no connection with the fire (which by itself, of course, is often

[15] For a discussion of this, cf. Cullmann, *Peter*, 123–31; Bruce, *BJRL* 50, 1968, 273–9.

[16] *De vir. ill.* 5. He based it on his own Latin translation of Eusebius' *Chronicle* (see below pp. 147–50).

[17] *Περιστεφάνων*, hymn 12, quoted by Edmundson, op. cit., 150.

[18] *Serm.* 296–7.

[19] Cf. also the quotation from *Acta SS. Jun.* 5, 423c, in Zahn, *INT* II, 76.

[20] This is well brought out by E. T. Merrill, *Essays in Early Christian History*, 1924, h. 4.

mentioned subsequently).[21] The fire is described in *Nero* 38, but the persecution of Christians is alluded to briefly in *Nero* 16 among a variety of public acts, chiefly legislative. As Hort dryly observed,[22] 'It comes between regulations about what might be sold in the cooks' shops and others about restraining the license of charioteers and the factions of clowns.' More remarkably there is no memory of its association with the fire preserved in any early Christian writer. None of the early references to the Neronian persecution, in Clement of Rome,[23] Melito of Sardis,[24] Tertullian,[25] Lactantius,[26] Eusebius[27] or Jerome,[28] makes any mention of the fire. The first link is in Sulpicius Severus,[29] whose *Chronicle* was completed *c.* 403 and which quotes Tacitus. In Eusebius' *Chronicle* the two events are separated by four years.

But we must return to the evidence of Tacitus, which is important enough to be set out in full. After giving a graphic and detailed description of the ravages of the fire and the immediate relief operations for the temporary rehousing of some hundreds of thousands of homeless (*Ann.* 15.38–41), he proceeds (15.42f.) to describe the rebuilding of the capital to a carefully thought-out plan with built-in fire precautions for the future, together with the construction by Nero of a palace for himself of unrivalled magnificence, the celebrated *Domus Aurea.*[30] Then, in 15.44, he goes on:

> So far, the precautions taken were suggested by human prudence: now means were sought for appeasing deity, and application was made to the Sibylline books; at the injunction of which public prayers were offered to Vulcan, Ceres, and Proserpine, while Juno was propitiated by the matrons, first in the Capitol, then at the nearest point of the sea-shore, where water was drawn for sprinkling the temple and image of the goddess. Ritual banquets and all-night vigils were celebrated by women in the married state. But neither human help, nor imperial munificence, nor all the modes of placating Heaven, could stifle scandal or dispel the belief that the fire had taken place by order. Therefore, to scotch the rumour, Nero substituted as culprits, and punished with the utmost refinements of cruelty, a class of men, loathed for their vices, whom the crowd styled Christians. Christus, the founder of the name, had undergone the death penalty in the reign of Tiberius, by sentence of the procurator Pontius Pilatus, and the pernicious superstition was checked for a moment, only to break out once more, not merely in Judaea, the home of the disease, but in the capital itself, where all things horrible or shameful in the world collect and find a vogue. First, then, the confessed members of the sect were arrested; next, on their disclosures, vast

[21] E.g. Pliny, *Nat. hist.* 17.5; Dio Cassius, *Hist.* 61.16–18.

[22] F. J. A. Hort, *The Apocalypse of St John I–III*, 1908, xxv.

[23] I Clem. 5f.

[24] In his Petition to Marcus Aurelius, cited by Eusebius, *HE* 4.26.9.

[25] *Apol.* 5.3f.; *Ad nat.* 1.7; *Scorp.* 15.

[26] *De mort. persec.* 2.

[27] *HE* 2.25.

[28] *De vir. ill.* 5.

[29] *Chronic.* 2.29.

[30] Described by Suetonius, *Nero* 31.

numbers were convicted, not so much on the count of arson as for hatred of the human race. And derision accompanied their end: they were covered with wild beasts' skins and torn to death by dogs; or they were fastened on crosses, and, when daylight failed, were burned to serve as lamps by night. Nero had offered his gardens for the spectacle, and gave an exhibition in his circus, mixing with the crowd in the habit of a charioteer, or mounted on his car. Hence, in spite of a guilt which had earned the most exemplary punishment, there arose a sentiment of pity, due to the impression that they were being sacrificed not for the welfare of the state but to the ferocity of a single man.[31]

It is quite clear from this account that a considerable interval of time must have elapsed before in desperation Nero rounded on the Christians. There is no need to assume that the building works were by then completed: indeed none was finished before Nero's death, and the *Domus Aurea* was demolished, uncompleted, by Vespasian. Yet in so far as we have any evidence for a connection between the fire and the persecution – and there is no good reason to question it – it is for a delayed reaction. At the very least, an interval of many months must be allowed for the various stages described by Tacitus, which from the time the fire finally died down at the end of July 64 brings us into 65 at the earliest. Yet almost universally, not only in the textbooks, but by giants like Lightfoot and Harnack and Zahn, the Neronian persecution is dated in 64. I myself became convinced that this could not be right, but it is one of the many merits of Edmundson's *Church in Rome in the First Century* that he exposes in careful argument what he calls this 'fundamental error on the part of almost every writer upon the subject'.[32] It is characteristic of the neglect of his book that what he says should also have been ignored ever since.

He demonstrates that it is no objection that Tacitus' treatment of the events of the year 65 appears to begin only at ch. 48, since it is this historian's practice, like that of others, 'to group together so as to form a single and complete episode in his narrative a series of events having close connection with one another but really spread over a considerable space of time'.[33] He shows how this applies to his compression of the Pisonian conspiracy into the events of 65; it is described as 'no sooner hatched than full-grown',[34] though it actually began in 63[35] and might well have led to the death of Nero during the fire of 64.[36] Certainly the ambitious programme for the rebuilding of Rome

[31] Tr. J. Jackson, Loeb Classical Library, 1937. For assessments of the passage by classical scholars, cf. B. W. Henderson, *The Life and Principate of the Emperor Nero*, 1903, 237–53, 434–49; H. Furneaux, *The Annals of Tacitus* II, Oxford 1907, 416–27.

[32] Op. cit., 125; cf. 123–44. [33] *Ibid.*, 126. [34] *Ann.* 15.48.

[35] *Ann.* 14.65. [36] *Ann.* 15.50.

described under the events of 64[37] could scarcely have got off the drawing-boards of Severus and Celer by the end of that year.

Among the points Edmundson makes are three which, he argues, help to date the spectacle in Nero's gardens as not earlier than the spring of 65. The first is the weather.

> One thing . . . may be regarded as certain: that such a nocturnal spectacle would not have been planned so long as the night air was chilly, nor would Nero with his scrupulous care for the preservation of his divine voice[38] have appeared at night in the open on a car in the garb of a charioteer in cold weather.[39]

The second is an argument, which he admits is speculative, that the account in *Ann.* 15.58 of 'continuous columns of manacled men dragged and deposited at the garden doors', which greatly exaggerates the actual numbers involved in the trial of the Pisonian conspirators in April 65, may have been confused by merger with the round-up of Christians at the same time. Thirdly, he draws attention to the fact that the Christian historian Orosius,[40] a younger contemporary of Sulpicius Severus, who had access to Suetonius, Tacitus and Josephus, follows his account of the fire and persecution with the words:

> Soon calamities in heaps began on every side to oppress the wretched state, for in the following autumn so great a pestilence fell upon the city that according to the registers [in the temple] of Libitina there were thirty thousand funerals.

Edmundson comments:

> These last words are a direct quotation from Suetonius,[41] who however as usual gives no date to the pestilence. This is however given by Tacitus, who thus concludes his narrative of the events of 65 AD[42]: 'The Gods also marked by storms and diseases a year made shameful by so many crimes. Campania was devastated by a hurricane . . . the fury of which extended to the vicinity of the City, in which a violent pestilence was carrying away every class of human beings. . . . Houses were filled with dead bodies, the streets with funerals.'[43]

None of this adds up to a demonstration that the persecution of Christians *was* in 65. It could have been later, though the plausibility of linking it with the crime of arson would steadily have diminished as the interval grew. But it may help to reinforce the strong inherent probability that it could hardly have been earlier. Tentatively then we may answer our first question by dating this initial assault upon the church in the spring of 65.[44]

[37] *Ann.* 15.42f.

[38] Cf. Suetonius, *Nero* 20; Pliny, *Nat. hist.* 19.6; 24.18; Tacitus, *Ann.* 15.22.

[39] Op. cit., 141. [40] *Hist. adv. pagan.* 7.7. [41] *Nero* 39.

[42] *Ann.* 16.13. [43] Edmundson, op. cit., 143.

[44] B. Reicke, *The New Testament Era*, ET 1969, 249, puts it 'around the beginning of 65'.

(*b*) Did Peter and/or Paul perish in this first attack? One could get the impression from I Clem. 5f. that Peter and Paul were actually in the van of the martyrs, but it is doubtful whether anything more than eminence causes their names to be put first. The other sources, when they mention names at all, do not discriminate, with the exception of Sulpicius Severus, who says:[45]

> Thus a beginning was made of violent persecution of Christians. Afterwards also laws were enacted and the religion was forbidden. Edicts were publicly published: 'No one must profess Christianity.' Then[46] Paul and Peter were condemned to death. The former was beheaded, Peter was crucified.

We shall have to come back to the legal enactments in another context.[47] The separation in so late a document of the deaths of the apostles from the initial violence would scarcely be significant if it were not for the somewhat confused evidence of the *Chronicle* of Eusebius. In his *History*[48] he mentions no dates, despite dating other events in the chapters that precede and follow. In the *Chronicle* we have varying evidence in the two versions.[49] The Armenian puts the fire of Rome (or rather 'many fires in Rome') in 63[50] and Nero's 'beginning of the persecution of Christians in which Peter and Paul suffer martyrdom at Rome' in 67. This however is rendered doubtful by a previous entry for 66, when Linus is recorded as succeeding Peter as Bishop of Rome. In Jerome's Latin version 'Nero sets fire to most of Rome' in 64, and the 'first persecution of Christians by Nero in which Peter and Paul perished gloriously in Rome' is in 68, and in the same year 'Linus becomes Bishop of Rome after Peter'. The Latin version is recognized to be generally the more reliable,[51] and in the reign of Nero it usually shows greater approximation to the dates supplied by Tacitus or Josephus. Indeed for two only, the

[45] *Chronic.* 2.29.3. Tr. J. Stevenson, *A New Eusebius: Documents Illustrative of the History of the Church to AD 337*, 1957, 6.

[46] But Barrett, *NT Background*, 17, translates 'at that time', thus eliminating the suggested interval.

[47] P. 234 below. [48] *HE* 2.25.

[49] For convenient comparison in parallel columns, cf. Schoene (ed.), II, 154–7.

[50] Eusebius' dates are expressed in terms of the regnal years of Nero. Working backwards, the last, Nero 14, must be 68, with Nero 1 as 54, and this calculation is supported by Finegan, *HBC*, 308. Lightfoot, *AF* I.1, 230, puts all the dates a year earlier; C. H. Turner, 'The Early Episcopal Lists', *JTS* 1, 1900, 187–92, a year later. Turner ingeniously works out that Eusebius must calculate the regnal year 1 of any emperor from about the 15th September *following* his accession. Since Nero did not become emperor till October 54 this means that Nero 1 = September 55–September 56. But on this calculation Nero 14 becomes September 68–9 and Nero would then not kill himself till 9 June *69* (during the reign of Vitellius!).

[51] So Lightfoot, *AF* I.1.232; Turner, op. cit., *JTS* I, 184–7; Finegan, *HBC*, 155f.

earthquake at Laodicea and the murder of Octavia, where it is four and five years out respectively, is there a discrepancy of more than a year or two.

The one thing that emerges clearly is that Eusebius does not associate the persecution with the fire (in both versions they are four years apart), but does associate the deaths of Peter and Paul with the general persecution. There is nothing in Tacitus actually to *rule out* a four-year interval between the fire and the persecution, though such a gap would have made any connection with the charge of arson incredible. The circumstantial, and much older, evidence of Tacitus must be preferred at this point, with the general persecution beginning, in all probability, in 65. But what of the later date for the apostles' death? There is absolutely no way of being certain, and Lightfoot, despite an exhaustive discussion of the early Roman episcopal succession,[52] declined to commit himself to choosing between 64 (as he dated the persecution) and 67 or 68.[53] Wisdom perhaps should dictate leaving it there, and there is certainly no place for Harnack's dogmatic assertion that the martyrdom of Paul in July 64 is 'an assured fact'.[54] But there are certain observations of greater or lesser probability that can be made.

1. It is questionable whether Eusebius had any basis for his dating except guess-work, and on the date of the general Neronian persecution he was almost certainly wrong by some three years. The limitation of a chronicle is that it allows no room for genuine uncertainty. In a history one can slur over one's ignorance; in an annual record one is forced to place things in one year or another. As we have seen, in his *History* Eusebius offers no date for the persecution, which may suggest that he did not have one. There are two reasons why in his *Chronicle* he could have decided to put it at the end of Nero's reign. In the Armenian version (and the Latin is similar) his entry for the persecution reads: 'On top of his other crimes Nero was the first to provoke persecutions of Christians; under him the apostles Peter and Paul suffered martyrdom in Rome.' Zahn comments:[55]

> Eusebius himself knows no more than what he says, namely, that Peter and Paul died under Nero, and does not intend that 67 shall be regarded as the year in which both apostles died, as is proved also by his remark at the year preceding (66) that Linus succeeded Peter as bishop of Rome. It was only his way of looking at the history, according to which the slaying of the Christians was the climax of Nero's crimes (*HE* 2.25. 2–5), that caused him in his *Chronicum* to place the persecution of the Christians at the end of that emperor's reign.[56]

[52] *AF* I.1, 201–345. [53] *AF* I.1, 351. [54] *Chron.*, 240. [55] *INT* II, 78.

[56] There may also have been the motive we have encountered before, which

The other reason, on which Harnack fastened,[57] is that the year 67 looks suspiciously as if it may be influenced by combining the traditions of a twelve-year stay of the apostles in Jerusalem and a twenty-five year 'episcopate' of Peter over Rome (30 + 12 = 42 + 25 = 67). Unlike the date 42, it is supported by no other evidence than that of Eusebius himself, and is therefore unreliable.

2. The evidence of Sulpicius Severus, though late, could be based on better sources. His reference to decrees is, as we shall see, borne out by Tertullian. Unlike Eusebius, he certainly had access to Tacitus, whose account he clearly echoes. But Tacitus had nothing about the death of Peter and Paul, and this may be the reason for Sulpicius' adding the notice of it apparently as a separate item at the end, following the decrees. In any case, if he intended an interval after the initial onslaught, there is absolutely no indication of its duration. It could have been but a few weeks.

3. As far as the death of Peter is concerned, the evidence points to its being associated with the mass violence of 65. Death by being 'fastened to crosses' is among the horrors listed by Tacitus, and the 'Quo Vadis?' legend,[58] to which we shall return,[59] and to which, Edmundson argues,[60] considerable credibility attaches, speaks of Peter seeking to save his life by leaving the city, only to be turned back by the vision of Christ to face crucifixion. This suggests that though he escaped the initial round-up mentioned by Tacitus he met his death before the end of the purge. There is no suggestion in any tradition that this was prolonged beyond the year (indeed in 66 Nero went to Greece and did not return till 68). So tentatively we may agree with Edmundson that the death of Peter took place 'some time during the summer of 65'.[61]

4. By contrast there is nothing specifically to connect the death of Paul with the Neronian *pogrom*. It was apparently a judicial execution following a trial and could have occurred at any time before, during, or after it. For what little it is worth, the evidence is in favour of Paul's death being somewhat later than that of Peter.[62] But many

---

reappears in the *Acts of Peter and Paul* (ed. L. F. K. Tischendorf, *Acta Apostolorum Apocrypha*, Leipzig 1851, 38), of suggesting that the death of Nero followed speedily upon his killing of the apostles: 'Know ye that this Nero will be utterly destroyed not many days hence and his kingdom given to another'; quoted by Ogg, *Chronology of Paul*, 199, who also doubts the evidence of Eusebius.

[57] *Chron.*, 241f. [58] *Acta Petr.* 35 (Hennecke, *NT Apoc.* II, 317f.).
[59] P. 214 below. [60] Op. cit., 151–3. [61] Ibid., 152.
[62] Cf. p 143., nn. 17–19, above; also *Acta Petr.* 40, which places Paul's return to Rome from Spain after Peter's death. It has been argued (cf. Cullmann, *Peter*, 94f.)

modern reconstructions, unlike those of the ancients who allowed only for a visit to Spain (which could easily have been fitted in between 62 and the Neronian persecution),[63] have been affected by the desire to leave time for further journeys east so as to satisfy the supposed requirements of the Pastoral Epistles.[64] There is really no way of telling. All we can say is that it was near enough to the death of Peter to be regarded by Clement as part of the same attack and later by Dionysius to have occurred 'about the same time'. Probably we shall not be far out in settling for some time in 66, or 67 at the latest.

It must be stressed again that all this is no more than a very tentative reconstruction in the absence of any firm evidence. It can but provide a provisional framework, which may have to be modified by the evidence from the Petrine epistles, to which we must turn.

I Peter

There is no question at any rate that the epistle claims to be by the apostle Peter (1.1) and purports therefore to be written during his lifetime. It is addressed to 'those of God's scattered people who lodge for a while in Pontus, Galatia, Cappadocia, Asia and Bithynia', and, in contrast with the epistle of James, the Christian *diaspora* evidently now includes a majority (probably) who were once Gentiles (1.14, 18; 2.9f.; 3.5f.; 4.3). The other thing that is reasonably certain is that it was written, or purports to have been written, from Rome. The 'greetings from her who dwells in Babylon, chosen by God like

---

that since the Old Testament examples of jealousy in I Clem. 4 are in chronological order, the mention of Peter before Paul implies that Peter died first. This is possible; but it would logically follow that both died before the mass of the martyrs, which is specifically denied by Sulpicius Severus. Cullmann never even discusses the question of dates.

[63] So Gunther, *op. cit.*, 147, who suggests not without plausibility (following Pherigo, *JBL* 70, 278) that Paul's imprisonment in Rome was terminated by a sentence of *relegatio* or temporary exile to a place of his choice. This would account for the 'exile' mentioned in I Clem. 5.6, which is otherwise difficult to fit in, and is in line with the tradition in *Acta Petr.* 1: 'Quartus, a prison officer, . . . gave leave to Paul to leave the city (and go) where he wished. . . . And when he had fasted for three days and asked of the Lord what was right for him, Paul then saw a vision, the Lord saying to him, "Paul, arise and be a physician to those who are in Spain"' (Hennecke, *NT Apoc.* II, 279). Subsequently, in 66, as Edmundson, op. cit., 160–2, points out, Apollonius of Tyana was also banished from Rome and 'turned westwards to the land which they say is bounded by the Pillars' (Philostratus, *Vit. Apol.* 4.47).

[64] Thus Lightfoot (*Biblical Essays*, 223) puts Paul's death on these grounds in the spring of 68 (?); Zahn (*INT* II, 67) in late 66–June 68; Edmundson (op. cit., 160–3 and 240) in 67.

you' (5.13) is almost universally agreed to be a disguise for the church in Rome. The pseudonym is indisputable in the book of Revelation (14.8; 16.19; 17.5; 18.2, 10, 21) as it is in other late-Jewish and Christian writings (II Bar. 10.1f.; 11.1; 67.7; II Esd. 3.1f., 28, 31; Orac. Sib. 5. 143, 159f.), and it was so understood here as early as Papias.[65] There is no need to spend time discussing alternative locations in Mesopotamia[66] or Egypt. The only question is why the disguise was felt to be necessary – as it never is, for instance, in the writings of Paul. The obvious answer is that it was resorted to for the same reason as in the Apocalypse, namely, that of security (however thin the veil). But this at once leads into a discussion of the main, and indeed the only, circumstantial evidence in the epistle which is relevant to its dating, the menace of persecution that everywhere pervades it.

Let it be said at once that this evidence *proves* nothing by way of dating. The references are such as could be explained by the kind of harassment at the hands of Jews and local magistrates that meets us constantly in Acts and Paul, and which might have occurred at any time or place. This has been emphasized by a number of recent writers,[67] for instance Selwyn,[68] Moule,[69] Kelly,[70] Best,[71] and van Unnik.[72] The last concludes:

> Once we rule out the possibility of identifying these sufferings with some particular persecution, we are left with no direct indication as to the date. The situation reflected in the letter could have happened at any time in the first or second century wherever a Christian group was found.

Indeed F. L. Cross goes so far as to say that 'the supposed references to persecution are false trails',[73] since he argues that the theme of suffering is supplied by the church's liturgical season rather than by external events.

But, even granting that there is a liturgical setting, this is surely to

[65] Eusebius, *HE* 2.15.

[66] A. Schlatter, *The Church in the New Testament Period*, ET 1955, 253–7, and J. Munck, *Paul and the Salvation of Mankind*, ET 1959, 275, are among those who have believed that Peter visited the Babylonian dispersion. But there is no other evidence for this – while there is plenty that he was in Rome.

[67] And earlier by Zahn, *INT* II, 178–85.

[68] E. G. Selwyn, 'The Persecutions in I Peter', *Studiorum Novi Testamenti Societas Bulletin*, 1950, 39–50.

[69] C. F. D. Moule, 'The Nature and Purpose of I Peter', *NTS* 3, 1956–7, 1–11; *Birth of the NT*, 114.

[70] J. N. D. Kelly, *The Epistles of Peter and Jude* (Black's NTC), 1969, 5–11, 29.

[71] E. Best, *I Peter*, 1971, 39–42. [72] *IDB* III, 762.

[73] F. L. Cross, *I Peter: A Paschal Liturgy*, 1954, 42.

present a false either/or. Moreover, though these are salutary warnings against identifying the references with any datable official persecution – and still more against the dogmatism of *precluding* a date because there is no record of a persecution in that particular area – it does seem that there is perhaps more to be said. For the preoccupation with suffering, and with Christian behaviour under it, is unique to I Peter. There is nothing quite like it in the Pauline epistles, or in any others, with the exception perhaps of Hebrews. But in Hebrews the persecution lies, partly at least, in the past, and the concern is for the danger of relapse it has brought in its train. Here it is potential, imminent or incipient (1.6; 2.12, 19f.; 3.13–17; 4.12–19; 5.8–10). What situation is reflected in Hebrews we must go on to discuss in the next chapter, but that it reflects a particular situation can hardly be doubted. So in I Peter, at least in 4.12, 'Do not be bewildered by the fiery ordeal that is upon you' (or is happening to you, ὑμῖν γινομένῃ), it seems evident that something specific is in mind. And while it is not limited to the recipients of the letter (5.9), it is nevertheless a new situation (4.17) for which they are not prepared (4.12). It may not be an official persecution, but it is clear that things are building up to a climax, indeed, in the author's view, to the final climax (4.7). Perhaps the nearest historical parallel to the kind of social and religious harassment that I Peter seems to presuppose is the phenomenon of anti-semitism; and this characteristically manifests itself in waves, erupting from time to time in sharp *pogroms* (whether or not officially 'inspired'). It is clear too that this persecution of Christians is not the sort that Paul mentions in I Thess. 2.14–16, and which Acts chronicles so frequently, as instigated specifically by Jews. Jews may have been involved, but there is nothing to say so. It is pagans who malign them as wrongdoers (2.12) and vilify them as spoilsports (4.3f.); it is the criminal code and the standards of good citizenship which they must be careful not to offend (2.12, 15f.; 3.16f.; 4.14f.), not the Mosaic law or Jewish susceptibilities.

Above all there is a wariness with regard to the state authorities (2.13f.) that suggests that Christians must be particularly careful to afford them no handle. If they have to suffer, they must be sure not to put themselves the wrong side of the law (4.14f.) and so give excuse to the adversary who is 'looking for someone to devour' (5.8). The parallel today might be a warning to Christians in South Africa to make certain that, if they are going to oppose *apartheid* (as of course they must), they do not allow themselves to be convicted for doing wrong rather than for doing good. And this approach, of being, in Jesus' words, as wise as serpents and harmless as doves, is entirely compatible with advocating and encouraging all *proper* respect for the state and its powers (2.13–17; cf. 3.15). The situation here is not that reflected in the book of Revelation, where the time is past when Christians can expect that such respect will bring them justice. Moreover, in contrast again with the Apocalypse, there is as yet no evidence of martyrdom or banishment, or indeed of any physical violence. Though hostility would obviously not be limited to insulting words (cf. 2.20, of the beating of slaves), the attack upon them 'as Christians' seems to have consisted primarily of slander and calumny. As Zahn pointed out:[74]

> Whenever a specific injury is mentioned which they suffered at the hands of the heathen, it is always of this character:– *καταλαλεῖν* (2.12; 3.16), *λοιδορεῖν* (3.9), and *ἐπηρεάζειν τὴν ἀγαθὴν ἐν Χρισῷ ἀναστροφήν* (3.16); *βλασφημεῖν* (4.4) and *ὀνειδίζειν* (4.14). They are to silence their slanderers by good conduct (2.15); they are to put them to shame (3.16); above all, they are not to answer reviling with reviling, but with blessing (3.9). The very first condition of a comfortable life is to refrain from evil and deceitful words (3.10). Even in the passage where the suffering of Christ is held up as an example especially to slaves, it is not said that he refused to use his power to defend himself against violence (Matt. 26.51–5; 27.40–4; John 18.36; Heb. 12.2f.); but that when he was reviled he reviled not again, and did not give vent to threatening words when he was compelled to suffer (2.23).

To sum up, there is no evidence of open state persecution. Yet there is a sense of tension with regard to the civic authorities which is missing from even the latest epistles of Paul and the end of Acts. I believe therefore that those are right who look for *some* climacteric to which a date may be put. Can we be more specific? Three main possibilities have been suggested, the situations under Trajan, Domitian and Nero.

1. We may begin with that under Trajan because we have a parallel which looks almost too good to be true. In his oft-quoted letter to the Emperor[75] Pliny the younger, who was governor of Bithynia-Pontus, a province specifically mentioned in the address of I Peter, asks whether, in dealing with those brought before him 'as Christians', 'punishment attaches to the mere name apart from secret crimes, or to the secret crimes connected with the name'; and he cites the oath by which Christians bound themselves, 'not for any crime, but not to commit theft or robbery or adultery'. This seems to parallel closely the situation described in 4.14–16:

> If Christ's name is flung in your teeth as an insult, count yourselves happy. . . . If you suffer, it must not be for murder, theft, or sorcery, nor for infringing the

[74] *INT* II, 180f. [75] *Epp.* 10.96. Trajan replies in 10.97.

> rights of others. But if anyone suffers as a Christian, he should feel it no disgrace, but confess that name to the honour of God.

Many have concluded with F. W. Beare that 'it would therefore seem unnecessary to look further for the persecution which called forth our letter',[76] and he dates it at the same time. J. W. C. Wand admits that this identification 'seems powerfully attractive'.[77] Yet both from Pliny's practice and from the Emperor's reply it is presupposed that Christianity is already a *religio illicita* and that this is nothing new – conditions that cannot be presumed from I Peter.[78] As Moule says,[79] it is illegitimate to draw the inference from 4.15 that being a Christian is itself a capital offence comparable with murder. To take care that you suffer unambiguously as a Christian no more implies this than it does in the parallel we suggested from South Africa today. Suffering for 'the name' is of course already to be found in Acts 5.41; 9.14; and Mark 13.13; and the wording of Matt. 5.11, 'How blest are you, when you suffer insults and persecution and every calumny for my sake', is particularly close to the situation in I Peter. The term 'Christian' too had become established well before this date (Acts 11.28; 26.28).[80] These parallels are the more significant if, as we have argued, Acts and the synoptic gospels are all to be dated before the mid-60s. The Trajanic setting would be compelling *if* there were any other reason to suggest a second-century date or if no other *Sitz im Leben* looked possible. Otherwise it cannot be said to be necessary, or indeed probable. (It is notable that the most thorough English commentary on the epistle in recent years, that of Selwyn, does not even mention it – Trajan comes into the index only in a quotation from Dante!) It will be proper therefore to suspend judgment until we have examined the evidence for the other alternatives.

2. The placing of I Peter under Domitian is really a compromise for those who can put it at neither of the other dates. Thus Kümmel, who has already ruled out apostolic authorship, writes:

[76] F. W. Beare, *The First Epistle of Peter*, Oxford ²1958, 14. Similarly, J. Knox, 'Pliny and I Peter: A Note on I Peter 4.14–16 and 3.15', *JBL* 72, 1953, 187–9; and A. R. C. Leaney, *The Letters of Peter and Jude*, Cambridge 1967, 8–10. Streeter, *PC*, 115–36, saw the epistle as republished (under the pseudonym of Peter) to meet this situation.

[77] J. W. C. Wand, *The General Epistles of St Peter and St Jude*, 1934, 15.

[78] For a careful study of the nature of the early persecutions of Christians, cf. A. N. Sherwin-White, *The Letters of Pliny*, Oxford 1966, 772–87.

[79] *Birth of the NT*, 113f. For other points in the same direction, cf. A. F. Walls in *The New Bible Dictionary*, edd. J. D. Douglas et al., 1962, 975.

[80] For a survey of the evidence inside and outside the New Testament, cf. Zahn, *INT* II, 191–4.

> The reign of Domitian should probably be taken as the time of writing, since the mention of the persecution 'as Christians' (4.16) is not sufficient ground for going down as late as the beginning of the second century, or even to the time of the persecution under Trajan. 90–5 is, therefore, the most probable time of composition.[81]

The reason, of course, for selecting the last years of Domitian's reign is that this is the only other period apart from the latter 60s associated in the tradition with the persecution of the church. What in fact this persecution amounted to we must examine more closely when we come to the book of Revelation,[82] which is usually connected with it. But there is no evidence that it affected Asia Minor[83] – and in this it is in exactly the same position as the Neronian persecution – *except* for the evidence of the Apocalypse. But equally, if the Apocalypse comes from the times of Nero, then its evidence, including the use of the pseudonym 'Babylon', would support a similar date for I Peter. For the moment therefore we must leave this evidence on one side. In any case, as we have seen, the state of affairs in I Peter is clearly not yet that of the Apocalypse. Reicke[84] makes the point that

> sacrifices to the emperor are not mentioned in First Peter as a problem confronting the Christians. If the epistle had been written during Domitian's persecution that well-known, grave issue could not have been passed over.

This is, of course, an equally valid objection to the Trajanic date, since Pliny specifically mentions 'supplication with incense and wine' to the statue of the emperor as an alternative to execution; and of this there is no hint in I Peter. Indeed it is scarcely credible that under either Trajan or Domitian the writer could have linked 'reverence to God' and 'honour to the emperor' in the positive and unqualified manner of 2.17.

There is in fact really nothing to be said for a date in Domitian's reign except as a last resort. I cannot resist quoting Wand's comment in this connection,[85] since it bears out what I have come to feel at many points in the course of this investigation:

> Is there not some danger of Domitian's reign becoming rather overloaded with otherwise undated bits of Christian literature? The Apocalypse, Hebrews and *I Clement*, to say nothing of *Barnabas* and the *Didache*, have all been ascribed to this period. It has in fact become the favourite dumping-ground for doubtful writings with a hint of persecution about them.

[81] *INT*, 425. [82] Pp. 231–3 below.

[83] Unless it be the straw at which some have (quite seriously) grasped, that Pliny reports that a number of those he was investigating had given up their Christianity 'some three years before, some a longer time, *one or two* even twenty years ago' (italics mine). The last date would bring us back to *c.* 95.

[84] *James, Peter and Jude*, 72. [85] *Peter and Jude*, 16.

But he is too modest in his list. The reign has also been pressed into service to accommodate Ephesians, Luke, Acts, Matthew, John and the Johannine epistles, and by many too James, Jude and the Pastoral Epistles! This is not because all these writings have common factors (not even persecution): they are widely different. Nor is it because we have such detailed information of the circumstances of the reign that we can see how and why they fit in. Indeed, from a Christian point of view, it is one about which we know remarkably little. Hence its attractiveness as a depository: it can accommodate almost anything. So let us pass on, to see whether we are really forced by lack of alternative to bring it into use for I Peter.

3. With a date under Nero the issue of authorship becomes a decisive factor – though in fact it is equally tied to the other two hypotheses, which are viable only on the assumption of pseudonymity or original anonymity (the name of Peter being subsequently attached). Inevitably, however, the arguments that it *cannot* be by the apostle tend to be held (or are capable of being stated) more decisively, not to say dogmatically, than the arguments that it *must* be by the apostle. For it is easier to preclude authorship than to prove it. Arguments against apostolicity are therefore often used (e.g. by Kümmel) to rule out a Neronian dating without further discussion. Beare, who commits himself to the statement that 'there can be no possible doubt that "Peter" is a pseudonym',[86] effectively dismisses this date on the sole ground that there is no evidence that this persecution extended to the provinces.[87] There is, to be sure, no evidence that the persecution of Nero had repercussions in Asia Minor (unless of course the Apocalypse *does* come – somewhat later – from this period). But the happy accident that so remote a province as Bithynia-Pontus had an exceptionally literary governor in the second decade of the second century whose correspondence has survived and touches at one point on the treatment of Christians can scarcely be used as an argument that silence elsewhere implies that there was nothing of the sort going on. In any case, the kind of suppressed tension which I Peter reflects, in contrast with open state persecution, is hardly likely to have featured prominently in the history books. The issue is whether the terror that erupted under Nero is the sort of which this situation could be the build-up, whether

[86] *I Peter*, 25.

[87] Ibid., 10–13. He appends some other arguments from W. Ramsay, *The Church in the Roman Empire before AD 170*, 1893, 196–295, which are about as unsubstantiated as that writer's eccentric conclusion that it was written *c.* 75–80 *by Peter*, who lived on into the reign of Vespasian!

or not it also broke out openly in Asia Minor. And here Tacitus' words in *Ann.* 15.44 already quoted deserve closer scrutiny.[88]

Apart from the obviously trumped-up charge of arson, there are two counts mentioned. One is 'hatred of the human race' (odium humani generis; cf. Tacitus' comment on the Jews in *Hist.* 5.5, 'adversos omnes alios hostile odium'). This is clearly a catch-all indictment (and the word 'convicti' seems to imply that it was framed as a legal charge) such as can succeed only if it can feed on, and foment, latent popular resentment and hostility (as with Hitler's incrimination of the Jews after the Reichstag fire). And this is precisely the kind of lurking, or rather prowling (5.8), hostility that I Peter reflects. Secondly, says Tacitus, 'first those were arrested who confessed' (primum correpti qui fatebantur). The context shows that this cannot mean confessed to arson, of which it is made clear they were innocent, but to their faith.[89] The situation was the same as with Pliny: 'I asked them whether they were Christians, and if they confessed, I asked them a second and third time with threats of punishment' – though Nero's procedures were certainly not designed to give them an incentive to recant, but rather to inform on their co-religionists. Admission to being a Christian was all that was needed. And, says the author of I Peter, let commission of *this* 'crime' be all that they can find against you: 'If anyone suffers as a Christian, he should feel no disgrace, but confess that name to the honour of God' (4.16). The parallel with the time of Nero is as close as with that of Trajan, and, assuming that open persecution has not yet broken out, the attitude of wary respect and duly discriminating honour for the authorities, 'whether it be to the emperor as supreme or to the governor as his deputy' (2.14–17), is *at this stage* entirely explicable. But such language, and even more that of 3.13, 'Who is going to wrong you if you are devoted to what is good?', would be incredible if the Neronian terror had already struck – or even if Paul had by then been executed.[90] And this is perhaps a further indication that the martyrdom of Paul did not precede the persecution.

All that is lacking (unless the Apocalypse supplies it) is specific evidence from Asia Minor. But is the clue to the writer's language to be sought in the epistle's destination – or in its source? There is no

[88] I am indebted for this comparison to the notable article on I Peter by F. H. Chase in *HDB* III, 784f. Cf. H. Fuchs, 'Tacitus über die Christen', *VC* 4, 1950, 65–93.

[89] This is generally agreed among the commentators. Jackson in the Loeb edition translates 'the confessed members of the sect'.

[90] So C. Bigg, *The Epistles of St Peter and St Jude* (ICC), Edinburgh 1901, 85.

suggestion that he speaks from personal acquaintance with his readers. We cannot tell whether he has ever paid them a visit, and he holds out no prospect of one.[91] Certainly he does not claim to have brought them the gospel: that has been the work of other preachers (1.12). But there is the further consideration, which many commentators have noted, that the epistle reads like material composed in the first instance as a homily – or more than one homily. The unity of the epistle is not our direct concern, but the resumption at 4.12, after a doxology, with matter that appears to reflect a more imminent or actual situation of persecution has suggested to some that two letters have been combined.[92] Absence of any textual evidence for this (in contrast to the very varied position of the doxology at the end of Romans) must weigh against any theory of *literary* division; but that the material represents addresses given on different occasions or to different groups is entirely plausible. Yet here the implications of the *place* of delivery are more relevant. For if it is material prepared in the first instance for speaking (however much it was adapted subsequently), then the situation it reflects will primarily be that of Rome rather than the obscurer parts of Asia Minor.

There have indeed been attempts to pin the occasion down still more specifically, notably by Cross,[93] who, however, makes no attempt to draw out the geographical implications for the situation of suffering, which, as we have seen, he regards as a false trail. There is no need here to go into the details of his theory that I Peter is originally material composed for the bishop's part at a paschal baptismal liturgy in Rome. They have been sharply criticized,[94] though I am inclined to think at some points he could have stated his case more cogently and in a form less open to objection.[95] But

[91] There is a somewhat greater probability that Mark sends his greetings (5.13) because he is known to them. Edmundson, op. cit., 121f, suggests that Mark visited at least some of them after his visit to Colossae (Col. 4.10); though cf. II Tim. 4.11. In any case there is no ground for thinking, with Edmundson, that he met Peter there. Speculations about the interrelationship at the time of Peter and Paul *via* Silvanus (Chase, *HDB* III, 790–2; cf. Zahn, *INT* II, 160–2) are fruitless.

[92] So Moule, op. cit., *NTS* 3, 1–11; cf. J. H. A. Hart, *EGT* V, 29f.

[93] *I Peter: A Paschal Liturgy*, building on, and applying to the Passover, the baptismal setting of I Peter argued by Perdelwitz, Bornemann, Windisch, Streeter, Beare and Preisker, references to whose works are given in the footnotes to Cross, op. cit., 28.

[94] E.g. by Moule, *NTS* 3, 1–11; W. C. van Unnik, 'Christianity according to I Peter', *ExpT* 68, 1956–7, 79–83; T. C. G. Thornton, 'I Peter, a Paschal Liturgy?', *JTS* n.s. 12, 1961, 14–26.

[95] Rather than the references to suffering being occasioned purely by the church's year, I believe the preacher is using the opportunity this provides to give teaching

whether this theory (or any modification of it) is *necessary* as an explanation of the epistle (and clearly it is not), it is at least worth considering the implications of some of the phraseology on the assumption that what shaped it was the experience of the writer's own pastoral situation in Rome rather than that of his distant, and highly diverse, readers. I believe there may be several hints of this, especially in the closing section of the epistle, which may have been addressed more specifically to the immediate needs of the local congregation as a whole.

The most striking phrase is that in 4.12 about 'the fiery ordeal that is upon you' (*τῇ ἐν ὑμῖν πυρώσει πρὸς πειρασμὸν ὑμῖν γινομένῃ*). It is indeed difficult to apply this to a general situation in every part of Asia Minor north and west of the Taurus mountains. Hence the theories that it may have been added for a particular province or church, though there is nothing else to suggest or confirm this. We must be wary of taking the metaphor too literally, since the *πύρωσις* takes up the metaphor of the assayer's fire in 1.7 (though why it was chosen there is still relevant). The use of the symbolism of 'the fire of testing' (*τὴν πύρωσιν τῆς δοκιμασίας*) for the eschatological ordeal occurs also in Did. 16.5, as, of course, in Paul (I Cor. 3.15) and elsewhere. Nevertheless 'the fiery trial' would be a grimly appropriate image for the Neronian terror, sparked off as it was by the fire of Rome and culminating in 'Christians fastened on crosses, and . . . burned to serve as lamps by night'.

If this part of the epistle does reflect a more circumstantial account of what had already begun in Rome (though not yet in Asia Minor), there could also be an echo of it in 5.8. There in a vivid metaphor (cf. I Cor. 15.32; II Tim. 4.17) the Christians' *ἀντίδικος*, or adversary in

which is very much related to his hearers' condition. Similarly, the sermon, while presupposing the external actions and imagery of the liturgy, is concerned to draw out the inward and spiritual meaning of the sacramental acts, many striking parallels for which are to be found in the later record of the early Roman rite in Hippolytus' *Apostolic Tradition*. Thus in 3.3f. the stress is on 'not in outward adornment'. The women have to plait their hair undone for the baptism, refasten the jewellery they have taken off, and put on their new robes: all this is part of the rite – now it has to be done not just externally but 'in the inmost centre of our being'. So in 2.2 the milk they have received is interpreted as spiritual (*λογικόν*), and in 2.5 the structure of the church and the *θυσίαι* (oblations?) as *πνευματικαί*. Finally in 3.21 baptism is seen not as a mere washing away of the bodily pollution but (if this is the right translation) a pledge to God proceeding from a good conscience. But, though the different moments of the rite provide the occasion for the teaching, there is no need (with Cross) to assume that the sermon was tied synchronistically to them.

court, is viewed as the devil (incarnate in the imperial power?) who, 'like a roaring lion prowls around looking for someone to devour'. Tacitus does not indeed specify the lions of the amphitheatre, but he does say that the Christians were 'covered with wild beasts' skins and torn to death by dogs'.

Finally, with great hesitation, I offer a suggestion on which nothing turns and which indeed I throw out mainly for a classicist with more knowledge than myself to refute or confirm. The phrase in the following verse, 5.9, translated in the NEB, 'remember that your brother Christians are going through the same kinds of suffering while they are in the world', or, in the RSV, 'throughout the world', has long struck me as odd. From opposite extremes of the critical spectrum Bigg[96] and Beare agree that 'this clause is full of difficulties; almost every word offers a problem'.[97] Yet neither of them, nor as far as I have discovered anyone else, observe the oddness in the phrase *ἐν κόσμῳ*. It has to be paraphrased to mean either 'while still in the world' or 'in the rest of the world' or 'in the whole world'. Yet when Paul wants to say this *to* Rome, he says it quite clearly: *ἐν ὅλῳ τῷ κόσμῳ* (Rom. 1.8). Could it possibly be a stock phrase (without the article) to mean the opposite of 'in town'? And if so is it a Latinism reflecting the usage of the place where Peter's successor still makes his allocution 'urbi et orbi'?[98] Was there anywhere else except 'the City'[99] where one could speak of the provinces as 'the world' without qualification? If so, it would be a further subtle pointer to the original context of the phraseology being supplied not by Asia Minor but by Rome.

The objection to this whole thesis is that it is inconceivable how, in Moule's words,

> a liturgy-homily, shorn of its rubrics . . . but with its changing tenses and broken sequences all retained, could have been hastily dressed up as a letter and sent off (without a word of explanation) to Christians who had not witnessed its original setting.[100]

But this objection loses much of its force on two conditions. The first

[96] *Peter and Jude*, ad loc.

[97] *I Peter*, ad loc.

[98] I confess I have made no progress in tracing this phrase back to the first century, but I am grateful for the negative results of my friends, particularly Dr Robert Sharples of the Department of Latin, University College, London.

[99] This usage for Rome (as for London) is of course well established. Cf. the derivation of the name Istanbul, which is a corruption of the modern Greek for *εἰς τὴν πόλιν*.

[100] *NTS* 3, 4.

is that one does not press the points in the argument that make it into a liturgy proper[101] but treats it more, with Reicke,[102] as 'a confirmation sermon' comparable, he suggests, with Ephesians (another Asian encyclical). Secondly, one must bear in mind that, as I read them, the circumstances are far from normal. The homily turned into a circular letter is dispatched, *via* Silvanus, 'our trusty brother, as I hold him', with the message 'I am saying very little in writing' (5.12), because, like Tychicus in Eph. 6.21, he will 'tell all' (πάντα γνωρίσει).[103] The situation is one of great urgency and danger, in a city that must already be disguised as 'Babylon', as the Neronian terror breaks. When would this be? We shall not be far wrong, I think, if we guess the spring of 65. Indeed if the paschal associations of I Peter, as of I Corinthians (cf. I Cor. 5.7f.; 16.8), are granted,[104] *whatever* its literary form, we may be more specific still. Passover that year was late, falling on April 12. If Edmundson is right, who argues for this same dating of I Peter,[105] the rounding up of Christians after the first 'confessions' became mixed up with the retribution vented on the Pisonian conspirators. This also came to a head, according to Tacitus, in April 65. We may then envisage Silvanus leaving hastily for Pontus on his round of the Asian churches[106] perhaps towards the end of that month.

But at this point we must reckon with factors which have seemed to many to make such a dating impossible. They focus mainly on the issue of authorship, but, first, what of any other indications in the epistle, or out of it, which might suggest a later date?

As regards external attestation, there is nothing to suggest that it was not known as early as almost any New Testament book. It is quoted several times (though not by name) in the epistle of Polycarp from the first part of the second century. Possible connections with Ephesians, Hebrews, James and I Clement are (it is now widely agreed) too sketchy or too general for asserting literary dependence

[101] In particular I would question the forced interpretation of νῦν (1.12; 2.10, 25; 3.21) and ἄρτι (1.6, 8; 2.2) to indicate 'a rite in actual progress' (Cross, op. cit., 30). 1.6 and 8 are surely impossible to take this way in any case.

[102] *James, Peter and Jude*, 74f.; cf. Streeter, *PC*, 123.

[103] Cf. Acts 15.27, also of Silvanus: 'We are therefore sending Judas and Silas, who will themselves confirm this by word of mouth'.

[104] See Cross, op. cit., 23–7. He cites in particular (and so interprets): 1.3–12, 13–21, 18f.; 2.9f., 11. Cf. A. R. C. Leaney, 'I Peter and the Passover: An Interpretation', *NTS* 10, 1963–4, 238–51 (especially 244–51).

[105] Op. cit., 118–44.

[106] Cf. F. J. A. Hort, *The First Epistle of Peter (1.1–2.17)*, 1898, 157–85, for the itinerary reflected in the order of the districts named.

either way. In any case the arguments are circular, depending on judgements made of the dates of these other documents.[107]

With regard to the internal evidence, it is remarkable how little even those like Beare who regard an early date as impossible can point to traits of doctrine or organization to support them. In fact, apart from asserting that the epistle's teaching on baptismal regeneration is (at some unspecified date) 'borrowed from the contemporary Hellenistic modes of thought,'[108] he fastens on the fact that the Spirit of God is mentioned only four times, which he interprets to mean that

> a writing in which the sense of the active presence of the Spirit has fallen into eclipse as it has in First Peter betrays by that indication alone that it is the product of a later generation. It is utterly inconceivable that to Peter, or to Silvanus for that matter, the doctrine of the indwelling Spirit was wholly unknown, or was not of the first importance for the moral life of the Christian.[109]

Seldom can the argument from silence have been made to cover so much. One might as well argue the same for Colossians, which does not refer to the Holy Spirit once.

Cross, on the contrary, as a scholar at home both in the biblical and the patristic periods, has no doubt as to the world to which I Peter belongs. I quote the summary that concludes his study:

> First, the theology of I Peter betrays many signs of great antiquity. There is a marked absence of later theologoumena, e.g. in the undeveloped doctrine of the Trinity in 1.2; while there are indications that the ordering of the Christian ministry is that of a very early date.[110] Secondly, the eschatological structure of the thought, with its close inter-penetration of future hope and present realiza-

[107] Thus E. J. Goodspeed, *New Solutions of New Testament Problems*, Chicago 1927, 115, regards I Peter as a response to Hebrews and puts both of them in the reign of Domitian. C. L. Mitton, 'The Relationship of I Peter and Ephesians', *JTS* n.s. 1, 1950, 67–73, sees I Peter as dependent on Ephesians which, like Goodspeed, he also places in the same reign. Beare, *I Peter*, 9f., 195f., follows him. Kümmel, *INT*, 423, though supporting a late date, dismisses literary dependence on Romans and Ephesians as 'improbable', 'because the linguistic contacts can be explained on the basis of a common catechetical tradition'.

[108] *I Peter*, 38. He toys (16–19) with theories of associations with the mystery cults of Cybele, especially the Taurobolium. He has to admit that the direct evidence is far too late, but still uses it to give substance to the statement that 'one is inclined to feel that he is indeed in the religious atmosphere of the second century'.

[109] *I Peter*, 36.

[110] The only reference to the ministry is in fact in 5.1–4, where the author, despite claiming to be an apostle (1.1), addresses the elders as a fellow-elder, exhorting them as shepherds of the flock under Christ, the chief shepherd, who is also in 2.25 the shepherd and ἐπίσκοπος of their souls. The contrast with the epistles of Ignatius, also from Asia Minor in the reign of Trajan, is very marked. Even if (contrary to the NEB) ἐπισκοποῦντες were part of the true text in 5.2, the function of ἐπισκοπή would be that of the presbyters, as in the whole of the New Testament.

tion, suggests the same conclusions. The ethics is still in the atmosphere of the last things, and we find that remarkable co-presence of the End as future and yet as already here, with no suggestion of the clear distinction between the *Prote* and the *Deutera Parousia* of Christ as we find it from Justin onwards, which is a mark of very early times. And thirdly, the whole tone of the work. If we ask: 'Does it breathe the spirit of the other Biblical writings which we use day by day in our Christian worship, or is it that of later days whose ethos, however sublime, is not that of the New Testament?' I think that most will have a ready answer; and it is this that matters most. Whether it is the work of Peter or of Silvanus or of someone else I will not here try to say.[111]

In the same way, Moffatt, who argues for a late first- or early second-century date for Ephesians, the Pastorals, Hebrews and James, is equally clear that this period does not fit I Peter:

An early date is favoured by the absence of any heretical tendencies among the readers, the naive outlook on the imminent end (4.17f.), and the exercise of charismatic gifts (4.10); . . . and by common consent it has the stamp of primitive Christianity more than any other, not only of the writings in the Petrine New Testament (Gospel, Acts, Epp., Apoc.), but of the post-Pauline writings.[112]

But what, finally, of the question of authorship, which is our concern only in so far as it rules out or reinforces the dating?

First, it is worth noting that while some, as we have seen, speak as though apostolic authorship (whether direct or through an amanuensis) were out of the question, there are other scholars supporting it here who deny it in other comparable cases. Indeed, if we leave out such questioned but nevertheless widely accepted letters as Colossians and II Thessalonians, this, with the possible exception of James, is the *least* likely New Testament epistle to be pseudonymous. Even Harnack,[113] who decided against apostolicity, nevertheless found the case of pseudonymity 'weighed down' by such insuperable difficulties that, if his own theory were unacceptable, he said that he would opt for Petrine authorship. This theory was of an originally anonymous writing (from between 82 and 93 – though conceivably some twenty years earlier) which was later (*c.* 150–175) attributed to Peter by the addition of 1.1f. and 5.12–14. These verses are certainly detachable and may well be what originally turned a liturgical sermon into a letter. But there is absolutely no textual or external evidence for the theory, and it leaves most of the problems where they are. It has won

[111] Op. cit., 43f. Kelly, another patristic scholar, concurs (*Peter and Jude*, 30). Moule, *NTS* 3, 11, after disagreeing with most of Cross's thesis, ends by saying: 'I am in whole-hearted agreement with the last two pages of Dr Cross's lecture, where he argues that at any rate the theology, the ethics and the "tone" of the writing are all in keeping with an early period of the Christian Church's existence.'

[112] *ILNT*, 344. [113] *Chron.*, 457–65.

little support,[114] and, as Chase comments in his perceptive summary and critique of it,[115] it is another sign (noticed by Mayor of Harnack's treatment of James) of the remnants of the Tübingen presuppositions from which Harnack at the time had not shaken himself free:

> It essentially belongs to a period of transition. It is the product, on the one hand, of the lingering influence of an older criticism, too thoroughly bent upon negative results to retain much delicacy of perception; and, on the other hand, of a keen literary and spiritual sense of the significance of a writer's matter and manner.

The objections to pseudonymity felt by Harnack are nowhere better stated than by Chase himself:[116]

> A close study of the document itself reveals no motive, theological, controversial, or historical, which explains it as a forgery. It denounces no heresy. It supports no special system of doctrine. It contains no rules as to Church life or organization. Its references to the words and the life of Christ are unobtrusive. It presents no picture of any scene in St Peter's earlier life, and does not connect itself with any of the stories current in the early Church about his later years. Why, moreover, should a forger . . . represent Silvanus as the amanuensis or the bearer of St Peter's letter, though in the Acts he nowhere appears as in any way connected with that apostle, but both in the Acts and in three Epistles (I and II Thess., II Cor.) as the companion of St Paul? Why, above all, should a forger give to Pauline thoughts and to Pauline language a prominent place in an Epistle bearing the name of St Peter?

Attempts have legitimately been made to defuse the suggestions of 'forger' (e.g. by Beare[117] and Leaney[118]). The question of whether or not pseudonymity was an accepted literary convention which deceived (or attempted to deceive) no one will best be kept for the discussion of II Peter. All one can say here is that whatever the intention, it seems in this case a particularly motiveless exercise,[119] which in fact (unlike II Peter) deceived everyone until the nineteenth century.

But what are the improbabilities (Harnack) or impossibilities (Beare and Kümmel) in the way of apostolic authorship? Apart from the circumstances of persecution already considered, they may be summarized briefly under three heads.

1. If the epistle were by an intimate associate of Jesus we should expect more direct references to his life and words. This is a very

[114] Cf. Beare, *I Peter*, 24: 'It has no positive evidence to support it, and very little to commend it.'

[115] *HDB* III, 786f.

[116] Ibid., 785f.

[117] *I Peter*, 29f.

[118] *Peter and Jude*, 11f.

[119] Kümmel, *INT*, 424, concludes: 'The fact of pseudonymity is not contradicted by our inability to perceive the motive for it.' But it is precisely this 'fact' that has to be established and rendered plausible.

subjective expectation, and ironically it is precisely because II Peter *does* contain such explicit reference that it is discredited. Certainly the fact that any claims or allusions are so indirect argues more strongly against pseudonymity than authenticity. In any case to say that it is inconceivable that Peter should not 'have referred to the example of Jesus in some way'[120] is not merely subjective but wrong. The reference in 2.23 to the example of Jesus under trial is a clear allusion to the passion story. Indeed it is one of a number of passages which Selwyn[121] cites as evidence of 'apostolic testimony'.[122] None of these, he admits, is unambiguous, and they will strike different people with different force. But two others, I think, are worth repeating. They are 1.8: 'You have not seen him, yet you love him; and trusting in him now without having seen him, you are transported with a joy too great for words.' It has been well remarked that Paul never writes, nor could ever have written, such words, with their implied contrast in status between writer and readers. Selwyn cites Hoskyns and Davey's comment[123] on the similar word of Jesus to the twelve in John 20.29: 'Those who have not seen and yet have believed are what they are because there once were men who believed because they did actually see.' The other passage is the highly ambiguous one of 5.1: 'I appeal . . . as . . . a witness of Christ's sufferings, and also a partaker in the splendour that is to be revealed.' It is difficult to believe that this refers merely to the common experience of all Christians described in 4.13 ('It gives you a share in Christ's sufferings . . . and when his glory is revealed your joy will be triumphant'). A 'witness' would naturally imply more, as in Peter's words in Acts 1.22 and 2.32. And this is fortified by Selwyn's interpretation[124] of the following phrase, 'who have also had experience of the glory that is to be revealed', as a reference to the transfiguration, viewed (as G. H. Boobyer has cogently argued)[125] as an anticipated vision of the *parousia*. If so, the veiled allusion, in contrast with the unmistakable reference in II Peter 1.16–18, fits with the modesty of the author's

[120] Kümmel, *INT*, 424.

[121] *I Peter*, 27–33.

[122] Cf. also R. H. Gundry, '"Verba Christi" in I Peter', *NTS* 13, 1966–7, 336–50, who argues that the underlying allusions to the 'words of Christ' are specially connected with narrative contexts in the Gospels where Peter is an active participant.

[123] E. Hoskyns and F. N. Davey, *The Fourth Gospel*, ²1947, 97.

[124] *I Peter*, ad loc.

[125] G. H. Boobyer, *St Mark and the Transfiguration Story*, 1942; 'The Indebtedness of II Peter to I Peter' in A. J. B. Higgins (ed.), *New Testament Essays: Studies in Memory of T. W. Manson*, Manchester 1959, 43. Cf. my *Jesus and His Coming*, 133.

whole approach in 5.1 ('I appeal to you as a fellow-elder'), though scarcely with the pretensions of one falsely claiming to be an apostle.

2. It is said that the Paulinism of the doctrine is incompatible with the known position of Peter. This 'Paulinism' has in any case been much exaggerated, when, as Selwyn says, 'we reflect that the Epistle is without allusion to what are commonly regarded as the characteristic ideas of St Paul' – and he lists justification; the contrast between faith and works, gospel and law; the distinctive Pauline connotations of grace and sin, the atonement and the body of Christ; and much in the ethical field.[126] For the rest he has persuasively demonstrated that the similarities reflect the common stock of early Christian teaching and catechetical patterns.[127] In any case, apart from one regrettable but temporary lapse (Gal. 2.11–14), neither in the Pauline epistles (cf. especially Gal. 2.6–10; I Cor. 1.12f.; 15.3–11) nor in Acts (cf. especially 15.6–11, where Peter puts the Pauline case) is the Petrine position regarded as fundamentally different from Paul's. If Peter had read Romans (which if it was sent to Rome some eight years before is more than likely) and indeed other Pauline epistles (as II Peter 3.15 at any rate says that he had), there is no reason why he should not reflect the thinking of one who was on all the evidence the more creative theologian.[128] But this is not to deny that he also had a theological position, particularly in regard to the sufferings and death of Christ, distinctively his own[129] – whether or not we allow any weight to the significant connections between I Peter and the Petrine speeches in Acts.[130]

(3) Finally, there is the vital question again of language. One objection over which time need not be spent is the fact that the Old Testament quotations follow the LXX rather than the Hebrew text. For, naturally, if a man is writing to Greek-speaking readers he follows 'their' Bible. 'Besides', as van Unnik observes from experience,[131] 'a foreigner writing in another language will usually stick to the standard translation for literal quotations and not dare to change it to suit his own text.' Beare's assumption[132] that there would be no

[126] *I Peter*, 20f. Similarly Kelly, *Peter and Jude*, 11–15; and earlier Bigg, *Peter and Jude*, 16–21; 52–67; Chase, *HDB* III, 788f.; Wand, *Peter and Jude*, 17–21.

[127] *I Peter*, 365–466. [128] Cf. Zahn, *INT* II, 175–7.

[129] Cf. Cullmann, *Peter*, 65–9.

[130] Cf. Wand, *Peter and Jude*, 26–8; Selwyn, *I Peter*, 33–6; and most recently S. S. Smalley, 'The Christology of Acts Again' in B. Lindars and S. S. Smalley (edd.), *Christ and the Spirit in the New Testament: In Honour of C. F. D. Moule*, Cambridge 1973, especially 84–93. The parallels are certainly more substantial than those between James and Acts.

[131] *IDB* III, 764. [132] *I Peter*, 26f.

occasion for Peter to have used the Greek scriptures except in addressing Gentiles (and that late in life) is astonishing. But, quotations apart, could Peter have written the Greek of I Peter? Again there is no way of saying dogmatically. Many of the issues are the same as those already discussed in relation to James, though the Greek of I Peter has perhaps a somewhat more 'classical' touch. But against the possibility or at least the probability of this there are two further arguments. The first is that, according to Acts 4.13, Peter and John were described by the high priests as ἀγράμματοι, though whether this means 'illiterate' or more likely, as in the NEB, 'untrained' (in the Law) cannot finally be determined. In any case, what struck the authorities was what they were capable of *despite* this. The second is that according to Papias[133] Peter had Mark as his 'interpreter' (ἑρμηνευτής), though again whether this means 'translator' is uncertain.[134] In any case, the purpose of the quotation is to stress Mark's closeness to Peter, not to provide information about Peter's linguistic abilities. It is noticeable that in none of Clement of Alexandria's references to this tradition[135] is this aspect mentioned: Peter preaches 'publicly' in Rome (with no mention of an interpreter) and Mark his follower 'remembers' and subsequently writes down what he said. But even if at one stage Peter used a translator, this incident may come from an earlier period. As we have seen, the only person to date it, Eusebius, places it back in the reign of Claudius,[136] and in his *Chronicle* as early as 42. Whatever Peter's educational limitations immediately after Pentecost, it is inconceivable that he can have exercised any kind of leading ministry in Antioch or even Jerusalem, let alone in Rome, without the use of Greek. Whether this means that he could or did write the good Greek of I Peter is, naturally, another matter. Suspension of judgment appears to be the only prudent course, and the fact that eminent authorities can be found on both sides of the argument suggests humility rather than dogmatism.

But, in contrast with the epistle of James, there is the ready way out (on which many have seized) of an amanuensis or ghost-writer in the person of Silvanus (5.13) – not, be it noted, Mark, who is mentioned in the next verse and whom on the basis of Papias' tradition one would have expected a pseudepigrapher to select.[137] But

[133] Eusebius, *HE* 3.39.15.

[134] For Jerome (see n. 137 below) 'interpretes' meant amanuensis.

[135] See above, pp. 108–10. [136] *HE* 2.14.6–15.1.

[137] Jerome, *Epp.* 120.11, uses the same word 'interpretes' for the different amanuenses to whom he attributed the diverse styles and vocabulary of I and II Peter. But he does not mention Silvanus or Mark.

the question is, What is the meaning of διὰ Σιλουανοῦ . . . ἔγραψα? Is Silvanus the carrier or the scribe (and therefore by extension the writer) of the letter? It would be safe to say that he is in any case envisaged as delivering the letter and is commended to the churches for this purpose. But did he also write it at Peter's dictation or behest?

On the analogy of the opening verses of I and II Thessalonians, one might expect Silvanus to have shared in the address if he was part-author, or to have added his own greeting, like Tertius in Rom. 16.22, if he was the amanuensis, though obviously these parallels cannot be pressed. The bearer of Romans is evidently Phoebe, who is similarly commended to the congregation (16.1f.), and it is significant that the subscription added to later manuscripts describes the epistle as ἐγράφη ἀπὸ Κορίνθου διὰ Φοίβης. It was her activity, not that of Tertius, that the scribes thought was properly described by the preposition διά. This is one of a number of parallels given by Chase in a careful note on the subject[138] which seems to have been conspicuously ignored (or misinterpreted) by those who have not agreed with its conclusion. The only other example in the New Testament (also as it happens associated with Silvanus) is in Acts 15.23 where γράψαντες διὰ χειρὸς αὐτῶν must in the context (cf. 15.22, 27) refer to the *sending* of the apostolic letter, *via* Judas Barsabbas and Silas, and mean, as the NEB rightly renders it, 'gave them the letter to deliver'. The same applies to the Epistle of Polycarp 14, 'I write these things to you by (per) Crescens, whom I commended to you recently and now commend to you', and to the only unambiguous instance in the letters of Ignatius: 'I write these things to you from Smyrna by the hand of (διά) the Ephesians who are worthy of all felicitation' (Rom. 10.1).[139] On the other side only two parallels, as far as I know, have been cited. One is the letter from Dionysius of Corinth[140] to the Romans, where he describes I Clement as having been written from the Roman church διὰ Κλέμεντος. But this means not that Clement was the amanuensis of some other author, but the representative of his church. Similarly in the Martyrdom of Polycarp 20 the church in Smyrna writes to the church in Philomelium and elsewhere 'through our brother Marcianus', and he is distinguished from Euarestus who 'wrote the letter' and, like Tertius in this capacity, sends his own greeting. Marcianus again is evidently the spokesman of the church and thus corresponds to Peter rather than Silvanus: he is no one's secretary. So Kümmel

[138] *HDB* III, 790.

[139] For discussion of this and the other instances (Philad. 11.2; Smyrn. 12.1) see Chase.

[140] Eusebius, *HE* 4.23.11.

seems to be right in saying that 'no one has yet proved that γράφω διά τινος can mean to authorize someone else to compose a piece of writing'.[141]

Until this can be shown, then to rely upon Silvanus as the real composer of the Greek is extremely hazardous.[142] It could be so. Yet Peter as the author (as the very personal address of 5.1ff. would suggest) must really be prepared to stand on his own feet. The doubts and difficulties will remain, and it seems impossible that they could ever be finally resolved either way. In the last resort I can only say that I find nothing decisive to outweigh the many other considerations to suggest that, whoever actually penned it, the epistle comes from Peter's lifetime and that he is in the fullest sense 'behind' it. I see therefore no reason from the evidence of the authorship to go back on the previous assessment of a date for the dispatch of the letter somewhere around the end of April 65.

II PETER AND JUDE

Turning to II Peter, we move into a much more complex set of problems and an area of the New Testament that from every point of view, including that of chronology, is a good deal murkier. We cannot expect it to shed much light on anything else; it is a question of what light other things can shed on it. II Peter cannot be considered except in conjunction with the epistle of Jude, with which, all would agree, it has a literary connection of some kind. What that is, and what is the relationship between them and I Peter, and whether either Jude or II Peter can sustain the claim to be written by the persons in whose name they stand, raise acutely debated issues which may not be burked. But with dating as our primary concern it may be helpful to to come at the matter from a different angle from that which has led to the concentration of the debate on the issue of pseudepigraphy.

Let us begin by leaving on one side for the time being the questions of authorship and literary dependence and look at the documents for the clues they afford which are relevant to placing them in 'period'. I deliberately put it that way, because neither II Peter nor Jude contains any positive indication of absolute dating. It is a question of where they belong in relation to other comparable literature, and more than usually therefore the arguments are in danger of being

[141] *INT*, 424.

[142] Selwyn's attempt, *I Peter*, 369–75, to show Silvanus to be the common literary factor between I Peter, I and II Thessalonians, and the decree of Acts 15.29, cannot be said to have succeeded. Cf. the telling criticisms of the whole 'Silvanus hypothesis' by Beare, *I Peter*, 188–92.

circular. If this other literature itself is dated late, then these epistles will follow; if early, then the same will be true. Yet II Peter has continued to remain an exception to almost every chronological scheme; and exceptions have value in proving a rule. *If* it is an exception, to what is it an exception, and why?

In asking what these two documents may have to tell us about dating, without prejudice to their interrelationship, we must begin with one or the other. Since the majority of scholars give priority to Jude over II Peter, let us start with the epistle of Jude, though keeping an open mind on the question.

Jude follows James, whose brother he claims to be (and there is general agreement that it is of this James that the claim is made), in calling himself simply a 'servant of Jesus Christ' (1.1; cf. James 1.1, 'servant of God and the Lord Jesus Christ') and in giving no other details either about himself or of those with him, or of the place of origin or destination of the letter. In fact it is even less informative. While there are clues in James that point, as we saw, to a Palestinian milieu, there is nothing in Jude that affords any hint of where the author is living. And while James at least indicates that the destination of his epistle is *not* a single locality, Jude appears to be addressing a particular group of Christians but gives absolutely no indication of where they might be.

The one thing that is clear is the *occasion* of the epistle, which was of sufficient urgency to make him turn aside from other more leisurely literary activity:

> My friends, I was fully engaged in writing to you about our salvation – which is yours no less than ours – when it became urgently necessary to write at once and appeal to you to join the struggle in defence of the faith, the faith which God entrusted to his people once and for all. It is in danger from certain persons who have wormed their way in (3f.).

The whole of the rest of the epistle, up to the notable doxology in 24f., is given over to an attack on these anonymous persons, referred to constantly as 'these men'. Almost all that can be said about them is summarized in the opening description:

> They are the enemies of religion (ἀσεβεῖς); they pervert the free favour of our God into licentiousness (ἀσέλγειαν), disowning (ἀρνούμενοι) Jesus Christ, our only Master and Lord (4).

Their menace, in other words, is religious, moral and doctrinal. It is also clear from the terms in which they are condemned and the warnings given from the past, that both they and the writer and presumably those to whom he is writing belong to a dominantly, if not exclusively,

Jewish–Christian milieu within the Hellenistic world. Yet we are a long way from the 'primitive' atmosphere of the epistle of James, where no problems of heresy or schism have seriously arisen. Here we are in a silver-age situation, where reversion and perversion are the dangers and where purity of doctrine and discipline are imperilled. It is evident too that the menace arises from a sort of gnosticizing Judaism. Like those in Corinth with whom Paul had to deal, these men 'draw a line between spiritual and unspiritual persons', despising others as ψυχικοί (19; cf. I Cor. 2.6–3.4; 8.1–3). Like them too, they take liberty for licence (4; cf. I Cor. 6.12; 10.23) and end up slaves of sensuality (8, 10, 16, 23; cf. I Cor. 6.9–20; II Cor. 12.21). Like them, they 'eat and drink without reverence' at the Christian love-feast (12; cf. I Cor. 11.17–43). Like them again, they flout the authority of those set over them in the Lord (8, 11; cf. I Cor. 4.8–13; 9.1–12) and themselves claim leadership (cf. II Cor. 11.13; 12.11). As 'shepherds who take care only of themselves' (12) they earn the condemnation of Israel's self-styled leaders (cf. Ezek. 34.8).

Yet though there are these reflections of the situation in Corinth in the mid-50s, things are evidently far further gone. In Pauline terms, the parallels are more with the Pastoral Epistles, where we have the same falling back upon the authorized deposit of 'the faith' (3, 20; cf. I Tim. 1.3; 4.6; II Tim. 1.13f.; 2.2; Titus 1.9) – though even this was for Paul by no means a wholly new emphasis (cf. Rom. 6.17; 10.8; 16.17; I Cor. 11.2; Gal. 1.23; 6.10; Eph. 4.5; Phil. 1.27; I Thess. 2.13; II Thess. 2.15; 3.6). The danger from false brethren who insinuate themselves (3), though again not new (cf. Gal. 2.4), is especially characteristic of the later apostolic age (Acts 20.30; Phil. 3.2; II Tim. 3.6; I John 2.18f.; 4.1; II John 7f.; Rev. 2.20f.; cf. Ignatius, Eph. 7.1; 9.1); and they have to be dealt with both firmly and with discrimination (22f.; cf. I Cor. 5; II Thess. 3.14f.; I John 4.1–6; II John 7–11; and Did. 2.7; Ignatius, Smyrn. 4.1).

Yet if we ask what precisely these heretics taught it is impossible to form any clear impression. We read that they 'deny Jesus Christ, our only Master and Lord' (4). But whether this was by faithlessness, like those referred to in Heb. 6.6 and 10.29 or II Tim. 2.12f. (cf. Titus 1.16; Rev. 2.13), or by doctrinal error, like those attacked in Col. 2.8 and I John 2.22f. and 5.6–12, or by dishonouring conduct, it is impossible to tell. But there is no reference to theoretical speculation and nothing to suggest any of the gnostic systems of the second century.[143] To infer from the phrases 'our only Master and Lord' (4) and 'the only God our Saviour' (25) that they believed in other mediators or a

[143] Kümmel, *INT*, 426, concurs.

second God or Demiurge is eisegesis rather than exegesis. Their threat seems to have been far more moral and religious than theological. If there is a parallel with other known sectarian groups it is not (as many earlier commentators tended to argue without our present knowledge of the gnostic texts) with the later forms of heresy listed by Irenaeus such as the Carpocratians,[144] but with those gnosticizing libertines attacked in the letters to the seven churches of the Apocalypse who 'hold to the teaching of Balaam' (Rev. 2.14; cf. Jude 11) and 'pollute their clothing' with immorality (Rev. 3.4; cf. Jude 23).

There are no other distinctive characteristics of second-century Christianity. There is no stress on the authority of the organized ministry, or even reference to it (in marked contrast at this point with the Pastoral Epistles), and the *agape* or love-feast still appears to be one with the eucharistic assembly. There are those[145] who have found in Jude 5 a reference to the destruction of Jerusalem: 'Let me remind you how the Lord, having once delivered the people of Israel out of Egypt, next time destroyed those who were guilty of unbelief.' But the natural interpretation in the context[146] is to refer this to the destruction of faithless Israel in the wilderness, as in the closely parallel warning of I Cor. 10.5–10. Again, to interpret *πάλαι προγεγραμμένοι* in Jude 4 of long past *Christian* writings[147] is wholly arbitrary: it evidently refers to the warnings that follow from 'scripture' (as the NEB rightly translates). The references in v. 9, apparently, to the Assumption of Moses and in v. 14, certainly, to I Enoch carry in themselves no implication for a late date, since both these documents were in existence well before the middle of the first century – though the free use made of them indicates that they had not come under the later suspicion of apocrypha felt by the church.[148]

The only passage which suggests a post-apostolic situation is that in 17f.:

> But you, my friends, should remember the predictions made by the apostles of our Lord Jesus Christ. This was the warning they gave you: 'In the final age there will be men who pour scorn on religion, and follow their own godless lusts.'

This could indeed imply that the apostolic age was now closed, but it cannot be said that it necessarily does so. From one who makes no claim to be an apostle (or indeed to kinship with Jesus, which later

[144] For the differences here, cf. already Zahn, *INT* II, 292f.

[145] E.g. Zahn, *INT* II, 252–5.

[146] So J. B. Mayor, *The Epistle of St Jude and the Second Epistle of St Peter*, 1907, ad loc.

[147] Again with Zahn, *INT*, 251f.

[148] Cf. Jerome, *De vir. ill.* 4.

interest in the person of Jude would surely have exploited),[149] it could refer to the sort of warnings of which the later apostolic age is full (Acts 20.29f.; I Tim.4.1; II Tim.3.1–5; 4.3; I John 2.18f. – leaving out of account for the moment II Peter 2.1–3; 3.3). The ἔλεγον ὑμῖν would most naturally refer to oral teaching, as in the parallel warning of Phil.3.18f.:

> As I have often told you (ἔλεγον ὑμῖν), and now tell you with tears in my eyes, there are many whose way of life makes them enemies of the cross of Christ. They are heading for destruction, appetite is their god, and they glory in their shame (cf. Rom. 16.18).

But even if reference were to written warnings, none of these other documents (leaving aside the Johannine epistles whose date we have yet to consider), excludes a dating in the 60s. Indeed as a provisional conclusion, on the scanty evidence of the epistle itself, I would concur with the estimate of Chase:[150]

> The general tone of the Epistle harmonizes best with a date somewhat late in the apostolic age. We shall not be far wrong if we suppose that it was written within a year or two of the Pastoral Epistles (assuming their genuineness), the Apocalypse (assuming the earlier date),[151] the First Epistle of St Peter, and the Epistle to the Hebrews.

Beyond that we cannot go until we have taken into account the link with II Peter, to which we must now turn.

II Peter affords as little direct information about its origin and destination as Jude, and its occasion is less specific. It purports to be 'from Simeon Peter, servant and apostle of Jesus Christ, to those who through the justice of our God and Saviour Jesus Christ share our faith and enjoy equal privilege with ourselves' (1.1). To the significance of 'Simeon Peter', in contrast with 'Peter' in I Peter 1.1, we must return. But on the face of it the form looks, or is intended to look, both Jewish and primitive. 'Servant and apostle' brings together the 'servant' of James 1.1. and Jude 1 and the 'apostle' of I Peter 1.1, but in itself is a typical apostolic greeting (Rom. 1.1; Titus 1.1) without significance for dating. There are no indications, in contrast with I Peter, of where the epistle was written to or from. The distinction implied in 'those who . . . enjoy equal privilege with ourselves' appears to be between readers and apostle, as in I John 1.3 ('so that you and we together may share in a common life'), rather than

[149] Cf. the story from Hegesippus quoted by Eusebius, *HE* 3.19f., whose point lies in this link.

[150] *HDB* II, 804.

[151] I.e., a date from the Neronian rather than the Domitianic persecution. For a discussion of this, cf. ch. VIII below.

between Jews and Gentiles, as in Acts 11.17; Col. 1.25–9; Eph. 2.11–3.6. Indeed it is impossible to be certain whether the recipients are Jewish or Gentile Christians, though (in contrast again with I Peter) the dominant atmosphere (as in Jude) appears to be Jewish–Christian. In 2.20 the words, 'They had once escaped the world's defilements through the knowledge of our Lord and Saviour Jesus Christ', have been taken to mean that the converts (or is it the heretics?) have come from what the NEB paraphrases in 2.18 as a 'heathen environment'. But the language no more necessarily implies a Gentile origin than when Paul says of his fellow-Jews in Eph. 2.3, 'We too were of their number: we all lived our lives in sensuality, and obeyed the promptings of our own instincts and notions', or when the writer of I John speaks to his predominantly Jewish–Christian readers of the evil world and its blandishments from which they have passed.

The prevailing atmosphere, as in Jude, is still that of the Pastoral Epistles, reflecting the same usage of πίστις and σωτήρ and εὐσέβεια, with particular stress on true insight and knowledge (ἐπίγνωσις and γνῶσις) (1.2f., 5f., 8; 2.20; 3.18), which characterizes not only the Pastorals (I Tim. 2.4; 6.20; II Tim. 2.25; 3.7; Titus 1.1) but Colossians (1.9f.; 2.2f.; 3.10) and Ephesians (1.17; 3.19; 4.13) and, in verbs rather than nouns, the Johannine epistles (*passim* but especially I John 2.20f.). The epistle's most distinctive phrase in this regard is 'partakers of the divine nature' (θείας κοινωνοὶ φύσεως) in 1.4, but it has been shown that this, like the whole so-called 'Asian' style in which II Peter is written, in no way lies outside the range of first-century Hellenistic Judaism.[152] Indeed, like the language of τὸ πλήρωμα in Col. 1.19 and 2.19 or σπέρμα θεοῦ in I John 3.9, it may well be being taken over and given Christian meaning.[153] In content it is not essentially different from the Christian's κοινωνία with the Father and the Son and his transformation into the divine likeness claimed by I John (1.3; 3.2). And this goal is achieved not, as in Platonism and later gnosticism, by escaping from matter as evil, but by moral union, *having* escaped (ἀποφυγόντες) from 'the corruption with which lust has infected the world'. The dualism, as in the Johannine writings, is not

[152] Cf. e.g. Philo and Josephus and in particular the Decree of Stratonicea in Caria to the honour of Zeus and Hecate, dated AD 22 (*Corpus Inscriptionum Graecorum* II, 2715). For the references and discussion, cf. A. Deissmann, *Bible Studies*, ET Edinburgh 1901, 360–8; Mayor, *Jude and II Peter*, cxxvii–cxxx and ad loc; E. M. B. Green, *II Peter Reconsidered*, 1961, 23; *II Peter and Jude*, 1968, 16–19; Reicke, *James, Peter and Jude*, 146f., 184; Kelly, *Peter and Jude*, ad loc.

[153] Kelly, *Peter and Jude*, 304, quotes C. H. Dodd's comment, *The Johannine Epistles*, 1946, on I John 3.2, that the writer 'is naturalizing within Christian theology a widely diffused mystical tradition'.

material and metaphysical but moral and eschatological.[154] The use of 'the world' is the same as that in John (e.g. I John 2.15–17) and does not imply any depreciation of the flesh *per se*. In fact neither in Jude nor in II Peter is there any sign of the ascetical denial of the flesh as evil (in contrast to its indulgence as indifferent) such as we find in Col. 2.18f. and I Tim. 4.3f.,[155] or of the docetic denial of matter as unreal of the Johannine epistles (I John 4.2; II John 7). In this again the persons attacked in II Peter as in Jude stand nearer to the libertines of Corinth: they promise freedom but the result is sensual slavery (2.19f.). In fact apart from their questioning of the *parousia* (3.4; cf. 1.16), there is nothing that suggests that the heretics in II Peter were any different from those in Jude or more 'advanced' in their teaching. The 'artfully spun tales' (μῦθοι) abjured in 1.16 recall the 'myths' attacked in I Tim. 1.4; 4.7; II Tim. 4.4; and Titus 1.14, which are linked with an interest in genealogies and angelology, and in the last passage specifically called 'Jewish'. As in Jude, we are in the sphere of a gnosticizing Judaism, countered by warning examples from Israel's history (2.1–16). We are not dealing with the developed systems of second-century Christian heresies. Summing up the teaching common to both epistles, Zahn concluded:[156]

> While there were numerous parties and sects representing libertinistic theories and practices in the second and third centuries, there is none that so closely resembles the seducers described in II Peter and Jude as the libertinistic movement with which we become acquainted in I Corinthians, and as the Nicolaitans of whom we learn hints in Revelation.[157]

So far then there would be nothing to cause us to date II Peter any later than Jude. It is, however, in the distinctive material of the epistle, particularly in three passages, 1.12–18; 3.1–4; and 3.15f., that the doubts arise.

[154] This point is made strongly and correctly by Green, *II Peter Reconsidered*, 14–21, and *II Peter and Jude*, 24f., against Käsemann, 'An Apologia for Primitive Christian Eschatology', *Essays on New Testament Themes*, 169–95, and especially such a remark as: 'It would be hard to find in the whole New Testament a sentence which, in its expression, its individual motifs and its whole trend, more clearly marks the relapse of Christianity into Hellenistic dualism' (179f.).

[155] How near the two apparently opposite extremes are is illustrated by the story Eusebius, *HE* 3.29, quotes from Clement of Alexandria about the founder of the Nicolaitans, who offered his young and lovely wife to others 'to renounce his passion': 'It was self-control . . . that taught him to say "abuse the flesh".'

[156] *INT* II, 283.

[157] Rev. 2.6, 15. They are evidently closely associated with those who hold to the teaching of Balaam (2.14; cf. II Peter 2.15f.; Jude 11) and with others who falsely claim both to be Jews (2.9; 3.9) and to be apostles of the church (2.2; cf. Jude 12).

1. Taken at its face value, the first passage actually contains nothing that would in itself require us to put the writing after the death of Peter. Yet it is the passage which has given greatest ground for suspicion that a forger is at work, inserting biographical detail for the sake of specious verisimilitude. Whether or not he is doing so cannot be decided except in relation to the whole question of authorship and pseudepigraphy from which at the moment we are prescinding. But let us examine the details without prejudgment.

> I will not hesitate to remind you of this again and again, although you know it and are well grounded in the truth that has already reached you. Yet I think it right to keep refreshing your memory so long as I still lodge in this body. I know that very soon I must leave it; indeed our Lord Jesus Christ has told me so. But I will see to it that after I am gone you will have means of remembering these things at all times.
>
> It was not on tales artfully spun that we relied when we told you of the power of our Lord Jesus Christ and his coming; we saw him with our own eyes in majesty, when at the hands of God the Father he was invested with honour and glory, and there came to him from the sublime Presence a voice which said: 'This is my Son, my Beloved, on whom my favour rests'. This voice from heaven we ourselves heard; when it came, we were with him on the sacred mountain (1.12–18).

Peter (it would be otiose to keep putting the name in inverted commas – any more than Jude or John) here uses the metaphor of the body as a tent (already found in Wisd.9.15 and Philo, and of course widely in pagan literature) which Paul uses in II Cor.5.1–4, and, like Paul, he combines it with that of taking off clothes. In his case, he knows, this putting off is to be *ταχινή* (swift), which could be interpreted to mean either 'soon' or 'sudden'. Zahn[158] argued strongly that it here refers to a sudden end, and this is supported by the only other occurrence of the word in the epistle (2.1) and indeed in the New Testament. The intimation upon which it is based, 'as our Lord Jesus Christ has shown me', appears (whether factually or fictionally) to be that alluded to in John 21.18f., where Jesus foretells that Peter will die an unchosen death when he has grown old (*ὅταν γηράσῃς*). By the seventh decade of the century this latter condition could already be said to obtain, but the concern to leave a record of his teaching behind him might be prompted by the expectation of an unprepared as much as by that of an imminent death. All we can say is that these are the words of a man for whom death is much in mind, and this would fit the 60s as the period when they were either written or supposed to be written. What he had in mind to leave, so that 'after I am gone you will have means of remembering these things', is equally

[158] *INT* II, 212–14.

unclear. Some[159] have seen in this a reference to St Mark's gospel (and the origin of the Papias legend). But the gospel of Mark can hardly be described as a reminder of 'these things', that is, the teaching of the present epistle (cf. 1.12). It would appear too to demand a writing by *Peter* (as the later pseudepigrapha like the Preaching of Peter and the Gospel of Peter supplied). Kelly[160] thinks that 'almost certainly the reference is to the epistle itself', though he admits that the future, σπουδάσω (according to the most probable reading), is difficult. It would naturally suggest a further document. For our purposes we may be content to suspend judgment, noting only that if a forger is at work he has laid some very elusive clues.

In the descriptive passage that follows, the transfiguration is regarded as an anticipation and pledge of the *parousia*, in the way that we argued it was, far less explicitly, in I Peter 5.1. It has also been said that the word ἐπόπται, eyewitnesses, echoes the ἐποπτεύοντες of I Peter 2.12 and 3.2; but this is very doubtful, since there it simply refers to pagans 'observing' the conduct of Christians. If the word has any overtones, it is more likely to take up the language of the mysteries and the claims of the heretics that in their visions (cf. the dreams or trances of Jude 8) they had direct experience of the deep things of God (cf. Rev. 2.24). But its immediate reference is to apostolic eyewitness, to which I John 1.1–3 also appeals in similar circumstances. It is generally accepted that the wording of the account of the transfiguration is independent of any of our gospel texts. The omission of the injunction 'hear him', common to them all, and of any reference to Moses and Elijah or to the three tents (σκηναί), which one would have thought irresistible after the σκηνώματος of 1.14, tells heavily against the use of the synoptists by a later hand. The only other touch, 'the *holy* mountain', which is said to betray veneration of the sacred site (for which there is in fact no evidence till *much* later), is hardly decisive for dating. As regularly with Zion or Sinai in the Old Testament, any mountain with which theophany is associated is for the Jew 'holy'.

The really significant parallel for dating purposes is that with the Apocalypse of Peter.[161] This document is usually put in the first half of the second century, perhaps *c.* 135. It is quite palpably dependent on the synoptic gospels, particularly Matthew.[162] This is true too of its

159 E.g. Bigg, *Peter and Jude*, ad loc.; Mayor, *Jude and II Peter*, cxlii and ad loc.

160 *Peter and Jude*, 315.

161 For the full text, see Hennecke, *NT Apoc.* II, 668–83.

162 Thus the opening verse contains clear echoes of Matt. 24.3: 'And when he was seated on the Mount of Olives, his own came unto him, and we entreated and

section on the transfiguration (15–17), which includes a highly elaborated account of the vision of the appearances of Moses and Elijah and quotes Peter's comment *verbatim* from the version in Matt. 17.4: 'My Lord, wilt thou that I make here three tabernacles, one for thee, one for Moses and one for Elias?'. By contrast its only verbal contact with the account in II Peter is the reference (and that in the Ethiopic version only) to 'the holy mountain'. If there is dependence either way, it seems quite clear that the Apocalypse is the later document. How Harnack can have thought otherwise[163] must be counted as one of those aberrations of scholarship which fresh discoveries induce,[164] and it has long since been abandoned even by those who view II Peter as a second-century document.[165] That even conservative scholars like W. Sanday[166] can have thought that the two came from the same pen, or like Chase[167] from the same school at approximately the same date, is incredible. Indeed if this is the sort of thing that was being produced in the first half of the second century it is the strongest possible argument for *not* placing II Peter there. As the writer of the article on the Apocalypse of Peter in *The Interpreter's Dictionary of the Bible* says,[168] 'one short sample will indicate the nature of the whole', and he quotes:

> And some there were there hanging by their tongues: and these were they that blasphemed the way of righteousness, and under them was laid fire flaming and tormenting them. And there was a great lake full of flaming mire, wherein were certain men that turned away from righteousness; and angels, tormentors, were set over them. And there were also others, women, hanged by their hair above that mire which boiled up; and these were they which adorned themselves for adultery.

He comments:

> That this writing, in all likelihood in no small part suggested by the canonical Revelation, and the product of perfervid imagination, aided by Orphic and

---

implored him severally and besought him, saying unto him, "Make known unto us what are the signs of thy Parousia and of the end of the world." ' The contrast with II Peter is at once evident.

[163] *Chron.*, 470–2. He dated the Apocalypse *c.* 120–40 (or 110–60) and II Peter *c.* 160 (or 150–175).

[164] At the time he only had the Akhmim fragment in Greek to go on, discovered in 1886, though this includes most of the relevant parallels. The complete text, in Ethiopic translation, was found in 1910. For a modern assessment, cf. C. Maurer in Hennecke, *NT Apoc.* II, 663–8.

[165] Moffatt, *ILNT*, 367, was a strange exception.

[166] W. Sanday, *Inspiration*, Oxford 1893, 347.

[167] *HDB* III, 815f. He is followed by McNeile-Williams, *INT*, 247.

[168] M. S. Enslin, *IDB* III, 758.

Pythagorean accounts of the future, is not later than the middle of the second century is universally admitted.

He agrees in fact that it is probably earlier than the Gospel of Peter – but interestingly *never even mentions* II Peter. Yet the same Dictionary's article on II Peter[169] continues to date this epistle *c.* 150 AD.! On the basis of this passage of II Peter alone some rethinking of critical presuppositions appears to be called for.

2. The second passage, II Peter 3.1–4, raises more difficulties. The writer starts with a reference, apparently, to I Peter:

> This is now my second letter to you, my friends. In both of them I have been recalling to you what you already know, to rouse you to honest thought. Remember the predictions made by God's own prophets, and the commands given by the Lord and Saviour through your apostles (3.1f.).

The relation to I Peter must engage us later. At this stage one need only say that if the writer is a Christian from a subsequent age then the reference *must* be to I Peter, since this is the only other Petrine letter of which there is any record in the tradition. Yet it is very far from obvious that the content of the two epistles *is* the same, and, if the allusion here is to I Peter 1.10–12 (the only likely passage), then the content of the prophecies there is the sufferings of Christ, not, as in the verses that follow in II Peter, the state of affairs at the end of the world. Again the pseudepigrapher does not lay his trail at all obviously.

The phrase in v. 2, 'your apostles', certainly reads oddly (quite apart from the tortuous grammar of the Greek) from one claiming himself to be an apostle, and it has seemed to most commentators to reflect the post-apostolic age. Yet we may say this with certainty only if it is agreed that Eph. 2.20 and 3.5 (where the apostles are also described as 'holy') *could* not have come from Paul, writing as an 'apostle of Christ Jesus' (Eph. 1.1). But, as we have seen, it is impossible to be so dogmatic. Moreover 'your apostles' need not, though it probably does, mean more than 'your missionaries' (cf. I Peter 1.12), and Paul (Rom. 16.7; II Cor. 8.23; Phil. 2.25), like Acts (14.14) and the Didache (11.3), continues to use the word in a wider sense. But assuming that it means those of the apostles particularly associated with you, this need not imply the end of the apostolic age, any more than when Paul says to the Corinthians, 'If I am not an apostle to others, at least I am to you' (I Cor. 9.2). In I Clem. 44.1 we have a similar usage of 'our apostles' (i.e., in Rome, Peter and Paul; cf. 5.3). All one can say is that the phrase itself is compatible with an apostolic or with a post-apostolic date. What is significant is that the apostles are

[169] J. C. Beker, *IDB* III, 769.

not contrasted in any way with a subsequent ordering of Christian ministry, as in I Clem. 44 (which speaks of their successors) or in the epistles of Ignatius (especially Rom. 4.3: 'I do not enjoin you as Peter and Paul did. They were apostles'). There is no more concern than in Jude with ministerial authority or its perpetuation.

But more serious as an objection to apostolic dating is the state of affairs reflected in the words of the scoffers that follow:

> In the last day there will come men who scoff at religion and live self-indulgent lives, and they will say: 'Where is now the promise of his coming? Our fathers (οἱ πατέρες) have been laid to their rest, but still everything continues exactly as it always has been since the world began.'

I cannot believe that it will do to say with Bigg[170] and Green[171] that 'the fathers' here means the ancestors of Israel. The context demands the sense[172] that ever since the first generation of *Christians* died things have continued as they always have been, whereas the specific promise had been given: 'This generation shall not pass away until all these things happen' (Mark 13.30 and pars.). It is true that elsewhere in the New Testament 'the fathers' refers to the Israelites. But in I John 2.13f. we have the usage of 'fathers' in contrast with the second and third generation of Christians, which stresses their special relationship as the founder-generation to the ἀρχή, in the way that in Acts 21.16 Mnason as one of the 'originals' is called an ἄρχαιος μαθητής. The death of Christians had always been a problem, as we know from Thessalonians and Corinthians, but the real crisis for the church must have come as that first promised generation was dying out and still nothing had happened. By the 60s a whole generation *had* elapsed. Naturally the difficulty did not then disappear.[173] But this is when the question must have been at its most acute, and there is no necessary reason to look to a later age. The theme of the master's delay, reflected in the church's adaptation of the parables, is already to be found in the 'Q' material of Matt. 24.28 = Luke 12.45, and also in Matt. 25.5, whose final editing we have seen no reason to place much after 60.

The details that follow in 3.5–13 of the *parousia* teaching do not in themselves require a late date. The notion of the destruction of the

[170] *Peter and Jude*, ad loc.

[171] *II Peter Reconsidered*, 29f.; *II Peter and Jude*, ad loc.

[172] So Mayor, *Jude and II Peter*, ad loc., strongly.

[173] Cf. I Clem. 23.3, quoting what it calls 'scripture': 'These things we did hear in the days of our fathers also, and behold we have grown old, and none of these things hath befallen us' (cf. II Clem. 11.2). But for the date of I Clement, cf. pp. 327–34 below.

world by fire, going back a long way in pagan literature, is now paralleled graphically in the Qumran Psalms (1QH 3.29–35).[174] Moreover Green is justified in pointing out[175] that the reference to Ps.90.4 is not given a chiliast interpretation (that the world would last for as many thousand years as there were days in creation) such as it regularly receives in later literature (e.g. Ep. Barn. 15.4, Justin, *Dial.* 81.3f., and Irenaeus, *Adv. haer.* 5.23.2; 28.3). As he says:

> If this Epistle had been written in the second century, when this doctrine was so widespread that it almost became a touchstone of Christian orthodoxy, is it likely that the author could have refrained from making any allusion to it whatever when quoting the very verse which gave it birth?

With the rest of II Peter's eschatology, including the coming of the day of the Lord as a thief (3.10; cf. Rev. 3.3; 16.15), the laying bare of the earth and all that is in it (3.10; cf. Rev. 6.12–17; 16.20; etc.), and the creation of new heavens and a new earth (3.13; cf. Rev. 21.1–4), this theme finds its nearest parallel in the book of Revelation (20.1–6), rather than in the extravagances of subsequent apocalypses, whether Jewish or Christian (including the Apocalypse of Peter).

3. It is the third passage (3.15f.), however, that presents the greatest difficulties of all:

> Bear in mind that our Lord's patience with us is our salvation, as Paul, our friend and brother, said when he wrote to you with his inspired wisdom. And so he does in all his other letters, wherever he speaks of this subject, though they contain some obscure passages, which the ignorant and unstable misinterpret to their own ruin, as they do the other scriptures.

We need not spend time at this hour refuting the Tübingen thesis that the genuine Peter could never have spoken of Paul in terms other than of hostility.[176] It is however relevant to ask whether a second-century writer would not have adopted an attitude either of attack or adulation (rather than bewildered affection). Typical of later descriptions are 'the blessed Paul' (I Clem. 47.1; Ep. Polyc. 11.3) or 'the blessed and glorious Paul' (Ep. Polyc. 3.2). 'Dear brother' and similar expressions are confined elsewhere in the New Testament to living fellow-workers (e.g. Eph. 6.21; Col. 4.7, 9; Philem. 16) and Paul himself is so addressed by James in Acts 21.20. The expression therefore *sounds* as if it comes from a contemporary, whether it does or not. Indeed Mayor, who himself argues for pseudepigraphy, says:[177]

174 The passage is quoted in full by Reicke, *James, Peter and Jude*, 176.

175 *II Peter and Jude*, ad loc. He is here, as often, following Bigg (*Peter and Jude*, 214).

176 Cf. Munck, *Paul and the Salvation of Mankind*, ch. 3.

177 *Jude and II Peter*, ad loc.

> There are many difficulties in the way of accepting the genuineness of this epistle; but the manner in which St Paul is spoken of seems to me just what we should have expected from his brother Apostle.

Again, the reference to the wisdom given to him implies not more than what Paul claimed for himself (e.g. I Cor. 2.6f.; 3.10; Gal. 2.9; Eph. 3.1–10). The contrast is striking with the self-depreciatory tone of the second century: 'Neither am I, nor is any other like unto me, able to follow the wisdom of the blessed and glorious Paul' (Ep. Polyc. 3.2). Moreover, whereas there can be no doubt that when Polycarp refers in the same passage to 'the letter he wrote to you' he means the epistle to the Philippians, the expression in II Peter 3.15 has baffled all the commentators. There is no obvious identification, unless indeed the reference to the Lord's patience with us being our salvation is meant to recall Rom. 2.4: 'Or do you think lightly of his wealth of kindness, of tolerance, and of patience, without recognizing that God's kindness is meant to lead you to a change of heart?'[178] In fact on this narrow basis alone Mayor argues for a Roman destination.[179] Yet there is no other hint that the epistle was written to Rome or from it. Either a genuine letter of Paul's has been lost or the imitator again is laying baffling or careless clues.

But the real problems start with the following phrase, ὡς καὶ ἐν πάσαις ἐπιστολαῖς. It is legitimate, with Zahn,[180] to point out that it is not (on the most likely reading) ἐν πάσαις ταῖς ἐπιστολαῖς. This would imply 'in *every* letter he wrote', whereas without the article the phrase could mean little more than *et passim* – though how much reliance should be placed on the presence or absence of the article in this writer is very doubtful.[181] It is not in any case implied that the *readers* knew all Paul's epistles, nor that these already formed a collection, let alone a canon. Talk here of 'the Pauline corpus' is premature. The present tense, 'whenever he speaks', is not of itself decisive, since Ignatius uses closely parallel language in Eph. 12.2, 'who in every letter makes mention of you in Christ Jesus', though Ignatius combines this with phrases that make it clear that Paul is long since dead: 'who was sanctified, who obtained a good report, who is worthy of all felicitation'. II Peter, in contrast, whether genuinely or fictionally, clearly

[178] But this is, of course, a Jewish commonplace; cf. e.g. Wisd. 11.23.

[179] *Jude and II Peter*, cxxxvii and ad loc.

[180] *INT* II, 290.

[181] Cf. Mayor, *Jude and II Peter*, xxx: 'I think we must recognize a failure to appreciate the refinements of the Greek article on the part of those whose mother tongue was not Greek and who may have also been influenced by the fact that Latin had no article.' Interestingly he does not even discuss this passage, following the longer reading (with the article) without demur.

implies that Paul is still alive. The misinterpretation of Paul's position, of which he speaks, in a gnosticizing, antinomian direction is of course plentifully attested in his lifetime (I Cor. 10.23; Rom. 3.8; 6.1; etc.), and, despite Paul's disclaimer, we may surmise between the lines of II Cor. 1.13f. that his readers *did* find parts of his epistles hard to understand. So far therefore there is nothing that *demands* a later date.

The crucial difficulty is the interpretation of the following phrase, *καὶ τὰς λοιπὰς γραφάς*, which certainly suggests that the Pauline epistles were already being viewed as 'scripture'. In view of the parallels for *γραφή* and *γραφαί* in the New Testament,[182] it is impossible, I believe, to argue[183] that the books of the Old Testament are *not* here being bracketed with the letters of Paul. The sole issue is whether the words imply that 'the writings' in question are seen as part of a canon, whether Jewish or Christian. This appears to be much more doubtful, and I would concur with the judgment of Mayor (who nevertheless thinks II Peter very late) when he says:[184]

> I incline to think that *γραφαί* is here used to denote any book read in the synagogue or congregation, including the letters of the Apostles (Col. 4.16; I Thess. 5.27) as well as the lessons from the Old Testament.

Certainly this would include the kind of apocryphal writings alluded to by Jude, one of which is described as a work of 'prophecy' (14). The work already referred to which is cited in I Clem. 23.3 ('these things did we hear in the days of our fathers also . . . and none of these things have befallen us') and which Lightfoot tentatively identified with *Eldad and Modad*,[185] is introduced with the words *ἡ γραφὴ λέγει*, and the same passage is designated in II Clem. 11.2 *ὁ προφητικὸς λόγος*. Certainly too if the quotations in James 4.5 ('the spirit which God implanted in man turns towards envious desires') and John 7.38 ('streams of living water shall flow out from within him'), each described as *ἡ γραφή*, are literal quotations, they do not come from the canonical Old Testament. Moreover texts from what appear to be the Old and New Testaments are already combined as citations of 'scripture' in I Tim. 5.18;[186] Ep. Barn. 13.7; I Clem. 36; Ep. Polyc. 12.1; etc. This does not by any means dispose of the

182 They are fully set out by Mayor, ad loc.

183 With Zahn, *INT* II, 277f., 290f. His arguments are countered by Chase, *HDB* III, 810.

184 *Jude and II Peter*, 168.

185 *AF* I.2, 80f.; cf. Hermas, Vis. 2.3.4.

186 'The labourer is worthy of his hire' could well however be a proverbial saying, not a quotation from Jesus.

difficulty. Yet Green at least puts up a good case when he argues:[187]

> For the writer of II Peter, the term ἡ γραφή denotes writings of men in touch with God, ὑπὸ πνεύματος ἁγίου φερόμενοι (1.21). He constantly correlates apostles and prophets – both are led by the Holy Spirit. In chapter 1 the apostolic testimony to the divine voice, and the divine voice through the Old Testament scriptures, are regarded in the same light. In chapter 2.1ff. the false teachers are accused of wresting the Old Testament; in chapter 3 of wresting Paul.

Most will probably not feel that this is a complete answer. But I am not at this stage attempting to come to a decision one way or the other. Having, however, started with the conviction that the so-called anachronisms in the epistle were almost certainly insuperable, I have been impressed, working through them, how open the verdict has constantly to remain. These passages certainly do not prove a first-century date: but they do not prove a second-century date either. Moreover they leave unresolved the question of authorship – for the absence of demonstrable anachronisms could merely indicate the skill of the imitator. Nor of themselves do they determine the epistle's relationship to I Peter or to Jude. To these wider issues we must now turn. For only then shall we be in a position to resolve more closely the question of dating.

The one thing on which virtually everyone is agreed is that I and II Peter cannot be written by the same hand. Even those who accept the apostolic authorship of both concede, with Jerome, that the difference of style demands an amanuensis with great liberty of expression for the composition of one if not of each – though a difficulty of this theory is that the greatest evidence for Petrine colouring in theology and expression comes in the epistle that might refer to an amanuensis (Silvanus), whereas the other mentions none.

Attempts have been made to minimize the differences between the two. Thus Green[188] quotes, *via* Mayor, B. Weiss' judgment that 'the Second Epistle of Peter is allied to no New Testament writing more closely than to his first'[189] (he presumably did not count Jude!). Yet this is also true of the book of Revelation and the gospel of John, but the differences of style and cast of mind have convinced most critics that they cannot be by the same man. Apparently impressive comparisons of word-counts have a habit of breaking down and tend simply to prove how variously statistics can be presented.[190] One is

[187] *II Peter Reconsidered*, 31. [188] Ibid., 12.

[189] *A Manual of Introduction to the New Testament*, ET 1887, II, 165.

[190] Thus Green adduces the findings of A. E. Simms, 'Second Peter and the Apocalypse of Peter', *The Expositor*, 5th series, 8, 1898, 460–71, that I and II Peter are as close on word-score as I Timothy and Titus, where few would question

inclined to apply Kelly's comment[191] on A. Q. Morton's disclosure,[192] also seized on by Green,[193] that the computer reveals the two epistles to be linguistically indistinguishable: 'Most readers of Greek would agree that this conclusion illustrates the limitations of the method.'[194]

Of course there *are* similarities of diction[195] – it would be astonishing if there were not – but, with the exception of the opening salutation 'grace and truth be multiplied to you' (I Peter 1.2; II Peter 1.2), most of them are fairly inexact or of the kind that might be found almost anywhere in the New Testament.[196] They certainly do not add up to what Green calls 'the extreme similarity in turn of phrase and allusion'.[197] Zahn, surveying the same evidence, concludes that 'the agreements in thought and language' are 'very few'.[198] Since Green cites Mayor's comment that in grammar and style 'there is not that chasm between them which some would try to make out',[199] it is only fair to give the full conclusion of his exhaustive examination:[200]

> On the whole I should say that the difference of style is less marked than the difference in vocabulary, and that again less marked than the difference in matter, while above all stands the great difference in thought, feeling, and character, in one word of personality.

---

unity of authorship: I Timothy has 537 words and Titus 399, with 161 in common; I Peter has 543 words and II Peter 399, with 153 in common. It sounds impressive until we look at the figures which Green does *not* quote from Mayor (lxix–lxxiv) that show that in the vocabulary of I and II Peter 'the number of agreements is 100 as opposed to 599 disagreements, i.e., the latter are just six times as many as the former' (lxxiv). It looks as if both sets of figures cannot be right (they may not be as far as I know: I have not counted). Yet though the former is for the total number of words and the latter for each individual word (however often it is used), Simms' proportion of 153 shared words out of a *combined* total for both epistles of 942 is still only a proportion of about 1:6 (indeed slightly less).

191 *Peter and Jude*, 235.

192 A. Q. Morton, 'Statistical Analysis and New Testament Problems', in *The Authorship and Integrity of the New Testament* (SPCR Theological Collections 4), 1965, 52f.

193 *II Peter and Jude*, 17.

194 On the place and limitations of the computer in biblical criticism, cf. Bruce, *BJRL* 46 (1964), 327–31.

195 For a detailed list, see Mayor, *Jude and II Peter*, lxix.

196 The next nearest parallel is between ἀμώμου καὶ ἀσπίλου in I Peter 1.19 and ἄσπιλοι καὶ ἀμώμητοι in II Peter 3.14. But, apart from the fact that one refers to Christ and the other to Christians, the words (in reverse order) are not even the same. ἀμώμητος is a *hapax legomenon* in the New Testament and suggests a different hand. The nearest true parallels for II Peter 3.14 are Col. 1.22; Eph. 1.4; I Tim. 6.14.

197 *II Peter and Jude*, 13.
198 *INT* II, 271.

199 *Jude and II Peter*, civ.
200 Ibid., cv.

I have laboured this because I wish to go on to support Green in his critique of pseudonymity. But that the two epistles can in any immediate sense be the product of the same mind, let alone of the same pen, seems to me highly improbable. Chase, to whom Mayor[201] paid the deserved tribute of saying, 'I have found . . . his articles on Peter and Jude in Hastings' *Dictionary of the Bible* by far the best introduction known to me', assessed the matter thus:[202]

> The difference between the two Epistles [viz., I and II Peter] in literary style and tone and teaching are, as it appears to the present writer, so numerous and so fundamental that no difference of amanuenses or 'interpreters' can account for them unless we are prepared to admit that, in the case of either one or both of these letters, the substance and the language alike were left absolutely in the hands of the apostle's companion.

So what is the alternative? There would appear only to be one. 'Scarcely anyone nowadays doubts that II Peter is pseudonymous', says Kelly;[203] 'though it must be admitted', he goes on, 'of the few who do that they defend their case with an impressive combination of learning and ingenuity.' Now if 'their case' is confined to doubting pseudonymity (as opposed to asserting identity of authorship), I believe indeed that there are points to answer which the proponents of pseudonymity pass over too hastily.

There is an appetite for pseudonymity that grows by what it feeds on. Thus M. Rist,[204] believing that possibly two-thirds of the New Testament writings are pseudonymous,[205] says, 'This, alone, [sic] shows the influence of pseudepigraphy in the early church.'[206] If you believe it is everywhere, you cease to have to argue for it anywhere. Perrin writes: 'Pseudonymity is almost a way of life in the world of the New Testament and also in the New Testament itself.'[207] Certainly it is among New Testament scholars! There is also a tendency to lump together very different categories of pseudepi-

[201] Ibid., ix. [202] *HDB* III, 813f. [203] *Peter and Jude*, 235.

[204] 'Pseudepigraphy and the Early Christians' in Aune, *Studies in the NT and Early Christian Literature*, 75–91 (89).

[205] As we have seen, van Manen went further and said of the Pauline epistles: 'They are all, without distinction, pseudepigrapha' (*EB* III, 3625).

[206] Op. cit., 89. Similarly Nineham, in Cross, *Studies in Ephesians*, 22, appeals to the 'very common . . . practice of pseudepigraphy', citing *inter alia*, from the New Testament, the book of Revelation (but this makes no claim to be by John *the Apostle*) and, from outside the New Testament, II Clement and the Epistle of Barnabas. But these latter are *anonymous*, and do not themselves purport to be by the writers to whom tradition has ascribed them: in this they are comparable with Hebrews, rather than Ephesians or I and II Peter.

[207] *NTI*, 119.

graphy.[208] Thus Jude, for instance, readily accepts, at any rate for the sake of the argument, that what we call I Enoch was written by 'Enoch, the seventh from Adam' (14). The convention of ascribing apocalypses to patriarchs, like psalms to David or wisdom to Solomon or prophecies to Daniel, was of course fully established. Indeed the novelty about the New Testament Apocalypse is that it is neither anonymous nor pseudonymous. Later, too, not only apocalypses but gospels, acts and epistles were freely ascribed to long dead apostles (and to no one less than Peter). But there is no firm evidence for this until the mid-second century. In heretical circles too there were documents claiming to be by apostles (like the gospels of Thomas and Philip), but these were never accepted as such by the church. If we ask what is the evidence for orthodox epistles being composed in the name of apostles within a generation or two of their lifetime, and for this being an acceptable literary convention within the church, the answer is nil – *unless* Ephesians, the Pastorals, I and II Peter, Jude, and any other canonical books one cares to add, are their own evidence. In each instance we have examined so far the case cannot be said to have been made. It really is necessary to have at least one hard example established on its own merits before relying on the cumulative argument. II Peter could well be that example and it is certainly the most promising. But, as Green[209] and Guthrie[210] quite legitimately argue, it would go against the stream of such evidence as we have rather than with it.

There is no doubt of what Paul thought of those who circulated letters claiming to come from him (II Thess. 2.2; 3.17): *he* knew of no harmless literary convention. Later Green quotes two instances which elucidate the church's attitude at the end of the second century. First, Tertullian[211] tells us that the author of the Acts of Paul and Thecla was deposed from the presbyterate for the sole reason that he had tried to pass this work off under Paul's name.

> The author of these *Acts*, like the author of II Peter, was orthodox; he, like the author of II Peter, made strenuous efforts after verisimilitude. He was, further-

[208] Even Mayor, usually so discriminating, is guilty at this point.

[209] *II Peter Reconsidered*, 32–7: *II Peter and Jude*, 30–5; cf. earlier Zahn, *INT* II, 270–3.

[210] D. Guthrie, 'Epistolatory Pseudepigraphy', in *NTI*, 671–84; 'The Development of the Idea of Canonical Pseudepigrapha in New Testament Criticism', *VE* 1, 1962, 43–59, reprinted in *The Authorship and Integrity of the New Testament*, 14–39. The latter article is a reply to K. Aland, 'The Problem of Anonymity and Pseudonymity in Christian Literature of the First Two Centuries', *JTS* n.s. 12, 1961, 39–49, also reprinted in *Authorship and Integrity*, 1–13.

[211] *De bapt.* 17.

more, inflamed with the noblest *pietas*, love of Paul, and it was with the best of intentions that he wrote. Yet he was deposed – for forgery.[212]

Secondly, Serapion, Bishop of Antioch, wrote a book *Concerning the So-called Gospel of Peter*, from which Eusebius quotes:[213]

For our part, brethren, we receive both Peter and the other apostles as Christ, but the writings which falsely bear their names (*ψευδεπίγραφα*) we reject, as men of experience (*ἔμπειροι*), knowing that such were not handed down to us.

Though the motive of his condemnation of it was the docetic heresy that he heard it was spreading, the criterion of his judgment, to which he brought the expertise in these matters that he claimed, was its genuineness as the work of the apostle. And this was the criterion employed a little later by Origen in relation both to II Peter and to II and III John.[214] He is doubtful of their genuineness; but there is no suggestion that if they had been pseudepigraphs, or he had known them to be such, it would have made no difference. Nor does he or any other Christian writer hint that there had earlier been any such convention. The fathers may have been uncritical (though hardly Origen) and been deceived, but there is no evidence that they were willingly deceived. In view of the significance usually attached to the lack of external testimony for individual books of the New Testament, it is surely much more significant that at no point is there the slightest external testimony to the collusion in innocent falsification to which appeal is so constantly made for documents like Ephesians, the Pastorals, James and I Peter. II Peter and Jude may still be the exceptions, but they have to be demonstrated as such.

Moving then from the general presumption to the particular evidence, what is to be said?

The very weakness of the external attestation for II Peter (albeit far stronger than that for any rejected writing)[215] suggests that Origen was not unjustified in doubting its genuineness – though these doubts are the most powerful evidence that the issue was not one that was not thought to matter. Certainly the epistle could be an attempt to silence latter-day scoffers and heretics in the name and authority of the chief of the apostles – although why anyone should resort for this purpose to the mantle of Jude is far from clear.[216] But it is fair

[212] *II Peter Reconsidered*, 34. [213] *HE* 6.12.3.

[214] Eusebius, *HE* 6.25.7–10.

[215] For the evidence, cf. the full surveys in Chase, *HDB* III, 799–807, and Mayor, *Jude and II Peter*, xcv–cxxiv. Eusebius, *HE* 3.3.1f., while placing II Peter among *ἀντιλεγόμενα*, or disputed books, has no hesitation in classing the Acts, Gospel, Preaching, and Apocalypse of Peter among the spurious (*τὰ νόθα*).

[216] Cf. Streeter, *PC*, 179f.: 'Jude is a person so obscure that no one, desiring to

comment that no other proven pseudepigraphs have this and no other motive. All, including the other pseudo-Petrine literature, had other axes to grind:

> They attempted to claim apostolic authority for heretical teaching, or to embody the secret tradition of the apostle concerned, or else to provide a romance, a sort of religious novel, or, perhaps, to answer some of the questions posed by a third generation's insatiable curiosity.[217]

II Peter does none of these things. Moreover, there are relevant questions to ask of this particular case. Why, for instance, does the author mention Paul in such brotherly terms and yet appear to be entirely uninfluenced by his theology – in marked contrast apparently with the author of I Peter? One would have expected him (like Ignatius and Polycarp) to quote or echo something from all those letters of his he claimed to know. As we have seen, he does not even identify the letter to the church to which he is writing – in contrast again to Clement, who when writing to Corinth reminds his readers of I Corinthians (I Clem.47. 1–4) and echoes its teaching (49.5). Were the epistle genuine, 3.15 could indeed allude to a lost letter, as might the reference in 3.1 to his previous epistle (on the analogy of I Cor. 5.9). But neither of these options is open to a pseudepigrapher, if he wishes to carry conviction. He must in the latter case have been referring to I Peter. Why then did he make so little use of it? Boobyer[218] makes a strenuous effort to show how he did use it – and on the hypothesis of pseudepigraphy this has to be done. But he himself quotes R. Knopf[219] and Windisch[220] for the judgment that the two epistles have little or nothing in common; and the connections which he finds are strained. Nor, as we have seen, does the author of II Peter make it clear to what other document he might be referring in 1.15 – unless he proposed to compose one himself and never did. To drop hints for the purpose of identification which merely baffle

---

give weight to his own views by publishing them under an authoritative name, would ever have thought of him, until and unless he had used up all the greater figures of the Apostolic Age. The epistle must therefore be the authentic work of a Christian leader actually named Judas.' He identifies him with a bishop of Jerusalem early in the reign of Trajan, regarding the words 'brother of James' as a marginal note incorporated into the text. There is of course no evidence for this, but as a last resort it is perhaps less incredible than pseudepigraphy.

217 Green, *II Peter Reconsidered*, 37.

218 G. H. Boobyer, 'The Indebtedness of II Peter to I Peter' in Higgins, *New Testament Essays*, 34–53.

219 R. Knopf, *Die Briefe Petri und Judä* (KEKNT 12), Göttingen [12]1912, 254.

220 H. Windisch, *Die katholischen Briefe* (HNT 15), Tübingen [3]1951, 99.

is scarcely a convincing procedure. The argument that the personal references in II Peter are too blatant to be credible (or, conversely, that in I Peter they are too obscure) is inevitably subjective. Moreover, one would expect clues to be laid both of place and personalia which would help to add verisimilitude (like the many such details in the Pastorals or the reference to Tychicus in Eph. 6.21f.). But there is nothing – except the curious form of the name 'Simeon Peter' in 1.1, which corresponds neither to the address of I Peter, the natural model for a copyist (as in the salutation of 1.2), nor to that of any later Petrine pseudepigraph. In particular, the absence of any reference to Rome, the obvious place of origin to claim on both historical and ecclesiastical grounds, is puzzling.

It is relevant too to ask about the circumstances in which such a pseudepigraph might be composed. We have already noted a number of points which make a second-century date look unlikely (the contrast with the Apocalypse of Peter and later gnostic systems, the lack of reference to chiliasm, and the absence of any concern for organization and the ministry). It is noticeable in fact that in recent commentaries the date is steadily dropping. Kelly[221] opts for 100–110, Reicke[222] for *c.* 90. The latter's choice of the reign of Domitian is this time neither because of references to persecution (of which there are none), nor because of the break between the church and the synagogue (of which again there is no sign – or, for that matter, of any post-70 situation), but ironically because in his reign prior to 95 the church had peace! II Peter and Jude, he thinks, are concerned to preserve a positive attitude to the state against those who would foment rebellion.

> Obviously their authors wish to oppose certain propaganda for political freedom, propaganda which they regard as hostile to the social order, and to which the Christians have been exposed by the magnates and their parties. This fits especially well into the latter half of Domitian's reign, during which the aristocrats and the senators of the empire fought with desperation against Domitian's tyranny (Suetonius, *Vit. Dom.* 10).[223]

Yet it is not at all 'obvious' that the persons under attack in these epistles were concerned for *political* freedom. The only evidence is that they 'flout authority' (*κυριότητα*) and 'insult celestial beings (*δόξας*)' (Jude 8; II Peter 2.10). Political disaffection could no doubt be so described on the spiritual level, but there is no suggestion that this in

[221] *Peter and Jude*, 236f. [222] *James, Peter and Jude*, 144f.

[223] Ibid., 145. He adds that the epistle of James 'seems to reflect the same political situation'. Yet it would scarcely be possible to find two documents which on the face of it are much more dissimilar in the conditions they presuppose. However Reicke now tells me that he would like to reconsider all these datings.

fact is what is in mind. On the contrary, it is the spiritual authority of the church they are challenging. They have 'rebelled like Korah' (Jude 11), that is, against the ordinances of God and the leaders of his people (Num. 16).[224] This is what κυριότης means in Did. 4.1, and the rejection of it there is linked with schism (4.3) – as in the split created by the insubordination of Diotrephes in III John 9f. who 'does not accept our authority'. Neither II Peter nor III John is to be dated by reference to the political scene.

Yet the further back II Peter is pushed into the first century (where all the parallels suggest it belongs), the harder it is, as with the Pastorals, to satisfy the basic condition of pseudepigraphy, namely, that the readers should, willingly or unwillingly, accept the deception. Indeed a comparison with the problem of the Pastorals is instructive. There we argued for the important difference between pseudepigraphy proper and the view that the letters or charges were composed for Paul in his name and with his authority. Under the former hypothesis the persons of Timothy and Titus and all the details of news and travel plans are part of the fiction (or genuine fragments incorporated to enhance the fiction). Under the latter hypothesis the persons and situations are entirely genuine but, for whatever reason, Paul may have got someone else to write the letters on his behalf, though probably dictating the personal messages. It has been suggested – I believe improbably – that this agent might be Luke. But it is the relationship that matters, and this relationship is not that of pseudepigraphy, nor is it the role of an amanuensis played by Tertius in Romans (16.22). Transferring the analogy from the Pastorals to II Peter, the distinction is not so clear, because there are no details by which to assess the genuineness of the situation, as distinct from the identity of the writer. But it is an analogy that I believe it is profitable to pursue. For it seems to have been assumed without question that there is no third term between Petrine authorship (whether through an amanuensis or not) and pseudepigraphy. And both of these alternatives, I believe, are open to almost equal objection – though if faced with the choice I think I should have, with even such conservative scholars as Chase, Mayor and Hort,[225] to plump for pseudonymity.

[224] Cf. the 'murmurers' (γογγυσταί) of Jude 16 with Num. 16.11 (and I Cor. 10.10).

[225] Cf. the characteristic remark of Hort's quoted by Sanday, *Inspiration*, 347, and cited by Mayor, *Jude and II Peter*, xxii, that, 'if he were asked he should say that the balance of argument was against the epistle; and the moment he had done so he should begin to think that he might be wrong.'

But at this point I should like to return to the relationship between II Peter and Jude. That there is some *literary* connection is indubitable, if only because all the parallels between the two epistles are virtually in the same order, as a glance at any reference Bible will show. Three main explanations have been advanced: (i) Jude is using II Peter (Spitta,[226] Zahn, Bigg); (ii) II Peter is using Jude (the vast majority of other scholars); (iii) Each is using a common source (E. I. Robson,[227] Reicke, Green[228]). The claims for priority can often be argued either way, as in the synoptic gospels (e.g. is smoothness or roughness, expansion or condensation, more likely to be original?). But it would seem that, on the assumption of direct dependence, II Peter is likely to be secondary, if only because it is difficult to see any good reason for writing Jude at all with so little fresh matter to add. The hypothesis of a common source, 'a sermon pattern formulated to resist the seducers of the church',[229] is attractive, but like that of 'Q' it is defensible only if it is necessary. There would appear to be no other evidence for such a document as, it is claimed, there is for catechetical summaries, scriptural testimonia, apocalyptic flysheets, or such a moral tract as seems to underlie the 'two ways' material of the Epistle of Barnabas and the Didache.[230] Moreover, what again was the point of producing the epistle of Jude if there was so little material in it independent of its source?

It should also be observed that, though the order of the common matter is the same, the degree of verbal correspondence is a good deal smaller than in those sections of Matthew and Luke that demand a literary and not just an oral connection. The relevant passages are conveniently set out in parallel columns in Moffatt's *Introduction to the Literature of the New Testament*.[231] It will be seen at once that, though the themes and many of the words are the same, there is no direct copying. As Guthrie, who supplies the statistics,[232] says,

> If II Peter is the borrower he has changed 70% of Jude's language and added more of his own. Whereas if Jude borrowed from II Peter, the percentage of alteration is slightly higher, combined with a reduction in quantity.

The relationship is much more like that of Ephesians and Colossians.

[226] F. Spitta, *Die zweite Brief des Petrus und der Brief des Judas*, Halle 1885.

[227] E. I. Robson, *Studies in the Second Epistle of Peter*, Cambridge 1915.

[228] Especially in his later book, *II Peter and Jude*, 53–5.

[229] Reicke, *James, Peter and Jude*, 190.

[230] Cf. pp. 323f. below.

[231] Op. cit., 348–50; also, in translation, in Leaney, *Peter and Jude*, 101–4. The complete Greek texts of Jude and II Peter are printed in parallel by Mayor, *Jude and II Peter*, 1–15.

[232] *NTI*, 926f.

It is the relationship not of a wooden imitator but of a creative re-shaper of the themes – *or* it represents a single mind writing at much the same time in a somewhat different context. It was the latter alternative that commended itself there, and I am astonished that it has apparently suggested itself to no one here. Let me then propose a hypothesis.

Jude begins by saying that he was fully engaged in writing to his readers about their common salvation when he was forced to break off to send them an urgent appeal to close ranks against the danger of false teachers from within (3f.). I suggest that what he was composing, in the name of the apostle, was II Peter. This was to be a general letter and testament, a 'recall to fundamentals' as the NEB styles I John. But, corresponding to the briefer II John to a more specific and somewhat less advanced situation, Jude also first wrote off a hurried letter on his own authority to counter the immediate menace of the new heretics. This he then incorporated (for the most part in a single block in ch. 2) in the more studied style of the formal encyclical. This would explain the fact that there is no discernible difference in the situation between the two epistles. Both are written to predominantly Jewish Christians in danger of 'losing their safe foothold' (II Peter 3.17), though not from persecution but from error. This similarity was noted by Mayor:[233]

> The moral corruption described in the two epistles is the same even in its minutest points; the cause of the corruption is the same, the misinterpretation and misuse of Paul's doctrine of God's free grace (Jude 4; II Peter 2.19; 3.16; cf. Rom. 3.5–8). The agents use the same methods and are described in the same terms.

He proceeds to detail them. Yet it does not appear to him to require explanation how or why the situations are identical at an interval, on his reckoning, of at least fifty years.[234] Moreover, apart from the less spontaneous and more pretentious level of writing in II Peter which often overreaches itself, the vocabulary and style are indistinguishable.[235] Mayor again in an exhaustive study of the 'grammar and style of Jude and II Peter'[236] observes no point at which the usage of the two epistles diverges. This is surely very remarkable, especially when compared with the strained efforts to show the similarities

[233] *Jude and II Peter*, clxxiv.

[234] He dates Jude 'nearer 80 than 70' (cxlv), II Peter in 'the second quarter of the second century' (cxxvii).

[235] An equivalent might perhaps be the difference in formality between Galatians and Ephesians.

[236] *Jude and II Peter*, xxvi–lxvii.

between I and II Peter. The only difference is the format in which the message is couched. When writing in his own name Jude says, 'Remember the predictions made by the apostles of our Lord Jesus Christ' (Jude 17); when writing with Peter's apostolic authority he says, 'Remember the predictions made by God's own prophets' (II Peter 3.2). Jude is representing Peter rather than impersonating him. But he leaves his own signature. For he calls him what *he* called him – Simeon. The only other person who is recorded as retaining this Hebraic use is his brother James (Acts 15.14): it was in the family.

In one sense this hypothesis is merely taking further the alternative at which Chase hinted when he said that no difference of amanuensis would be a sufficient explanation unless 'the substance and the language alike were left *absolutely* in the hands of the apostle's companion' (italics mine). In other words, he would not be an amanuensis but an agent. The relationship perhaps was best described by Origen,[237] who saw this as a possible (though we should think needless) way of holding that the anonymous epistle to the Hebrews could still be Pauline:

> I should say that the thoughts are the apostle's, but that the style and composition belong to one who called to mind the apostle's teachings and, as it were, made short notes of what his master said. If any church, therefore, holds this epistle as Paul's, let it be commended for this also. For not without reason have the men of old time handed it down as Paul's. But who wrote the epistle, in truth God knows.

He then goes on to record suggested guesses of who the agent might be – Clement of Rome and (again!) Luke.

Now if such a solution is possible to the problem of the Pastorals, whether or not it is *necessary*, it cannot be ruled out for II Peter. And in this case one may produce the identity of the agent with a good deal more plausibility. For with Jude the glove fits precisely – even when he is wearing a different hat. Whether Silvanus also stood in the same relationship to I Peter it is impossible to be sure, for we have nothing which comes solely from his pen by which to test it. But it is improbable. For in I Peter 5.12 the 'I' of the writer is clearly distinguished from that of the amanuensis (*if* indeed this is what *διά* means). The relationship is subtly but fundamentally different. As we have seen, the amanuensis can insert his own greeting (Rom. 16.22; Mart. Polyc. 20.2). But, like the political speech-writer or composer of an episcopal charge, the apostolic delegate must submerge his identity.

The hypothesis would also help to explain the doubts and hesita-

[237] Apud Euseb. *HE* 6.25.13f.

tions over II Peter in the church – in striking contrast with the remarkably good attestation of the minor and apparently less authoritative epistle of Jude.[238] For the latter authenticated itself – and there really is no case here for pseudonymity, unless again the Greek is, arbitrarily, deemed to be beyond a brother of the Lord. But II Peter *is* very puzzling. Try to fit it into the style or the situation of I Peter and it is bound to appear doubtful. Indeed, unless it is written by an agent, it must be written by a pretender – and for that, as we have seen, there is precious little motivation or plausible setting.

What then may we say is the setting of II Peter? I believe that Zahn was correct in refusing to see in 3.1 a reference to I Peter (though I think he was incorrect in dating Jude so much later). For the contents of I and II Peter are patently different, whereas the situation presupposed by Jude and II Peter is the same. The latter epistles are addressed to predominantly Jewish Christians in acute danger not from persecution but heresy; whereas I Peter is addressed to predominantly Gentile Christians in acute danger from persecution but with no mention of heresy nor whiff of a gnosticizing menace. To what then is the allusion in II Peter 3.1, where the epistle is described as being the 'second letter' to the same persons on the same subject? I believe two explanations are possible. Either it will refer to a lost letter, for which indeed there is sufficient precedent in Paul's extended correspondence with the church at Corinth. Or – and this is a solution I commend for serious consideration – it refers to the epistle of Jude, which would certainly qualify as far as description of contents is concerned.[239] If then it is asked how the earlier letter could be described as one which the same 'I' sent to the same readers, we should remember that in Jude 3 the author said '*I* was fully engaged in writing *to you*' what on this hypothesis is II Peter. The references are merely reversed. The principal and his agent are as one man. This may seem strange to us – though is it really so unusual in literary or official circles today? But it was established Jewish doctrine that, as the Mishnah puts it, 'a man's agent is as himself'.[240]

Whichever alternative is adopted, the necessity is removed, as Zahn saw, for having to find a setting for II Peter *after* I Peter. The most notable difference between Jude and II Peter on the one hand

[238] Cf. Streeter, *PC*, 179: 'So far as external evidence is concerned, Jude is one of the best authenticated of the catholic epistles.'

[239] Another possibility that has been canvassed is that II Peter is composite, chs. 1–2 or 2 constituting the previous letter. But for such a division there is no evidence, either in the manuscript tradition or even, as at I Peter 4.12, in the suggestion of a fresh start after a closure.

[240] *Ber.* 5.5.

and the book of Revelation on the other is that, while they all speak of a similar danger from gnosticizing Judaism, the former two breathe no air of persecution. In this they stand much nearer to the attitude to the civic authorities in the Pastorals (cf. I Tim. 2.1f.) and the closing chapters of Acts. Indeed the atmosphere of II Peter, with the apostle's warning of danger from error and perversion 'after my departure', is closer than anything else to Paul's speech in Acts 20.29f. and to II Tim. 4.6–8. Though in their contexts both *μετὰ τήν ἐμὴν ἔξοδον* in II Peter 1.15 and *μετὰ τὴν ἄφιξίν μου* in Acts 20.29 must carry allusion to the apostles' deaths, there is no reason why they should not also mean at the literal level 'after I have left you'. The same applies to 'the time of my departure' (*ὁ καιρὸς τῆς ἀναλύσεώς μου*) in II Tim. 4.6. II Peter 1.14 has been taken to imply that Peter is writing (or is purporting to write) on the point of death, though, as we have seen, this is by no means necessarily the implication of *ταχινή*. In any case, we have argued that the similar language of II Tim. 4.6–8 (reflected also in Acts 20.24f.) came from 58 – a number of years before Paul's death. May it not be that II Peter also represents that apostle's parting testimony to the Christians of Asia before he leaves for Rome? For there is absolutely no suggestion that II Peter comes *from* Rome, unlike I Peter. Where he was at the time of its writing or why he had an occasion to use an agent (unless he was on a missionary tour, whereas later he was settled in the capital) it is useless to speculate. Unfortunately, unlike Paul, he had no Boswell in Luke. Yet it seems highly improbable that neither Acts nor Paul's Caesarean correspondence would have mentioned his presence in Jerusalem in 57–9 had he been there. Nor could he credibly have been in Rome in 57 without the exhaustive greetings of Rom. 16 including him. Moreover Acts 28.15–31 could scarcely have been written as it is, especially when the Jews say in 21f., 'We have had no communication from Judaea, nor has any countryman of ours arrived with any report or gossip to your discredit', if Peter was there preaching to 'the circumcision' (cf. Gal. 2.9) either on Paul's arrival in 60, or, in all probability, during the two years following.

If we ask to what area the internal evidence points for the epistle's destination, the only parallels we have for the kind of gnosticizing tendencies found in II Peter and Jude are either in Corinth (I and II Corinthians) or Asia Minor (Acts 20, Colossians, I and II Timothy, I and II John, Revelation 1–3). We may be fairly sure that Peter had been in Corinth in the early 50s (I Cor. 1.12; 3.22), and the reference in I Cor. 9.5 to him and the Lord's brothers, as examples familiar to the Corinthians of missionaries who had brought their wives, could suggest that even then he had had with him Jude, the only one of the brothers whom we *know* to have been married.[241] For all along Peter seems to have been particularly closely associated with the Lord's brothers (Acts 1.13f.; 12.17; 15; Gal. 1.18f.; 2.9, 11f.; and cf. Mark 16.7 with Matt. 28.10; John 20.17). Corinth therefore is a perfectly possible destination for II Peter and Jude – in which case 'your apostles' will be Paul and Silvanus and Timothy (II Cor. 1.19), and Peter's disavowal of 'artfully spun tales' in his preaching to them will parallel Paul's disclaimer of 'the language of worldly wisdom' in I Cor. 1.17; 2.1. Nevertheless it seems improbable that Peter would have addressed so distinctive (and divided) a church as Corinth without any hint or mention of it (contrast again I Clement). For II Peter and Jude share the same anonymity of audience as the Johannine epistles and appear to reflect more scattered communities. In date too the emergence, as far as our evidence goes, of such gnosticizing tendencies in Asia Minor in the latter 50s and early 60s better fits the period we are looking for, and the 'Asian' style which II Peter in particular affects[242] points in the same direction.

Let us then surmise that Peter and Jude, wherever they may be (together or apart), are addressing a final word of apostolic testament to Jewish Christians in Asia Minor prior to Peter's departure for Rome for the last time. Can we put any date to this? We have already seen reason to think that he cannot have gone to Rome before 60 (and probably 62). There is ground too for believing that Jude is unlikely to be writing after 62. For he introduces himself simply as 'brother of James'. This in itself give no indication of whether James is alive or dead. But if he had already suffered martyrdom at the hands of the Sanhedrin, an event to whose impact on the Jews even Josephus testifies,[243] quite apart from its traumatic effect on Christians,[244] it would seem incredible that no hint of the tensions it created or of any posthumous epithet, such as *μακάριος* (as in I Clem. 47.1) or *ἀγαθός* (as in I Clem. 5.3) or, particularly in his case, *δίκαιος*,[245] should have crept into a letter written to Jewish Christians by his own brother. Indeed, as I have said, the most notable absence from these epistles is any reference to persecution, or for that matter

[241] Cf. again Eusebius, *HE* 3.19f.; 3.32.5, quoting Hegesippus.

[242] Cf. Deissmann, *Bible Studies*, 366–8.

[243] *Ant.* 20. 200–3.

[244] Cf. again Hegesippus, and the space Eusebius devotes to his testimony in *HE* 2.23.

[245] Cf. Hegesippus, apud Euseb. *HE* 2.23.4: 'He received the name of "the Just" from all men, from the time of the Lord even to our own; for there were many called James.'

any echo of the Jewish war, let alone the fall of Jerusalem. If these facts are taken into account, then 62 becomes a *terminus ad quem*, and we may date Jude and II Peter in fairly close succession (as Jude 3 indicates)[246] between 60 and 62. Since Peter is about to leave, we may put them nearer to the end of that period than the beginning, let us say in 61–2.

Now this is precisely the period to which II Peter was assigned by independent reasoning by Zahn.[247] I confess that when I first read him I was incredulous. I expected when I began this chapter that II Peter would either remain a pseudonymous exception (and have to be slotted somewhere into the late first century) or would belong to the gap (if any) between I Peter and the apostle's death. So early a dating will still probably seem incredible to many. Indeed, if the Pastoral Epistles are placed, as Zahn placed them,[248] in the mid-60s (let alone much later), it *is* implausible. But if, as we have argued, these come from 56–8, then there is nothing improbable about putting II Peter some five years later. Yet all this is likely to carry conviction only if, as we have also argued, the gospels and Acts too come from before this date, and if the other comparable documents to which we have been referring, the Johannine epistles and Revelation, are not much later. The dating of Peter and Jude is, as I warned at the beginning, bound, on any chronology, to reflect that of other documents. Yet I believe they have more light of their own to shed than their unpromising matter might at first suggest.

To sum up, then, we may say that Jude and II Peter were written, in that order, to predominantly Jewish-Christian congregations in Asia Minor *c.* 61–2. Whether Peter then set out for Rome as he hoped or was delayed in Jerusalem to assist, as Eusebius suggests,[249] 'with all the surviving apostles and disciples of the Lord' in finding a successor to James, we cannot say. But there is nothing improbable about that. By 64–5 at any rate he was evidently in the capital, from where, we have argued, he adapted preaching material, prepared for the church in Rome under the urgent shadow of the Neronian persecution in the spring of 65, for dispatch as an encyclical to different and more mixed congregations in northern Asia Minor, which there is no

[246] So Bigg, *Peter and Jude*, 315–17: 'Jude is practically contemporaneous with II Peter.' But then he has to say, quite arbitrarily, that 'the two Epistles were addressed to different Churches'.

[247] *INT* II, 210. He actually says 60–3, but then he dated Paul's arrival in Rome in 61. He ignores the relevance of the death of James, regarding Jude as written quite separately as late as 75.

[248] *INT* II, 67. He dated them in 65–6.

[249] *HE* 3.11.

firm evidence to suggest that he had ever visited.[250] The Petrine epistles therefore throw no further light on the closing months or years of Peter's life and do nothing to modify the provisional conclusions which previously we reached. But whether he or Paul, who appears unlikely to have been martyred by the time of I Peter (cf. 3.13) and may well have been out of Rome at the time (*possibly* in Spain), perished soon afterwards will have some bearing on the dating of the remaining books of the New Testament yet to be considered.

[250] Eusebius' statement in *HE* 3.1.2 that 'Peter, it seems, preached in Pontus and Galatia and Bithynia, in Cappadocia and Asia', is obviously only a guess derived from I Peter 1.1.

VII

The Epistle to the Hebrews

APART FROM THE prophecies of the fall of Jerusalem in the synoptic gospels, there is no other piece of New Testament literature that raises so acutely as does the epistle to the Hebrews the question of its relation to the events of 70. Whereas a moral tract like the epistle of James could reasonably omit all reference to the temple and its fate without its silence being significant, the whole theme of Hebrews is the final supersession by Christ of the levitical system, its priesthood and its sacrifices. The destruction of the sanctuary which physically brought this system to an end must surely, if it had occurred, have left its mark somewhere.

It is generally accepted that there is no such reference or allusion; and yet the epistle to the Hebrews is among those books of the New Testament regularly set, as Harnack was content to put it without seeing need for further specification, 'under Domitian'.[1] Indeed the balance of opinion in Introductions to the New Testament or Bible Dictionaries is astonishingly one-sided (much more so than I had imagined), and the consensus cuts across many of the other lines of division between conservatives and liberals (e.g. on I Peter). On a quick round-up of the reference-books listed earlier, all the following give support to a dating after 70: Harnack, Jülicher, Zahn, von Soden, the *Encyclopaedia Biblica*, (W. Robertson Smith) Bacon, Moffatt, Feine, K. and S. Lake, Goodspeed, Michaelis, Wikenhauser, the *Interpreter's Dictionary of the Bible*, Kümmel, Marxsen, Fuller, Klijn, Selby and Perrin. On the other side are only: Hastings' *Dictionary of the Bible* (A. B. Bruce), *Peake's Commentary on the Bible* (F. F. Bruce),

[1] *Chron.*, 718. But he admitted it might be earlier. Cf. 475–9, where he holds open the whole period 65–95.

Guthrie, Grant and Harrison.[2] Yet this weighting is remarkably unrepresentative of those who lately have studied the epistle more closely, and the difference could reflect the fact that the text-books have not yet caught up on a detectable swing. Thus in recent years the following have all put it, at varying dates and places, before 70: T. W. Manson,[3] W. Manson,[4] Spicq,[5] Moule,[6] Montefiore,[7] F. F. Bruce,[8] J. Héring,[9] G. W. Buchanan[10] and Strobel.[11]

So, before seeking to be more specific on either destination or date, we may adopt the same method of approach followed in relation to the synoptic gospels. Let us look first at the question of its over-all relation to the events of 70 and then at other indications of a more precise placing.

Whereas in the gospels it is the positive references to the events of 70, albeit in the future, which have led scholars to infer that they must be reflected in retrospect, in Hebrews ironically it is the absence of references on which the issue turns. The exercise consists not in explaining the 'prophecies', but in explaining away the silence.

First, however, there is one reference which has been seized on by some as a positive indication of absolute dating. This is the reference in Heb. 3.7 – 4.11 to the forty years of Israel's disobedience, leading to the oath that they should never enter into God's rest. This is interpreted typologically as an allusion to the forty years of Jewish history AD 30–70. Yet there is not a hint of this in the author's exegesis. Indeed he specifically asks the question, 'And with whom was God indignant for forty years?', and answers it: 'With those, surely, who had sinned, whose bodies lay where they fell in the desert' (3.17). There is no suggestion of a secondary application, any more than there is in I Cor. 10.1–13, where Paul also adduces Israel's wilderness experiences as a warning to Christians, not as a judgment

[2] Heard, Sparks and McNeile-Williams are undecided, as are A. S. Peake, *A Critical Introduction to the New Testament*, 1909, and F. B. Clogg, *An Introduction to the New Testament*, 1937.

[3] T. W. Manson, 'The Problem of the Epistle to the Hebrews', *BJRL* 32, 1949, 1–17; reprinted in *Studies in the Gospels and Epistles*, 242–58, to which page references are given.

[4] W. Manson, *The Epistle to the Hebrews*, 1951.

[5] C. Spicq, *L'Épître aux Hébreux* (Études Bibliques), Paris 1952–3.

[6] *Birth of the NT*, 44, following A. Nairne, *The Epistle of Priesthood: Studies in the Epistle to the Hebrews*, Edinburgh 1913.

[7] H. W. Montefiore, *Hebrews* (Black's NTC), 1964.

[8] F. F. Bruce, *Hebrews*, 1964. [9] J. Héring, *Hebrews*, ET 1970.

[10] G. W. Buchanan, *Hebrews* (Anchor Bible), New York 1972.

[11] A. Strobel, *Hebräerbrief*, Göttingen 1975.

on contemporary Judaism. In any case this interpretation, which has attracted little support, yields no agreed conclusion as to dating. Zahn[12] deduced from it a date of *c.* 80, A. B. Bruce[13] one of 70 (just prior to the fall of Jerusalem), while Gaston[14] regards it as 'a very strong argument for a pre-70 date'.

So we may proceed to the negative evidence and to the way in which its apparent force has been turned. This has followed three lines.

1. The fact that the entire levitical system is spoken of throughout the epistle in the present tense, with no hint that it lies now in ruins, is said to have no chronological significance. It is indeed true that many of the present tenses are timeless descriptions of ritual arrangements (e.g. 5.1–4; 8.3–5; 9.6f.; 10.1). Josephus writing well after the destruction of the temple gives a long account of the system in similar terms[15] and there are later Christian parallels for the same way of speaking.[16] If we were simply dealing with a discussion of scriptural and other ordinances, this would be a complete answer. But it is clear that in some passages at least the writer is appealing to existing realities, whose actual continuance is essential to his argument. If, he says, the levitical system had really been able to bring perfection,

> these sacrifices would surely have ceased to be offered, because the worshippers, cleansed once for all, would no longer have any sense of sin. But instead, in these sacrifices year after year sins are brought to mind (10.2f.; cf. 10.11,18).

Had the sacrifices in fact ceased to be offered, it is hard to credit that these words could have stood without modification or comment. For their termination would have proved his very point.

2. It has been maintained that some sacrifice *did* continue after 70.[17] But a recent Jewish investigator sums up the situation thus:[18]

> Although scattered evidence points to the presence of private sacrifices after the fall of the Temple, at least sporadically, . . . the Halakhah presupposes the

[12] *INT* II, 320–3, 337f.

[13] *HDB* II, 337.

[14] *No Stone on Another*, 467; W. Manson, op. cit., 55f., inclines in the same direction, saying that the argument 'should not be dismissed'.

[15] *Ant.* 3.224–57; cf. *Contra Apion.* 2.77 and 193–8.

[16] I Clem. 41.2; Ep. Barn. 7f.; Ep. Diognet. 3. But for the date of I Clement in this connection, cf. pp. 329f. below.

[17] K. W. Clark, 'Worship in the Jerusalem Temple after AD 70', *NTS* 6, 1959–60, 269–80. But his use of Hebrews, 'written in the reign of Domitian' (275f.), as *evidence* for this is clearly circular.

[18] A. Guttmann, 'The End of the Jewish Sacrificial Cult', *HUCA* 38, 1967, 137–48 (140).

cessation of these. . . . The Talmudic evidence for the cessation of the public sacrifices after 70 CE is crystal clear.

Schürer,[19] after investigating the indications to the contrary, is unequivocal:

In an enumeration of Israel's black days it is stated simply that 17 Tammuz saw the end of the daily sacrifice;[20] and there is nowhere any mention of its being subsequently restored. . . . When Christian writers and Josephus, long after the destruction of the Temple, speak in the present tense of the offerings of sacrifice, they are merely describing what was lawful, not what was actually practised. Precisely the same happens in the Mishnah, from the first page to the last, in that all legally valid statutes are presented as current usage, even when as a result of prevailing circumstances their performance was impossible.

But even if there were residual attempts to perpetuate the system, it is surely extraordinary that the body-blow that effectively finished it should have left no impact on the epistle. Above all, whatever else happened, the succession to the high priestly office was unquestionably terminated, and it is difficult to believe that this would not have left some trace on the argument of 7.11–28, which contrasts Christ's high priesthood, which remains for ever, with that which in order to keep going requires continual replacement and daily repetition. If the latter had in fact failed to be replaced, it is hard to think that this would have gone unobserved.

3. It is said, with truth, that in discussing the details of the 'material sanctuary' (9.1–7) the writer is describing not Herod's temple but the scriptural blue-print of outer and inner 'tents' on which the later structure was modelled.[21] It is these two chambers that he means by the first and second tents. When therefore he remarks that it is 'symbolic of the present time' that 'the first tent still stands' (9.8f.),[22] he is referring not to the continued existence of the Jerusalem temple but to the externality of the ordinances at present in force (9.10). Nevertheless, he sees these arrangements as temporary 'until the time of reformation' (9.10). They belong to the first covenant; and 'by speaking of a second covenant' God 'has pronounced the first one old; and anything that is growing old and ageing will shortly disappear' (8.13). If it *had* disappeared it is surely incredible that he

19 *HJP* I, 522f.

20 Mishnah, *Taan.* 4.6. The reference is to August 70; cf. Josephus, *BJ* 6.94.

21 Cf. the diagrams and discussion in Buchanan, *Hebrews*, 140–5; and Josephus, *BJ* 5, 184–236.

22 The NEB's translation 'the earlier tent' in 9.8 is misleading. It is the same phrase (ἡ πρώτη σκηνή) rendered 'the first tent' in v.6, and if a paraphrase is needed it should be, as in the RSV in both instances, 'the outer tent'.

would not have used this fact to rub in what he says in his 'main point', namely, that the shadow *must* soon give way to the reality (8.1–13). Moreover, though, for the purpose of his allegory, he is talking of the tent rather than the temple, it is clear that he is not merely indulging in abstract argument. For the one is symbolic of the other, and when he insists that 'our altar is one from which the priests who serve the tent have no right to eat' (13.10) there can be no real doubt as to whom he is referring.[23] As Schlatter correctly expressed it,[24]

> It is true that the writer based his warnings not on what actually went on at Jerusalem, but on the utterances of scripture. He expounded 'the Law'. For it was not what the Jew did, but what God commanded – not Jewish practice, but the will of God – which justified the action and made necessary the sacrifice which the author required of the Jewish Christians. . . . But the author to the Hebrews was not . . . so completely immersed in his texts as to forget contemporary conditions and happenings altogether. Every word is written with an eye on the situation of his readers, and they would hardly have been indifferent as to whether the Temple was still standing and the priests still officiating; or whether the Temple had been destroyed and the sacrificial worship had ceased.[25]

The nearest parallel to the Epistle to the Hebrews in early Christian literature is the Epistle of Barnabas,[26] whose theme too is the relationship of Christianity to the ritual ordinances of Judaism. It makes the point explicitly that the temple was destroyed by the Romans as a consequence of the Jewish rebellion (16.4). Had this event occurred by the time that Hebrews was written, it would have dotted the i's and crossed the t's of everything its author was labouring to prove. For, as Athanasius was to put it centuries later,[27]

> It is a sign, and an important proof, of the coming of the Word of God, that Jerusalem no longer stands. . . . For . . . when the truth was there, what need any more of the shadow? . . . And this was why Jerusalem stood till then – namely, that they [the Jews] might be exercised in the types as a preparation for the reality.

[23] So, emphatically, G. A. Barton, 'The Date of the Epistle to the Hebrews', *JBL* 57, 1938, 195–207. H. Koester, '"Outside the Camp": Hebrews 13.9–14', *HTR* 55, 1962, 299–315, argues that it refers not to the Jewish priesthood but to any, including Christians, who rely on cultic and ritual performances for salvation. But I do not find him at all convincing at this point.

[24] *The Church in the New Testament Period*, 240f.

[25] Cf. Montefiore, *Hebrews*, 3: 'After the destruction of the Jewish Temple in AD 70, and the consequent cessation of the high priesthood, it is inconceivable that the author of Hebrews should have written with such indifference to what actually happened.' Similarly M. Dods, *Hebrews*, *EGT* IV, 243; T. W. Manson, op. cit., 251f.; Spicq, *Hébreux* I, 254–7.

[26] For the dating of this, cf. pp. 313–9 below.

[27] *De Incarn.* 40.

The argument from silence can of course prove nothing. In this case, however, it can create what I believe is a very strong presumption. The burden of proof must rest on those who would date the epistle after 70. But the actual date must depend on closer examination of the positive indications in the epistle itself.

The very fact that commentators have differed so widely on both date and place makes it clear that there is nothing that points conclusively to any single solution. The one thing that is clear (for once) is the upper limit on dating. For Hebrews is quoted without question in I Clement (36.2–5, which cites excerpts from Heb. 1.3–13) and practically no one wishes to put I Clement later than 96. The reign of Domitian is therefore the *terminus ad quem*, as well as being for most the *terminus a quo* (e.g. Kümmel). But the reign of Nero is also favoured (e.g. Guthrie), and Montefiore has recently argued for that of Claudius. Of the three most recently discussed destinations, Rome (Kümmel and Guthrie, on balance), Jerusalem (Buchanan) and Corinth (Montefiore), Rome is not even listed as a possibility by Montefiore, Jerusalem is the one place 'certainly' ruled out by Kümmel,[28] while Buchanan is prepared to consider no alternative!

The first issue upon which a judgment has to be made is the integrity of the epistle. As B. F. Westcott recognized long ago,[29] 'the thirteenth chapter is a kind of appendix to the Epistle, like Rom. 15 and 16'. It converts what would otherwise be (and what may have started as) a homily into a letter.

That this last chapter is a postscript is not seriously in doubt. The only questions are whether it was written to the same persons as the main body of the epistle and by the same author. In the case of Romans, cited as a parallel by Westcott, there is more than enough manuscript confusion to suggest that ch. 16 and possibly ch. 15 may have been composed for separate recensions or recipients – though no one doubts Pauline authorship, except for the closing doxology of 16.25–7.[30] Yet even so the balance would seem in the end to be in favour of the integrity of the entire epistle down at any rate to 16.23. In the case of Hebrews 13 there is not the slightest sign in the manuscript tradition that it did not originally belong with the rest. And though the level of writing is, naturally, different as it moves from sermon to correspondence, there is no evidence for a change of style.

[28] *INT*, 399. For the powerful arguments against Jerusalem, cf. Zahn, *INT* II, 342f.; Guthrie, *NTI*, 712.

[29] B. F. Westcott, *Hebrews*, 1889, 429.

[30] *Perhaps* added by disciples of Marcion to round off the epistle when he truncated it at the end of chapter 14.

Kümmel says summarily, 'Nothing suggests the addition of a conclusion by another hand.'[31] The allusions in 13.10–16 (to the tent and the high priest, the blood of Jesus, and the city which is to come) echo the themes of the rest of the epistle, and F. V. Filson has made this unity the subject of an entire study.[32] The arguments for separation put forward by Buchanan[33] depend on internal contradictions to his own, I believe, quite implausible thesis that in chs. 1–12 the physical city of Jerusalem is, for the author and his readers, the location of the heavenly city,[34] whereas in ch. 13[35] it is not. We may safely, therefore, use what hints there are in ch. 13 as evidence for the dating and destination of the whole.

A tantalizing clue to the location of the readers is given in the laconic message of 13.24, which should probably be translated: 'Those who come from Italy (οἱ ἀπὸ τῆς Ἰταλίας) greet you.' It could be understood – as it has been[36] – as a greeting from Italy. But in a letter, say, from London to a congregation abroad it would hardly be natural to write 'those from England' (i.e. all Englishmen) send their greetings. It would be more natural in a letter *to* London for the Englishmen with the writer to join him in sending their love to those back home. Montefiore[37] (who holds that the epistle was written to Corinth from Ephesus) thinks that it refers to neither, but to Aquila and Priscilla, who are specifically said to have arrived in Corinth originally 'from Italy' (Acts 18.2) and whose greetings Paul also sends from Ephesus to Corinth in I Cor. 16.9. This indeed is quite possible, though the anonymity is odd when the couple are named so freely elsewhere. However, as we have seen, greetings are sent to them also in Ephesus (II Tim. 4.19) and in Rome (Rom. 16.3), where they had a house and were evidently as well known as in Corinth. In fact the most natural supposition to be drawn from the message, that the letter was sent to Rome, is the one, I believe, that yields the most fruitful results. When it is made, a good deal else falls into place. All that we can expect

[31] *INT*, 397.

[32] F. V. Filson, *Yesterday: A Study of Hebrews in the Light of Chapter 13* (SBT 2.4), 1967; cf. R. V. G. Tasker, 'The Integrity of the Epistle to the Hebrews', *ExpT* 47, 1935–6, 136–8; C. Spicq, 'L'Authenticité du chapitre XIII de l'Épître aux Hébreux', *CN* 11, 1947, 226–36.

[33] *Hebrews*, ad loc.

[34] He takes 'you have come to mount Sion' (12.22) literally of a migration of *diaspora* Jews to Jerusalem to await the *parousia*.

[35] In 13.14 'we have *here* no abiding city' is taken to refer to the city of Jerusalem.

[36] So e.g. Spicq, *Hébreux* I, 261–5.

[37] *Hebrews*, ad loc.; cf. F. Lo Bue, 'The Historical Background of the Epistle to the Hebrews', *JBL* 75, 1956, 52–7.

here is not a conclusive demonstration but a hypothesis that gives the most reasonable explanation for the largest amount of the data. I am persuaded that the one that does this is that which postulates that the epistle was written to a group or synagogue of Jewish Christians[38] within the church of Rome[39] in the late 60s.

We may start from the quite extraordinary severity of tone with regard to those who fall away after baptism.

> For when men have once been enlightened, when they have had a taste of the heavenly gift and a share in the Holy Spirit, when they have experienced the goodness of God's word and the spiritual energies of the age to come, and after all this have fallen away, it is impossible to bring them again to repentance; for with their own hands they are crucifying again the Son of God and making mock of his death (6.4–6; NEB margin).

There are similar passages of equal severity in 10.26–31 and 12.15–29.

This language is unparalleled in the New Testament and indeed outside it until the Novatianist controversy over the lapsed at the time of the Decian persecution in 250. It is explicable surely only if it is occasioned not by everyday post-baptismal failure but, as later, by apostasy under exceptional and dangerous circumstances, involving the betrayal of fellow-Christians. The only situation in the first century which would fit this for which we have evidence is the Neronian persecution in Rome. Describing it, Tacitus, it will be recalled, spoke of the 'information' given by those who confessed which led to the conviction of their fellow-believers. Clement, reflecting on the same sad story from the Christian side, speaks of

> a vast multitude of the elect, who through many indignities and tortures, being the victims of jealousy, set a brave example among ourselves (I Clem. 6.1).

And he attributes the persecution and death of the pillars of the church, Peter and Paul, to the same jealousy, envy and strife (I

[38] With Westcott long ago (*Hebrews*, xxxv), I find it hard to take too seriously the widely canvassed suggestion that it was addressed to Gentiles (e.g. H. von Soden, *Hebräerbrief*, Freiburg 1899; E. F. Scott, *The Epistle to the Hebrews: Its Doctrine and Significance*, Edinburgh 1922; J. Moffatt, *Hebrews* [ICC], Edinburgh 1924). Buchanan's commentary has the merit of bringing out once again the depth of immersion in rabbinic and sectarian Judaism presupposed both in the author and his audience. As F. F. Bruce says, *PCB*, 1008, 'Had they been Gentile Christians who were inclined to lapse, their only response to such an argument as "Now if perfection had been obtainable through the Levitical priesthood . . ." (7.11) would have been: "We never thought it was!"' Cf. W. Manson, *Hebrews*, 18–23, who also makes the point that there are no signs of Jew-Gentile conflict or of pagan aberrations.

[39] So also e.g. Harnack, Zahn, Jülicher, Dods, Edmundson, Peake, W. Manson, F. F. Bruce and Filson.

Clem. 5). In the course of an extended discussion, Cullmann comments:[40]

> This in the context of our letter can only mean that they were victims of jealousy from persons who counted themselves members of the Christian Church. In saying this we naturally do not mean that they were martyred or perhaps murdered by other Christians, but that the magistrates were encouraged by the attitude of some members of the Christian Church, and perhaps by the fact that they turned informers, to take action against others.

The author of the Shepherd of Hermas, also written from Rome, appears to allude some years later[41] to the same crisis and to the divisions it evoked, and in phrases that seem to have attracted remarkably little notice in this connection he echoes many of the reactions of the writer to the Hebrews, without (unlike Clement) giving any direct quotation. He speaks of those who had suffered 'stripes, imprisonments, great tribulations, crosses, wild beasts, for the Name's sake' (Vis. 3.2.1), but talks too of those who had been double-minded,[42] betrayed parents and denied their Lord (Vis. 2.2.2). He refers to 'the renegades and traitors to the Church that blasphemed the Lord in their sins, and still further were ashamed of the Name of the Lord, which was invoked upon them' (Sim. 8.6.4). Some were 'mixed up in business and cleaved not to the saints'; being divided in their loyalties (Sim. 8.8.1) they caused dissensions (Sim. 8.8.5). 'But some of them altogether stood aloof. These have no repentance; for by reason of their business affairs they blasphemed the Lord and denied him' (Sim. 8.8.2). They were 'betrayers of the servants of God. For these there is no repentance, but there is death' (Sim. 9.19.1). Yet Hermas is prepared to give each group the benefit of the doubt, and even 'for those who denied him a long time ago repentance seemeth to be possible' (Sim. 9.26.6). In his vision all those who 'suffered for the name of the Son of God' had their 'sins . . . taken away' (Sim. 9.28.3) – even though the fruit of their actions was reduced by their vacillation. Looking back, he pictures vividly the various sections under pressure:

> As many . . . as were tortured and denied not, when brought before the magistracy, but suffered readily, these are the more glorious in the sight of the Lord; their fruit is that which surpasseth. But as many as became cowards, and were lost in uncertainty, and considered in their hearts whether they should deny or confess, and yet suffered, their fruits are less, because this design entered into

[40] *Peter*, 89–109 (102).

[41] For the first-century dating of this document and the reasons for thinking that it refers to the Neronian persecution, see below pp. 319–22.

[42] διψυχία (with its cognates διψυχέω and δίψυχος) is the great enemy for Hermas, who returns to it constantly. It is also attacked in I and II Clement.

their heart; for this design is evil, that a servant should deny his own lord (Sim. 9.28.4).

This same setting appears to fit the concern of the writer to the Hebrews, with his grave warnings to 'see to it that there is no one among you that forfeits the grace of God, no bitter, noxious weed growing up to poison the whole' (12.15)[43] and his exhortations not to be 'among those who shrink back and are lost' (10.39) but, like the Lord himself (3.1; 4.14), to be 'firm and unswerving in the confession of our hope' (10.23). If then tentatively we make this identification, it may illuminate other phrases in the epistle which, while not demanding this reference, would certainly suit it.

In 13.7 the writer says:

> Remember your leaders, those who first spoke[44] God's message to you; and reflecting upon the outcome of their life and work, follow the example of their faith.

The word translated 'outcome' (ἔκβασιν) is ambiguous, but it is most natural to take it to mean death, as in the closely reminiscent description of the righteous man in Wisd. 2.17–20:

> Let us test the truth of his words, let us see what will happen to him in the end (πειράσωμεν τὰ ἐν ἐκβάσει αὐτοῦ); for if the just man is God's son, God will stretch out a hand to him and save him from the clutches of his enemies. Outrage and torment are the means to try him with, to measure his forbearance and learn how long his patience lasts. Let us condemn him to a shameful death, for on his own showing he will have a protector.

Similarly our author, like Clement, could be appealing here to the 'notable pattern of patient endurance' set by the leaders of the Roman church, and in particular 'the good apostles' Peter and Paul (I Clem. 5). It is to be observed that the use of the word 'leaders' or 'chief leaders' to designate the ministry of the Christian church is confined to documents associated with Rome[45] – though obviously the terms are too general for any specific conclusion.

The writer's reiterated plea is for 'firmness to the end' (Heb. 3.14)

[43] Cf. P. S. Minear, *The Obedience of Faith*, 1971, ix, who says of the Roman church: 'All the evidence points to the existence of several congregations separated from each other by sharp mutual suspicions.' The seeds of this are already evident in Rom. 14.1–15.13, where the tensions and recriminations between those who eat meat and those who do not could be reflected in the 'scruples about what we eat' in Heb. 13.9. Cf. also W. Manson, op. cit., 172–84.

[44] The word 'first' is not in the Greek: it is only a possible implication of the aorist ἐλάλησαν.

[45] ἡγούμενοι: Heb. 13.7,17, 24; I Clem. 1.3; προηγούμενοι: I Clem. 21.6; Hermas, Vis. 2.2.6; 3.9.7.

in the face of 'testing'. For this he appeals not only to the 'day of testing' in the wilderness (3.8f.) and to the Old Testament heroes of faith (especially 11.17,36f.) but supremely to Jesus:

> For since he himself has passed through the test of suffering, he is able to help those who are meeting their test now (2.18).

> For ours is not a high priest unable to sympathize with our weaknesses, but one who has been tested every way, as we are, only without sin (4.15, NEB margin).

> Think of him who submitted to such opposition from sinners: that will help you not to lose heart and grow faint (12.3).

He goes on in this last passage:

> In your struggle against sin, you have not yet resisted to the point of shedding your blood (12.4).

In other words (as is clear from the association of blood with death throughout the epistle), their community had not yet had its martyr. And, reading between the lines, we may hear the suggestion that they had been holding back and standing apart while others paid the supreme penalty. Yet it was not always thus:

> Remember the days gone by, when, newly enlightened, you met the challenge of great sufferings and held firm. Some of you were abused and tormented to make a public show, while others stood loyally by those who were so treated. For indeed you shared the sufferings of the prisoners, and you cheerfully accepted the seizure of your possessions, knowing that you possessed something better and more lasting (10.32–4).

But now they have to be reminded of their solidarity with their fellow Christians:

> Remember those in prison as if you were there with them; and those who are being maltreated, for like them you are still in the world (13.3).[46]

What this earlier occasion was when they were 'abused and tormented to make a public show', it is impossible to say with certainty. At first sight indeed it might seem to be referring to the Neronian persecution itself; and this is one of the arguments used by those who wish to date Hebrews much later. The phrase 'the former days' (τὰς πρότερον ἡμέρας) is entirely vague and the implication '*newly* enlightened', though probable, is again only read into the aorist φωτισθέντες. Yet the contrast is clear between their response then and

[46] Cf. I Peter 5.9: 'Remember that your brother Christians are going through the same kinds of suffering while they are in the world'. For the parallels between I Peter and Hebrews, arising, I believe, out of their common context and temporal proximity, cf. Selwyn, *I Peter*, 363–6.

now, and the appeal appears to be the same as that of the seer of Revelation to the church at Ephesus: 'I have this against you: you have lost your early love' (Rev. 2.4). There is no suggestion that at that time anyone was actually killed. Indeed this is implicitly denied by the fact that they still have not resisted to the point of bloodshed – for *then* they shared everything that was going. Reference to the Neronian terror would seem therefore to be positively excluded. Public exposure to abuse, torment, imprisonment and dispossession is all that is mentioned. This could well describe the sort of anti-semitic upsurge that led to the expulsion of the Jews from Rome in 49, perhaps as a result of disturbances caused by the preaching of Christ – if indeed this is the meaning of Suetonius' notoriously ambiguous 'impulsore Chresto assidue tumultuantes'.[47] This identification of the earlier crisis to which the author of Hebrews alludes is made by W. Manson, who writes:

> The Jews were protected by the privilege of *religio licita* so long as they kept the peace, and this privilege they had forfeited by their intra-synagogal disputes. The most plausible explanation of the whole episode is that Christian propaganda had been introduced into the synagogues at Rome and had created considerable ferment.[48]

If so, then the writer seems to be looking back to the 40s, when these Christian Jews could have been among those converted by the mission preaching of Peter and Mark. And this would fit with an earlier passage where the author appears to link himself with his readers in attributing their Christianity to those who themselves had heard Jesus:

> We are bound to pay all the more heed to what we have been told for fear of drifting from our course. . . . For this deliverance was first announced through the lips of the Lord himself; those who heard him confirmed it to us (2.1–3).

If we ask why now they were holding back from 'love and active goodness' and 'staying away' from assembling with their fellow Christians (10.24f.),[49] we may recall that in his description of the persecutions Hermas speaks of those who 'were mixed up in business and cleaved not to the saints'; they 'stood aloof . . . by reason of their business affairs' (Sim. 8.8.1f.); 'from desire of gain they played the hypocrite' (Sim. 9.19.3). 'Some of them' he sees in his vision 'are wealthy and others are entangled in many business affairs'; and the wealthy 'unwillingly cleave to the servants of God, fearing lest they

47 *Claud.* 25.4. 48 Op. cit., 41; cf. 71.

49 With the ἐπισυναγωγή here cf. the continuing use of συναγωγή for Christian worship in Hermas, Mand. 11.9.13f.

may be asked for something by them' (Sim. 9.20.1f.).

Those addressed in Hebrews were also evidently men of possessions (10.34), with a generous record of Christian aid (6.10). But now they have to be told: 'Do not live for money; be content with what you have' (13.5), and 'Share what you have with others' (13.16). The writer's metaphors too seem calculated to appeal to those who thought naturally in terms of profit and loss. God himself is a 'wage-payer' (μισθαποδότης) (11.6), and this word or its cognates appears four times in Hebrews and nowhere else in biblical literature. Moses, he says, had 'his eyes . . . fixed upon the coming day of recompense' (ἀπέβλεψεν εἰς τὴν μισθαποδοσίαν), when he reckoned 'the stigma that rests on God's Anointed greater wealth than the treasures of Egypt' (11.26), and the readers are commended for having made the same calculation (10.35). His main metaphor for salvation is drawn not, as with Jesus, from the family, nor, as with Paul, from the courts, but from the world of property: coming into, or getting possession of, an inheritance (1.2,4,14; 6.12, 17; 9.15; 11.7f.; 12.17). Even obedience to their leaders is commended in the language of commerce: 'Obey your leaders . . . as men who must render an account' (λόγον ἀποδώσοντες).[50] 'Let it be a happy task for them, and not pain and grief, for that would bring you no profit' (ἀλυσιτελές, again, uniquely here in biblical literature) (13.17). We are unlikely to be wrong then in guessing that (not for the first or last time) the Jewish community in Rome had a strong business sense, which was reflected in its Christian members. Their temptation was to allow racial and economic connections to outweigh the commitment of their Christian faith.[51] In W. Manson's phrase, they sought to shelter under the 'protective colouring' of the *religio licita* of Judaism.[52] Our author's appeal to them is to prefer like Moses (11.25) 'hardship with the people of God' to the solidarities of this world:

[50] Cf. Luke 16.2 of the unjust steward; and again Hermas, Vis. 3.9.4–10: 'This exclusiveness therefore is hurtful to you that have and do not share with them that are in want. . . . Look ye therefore, children, lest these divisions of yours deprive you of life. . . . Have peace among yourselves, that I also may . . . give an account concerning you all to your Lord'; and Mand. 2.4f.

[51] We suggested earlier that it was the refusal of the Jewish-Christian businessman Onesiphorus when in Rome to be 'ashamed' to seek out one shut up like a common criminal (II Tim. 1.16–18; 2.9) that so impressed Paul.

[52] That there was pressure also on Jews throughout the empire at this time (66–70) to close ranks in face of the common enemy in Palestine must certainly have been true, but I fail to find with Nairne, *Epistle of Priesthood*, 207, evidence of a Palestinian milieu or any specific allusion to the Jewish war. The troubles in Rome are enough to fill the picture.

Jesus also suffered outside the gate.... Let us then go to him outside the camp,[53] bearing the stigma that he bore. For here we have no permanent home, but we are seekers after the city which is to come (13.12–14).

That the contrast between the two cities, 'here' and 'to come' related to what was for the Roman world 'the city'[54] *par excellence* is perhaps reinforced by a further interesting passage from the Shepherd of Hermas. Without actually quoting the epistle, he suggests some remarkably parallel ideas. He is again addressing those who are in spiritual danger from excessive material attachments:

Ye know that ye, who are the servants of God, are dwellers in a foreign land;[55] for your city is far from this city [i.e. Rome]. If then ye know your city, in which ye shall dwell, why do ye here prepare fields and expensive displays and buildings and dwelling-chambers which are superfluous? He, therefore, that prepareth these things for this city does not purpose to return to his own city.[56] O foolish and double-minded and miserable man, perceivest thou not that all these things are foreign, and are under the power of another? For the lord of this city shall say, 'I do not wish thee to dwell in my city; go forth from this city,[57] for thou dost not conform to my laws.' Thou, therefore, who hast fields and dwellings and many other possessions, when thou art cast out by him,[58] what wilt thou do with thy field and thy house and all the other things that thou preparest for thyself? For the lord of this country saith to thee justly, 'Either conform to my laws, or depart from my country.' What then shalt thou do, who art under law in thine own city? For the sake of thy fields and the rest of thy possessions wilt thou altogether repudiate thy law, and walk according to the law of this city? Take heed, lest it be inexpedient to repudiate thy law; for if thou shouldest desire to return again to thy city, thou shalt surely not be received [because thou didst repudiate the law of thy city], and shalt be shut out from it. Take heed therefore; as dwelling in a strange land prepare nothing more for thyself but a competency which is sufficient for thee, and make ready that, whensoever the master of this city may desire to cast thee out for thine opposition to his law, thou mayest go forth from his city and depart into thine own city, and use thine own law joyfully, free from all insult (Sim. 1.1–6).

None of this adds up to proof that Hebrews was addressed to Rome in the late 60s, but if this is so it could possibly throw some light on the curious phrase in 6.6, that those who apostasize 'crucify the Son

[53] For *possible* echoes of the 'synagogue of the Hebrews' and the 'campus Judaeorum' outside the *Porta Portese* in Rome, cf. Edmundson, *The Church in Rome*, 155. For the ancient tradition behind the title πρὸς Ἑβραίους, cf. Zahn, *INT* II, 293–8.

[54] Cf. the contrast between 'the great city' and 'the heavenly city' of Rev. 16–18 and 21–2. There is also of course the contrast for the writers of both the Apocalypse and the epistle to the Hebrews between the earthly Jerusalem and the heavenly. Paul too makes use of both contrasts: Phil. 3.20; Gal. 4.25f.

[55] Cf. Heb. 11.9,13; and if originally also addressed, we have argued, to citizens of Rome, I Peter 1.11, 'I beg you, as aliens in a foreign land'; and later Ep. Diognet. 5f.

[56] Cf. Heb. 11.15f. [57] Cf. Heb. 11.8,10. [58] Cf. Heb. 10.34.

of God again' (ἀνασταυροῦντας; NEB margin). At least this is the translation (rather than simply 'crucify', as non-biblical usage would suggest) which the context seems to demand and which the ancient versions and the Greek fathers support. Without, obviously, being able to demonstrate its historicity, Edmundson makes the interesting suggestion that this may reflect the well-known 'Quo Vadis?' legend about Peter seeking to save his life by leaving the city.

> As he went out of the gate he saw the Lord entering Rome; and when he saw him he said, 'Lord, whither (goest thou) here?' And the Lord said to him, 'I am coming to Rome to be crucified.' And Peter said to him, 'Lord, art thou being crucified again?' He said to him 'Yes, Peter, I am being crucified again.'[59]

The solemn words of the author to the Hebrews, says Edmundson,[60]

> recalling, as they did, the very words which had caused Peter to turn back and welcome martyrdom, would strike home to the hearts and consciences of any waverers that heard them. For the *Quo Vadis?* story, if in any sense historical, must have been widely known from the first.

Behind this tradition, he suggests, lies the dialogue recorded in John 13.36f.:

> Simon Peter said to him, 'Lord, where are you going?' Jesus replied, 'Where I am going you cannot follow me now, but one day you will.' Peter said, 'Lord, why cannot I follow you now? I will lay down my life for you.'

And he adds:

> Two questions at once come into the mind: (1) Was the echo of those words haunting Peter's memory when he saw the vision? (2) Did his knowledge of the cause of Peter's voluntary return to death move the Fourth Evangelist to insert those verses in his narrative? Possibly both questions should be answered in the affirmative.

For a further echo is to be found in the allusion to Peter's death by crucifixion in John 21.18f., which we shall have occasion to argue[61] comes from the period immediately after it. If Hebrews comes from the same period, there is no reason why it too should not carry overtones of the same tradition. Clearly nothing can be built on this, but that the epistle reflects the deaths of Peter and Paul (cf. 13.7) is, as we have seen, on other grounds the most likely hypothesis. Edmundson supposes Paul still to have been alive, but for no good reason that I can see. Some reference to him in Rome would surely have been expected, especially since the author evidently comes from the Pauline circle and gives news of the release of 'our friend' Timothy as of special joy to his readers (13.23).

[59] *Acta Petr.* 35; Hennecke, *NT Apoc.* II, 317f.
[60] Op. cit., 153. [61] Pp. 279–82 below.

The precise dating is again hampered by our uncertain knowledge of just when the two apostles died. But as an estimate we suggested 65 for Peter and 66+ for Paul. Unlike the book of Revelation, the epistle to the Hebrews shows no sign of the relief or rejoicing brought by the suicide of Nero in June 68. We may therefore date it tentatively *c*. 67.[62]

The question of authorship, more vexed and elusive here than in the case of any other New Testament document, is in principle separable and does not affect the dating. Yet it is clear that if *we* do not know who the author was the recipients of the epistle did. His identity is therefore of a piece with the entire situation to which he writes. For the epistle is composed not as an abstract theological discourse but as an urgent pastoral plea. The doctrinal exposition, however impressively argued for its own sake, is set in the context of frequent and extended warnings and encouragements (2.1–4; 3.7–4.11; 4.12–16; 5.11–6.12; 10.19–39; 12.1–13.25), born of long spiritual knowledge of and care for his readers, though he makes no claim to have been their only or their original evangelist. And he ends with the hope of being 'restored' to them (13.19). If then any light can be shed on the author, it must help to fill in and confirm the picture of the destination and date.

Origen may have said the last word on the subject when he made his famous remark, 'But who wrote the epistle, in truth, God knows.'[63] Yet this did not stop him recording guesses, which have persisted into modern times. One of the more intriguing was Harnack's conjecture of Aquila and Priscilla,[64] which sought to make capital out of the

[62] Spicq, *Hébreux* I, 257–61, also reaches the date of 67, but on the basis of similarities with the gospel apocalypses reflecting, as he supposes, the Jewish war. W. Manson, op. cit., 162–70, who argues for the same destination as we have, plumps for a date of *c*. 60, on the ground that 12.4 ('You have not yet resisted to the point of shedding your blood') implies that the Neronian persecution had not yet taken place. Yet we know of nothing as early as 60, in Rome or elsewhere, which would account for the grim crisis to which Hebrews alludes. He dismisses the argument that the readers had lain low during the attack: 'Had the group addressed been guilty of such dissembling under the colour of the Jewish religion, it is inconceivable that fuller notice would not have been taken of it by the writer. We should have expected the infamy to resound through every page of his letter' (165). Though 'infamy resounding' may be too strong an expression, it seems to me that this is precisely what we do get.

[63] Quoted by Eusebius, *HE* 6.25.14.

[64] A. Harnack, 'Probabilia über die Addresse und den Verfasser des Hebräerbriefs', *ZNW* 1, 1900, 16–41. It was trenchantly criticized by Zahn soon afterwards (*INT* II, 365f.), but adopted by Dods, *EGT* IV, 228, and A. S. Peake, *Hebrews*, Edinburgh 1914, 36–8.

alternation between 'we' (2.5; 5.11; 6.1,3,9,11; 13.18) and 'I' (11.32; 13.19,22f.) to designate the author (though why is only one of them planning to make the visit, and which?) and argued that prejudice against women teachers in the church led to the suppression of the names (though why not only of hers?).[65] Much more plausible is Luther's guess of Apollos,[66] which has recently been built by Montefiore[67] into an argument for a very early date indeed. He believes that Apollos is addressing that section of the Corinthian church which was looking to him as their man (I Cor. 1.12; 3.4–6) and that the epistle was written prior to I Corinthians, which he thinks takes up its arguments. But apart from anything else, the time available is extremely short. Paul, as we have seen, was first in Corinth from late 49 to the latter part of 51. Apollos did not arrive there until after Paul left (Acts 18.24–19.1), let us say, early in 52. If I Corinthians was written in the spring of 55, the epistle to the Hebrews could not have been composed later than 54. While arguments for the time required for development are notoriously subjective, two to three years at most is a very brief period for so much to have happened. It is reasonable to expect that they should by then have progressed from the rudiments of Christianity to maturity and become teachers of others (5.12–6.3), for Paul uses the same argument in I Cor. 3.1–4. Instead, however, they have fallen into serious danger of relapse, apostasy and 'all sorts of outlandish teachings' (2.1–13; 3.12–14; 5.11–6.12; 10.23–39; 12.3, 12–17; 13.7–9), of which there is little or no trace in I Corinthians. Above all there is the appeal to 'remember the days gone by' when they were 'newly enlightened' (10.32) when their response to persecution was so different from what it is now. Then we are faced with what we are to make of the 'outcome' of their leaders' life and faith (13.7). A longer perspective seems indicated. Moreover, though the qualifications of Apollos as 'a Jew, . . . an Alexandrian by birth, an eloquent (or learned) man, powerful in his use of the scriptures' (Acts 18.24) are most attractive, he, no more than Aquila and Priscilla, could as far as we know claim to have had the Christian message confirmed to him by those who had 'heard the Lord' (Heb. 2.3) – rather, in fact, the opposite (Acts 18.25f.). Moreover, if Apollos had been the author, we might have expected that Clement, who refers to Paul as having in his letter to the Corinthians charged them 'concerning himself and Cephas and Apollos' (I Clem. 47.1), would equally

[65] The writer of 11.32 (διηγούμενον) is certainly masculine.

[66] It has also been favoured by, among many others, Zahn, *INT* II, 356; T. W. Manson, op. cit., 254–8; and Spicq, *Hébreux* I, 209–19.

[67] *Hebrews*, 9–31.

have mentioned Apollos when he quotes *his* letter.[68] The church at Alexandria too would surely have preserved some memory of his association with the epistle as one of its most distinguished scions. Yet Clement of Alexandria and Origen regularly quote it as Paul's and Origen evidently knew of no guess linking it with Apollos. Finally there is nothing in the tradition to connect Apollos with Rome, if that is the situation addressed.

At this point it is worth considering seriously the evidence which Harnack favoured before he had his wild surmise,[69] and which was also supported strongly by Edmundson,[70] namely, the statement of Tertullian that the author of the epistle was Barnabas.[71] They both agree that this is the only attribution ancient or modern that does not ultimately rest upon guesswork. As we have seen,[72] Edmundson earlier argued the case[73] for supposing that Barnabas accompanied Peter on a visit to Rome, after they left Corinth,[74] following the death of Claudius in October 54. He is also prepared to give credence to the tradition that Barnabas was responsible for the conversion there of Clement. The author of the Clementine Recognitions, usually historically worthless, relates that Clement was converted in Rome by the preaching of Barnabas, who later at Caesarea introduced him to Peter.[75] As Edmundson says,

> the object of the author of the 'Recognitions' is to magnify the authority and orthodox teaching of Peter, so that the introduction here of Barnabas, who is never mentioned again, is purely gratuitous, and indeed inexplicable in such a narrative unless the fact recorded were one based on a received and ancient tradition too well known to be ignored.[76]

This would help to explain the association of this epistle with Clement, who not only evidently had an early and intimate acquaintance with it but was later one of those surmised, by those in the east who doubted its Paulinity, to have translated it[77] or even written it.[78] But in the west it was known from the beginning not to be Pauline – and therefore not regarded as having apostolic authority[79] or for a long

[68] So Peake, *Hebrews*, 35f.; W. Manson, op cit., 172.

[69] *Chron.*, 477–9. [70] Op. cit., 157–60.

[71] *De pudic.* 20. For the text and for further later evidence, cf. Edmundson, 157. A full list of those favouring this view (though overlooking Edmundson!) is given by Spicq, *Hébreux*, 199f.

[72] Pp. 113f. above. [73] Op. cit., 80–2.

[74] Cf. the mention in the same breath in I Cor. 9.5f. of both Peter and Barnabas as being known to the Corinthians.

[75] *Recog.* 1. 7–13. [76] Op. cit., 81.

[77] Eusebius, *HE* 3.38.1–3. [78] *HE* 6.25.14; Jerome, *De vir. ill.* 15.

[79] It is remarkable, as Edmundson says, that Hebrews was never cited by

time the right to a place in the canon.[80] Tertullian, much as it would have suited him to attribute it to Paul,

> quotes the epistle as the work of a man whose credentials are simply that he was a companion and fellow-worker with Apostles. But on the question of authorship there is not a sign that he was making an assertion about which there was any doubt. He assumes that his readers were aware of it and would admit it. In fact as he is inveighing, as a Montanist, against what he regarded as 'the lax discipline of the Church of Rome', he would not be likely to have quoted this passage [Heb. 6.4–6] in support of his argument as written by Barnabas, unless he knew that his opponents would not impugn his assertion.[81]

Edmundson goes on to argue that what the writer himself calls his 'word of exhortation' (13.22) fits admirably this Greek-speaking Cypriot Jew, with relatives in Jerusalem and a Levite by descent.[82] The nickname given him by the apostles meaning 'son of exhortation' (Acts 4.36), betokens one with a gift for this form of synagogue exposition,[83] or perhaps, as R. O. P. Taylor has argued,[84] the 'born' trouble-shooter, the 'one called in' (παράκλητος) to sort things out. For the letter is both a reprimand and an *eirenicon* (Heb. 12.14; 13.1, 20), from one who previously had proved himself a natural mediator in the church (Acts 9.26–30; 11.22–30; 15.22–39), with a view to healing a breach that had already inflicted such crippling damage on the Christian community in Rome. If we are right in supposing that one of the main 'roots' of this 'bitterness' (illustrated by the 'worldly-minded' Esau who 'sold his birthright for a single meal'; Heb. 12.15–17) was the temptation to allow business attachments to override Christian associations, Barnabas would have been exceptionally strongly placed to administer rebuke. Not only had he been a leader in a notable act of Christian sharing (Acts 11.29f.) to which he calls

---

Novatian at Rome or by Cyprian at Carthage in their controversy about the lapsed in the third century, to which 6.2–6 would have been particularly relevant.

[80] It is implicitly excluded by the Muratorian Canon which speaks of the 'seven' churches to which Paul wrote.

[81] Edmundson, op. cit., 158. Zahn, *INT* II, 302f., argues that this was Montanist tradition, but Edmundson's point still stands.

[82] The special connection of Hebrews with the thought of Philo of Alexandria which is the strongest point of Apollos' claim has of late been questioned, especially since the evidence of its common ground with Essene-type sectarian Judaism has broadened the field. Cf. R. R. Williamson, *Philo and the Epistle to the Hebrews*, Leiden 1970; and Buchanan, *Hebrews*.

[83] Cf. Acts 13.2,15; and also 11.23, where at Antioch Barnabas 'exhorted them all to hold fast to the Lord with resolute hearts' – very much the tenor of Hebrews.

[84] *The Groundwork of the Gospels*, 115–40.

his readers,[85] but from the first he had been prominent among those who had made 'the sacrifice of which God approves' (Heb. 13.16), of selling his estate and giving away the entire proceeds (Acts 4.34–7), thereby binding himself to work for his living (I Cor. 9.6).

The statement in Heb. 2.3 that 'those who heard [the Lord himself] confirmed it to us', which has quite illegitimately been taken to mean 'a second-generation Christian'[86] and therefore to argue a post-apostolic date, would suit Barnabas admirably. For he was among those in Jerusalem who had 'heard the message' from the apostles Peter and John (Acts 4.4) and in those pentecostal days had seen it 'confirmed' by God, who, as the writer says, 'added his testimony by signs, by miracles, by manifold works of power, and by distributing the gifts of the Holy Spirit at his own will' (Heb. 2.4). Moule[87] makes the same point, but applies it to Stephen. But I confess I do not see the close connection with the movement and theology of Stephen, for which W. Manson in particular argued.[88] Our author belongs to the Pauline circle, as the traditional attribution of his epistle attests, and as the reference to Timothy as his travelling companion shows (13.23). Yet Paul is not mentioned. Moreover, Timothy has apparently been in prison. We seem to be in a situation later than that of I and II Timothy or Philippians, for otherwise we might have expected this to be listed in Timothy's 'record . . . in the service of the Gospel' (Phil. 2.22). Where too the writer is we cannot tell, unless indeed it be (as Montefiore argued) in the Ephesus area, where both Apollos and Priscilla (included among 'those from Italy'?) and Timothy were last heard of (II Tim. 4.9–19). But that on our reckoning was nearly ten years earlier. Meanwhile the mantle of the Apostle has in part fallen upon the writer himself. He can address his readers with a pastoral authority superior to that of their own leaders and with a conscience clear of local involvement (Heb. 13.17f.), and yet with no personal claim to apostolic aegis. There cannot have been

[85] With the phrase *διακονήσαντες τοῖς ἁγίοις καὶ διακονοῦντες* in 6.10 cf. the expressions used by Paul of the collection for the saints at Jerusalem in I Cor. 16.15; II Cor. 8.4; 9.1,12f. Zahn, *INT* II, 317, 336, actually supposed the readers had taken part in this collection, but of this there is no evidence, and the present tense indicates a continuing commitment to which the author now recalls them. For the financial implications of *κοινωνία* in 13.16, cf. Rom. 12.13; 15.26f.; II Cor. 8.4; 9.13; Gal. 6.6; Phil. 4.15; I Tim. 6.18.

[86] So even Harnack, *Chron.*, 475; Spicq, *Hébreux* I, 201; and Kümmel, *INT*, 403.

[87] *Birth of the NT*, 76.

[88] Op. cit., ch. 2. Here I would agree with Kümmel, *INT*, 402, when he says 'there is not even more than occasional contact with the speech of Stephen in Acts 7'.

too many of such men around. With the entirely proper desire of the church to see that his work had a place in the canon, the crucial test of apostolicity subsequently required its ascription to Paul himself – though the churches of the west that knew it best knew otherwise. In compensation perhaps he himself became credited with that equally anonymous but much inferior homily on the same theme which we now know as the Epistle of Barnabas.[89]

Yet the date and occasion of the epistle to the Hebrews are ultimately independent of this or any other hypothesis of authorship, and for the purpose of our argument nothing hangs upon it. Whoever wrote it, it seems to belong to that uneasy interval between the deaths of Peter and Paul and that of Nero which will be directly relevant also to the dating of the two major books of the New Testament still outstanding, the Apocalypse and the gospel of St John, to which finally we must turn.

[89] For an instructive comparison and contrast, cf. Westcott, *Hebrews*, lxxx–lxxxiv.

VIII

The Book of Revelation

THE BOOK OF Revelation is unique among the New Testament writings in being dated in early tradition. Considering the large number of external testimonies to authorship, this fact alone is remarkable; though considering also how varied is the weight that can be attached to the testimonies to authorship, there is no good reason to suppose that this fact alone settles the issue. As always, the external testimony is only as strong as the internal and must be assessed critically. For what it is worth, however, the credit of this witness is good. Irenaeus, himself a native of Asia Minor, who claims to have known Polycarp who knew John,[1] writes in *c.* 180+ with regard to the name of the Beast in Rev. 13.18:

> If it had been necessary that his name should be publicly proclaimed at the present season, it would have been uttered by him who saw the Apocalypse. For it was seen no such long time ago, but almost in our own generation, at the end of the reign of Domitian.[2]

This is twice quoted by Eusebius,[3] who supplies us with the original Greek. The translation has been disputed by a number of scholars,[4] on the ground that it means that *he* (John) was seen; but this is very dubious.[5] One must assume that Irenaeus believed the Apocalypse to

[1] *Adv. haer.* 3.3.4, quoted Eusebius, *HE* 4.14.3–8; Letter to Florinus, quoted *HE* 5.20.4–8.

[2] *Adv. haer.* 5.30.3. Tr. Hort, *Apocalypse*, xivf.

[3] *HE* 3.18.2f.; 5.8.6.

[4] E.g. F. H. Chase, 'The Date of the Apocalypse: The Evidence of Irenaeus', *JTS* 8, 1907, 431–5. For other references, going back to J. J. Wettstein, *Novum Testamentum Graecum*, Amsterdam 1751, II, 746, cf. Moffatt, *ILNT*, 505; also Edmundson, *The Church in Rome*, 164f.

[5] In favour of it is the fact that earlier (*Adv. haer.* 5.30.1) Irenaeus has been appealing for the correct text of the number 666 to the testimony of 'those who

have come from *c.* 95, although unlike Eusebius he does not link it with Domitian's persecution nor specifically with his fourteenth year, of which Eusebius's *Chronicle* records: 'Persecution of Christians and under him the apostle John is banished to Patmos and sees his Apocalypse, as Irenaeus says.'

But before accepting this date at its face value one must recognize that Irenaeus is making three statements: (i) that the author of the Apocalypse and of the fourth gospel are one and the same person; (ii) that this person is the apostle John; and (iii) that the Apocalypse was seen at the end of Domitian's reign. There are few scholars who would accept all three statements, and many who would reject both the first two. Hort was able to accept the first two only because he rejected the third: 'It would be easier to believe that the Apocalypse was written by an unknown John than that both books belong alike to John's extreme old age.'[6] We may leave the question of authorship till we come to the relation of Revelation to the other Johannine writings. But whatever the relationship, it is difficult to credit that a work so vigorous as the Apocalypse could really be the product of a nonagenarian, as John the son of Zebedee must by then have been, even if he were as much as ten years younger than Jesus. So if Irenaeus' tradition on authorship is strong, his tradition on dating is weakened, and *vice versa*.

Even more difficult to attach to a Domitianic date is the tradition which Eusebius goes on to quote from Clement of Alexandria:[7]

> When on the death of the tyrant he removed from the island of Patmos to Ephesus, he used to go off, when requested, to the neighbouring districts of the Gentiles also, to appoint bishops in some places, to organize whole churches in others, in others again to appoint to an order some one of those who were indicated by the Spirit.

To illustrate the last Clement then tells the tale of a young man whom John persuaded the local bishop to sponsor and bring up as his

---

have seen John face to face', and this is cited in the immediately preceding paragraph by Eusebius in *HE* 5.8.5 – though Eusebius himself evidently takes it to refer to the date of the book in *HE* 3.18.3f. Against it is the fact that Irenaeus twice says that John lived to the reign of Trajan, and not merely Domitian (*Adv. haer.* 2.22.5; 3.3.4; quoted Eusebius, *HE* 3.23.3f.). The Greek is much more naturally taken to refer to the Apocalypse than the person. Moreover the Latin translation ('visum') is definitely against the person, though if referring to the Apocalypse it should be 'visa'. 'Visum' would have to refer to the 'nomen' of the Beast. Chase rather weakly argues that it is a corruption of 'visus'.

[6] *Apocalypse*, xl.

[7] *Quis div. salv.*? 42.1–15; Eusebius, *HE* 3.23.5–19.

protegé. The story covers a number of years, over which this youth went to the bad, and it ends with the apostle going to visit him on horseback and then chasing him 'with all his might'! All this is inconceivable after 96. Clement, however, nowhere mentions the name of 'the tyrant'. He could have been an earlier emperor: it is only Eusebius who identifies him with Domitian.

This is not of course to say that Eusebius was the source of this identification. Apart from quoting Irenaeus, he refers to 'the record of our ancient men'[8] (i.e. in all probability the *Memoirs* of Hegesippus)[9] for the tradition that 'the apostle John also took up his abode once more at Ephesus after his exile' under Domitian's successor Nerva. Moreover Victorinus,[10] who antedates Eusebius, says that John was 'condemned to the mines in Patmos by Domitian Caesar' where he saw his Apocalypse, which he published after being released upon the death of the emperor.

Yet the identification is by no means solid. Clement's disciple Origen writes in his *Commentary on Matthew*[11] that 'the emperor of the Romans, as tradition teaches, condemned John to the isle of Patmos', adding that John does not say who condemned him. This does not of course prove that Origen did not know, but the absence of a name is again to be noted, especially since Origen does name Herod as having beheaded John's brother James.

The fact that the condemnation is seen as the direct act of the emperor may link up with the tradition preserved earlier by Tertullian[12] that John's banishment was from Rome,[13]

> where Peter suffered a death like his Master [i.e., crucifixion], where Paul was crowned with the death of John [the Baptist] [i.e., execution],[14] where the apostle John, after being plunged in burning oil and suffering nothing, was banished to an island.

This is the only association in ancient tradition of John with Rome. Jerome[15] in quoting the passage interprets Tertullian to mean that

[8] *HE* 3.20.8f. [9] Cf. Lawlor and Oulton, op. cit., II, ad loc.

[10] *In Apoc.* 10.11. [11] *In Matt.* 20.22. [12] *Praescr.* 36.3.

[13] More vaguely but in the same sense Hippolytus, *De Chr. et Antichr.* 36, speaks of 'Babylon' having exiled him.

[14] 'Ubi Paulus Johannis exitu coronatur.' The translation follows that of P. de Labriolle in Tertullian, *Praescr.*, ed., R. F. Refoulé (Sources Chrétiennes 46), Paris 1957, which gives excellent sense. F. Oehler, ed., Leipzig 1854, ad loc., refers to his note on *Scorp.* 9 for the fact that in Tertullian 'exitus' regularly means 'death'. For a strong defence of Tertullian's reliability at this point by a fellow lawyer, cf. K. A. Eckhardt, *Der Tod des Johannes*, Berlin 1961, 73–9. I am grateful again to Bammel for calling my attention to this strange but erudite book.

[15] *Contra Jovin.* 1.26.

John's suffering, like that of Peter and Paul, occurred under *Nero* – despite his own acceptance from Eusebius' *Chronicle* of the Domitianic date.[16]

Epiphanius, a contemporary of Jerome's, whom Hort[17] describes as 'a careless and confused writer but deeply read in early Christian literature', refers to John's banishment and prophecy as having taken place under 'Claudius Caesar'[18] – though he also seems to imply that Claudius was emperor in John's extreme old age! Whatever Epiphanius may have meant, it has been credibly argued that his source may have intended Nero, whose other name was Claudius (just as Claudius' other name was Nero). For what it is worth, both the title to the Syriac version of Revelation[19] and the *History of John, the Son of Zebedee* in Syriac[20] say that it was Nero who banished John.

Hort, who surveys the evidence with scrupulous fairness, sums up as follows:[21]

> We find Domitian and Nero both mentioned, as also an emperor not named. The matter is complicated by the manner in which St John is brought to Rome, or his banishment referred to the personal act of the emperor. It is moreover peculiarly difficult to determine the relation of the legend of the boiling oil to the Roman tradition of a banishment from Rome. On the one hand the tradition as to Domitian is not unanimous; on the other it is the prevalent tradition, and it goes back to an author likely to be the recipient of a true tradition on the matter, who moreover connects it neither with Rome nor with an emperor's personal act. If external tradition alone could decide, there would be a clear preponderance for Domitian.

Yet, despite this, Hort, together with Lightfoot[22] and Westcott,[23] none of whom can be accused of setting light to ancient tradition, still rejected a Domitianic date in favour of one between the death of Nero in 68 and the fall of Jerusalem in 70. It is indeed a little known fact that this was what Hort calls[24] 'the general tendency of criticism' for most of the nineteenth century, and Peake cites the remarkable

[16] *De vir. ill.* 9. [17] *Apocalypse*, xviii. [18] *Haer.* 51.12 and 33.

[19] J. Gwynn (ed.), *The Apocalypse of St John in a Syriac Version hitherto Unknown*, Dublin 1897, 1.

[20] W. Wright (ed.), *Apocryphal Acts of the Apostles*, 1871, II, 55–7. It is of course historically worthless but interesting at this and other points (see below, pp. 258f.) as an alternative and apparently independent tradition.

[21] *Apocalypse*, xixf. For similar surveys, cf. Zahn, *INT* III, 201f.; A. S. Peake, *The Revelation of John*, 1919, 71–7; E. B. Allo, *L'Apocalypse*, Paris ^{3}1933, ccxxii–ccxxix.

[22] J. B. Lightfoot, *Biblical Essays* (in lectures of 1867–72), 52; *Essays on the Work entitled Supernatural Religion*, 1889, 132. Even the author attacked in the latter book agreed this date to be 'universally accepted by all competent critics'.

[23] B. F. Westcott, *The Gospel according to St John*, 1882, lxxxvii.

[24] *Apocalypse*, x.

consensus of 'both advanced and conservative scholars' who backed it.[25] Since then the pendulum has swung completely the other way. In his learned and exhaustive commentary[26] Charles never even alludes to Hort's presentation of the case for an early dating, and in the course of my investigations I have not come across a single modern New Testament scholar who comes down in favour of it – apart from Torrey, and now most recently and eccentrically J. Massyngberde Ford.[27] Yet though the theologians may have forsaken it, the classicists have not. It was powerfully argued by Henderson, in his classic study of the reign of Nero,[28] and he reaffirmed his belief in it many years later,[29] commending and endorsing the strong statement of the same thesis by Edmundson[30] which had appeared in the interval. It was also accepted by A. D. Momigliano in the *Cambridge Ancient History*[31] and A. Weigall in his biographical study of Nero.[32] It has also commended itself recently to the distinguished German jurist K. A. Eckhardt.[33] It will not perhaps therefore be inappropriate to argue the question of date by examining again the strength

[25] *Revelation*, 70. It must have been one of the few things on which Baur and Lightfoot agreed! He quotes Harnack as having to plead in defence of the Domitianic date in a review of 1882 'that the ancient tradition as to the origin of the Book is perhaps not entirely to be surrendered'. W. H. Simcox, *Revelation*, Cambridge 1893, li, sums up the position at that time by saying, 'Most critics are disposed to admit both St John's authorship of Revelation and its early date. In England, indeed, many, perhaps most, orthodox commentators still adhere to the Irenaean or traditional date.' He has to urge that the early date should not be rejected just because it is espoused by the radicals! But it was rapidly losing ground, though still advocated by E. C. Selwyn (father of the commentator on I Peter) in *The Authorship of the Apocalypse*, Cambridge 1900, and *The Christian Prophets and the Prophetic Apocalypse*, 1900, despite his denying unity of authorship with the fourth gospel (though not with II and III John!). In 1908 Sanday in his preface to Hort's commentary, iv, asked: 'Will not this powerful restatement of an old position compel us to reconsider the verdict to which the present generation of scholars appears to be tending?'

[26] R. H. Charles, *Revelation* (ICC), 1920, I, xciii.

[27] J. Massyngberde Ford, *Revelation* (Anchor Bible), New York 1975. She thinks that, with the exception of the Christian addition of chs. 1–3, it was composed between 60 and 70 by a disciple of John the Baptist on the basis of a revelation (chs. 4–11) given to John before the public ministry of Jesus! Grant, *INT*, 237, is prepared to say 'a situation between 68 and 70 is not excluded', and Bruce tells me that he now inclines in this direction.

[28] *Nero*, 439–43.

[29] B. W. Henderson, *Five Roman Emperors*, Cambridge 1927, 45.

[30] *The Church in Rome*, 164–79. I owe my discovery of Edmundson to Henderson's reference – though even he spelt his name wrong!

[31] *Cambridge Ancient History* X, Cambridge 1934, 726.

[32] A. Weigall, *Nero: Emperor of Rome*, 1930, 298f.

[33] Op. cit., 58–72.

of this case against those who have dismissed it, or more often ignored it.[34]

In turning to the evidence supplied by the book itself, we may consider first the historical and geographical situation which occasioned its writing. This demands to be considered under two heads. First there is the situation presupposed by chs. 1–3, together with the coda of 22.6–21; and secondly there is the situation presupposed by the main body of the book, the visions of 4.1–22.5. In the former the scene is set in Asia Minor; in the latter the focus, in so far as it is upon earth at all, is in Rome and to a lesser extent in Jerusalem.

In this the book of Revelation corresponds to what we observed in I Peter. There we argued that while the opening and closing verses were directed towards the recipients of the epistle in Asia Minor, the background for understanding the homiletic material which makes it up was to be located rather in Rome. In fact the parallels between these documents are instructive. Both are dominated by a political situation that calls for the symbolic pseudonym of 'Babylon' and by an eschatological situation that compels the hope that the consummation cannot now be long delayed (I Peter 4.7; Rev. 1.7; 3.11; 22.6f.,12,20). Both also presuppose that persecution has gone a good deal further in Rome than in Asia. Yet there are differences too. The area of Asia Minor is different, northern in I Peter, western in Revelation; and the author of the latter clearly reveals an informed personal acquaintance with place and circumstance of which the author of the former shows no sign. Above all the whole situation is considerably further advanced. In I Peter the judgment is only now beginning with the household of God, even in Rome (4.17); in Revelation Babylon is already gorged with the blood of the apostles and prophets and people of God (16.6; etc.). In Asia Minor too things have clearly gone beyond the verbal abuse that in I Peter mainly characterized the attack on Christians – though still in Revelation the pressure for some consists of slander, with the suffering (confined to a symbolic ten days in jail) yet to come (2.9f.); and in all the churches there is as yet but one martyr to record (2.13). But what has decisively changed is the attitude to the state – from one of guarded reverence to one of open hostility. Yet there is nothing here so far to demand an interval of more than a few years the other side of that fiery ordeal which Peter had already recorded as starting (4.12) and

[34] An intermediate dating in the reign of Vespasian has been argued by a few, e.g. C. A. Anderson Scott, *Revelation*, Edinburgh 1905 (*c.* 77); Michaelis, *Einleitung*, 315–19 (possibly 80+); S. Giet, *L'Apocalypse et l'histoire*, Paris 1957 (74–5). But this seems to get the worst of both the external and the internal evidence.

which we saw good reason to identify with the Neronian *pogrom* of 65.

A further instructive parallel is provided by the situation presupposed in Jude and II Peter, which we gave grounds for supposing to be addressed to Jewish Christians in some part of Asia Minor in 61–2. At that time indeed there was no hint of persecution, but there was plenty of evidence of insidious attack from gnosticizing, Judaizing heretics who were making false claims to leadership of the church and were scoffing at the Christian hope. We have already seen that the nearest parallels both for the gnosticizing tendencies and for the eschatological teaching in these epistles is not with second-century literature but with other New Testament writings to be dated in the late 50s and 60s – and with the book of Revelation. The themes in common with the last are sufficiently striking to merit more extended treatment.

In both, the false teachers are accused of the error of Balaam (Jude 11; II Peter 2.15; Rev. 2.14), which in Revelation is closely associated with the teaching of the Nicolaitans (2.6,15). In both Christians are described as being lured into immorality (II Peter 2.14, 18; 3.17; Rev. 2.20), into contaminating their clothing (Jude 23; Rev. 3.4), and into disowning their Master (Jude 4; II Peter 2.1; Rev. 2.13). There is the same contrast between the true and false γνῶσις (Jude 8; II Peter 1.2f., 16; Rev. 2.17,24). The heretical teachers are claiming to be shepherds and apostles of Christ's flock (Jude 11f.; Rev. 2.2), and there is a similar appeal to remember the teaching of the true apostles (Jude 17; II Peter 1.12; 3.1f.; Rev. 3.3), who are the foundation of the church and of its faith (Jude 3; Rev. 21.14). The eschatological symbolism too shows remarkable parallels, with the day of Christ being likened not only, as in the common Christian tradition, to the thief (II Peter 3.10; Rev. 3.3; 16.15) but uniquely in these two documents to the morning star (II Peter 1.19; Rev. 2.28; 22.16). In both the existing heavens and earth disappear (II Peter 3.10; Rev. 6.14; 16.20; 20.11) to be replaced by new (II Peter 3.13; Rev. 21.1); in both the fallen angels are chained in the depths of hell (Jude 6; II Peter 2.4; Rev. 20.1–3, 7), and appeal is made to the theme of a thousand years (II Peter 3.8; Rev. 20.2–7).

All this could doubtless have come from almost any period, and if II Peter and Jude are not early the argument falls. Yet there is good reason to suppose that the Apocalypse too presupposes a time when the final separation of Christians and Jews had not yet taken place. For is it credible that the references in Rev. 2.9 and 3.9 to those who 'claim to be Jews but are not' could have been made in that form after 70? For the implication is that Christians are the real Jews, the fullness of the twelve tribes (7.4–8; 21.12), and that if these Jews were genuinely the synagogue of Yahweh (as they claim) and not of Satan they would not be slandering 'my beloved people'. Even by the time of the Epistle of Barnabas,[35] which, unlike the book of Revelation, clearly presupposes the destruction of the temple (16.1–4) and the irrevocable divide between 'them' and 'us' (cf. 13.1, *ἡ διαθήκη εἰς ἡμᾶς ἢ εἰς ἐκείνους*), such language is no longer possible. Hort makes this point in his commentary on Rev. 2.9, but I have not noticed anyone else who does – apart again from Torrey.[36] If it is valid, it helps to confirm that the remainder of this language belongs, as we argued earlier, to this same period.

The most noticeable feature in the account of what has actually been suffered by the churches of Asia, or is immediately likely to be, is the absence of any clear reference to the imperial cult, which pervades the rest of the book. There is nothing in the warnings and encouragements given to the congregations that requires us to presuppose more than Jewish harassment, the action of local magistrates, and general pagan corruption. Even in Pergamon, which is stated to be 'Satan's throne' (2.13), there is no compelling evidence that the allusion is to emperor-worship. In so far as Satan is characteristically for this writer 'the old serpent' (12.9; 20.2), the allusion may well be to the snake-worship associated with the shrine of Asclepius, of which the city was a centre.[37] Even if, as later commentators tend to argue, the reference is to the temple consecrated there to 'the divine Augustus and the goddess Roma',[38] this had been founded in 29 BC [39] and does not of itself require a late date. Yet though emperor-worship can be read into the letters to the seven churches it is not demanded by them (in strong contrast with the visions that follow). Even if a gigantic statue of the Emperor Domitian was indeed erected in a temple at Ephesus,[40] there is absolutely nothing in the letter to the Christians there to suggest that this was the issue they faced: their struggle was not with the state but with false apostles, the Nicolaitans, and loss of fervour within the church (2.1–7). This is not, of course, to deny that for the seer the final battle with the 'beast' underlay everything else. But the development of emperor-worship in the province of Asia can-

[35] For the date of this, cf. pp. 313–9 below. [36] *Apocalypse*, 82f.

[37] So Hort, ad loc.; Zahn, *INT* III, 411f.

[38] I. T. Beckwith, *The Apocalypse of John*, New York 1919, 456, notes that Pergamon was the first place in the province of Asia to have such a temple. Yet Augustus also sanctioned temples in Ephesus and Nicea with the inscription 'To the goddess Roma and the divine Julius' (Dio Cassius, *Hist.* 51.6).

[39] Tacitus, *Ann.* 4.37; cf. 3.63; 4.55; and Suetonius, *Aug.* 52.

[40] Cf. Reicke, *NT Era*, 279, for the references.

not be used for determining the historical context into which the letters fit.

While on the subject of the letters to the churches, it will be appropriate to consider the objection often raised that they presuppose a state of affairs so far beyond that of Paul's time as to point to a later generation.[41] This is one of those contentions that it is very difficult to handle. How much time is required for the Galatians 'so quickly' to have followed a different gospel (Gal. 1.6), or for the church of Ephesus to have lost its early love (Rev. 2.4), or for the church of Laodicea to have grown lukewarm (Rev. 3.15f.)? – especially since what we can tell about the state of the last from the epistle to the Colossians (2.1; 4.13–16), our only other source, amounts to precisely nothing. It is obviously impossible to set any firm figure. Yet considering all that we know happened to the only well-documented church, that of Corinth, in the seven and a half years between late 49 and early 57, the ten and a half years from mid-58 (on our reckoning, the date of Colossians) to late 68 (the earliest date for the Apocalypse) could surely have seen quite as many changes in the Asian churches – changes indeed which, according to Acts 20.29f. and II Tim. 4.3f., Paul himself clearly foresaw, and of which the Petrine epistles have already given us more than a glimpse. And, as we have said, there is nothing to suggest that there is any great interval between where these last leave off and the letters of Rev. 1–3 begin.

One objection however can be dismissed, which is constantly repeated from one writer to another.[42] This is that Polycarp in his epistle to the Philippians (11.3) states that his own church at Smyrna had not been founded till after the death of Paul – so that it could not therefore be addressed as it is in Rev. 2.8–11 as early as the late 60s. But, as Lightfoot[43] observed long ago, all that Polycarp actually says[44] is that 'the Philippians were converted to the Gospel before the

[41] So e.g. Beckwith, *Apocalypse*, 207, who refers vaguely to 'a considerably long interval'.

[42] E.g. Zahn, *INT* III, 412f.; Moffatt, *Revelation*, *EGT*, V, 317; *ILNT*, 507; Charles, *Revelation* I, xciv; McNeile-Williams, *INT*, 262; Kümmel, *INT*, 469; and most recently even the conservative L. Morris, *The Revelation of St John* (Tyndale NTC), 1969, 37.

[43] *AF*, 166.

[44] His words are (in Lightfoot's translation): 'But I have not found any such thing in you, neither have heard thereof, among whom the blessed Paul laboured, who were his letters from the beginning. For he boasteth of you in all those churches which alone at that time knew the Lord; for we knew him not as yet.' Other editors prefer to supply a word in the difficult phrase 'qui estis in principio epistulae eius' and take it to mean 'who are praised (or mentioned) in the beginning of his Epistle'; but this does not affect the issue of dating.

Smyrneans – a statement which entirely accords with the notices of the two churches in the New Testament'.[45] It is astonishing that so much has continued to be built on so little.

A similar objection has sometimes been brought[46] against a date in the 60s from the fact that Laodicea, almost totally destroyed in the earthquake of 60–1, is addressed as an affluent church. But the city took pride in having rebuilt itself without waiting for help from imperial funds,[47] and by the end of the decade might well have boasted, 'How well I have done! I have everything I want in the world' (Rev. 3.17). Ironically Moffatt[48] holds that it is irrelevant to connect this with the reconstruction after the earthquake because by the 90s 'the incident is too far back'! This is an instance of how arbitrary dating procedures so often are. In contrast Charles[49] regards the letters to the churches as having been written 'at a much earlier date than the Book as a whole'[50] and re-edited in the reign of Domitian.[51] For their outlook, he says, is one in which Christians could still be expected to survive to the *parousia* ('Only hold fast to what you have, until I come', 2.25) and in which – a significant admission – 'there is not a single reference' to the imperial cult.[52]

So much then for the situation in Asia Minor presupposed in the letters. But what of the rest of the book? For there clearly Christians have already suffered harrowing persecution, and emperor-worship is at the heart of the attack. Are we not here in the presence of something much later? Let us consider these two issues, of persecution and the cult, in turn.

One thing of which we may be certain is that the Apocalypse,

[45] This is recognized by Torrey, op. cit., 78f., and also by Guthrie, *NTI*, 955.

[46] E.g. again by Kümmel, *INT*, 469.

[47] Tacitus, *Ann.* 14.27; cf. Orac. Sib. 4.107f.: 'Miserable Laodicea, thee too an earthquake shall one day raze in precipitate ruin, but thou shalt stand built up again as a city.'

[48] *EGT* V, 371. [49] *Revelation* I, 43–6 (44).

[50] 'In the closing years of the reign of Vespasian (75–9) but hardly earlier.' He bases the last qualification solely on the supposedly late foundation of the church of Smyrna (I, xciv).

[51] His grounds for this re-editing are simply that (*a*) the reference in 3.10 to 'the ordeal that is to fall upon the whole world' (long previously, one would have thought, a stock feature of Jewish apocalyptic) presupposes the later outlook of the book as a whole, and (*b*) the beginnings and endings of the letters contain allusions to the thought and diction of 1.13–18 and other passages from the main body of the book. So without a shred of evidence, textual or stylistic, he regards these as later additions. This is characteristic of his procedure with any passage that will not fit his scheme.

[52] Similarly Michaelis, *Einleitung*, 316, who sees no evidence of state persecution in the letters and regards a Domitianic date for them as too late.

unless the product of a perfervid and psychotic imagination, was written out of an intense experience of the Christian suffering at the hands of the imperial authorities, represented by the 'beast' of Babylon. That violent persecution has already taken place and cries aloud for vengeance is an inescapable inference from such texts as 6.9f.; 16.6; 17.6; 18.20,24; 19.2; and 20.4. They presuppose that the blood of apostles and prophets and countless Christians, including some 'who had been beheaded for the sake of God's word and their testimony to Jesus', had saturated the streets of the capital itself. This of course is not the language of factual reporting; yet if something quite traumatic had not already occurred *in Rome* which was psychologically still very vivid, the vindictive reaction, portraying a blood-bath of universal proportions (14.20), is scarcely credible. The sole question is what terrible events are here being evoked.

The impact of the Neronian terror, already cited from Tacitus and Clement, immediately comes to mind, and one is tempted to ask what further need we have of witnesses. Indeed Zahn, who holds that the book comes from thirty years later, still believes that 'the author refers to the Roman martyrs of the time of Nero, and especially to Peter and Paul'.[53] But most of those who have argued for a Domitianic date take the reference to be to the persecution under that emperor. This is especially true of Sir William Ramsay, who painted a gruesome picture of what he called 'the Flavian persecution'. This, as he depicted it, was

> not a temporary flaming forth of cruelty: it was a steady uniform application of a deliberately chosen and unvarying policy, a policy arrived at after careful consideration, and settled for the permanent future conduct of the entire administration. It was to be independent of circumstances and the inclination of individuals. The Christians were to be annihilated, as the Druids had been.[54]

Unfortunately however the scene is one that is drawn largely from his own imagination playing upon the evidence of the Apocalypse *already interpreted* as Domitianic material.[55] The primary sources[56] present a rather different picture.

[53] *INT*, III, 410. So Bruce, *NT History*, 400.

[54] W. M. Ramsay, *The Letters to the Seven Churches of Asia*, 1904, 91.

[55] In his earlier and more sober account in *The Church in the Roman Empire*, 277, he asks, 'How then is it that the Christians are silent about this continuous persecution?' He adduces I Peter, which he dated, as we saw, *c.* 75–80, as evidence for this period, since he believed in 'a practically continuous proscription of Christians from 64 onwards'; but his *a priori* approach is disclosed in the revealing comment: 'The persecution of Domitian burned itself ineradicably into the memory of history; it may be doubted by the critic, but not by the historian. . . . So strong and early a tradition as that which constitutes Domitian the second great persecutor cannot

According to Eusebius,[57] Domitian was the second after Nero to stir up persecution against Christians, and he quotes Melito of Sardis to the same effect.[58] Yet while Eusebius speaks of the death and banishment of 'no small number of well-born and distinguished men at Rome', he does not mention the *death* of a single Christian.[59] He records that 'Flavia Domitilla, the daughter of a sister of Flavius Clemens,[60] who was one of the consuls of Rome at that time, was committed by way of punishment to the island of Pontia because of her testimony for Christ.' He also says that the descendants of Jude, on the ground that they were of the family of David, were brought before the Emperor; but he 'in no way condemned them, but despised them as men of no account, let them go free, and by an injunction caused the persecution against the church to cease'.

The facts of the case of Domitilla and Clemens are by no means clear.[61] Domitilla was probably a Christian, Clemens possibly a sympathizer. But there is now widespread agreement among historians that, while Domitian may indeed have had an axe to grind against 'atheism' and 'Jewish manners',[62] his action against prominent individuals in Rome was motivated by reasons of state rather than by any odium against the church. In Reicke's words,[63] 'Domitian's purpose was domination of the Roman aristocracy, not an attack upon the Christian faith'. In fact recent studies have been strongly in the direction of showing that 'the evidence for a widespread Christian

---

be discredited without wrecking the foundations of ancient history. Those who discredit it must, to be consistent, resolve to dismiss nine-tenths of what appears in books as ancient history, including most that is interesting and valuable' (259).

[56] Set out in full by Lightfoot, *AF* I.1,104–15.

[57] *HE* 3.17–20.

[58] *HE* 4.27.9.

[59] In his *Chronicle* he says sweepingly, 'Many Christians martyred and Flavia Domitilla and Flavius Clemens banished.' In fact Flavius Clemens was executed (Suetonius, *Dom.* 16).

[60] Another confusion. She was the wife of Clemens and niece of Domitian.

[61] They are carefully assessed by Reicke, who believes in a Domitianic date for Revelation, in his *NT Era*, 295–302. Cf. also P. Prigent, 'Au temps de l'Apocalypse: I. Domitien', *RHPR* 54, 1974, 455–83 (especially 470–4).

[62] Dio Cassius, *Hist.* 67.14.2. Yet Edmundson rightly says, *The Church in Rome*, 222 (cf. 221–37): 'The origin of the persecution under Domitian was not so much religious as fiscal.' In a search for new sources of income he insisted on a stricter exaction of the *didrachma* tax not merely from practising Jews but from all who lived in the Jewish manner (including among them no doubt converts to Christianity as well as 'God-fearers'). Cf. E. M. Smallwood, 'Domitian's Attitude toward the Jews and Judaism', *Classical Philology* 51, 1956, 1–13.

[63] Op. cit., 302.

persecution under Domitian is late [and] probably exaggerated'.[64] In his later book Henderson concludes:

> All that is left as authority for the 'squall of persecution' under the Flavian Emperor is too remote to be of value. . . . Let who will credit the talk of a general persecution of Christianity under Domitian.[65]

It is not in fact till Orosius, a Christian historian of the fifth century, that we hear tell of 'the cruellest persecution throughout the whole world'.[66] Tertullian is far more restrained:

> Domitian also with a share of Nero's cruelty had tried on one occasion to do the same as Nero. But being, as I imagine, possessed of some intelligence, he very soon ceased, and even recalled those whom he had banished.[67]

When this limited and selective purge, in which no Christian was for certain put to death, is compared with the massacre of Christians under Nero in what two early and entirely independent witnesses speak of as 'immense multitudes',[68] it is astonishing that commentators should have been led by Irenaeus, who himself does not even mention a persecution, to prefer a Domitianic context for the book of Revelation.

But, of course, it is not simply the state of persecution but the

[64] P. Richardson, *Israel in the Apostolic Church*, Cambridge 1969, 40f. In one of the better of his uneven *Essays in Early Christian History*, ch. 6, Merrill argues a powerful case against a Domitianic persecution of Christians. He makes the point (172) that Suetonius who was resident in Rome during the latter part of Domitian's reign nowhere mentions Christianity in connection with the terror, despite recording Nero's treatment of what he (Suetonius) regarded as this 'baleful superstition'. Similarly Pliny, who was also in Rome and a member of the senate at the time, stated later that he had never had anything to do with the trial of Christians (*Epp.* 10.96). Among subsequent studies in the same direction, cf. R. L. P. Milburn, 'The Persecution of Domitian', *CQR* 139, 1945, 154–64; J. Knudsen, 'The Lady and the Emperor', *CH* 14, 1945, 17–32; W. H. C. Frend, *Martyrdom and Persecution in the Early Church*, Oxford 1955, 212–17; G. E. M. de Ste Croix, 'Why were the Early Christians Persecuted?', *PP* 26, 1963, 6–38; B. Newman, 'The Fallacy of the Domitian Hypothesis', *NTS* 10, 1963–4, 133–9; T. D. Barnes, *Tertullian*, Oxford 1971, 143–63; Prigent, *RHPR* 54, 455–84; though cf. L. W. Barnard, 'Clement of Rome and the Persecution of Domitian', *NTS* 10, 1963–4, 251–60, against exaggerated statements of this thesis.

[65] *Five Roman Emperors*, 45; cf. 43–53. Barnes, op. cit., 150, believes that the Domitianic persecution was employed (or even invented) by Melito 'to justify his argument that only bad emperors condemned Christians'. Similarly Prigent, *RHPR* 54, 481.

[66] *Hist. adv. pag.* 7.10.1.

[67] *Apol.* 5, as quoted by Eusebius, *HE* 4.20.7. In the original Tertullian has 'because he also had some humanity' (qua et homo).

[68] Tacitus, *Ann.* 15.44; I Clem. 6.1.

relation of Christians to the imperial religion that has led to this preference.

Here again we may start with Tertullian. Earlier in the same passage of his *Apology* he refers pagans to their own records ('commentarios vestros') for the fact that Nero was the first to attack Christianity at Rome 'with the utmost ferocity of the imperial sword'.[69] Elsewhere, in a discussion concerned to show that from an early date Christianity was no obscure provincial sect but attracted the attention of the imperial authorities, he makes the point that the sole decree of Nero ('institutum Neronianum') not rescinded on his death was one against Christians.[70] The only other reference to any such legal act occurs in the passage of Sulpicius Severus[71] which we have already had occasion to quote:

> Thus a beginning was made of violent persecution of Christians. Afterwards laws were enacted and the religion was forbidden. Edicts were publicly published: 'No one must profess Christianity'.

This evidence is otherwise unsupported and has generally been treated with scepticism.[72] Speaking of Tertullian's 'institutum Neronianum', Sherwin-White says, 'Though this theory might explain persecution at Rome it fails to explain it in the provinces.'[73] But then it is not required to explain it in the provinces. The only hint in Revelation of any such executive decree is in 'Babylon' itself, and it is difficult to believe that *something* of the kind does not lie behind the language of 13.14–17. There, speaking of the second, subordinate beast, the seer says:

> It . . . made them erect an image in honour of the beast that had been wounded by the sword and yet lived. It was allowed to give breath to the image of the beast, so that it could speak, and could cause all who would not worship the image to be put to death. Moreover, it caused everyone, great and small, rich and poor, slave and free, to be branded with a mark on his right hand or forehead, and no one was allowed to buy or sell unless he bore this beast's mark, either name or number.

He then goes on to supply the reader with the clue to the identity of the beast 'that had been wounded by the sword and yet lived':

[69] *Apol.* 5.3.

[70] *Ad nat.* 1.7.9. For a full discussion of this vexed passage, with bibliography, cf. A. Schneider, *Le premier livre* ad Nationes *de Tertullien*, Neuchâtel 1968, 171–3; also P. Prigent, 'Au temps de l'Apocalypse: III. Pourquoi les persécutions?'. *RHPR* 55, 1975, 353f.; he agrees in concluding that the passage, while not in itself sufficient to establish such an 'institutum', must strengthen any other indication.

[71] *Chronic.* 2.29.3.

[72] E.g. Merrill, op. cit., ch. 5.

[73] 'Early Persecutions and Roman Law Again', *JTS* n.s. 3, 1952, 202.

> Here is the key; and anyone who has intelligence may work out the number of the beast. The number represents a man's name, and the numerical value of its letters is six hundred and sixty-six (13.18).

Though there can be no final certainty, far the most widely accepted solution to the conundrum is that the figure represents the sum of the letters in Hebrew (or Aramaic) (the language evidently in which this barbarous Graecist thought) of the name 'Neron Caesar'.[74] The reference to Nero, who killed himself by his own sword, is further confirmed by the fact (strangely ignored by the commentators) that Suetonius cites a parallel puzzle based on the aggregate of the letters in Greek (1005), as current in Nero's own lifetime:

> Count the numerical values
> Of the letters in Nero's name,
> And in 'murdered his own mother':
> You will find that their sum is the same.[75]

This strongly suggests that Rev. 13.18 is the Christian version of a familiar game.[76]

Further, for the naming of Nero as 'the beast' there is the interesting parallel, quoted by Edmundson,[77] from Philostratus' *Apollonius of Tyana*. Apollonius is represented as saying on his arrival in Rome at this time:

> In my travels, which have been wider than ever man yet accomplished, I have seen many, many wild beasts of Arabia and India; but this beast, that is commonly called a Tyrant, I know not how many heads it has, nor if it be crooked of claw, and armed with horrible fangs. However, they say it is a civil

[74] The Hebrew form 'Nrōn qsar' is now further confirmed from Qumran; cf. *Discoveries in the Judaean Desert of Jordan* II, edd. P. Benoit, J. T. Milik an dR. de Vaux, Oxford 1961, 18, plate 29. The alternative reading 616 (already known to Irenaeus, *Adv. haer.* 5.28.2) neatly fits the Latin form 'Nero Caesar'. Peake, *Revelation*, 309–34, gives a history of this and other interpretations which reveals his combination of learning and sound judgment. It is a pity that his book appears to have been overshadowed by Charles' erudite but unbalanced commentary the following year.

[75] *Nero* 39; tr. R. Graves, *The Twelve Caesars*, 1962.

[76] Cf. also Orac. Sib. 1.324–31, where the numerical value of the name Ἰησοῦς is given in contrast as 888. These parallels must count against the argument of Reicke, 'Die jüdische Apocalyptic und die johanneische Tiervision', *RSR* 60, 1972, 173–92 (especially 189–91), that the solution lies not in *gematria* (the numerical value of the letters) but in the properties of the 'triangular' number 666 ($= 1 + 2 + 3 \ldots 36 = 6 \times 6$). But the pinning of this mysterious number of evil on to Nero (with which Reicke agrees) can only be achieved by showing that it is *also* the sum of the letters of his name.

[77] Op. cit., 173.

beast, and inhabits the midst of cities; but to this extent it is more savage than the beasts of mountain and forest, that whereas lions and panthers can sometimes by flattery be tamed and change their disposition, stroking and petting this beast does but instigate it to surpass itself in ferocity and devour at large. And of wild beasts you cannot say that they were ever known to eat their own mothers, but Nero has gorged himself on this diet.[78]

Yet, though few doubt that the primary reference of 'the beast' in Revelation is to Nero, there is still a reluctance to date from his time the decree to worship the emperor or his statue (Rev.13.4, 12,15; 14.9–11; 15.2; 16.2; 19.20; 20.4). The growth of the imperial cultus is again something which it is almost impossible to date with confidence. The first hard evidence that this was required of *Christians* is not indeed until the reign of Trajan; but by then it is treated as a stock test of loyalty. As Pliny puts it in his afore-mentioned letter to the Emperor, 'At my dictation they invoked the gods and did reverence with incense and wine to your image, which I had ordered to be brought for this purpose along with the statues of the gods.' In some form however the claim to divine honours and the setting up of the emperor's statue in provincial temples goes back as far as Augustus. Caligula indeed was actually threatening in 40 to have his image imposed upon the temple at Jerusalem – a blasphemy averted only by his timely death. According to Tacitus,[79] a statue of Nero was in 55 set up in Rome of the same size as that of Mars the Avenger and in the same shrine – 'thus', in Reicke's words, 'introducing the emperor cult into the city of Rome'.[80] It is certainly true that Domitian ordered himself to be called 'our Lord and our God' (dominus ac deus noster).[81] 'But', as Bruce salutarily reminds us, 'there is no record that this precipitated a clash between him and the Christians.'[82] The book of Revelation would fit into what we know of his reign. But the dogmatism of so many commentators[83] that such developments *could*

[78] *Vit. Apol.* 4.38; tr. J. S. Phillimore, Oxford 1912, II, 38.

[79] *Ann.* 13.8. Cf. 15.29 for quasi-religious homage to an image of Nero.

[80] *NT Era*, 241, referring to G. Wissowa, *Religion und Kultus der Römer*, Munich ²1912, 82. Dio Cassius stresses what a very different matter this was from the same practice in the provinces (*Hist.* 51.8f.). He also describes Nero as being addressed as divine (*Hist.* 62.5.2).

[81] Suetonius, *Dom.* 13. Eusebius' *Chronicle* dates this in the year 86. Cf. L. Cerfaux and J. Tondriau, *Le culte des souverains dans la civilisation gréco-romaine*, Tournai 1957, 355–7, for other references.

[82] *NT History*, 391. The phrase in Rev.4.11, *ὁ κύριος καὶ ὁ θεὸς ἡμῶν*, has been seen as the Christian 'answer' to it. But 'the Lord our God' is a title already so deeply rooted in the Old Testament that nothing can be built on this.

[83] E.g. Zahn, *INT* III, 412, 422; Beckwith, *Apocalypse*, 201; Charles, *Revelation*, I, xciv; Kümmel, *INT*, 467; G. B. Caird, *Revelation* (Black's NTC), 1966, 6, 166.

not have occurred till then is misplaced (and unargued). Peake sticks to the facts when he says,[84] 'It is possible that the demand for some act of worship of the emperor was introduced in Domitian's reign as a test for the detection of Christians.' Beyond that we cannot go. The purple passages in which E. Stauffer[85] reconstructs the scene by which John (in his view the apostle) was confronted in Ephesus under Domitian are, alas, highly imaginative if not wholly imaginary.[86] They are marked by turns of phrase which constantly slur the evidence[87] and at points force[88] and distort it.[89] When a great scholar is driven to such lengths one may suspect that his case is weak. He has his own elaborate interpretation of the cipher 666 as referring to Domitian,[90] but offers no explanation of how he can possibly be the 'sixth king' who 'is now reigning' (Rev. 17.10).[91] All one can say is that while the evidence from the imperial cultus does not rule out a

84 *Revelation*, 121.

85 E. Stauffer, *Christ and the Caesars*, ET 1955, 147–91.

86 So too P. Prigent, 'Au temps de l'Apocalypse: II. Le culte impérial au 1er siècle en Asie Mineure', *RHPR* 55, 1975, 221. The same applies, as we have said, to Ramsay's account of 'The Flavian Persecution in the Province of Asia as depicted in the Apocalypse', *Letters to the Seven Churches*, ch. 9. He is candid enough to admit that most of the statements derived from the Apocalypse are 'entirely uncorroborated: no even indirect evidence supports them. . . . We are reduced to mere general presumptions and estimate of probabilities. . . . This is the one contemporary account that has been preserved of the Flavian procedure' (99). If that is *not* contemporary, we have nothing.

87 Thus, in the course of a single page (171f.) occur the following: 'one may suppose that', 'may be presumed to', 'of some such kind', 'it is likely that', 'would certainly', 'was without doubt . . . the obvious man to', 'was perhaps', 'one may be assured that', 'had every chance of'.

88 Of the beast that was mortally wounded but whose wound was healed we are told, 'This seems to refer clearly enough . . . to the abortive conspiracy of 88–90' (178)!

89 Thus, it is said (161f.) that Domitian 'diverted the temple tax, which the Jews of the whole world had paid for the temple on Mount Zion, to the temple of Jupiter on the Capitol'. But this had been done by Vespasian in 70 (Josephus, *BJ* 7.218): Domitian merely exacted it more rigorously (Suetonius, *Dom.* 12). Again, Stauffer elaborates Tertullian's passing reference to John's torture and expulsion from Rome, adding (175): 'There is no reason to doubt the truth of the account, corresponding as it does to our knowledge of Domitian's character and of the facts of the persecution that year' (viz. 95). But Tertullian, as we have seen, relates this to the deaths of Peter and Paul, and Jerome takes him to be referring to Nero.

90 A(utokrator) KAI(sar) DOMET(ianos) SEB(astos) GER(manikos) (179; cf. his article, '666', *CN* 11, 1947, 237–41). Like many another ingenious attempt it cannot be disproved, but, as Caird says, *Revelation*, 175, 'Apart from its complexity it has only one flaw: although each of these abbreviations by itself is well attested, there is no single coin on which all five occur together.'

91 On the interpretation of this, see below, pp. 242–52.

Domitianic dating, it does not establish it either.[92] The language of compulsory emperor-worship throughout the world on pain of death is in any case not meant to be taken literally. The role of the seer is to descry, not to describe. What he sees in his vision no more happened in the time of Domitian than in the time of Nero: he is projecting upon the end – the era of Nero *redivivus* – the inevitable outcome of a totalitarian tyranny.

This is perhaps the point to mention a tiny piece of evidence that Moffatt[93] goes so far as to call a 'water-mark of the Domitianic period'. In Rev. 6.6 a voice is heard saying, 'A whole day's wage [literally, a denarius] for a measure of flour, a whole day's wage for three measures of barley-meal. But spare the olive and the vine'. 'The immunity of wine', he says, 'may be a local allusion to Domitian's futile attempt (in AD 92) to check the cultivation of the vine in the Ionian provinces.' One is bound to confess that it does not immediately sound like it,[94] and both Beckwith and Charles, though it suits their dating, reject it. The allusion is evidently to some situation of acute cereal shortage, and if one wants one that fits one could just as well look to the account which Josephus gives of the final stages of the siege of Jerusalem: 'Many clandestinely bartered their possessions for a single measure – of wheat, if they were rich, or barley, if they were poor';[95] and later he tells[96] of the sacred wine and oil being distributed and drunk. Almost certainly there is no specific reference to these events. But it does raise the question of what relation, if any, the Apocalypse bears to the situation obtaining at this time at the other end of the empire, in Jerusalem. And to this we may turn before coming back to the crucial passage for its dating which speaks of the sequence of Roman emperors in ch. 17.

In 11.1f. the seer is told:

> Go and measure the temple of God, the altar, and the number of the worshippers. But have nothing to do with the outer court of the temple; do not measure that; for it has been given over to the Gentiles, and they will trample the Holy City underfoot for forty-two months.

[92] So Guthrie, *NTI*, 950f. Prigent in his important survey of the imperial cult in Asia Minor, *RHPR* 55, 215–35, while himself believing that the Apocalypse comes from the reign of Domitian, argues that this emperor introduced at this point nothing distinctive (221). In his subsequent article on the causes of persecution (*RHPR* 55, 341–63, especially 357–62) he plays down the blasphemous significance of the title 'Kyrios Kaisar' and never even mentions Domitian's claim to that of 'dominus ac deus noster'.

[93] *ILNT*, 507, following S. Reinach.

[94] What, in any case, about the olives? Moffatt dismisses this as 'probably an artistic embodiment, introduced in order to fill out the sketch'!

[95] *BJ* 5.427. [96] *BJ* 5.565.

It is clear from what follows that this is the old temple of the earthly city. The picture of its being trampled underfoot is taken, like so much else in this book, from the Old Testament (Dan. 8.10–14; Zech. 12.3 [LXX]; Isa. 63.18; Ps. 79.1) – as, we have argued, it is in Luke 21.24.[97] The period of forty-two months, or 1260 days, or three and a half years, is, of course, a stock time for the reign of evil, derived again from Daniel (7.25; 12.7, 11f.), and is not to be taken as prediction before or after the event. Yet both here and in 12.6 and 14 (where for the same period the woman, the church or true Israel who gives birth to the Messiah, flees into the wilds to 'a place prepared for her by God' to be sustained out of the reach of the serpent), it looks as if the reference is to the flight from Jerusalem enjoined in the synoptic apocalypses.[98] Here however we seem to be at a later stage,

[97] The author of Revelation has certainly not derived it from Luke 21.24, any more than he has derived the shutting up of the sky for three and a half years in 11.3 and 6 from Luke 4.25 (or James 5.17). It is hopeless to attempt to date the book of Revelation by its dependence on the synoptists or other New Testament writings. Charles, *Revelation* I, lxxxiii–vi, claims: 'Our author appears to have used Matthew, Luke, I Thessalonians, I and II Corinthians, Colossians, Ephesians and possibly Galatians, I Peter and James'; and the same list is simply taken over (without even the 'possibly'!) by J. W. Bowman, *IDB* IV, 61. Yet here above all there is no firm case for literary dependence, only for common tradition. Cf. L. A. Vos, *The Synoptic Traditions in the Apocalypse*, Kampen 1965; and Guthrie, *NTI*, 956.

[98] There is a most interesting parallel to this in the Ascension of Isaiah, which merits reproduction: 'After it [the world] is consummated, Beliar the great ruler, the king of this world, will descend, who hath ruled it since it came into being; yea, he will descend from his firmament in the likeness of a man, a lawless king, the slayer of his mother [i.e., Nero; cf. Orac. Sib. 4.121; 5.145, 363]: who himself (even) this king will persecute the plant which the Twelve Apostles of the Beloved have planted. Of the Twelve one [i.e., Peter] will be delivered into his hands. This ruler in the form of that king will come and there will come with him all the powers of this world [cf. Rev. 16.14; 20.7–9], and they will hearken unto him in all that he desireth. And at his word the sun will rise at night and he will make the moon to appear at the sixth hour [cf. II Esd. 5.4]. And all that he hath desired will he do in the world: he will do and speak like the Beloved [cf. Rev. 13.11] and he will say: "I am God and before me there has been none" [cf. Rev. 13.6]. And all the people in the world will believe in him. And they will sacrifice to him and they will serve him saying: "This is God and beside him there is no other" [cf. Rev. 13.4, 8, 12]. And the greater number of those who shall have been associated together in order to receive the Beloved, he will turn aside after him [cf. Rev. 13.14; Mark 13.22]. And there will be the power of his miracles in every city and region. And he will set up his image before him in every city [cf. Rev. 13.14; 19.20]. And he shall bear sway three years and seven months and twenty-seven days [cf. Rev. 13.5]. And many believers and saints having seen him for whom they were hoping, who was crucified, Jesus the Lord Christ, . . . and those also who were believers in him [cf. John 20.29] – of these few in those days

for the temple area is already envisaged as under partial occupation. Yet if Jerusalem had actually been destroyed, it is surely incredible that the worst judgment upon it should be that in a violent earthquake (and not by enemy action) 'a tenth of the city fell' (11.13).[99] Rather, we should expect, as Moule has said,[100] a description of the doom of the city 'where the Lord was crucified' parallel to that other 'great city', also with its allegorical name of evil (cf. 11.8 with 18.10), where 'the blood of the prophets and God's people was found' (18.24). If in the case of Jerusalem 'the smoke of her conflagration' (18.9, 18), so vividly described by Josephus,[101] had already been seen, it is astonishing that it receives no mention.

It is indeed generally agreed that this passage must bespeak a

---

will be left as his servants, while they flee from desert to desert [cf. Rev. 12.6,14], awaiting the coming of the Beloved. And after (one thousand) three hundred and thirty-two days the Lord will come with his angels and with the armies of the holy ones from the seventh heaven with the glory of the seventh heaven, and he will drag Beliar into Gehenna [cf. Rev. 19.20] and also his armies' (4.2–14; vv. 15–18 contain further parallels; tr. R. H. Charles, with an introduction by G. H. Box, *The Ascension of Isaiah*, 1917, 37–9). Charles, *The Ascension of Isaiah*, 1900, 30f., dated this vision, the so-called 'Testament of Hezekiah' (3.13–4.18), between 88 and 100, on the grounds that it presupposes 'a form of the Antichrist myth' that 'could hardly have arisen earlier than 88 AD' (but this is a very dubious judgment; cf. pp. 245f. below) and the continued survival of believers who had seen Christ in his lifetime (4.13), the last of whom would have died *c.* 100. But it could well be considerably earlier. It seems to be set during the desert-flight and to be expecting the *parousia* about three and a half years after the death of Peter. In this case it would be contemporary, on our dating, with the book of Revelation, whose themes it echoes so closely yet without quoting or copying (as one would expect if it were later). Observe the subtle differences in the names (Beliar, the Beloved, Gehenna, none of which are in Revelation) and in the figure for the reign of evil (1332 as opposed to 1290). This last differs also from the 1335 of Dan. 12.12; but, rather than being a scribal error, as Charles suggested, 1332 appears to represent the double of 666 (A. Bosse, 'Zur Erklärung der Apocalypse der Asc. Jesaiae', *ZNW* 10, 1909, 320–3) and thus again to presuppose a common tradition with Rev. 13.18 (so Reicke, *RSR* 60, 188f., who also argues that the two writings are contemporary – though from the reign of Domitian). In contrast with the self-authenticating quality of the Revelation of John, the Ascension is attributed to Isaiah, because he saw 'the vision of Babylon' (Isa. 13–14), to which the reader is specifically referred (4.19). If the Ascension really does come from the latter 60s, then it has interesting implications for the dating not only of the Apocalypse but of other parts of the New Testament tradition (especially the Matthean tradition in 3.14 and 18, and that represented by the Pastorals in 3.21–31) which it appears to presuppose, though again without quoting.

[99] Contrast the earthquake 'like none before it in human history' which marks the complete destruction of Babylon in 16.17–20.

[100] *Birth of the NT*, 123. [101] *BJ* 6.164–434.

pre-70 situation. But the solution has been to date the oracle (or oracles)[102] of ch. 11 (like that of ch. 12) earlier than the book as a whole and to see them as originally Jewish rather than Christian. Indeed it has been confidently maintained that the prophecy that the temple would survive *could* not have been spoken by a Christian, who would have known that Jesus had foretold its destruction.[103] Following Wellhausen, Charles took 11.1f. to be an oracle by a Zealot prophet predicting that though the city and the outer court of the temple would fall, the sanctuary and the Zealots who occupied it would be preserved.[104] But there is nothing in the passage that predicts the survival of the temple. True, there is to be a sort of temporary ring-fence within which the two prophets, fulfilling the roles of Elijah and Moses,[105] can utter in safety a final call to repentance. But to interpret the command to 'measure' the temple as a promise of preservation is to ignore the Old Testament background of the imagery. Often indeed the measuring-line and plummet are symbols rather of judgment and destruction (cf. II Kings 21.13; Isa. 34.11; Lam. 2.8; Amos 7.7–9). But the background here is clearly Ezek. 40–45, where the point of the action laid upon the prophet is not preservation but purification – 'to teach my people to distinguish the sacred from the profane' (44.23):[106] 'So tell the Israelites, man, about this temple, its appearance and its proportions, that they may be ashamed of their iniquities', iniquities which include, above all, the

[102] Charles, *Revelation*, ad loc., argues that 11.1f. and 3–13 are separate fragments.

[103] So Zahn, *INT*, III, 439; Peake, *Revelation*, 30f.

[104] Similarly Peake, *Revelation*, 291f. Beckwith, *Apocalypse*, 584–8, agrees that the prophecy cannot originally have been Christian but questions the specific solution, which Caird, *Revelation*, ad loc., goes so far as to call 'improbable, useless and absurd'.

[105] The reference of the death of the two witnesses (*μάρτυρες*) to the martyrdoms of Peter and Paul brilliantly argued by Munck, *Petrus und Paulus in der Offenbarung Johannis* (and previously proposed by C. H. Turner, *Studies in Early Church History*, Oxford 1912, 214, though Munck makes no mention of this), would, of course, suit a Neronian dating; but it is highly speculative. There seems no evident connection between Peter and Paul and the roles of the two prophets in shutting up the sky and turning water into blood (11.6). Above all, it all appears to happen in Jerusalem, not Rome; and to say with Munck (op. cit., 30–5) that the description of the city as the place 'where their Lord was crucified' (11.8) is either an interpolation or refers to the guilt of Rome's involvement in the crucifixion or means 'spiritually crucified' (as in the 'Quo vadis?' legend) is very unsatisfactory. In any case 11.3–13 has to be separated from 11.1f., where the scene is clearly 'the Holy City' with its temple. The most we can say is that the Christian reader may have been intended to read this prophecy in the light of the martyrs' death, but he is not given much help in this direction.

[106] Yet contrast Ezek. 42.1ff. and Rev. 11.2, where this time the outer court is deliberately given over to profanation.

failure to remove the corpses of their kings (43.7–10). But the testimony of the two witnesses of Revelation ends in failure: *their* corpses are left unburied in the streets; and it is only by God's resurrection of them to heaven that their enemies are scared into homage (11.7–13).[107] There would appear to be nothing here out of line with the saying of Jesus after the transfiguration (where Moses and Elijah also appear as witnesses) that, though the promised Elijah had indeed been sent to the Jews prior to the end 'to set everything right', 'they have worked their will upon him, as the scriptures say' (Mark 9.11–13).[108] There seems therefore no reason why the oracle should not have been uttered by a Christian prophet as the doom of the city drew nigh to predict that, despite God's care for his people, the final offer of repentance would inevitably be spurned by the representatives of 'the Jerusalem of today', which the seer, like Paul, contrasts with 'the heavenly Jerusalem' (Gal. 4.25f.; cf. Rev. 21.2f.).

The resort of commentators to treating anything that will not fit a Domitianic date as the incorporation of earlier material, though (for reasons they do not explain) without subsequent modification, is invoked still more arbitrarily in the passage to which we must now return in ch. 17, which is crucial for any more precise determination of the date of the book.

The central verses are 17.9–11, which supply 'the clue for those who can interpret it' to the vision of the scarlet woman, whose name is Babylon, 'the great city that holds sway over the kings of the earth':

> The seven heads are seven hills on which the woman sits. They represent also seven kings (*or* emperors), of whom five have already fallen, one is now reigning, and the other has yet to come; and when he does come he is only to last for a little while. As for the beast that once was alive and is alive no longer, he is an eighth – and yet is one of the seven, and he is going to perdition.

Much ink has been spilt over this passage, but the issues are succinctly summed up in Beckwith's note on the subject.[109] On the assumption that the words have a reference to Roman history, there are two questions to dispose of in advance: (i) With whom does the list of the emperors begin? and (ii) Are the three emperors of 68–9 between Nero and Vespasian (Galba, Otho and Vitellius), who lasted only a few months each, to be included in the count?

[107] Despite Beckwith and Caird, it is difficult to believe that this is intended to indicate true repentance. The Danielic phrase 'they gave glory to the God of heaven' suggests much more the reluctant obeisance of a Nebuchadnezzar.

[108] Cf. the same connection made with the fate of the Son of Man in Rev. 13.8: 'where *also* their Lord was crucified'.

[109] *Apocalypse*, 704–8; cf. Allo, *L'Apocalypse*, 275–86.

The first question is theoretically in doubt but may be settled quite quickly. Though the Roman empire (following upon the republic) is normally regarded as starting with Augustus,[110] Julius Caesar, who claimed the title 'imperator', was emperor *de facto* and is included in Suetonius' *Lives of the Twelve Caesars*. More importantly, from our point of view, the comparable lists of kings in Orac. Sib. 5.12 and II Esd. 12.15 (where the second reigns the longest and must be Augustus)[111] begin with Caesar. The same appears to be true of the calculation in the Epistle of Barnabas (4.4), where the tenth king is probably Vespasian, starting from Caesar. But in Revelation it is clear that the first king must be Augustus. Otherwise Nero would be the sixth; and if one thing is certain it is that Nero is dead and not 'now reigning'.

The second question can also, I believe, be resolved with reasonable certainty. The sole ground ever given for excluding the three emperors of 68–9 is that Suetonius is interpreted as speaking disparagingly of them as 'rebellious princes'[112] who constituted a kind of interregnum. Yet Suetonius himself includes them in his *Lives of the Twelve Caesars*, and neither Tacitus[113] nor Josephus[114] has any hesitation in putting them on a par with the rest. More significantly they are included without reservation in the catalogue already referred to in Orac. Sib. 5.35 and also in II Esd. 12.20f.

'It requires then', as Beckwith says,[115] 'a certain degree of arbitrariness to avoid making the sixth king either Nero or Galba' – and, as we have seen, Nero may be ruled out without any arbitrariness. Now Galba reigned from June 68 to January 69. 'The other' who 'has yet to come' and 'when he does come is only to last for a little while' would then be Otho (who reigned from January to April 69). The only way to get round this would be to discount the three short-lived emperors, regard the sixth as Vespasian (69–79), the seventh who lasted only a little while as Titus (79–81), and see Domitian (81–96) as the 'eighth who is also one of the seven', i.e. Nero *redivivus*.[116] Yet even Charles, though supporting a Domitianic date, is convinced that 'Domitian cannot be identified with Nero *redivivus*. Not a single phrase

[110] Thus Tacitus, *Ann.* 1.1; *Hist.* 1.1.

[111] Josephus, *Ant.* 18.32, also describes him as 'the second emperor of the Romans'.

[112] *Vesp.* 1.

[113] Cf. his famous epigram on Galba in *Hist.* 1.49: 'omnium consensu capax imperii nisi imperasset.'

[114] *BJ* 4.491–6. [115] *Apocalypse*, 705.

[116] Cf. Juvenal, *Sat.* 4.37f., where Domitian is called a bald-headed Nero, and Martial, *Epig.* 11.33, who refers to Domitian's as 'Nero's death'.

descriptive of the latter can be rightly applied to Domitian.'[117] Moreover the statement, 'one', namely the sixth, 'is now reigning', becomes meaningless mystification – unless it is intended to look like prophecy by a deliberate antedating of the real time of writing.[118]

There have been various ways in which scholars have sought to evade what seems the obvious conclusion.

1. The commonest is to say that the passage was indeed written under Galba (or, by discounting the three, under Vespasian) but has been incorporated in the later work. This is the line taken, for instance, by Peake, who says: '17.10 was probably written under Vespasian and 17.11 under Titus. But there are touches which carry us down to the reign of Domitian'.[119] Why the whole was not properly taken in hand and revised in the light of events (or non-events) no one explains. As Kümmel says:[120]

> None of these hypotheses can make clear why an author would have added to or inserted into a later writing an early writing of his own, without correcting it, so that by this route we have no access to a solution of the literary problem of Revelation.

2. Another way has been to deny that the count of the emperors starts at the beginning. Thus Strobel[121] begins with Caligula on the grounds that he was the first to 'fall' (by violent death) and was also the first emperor to begin to reign in the post-messianic, or Christian, age, and, by omitting the three of 68–9, he succeeds in making Domitian the sixth. Reicke,[122] following Allo,[123] argues that Nero is the first (and sum) of the evil emperors, but this yields Domitian as the sixth only by treating Otho and Vitellius as one. And, if the knowledge is so vital to the calculation, why is Nero merely called 'one of the seven' and not the first (or even 'the first and the last, the Alpha and the Omega' of evil)? A weakness of this alternative in any form[124] is that all the comparable extra-canonical counts, Jewish or Christian, start at the beginning.

[117] *Revelation* I, xcvif. Similarly Peake, *Revelation*, 132f.

[118] So H. B. Swete, *The Apocalypse of St John*, 1906, ad loc.

[119] *Revelation*, 348; similarly Charles, *Revelation*, ad loc. M.-E. Boismard, ' "L'Apocalypse" ou "les Apocalypses" de S. Jean', *RB* 56, 1949, 507–41, and 'Notes sur l'Apocalypse', 59, 1952, 161–81, argues for two parallel visions, one dating from the time of Nero, the other from Vespasian or the beginning of Domitian. In contrast to Charles he puts the letters to the seven churches still later.

[120] Kümmel, *INT*, 464.

[121] A. Strobel, 'Abfassung und Geschichtstheologie der Apokalypse nach Kap. XVII. 9–11', *NTS* 10, 1963–4, 433–45 (especially 439–41).

[122] *RSR* 60, 175–81; anticipated again by C. H. Turner, op. cit., 217.

[123] *L'Apocalypse*, 270, 281f.

[124] For one starting with Claudius, see below pp. 249–52.

3. The third way, which seems to be gaining in favour with recent commentators[125] and is at least more straightforward, is to give up the whole business of trying to trace any reference to specific emperors at all and view the whole thing as *purely* symbolic. The sixth king is then the last but one before the end-time, whoever he may happen to be. But this way of cutting the knot does less than justice to two factors.

The first is that, as virtually all agree, there must be a reference to Nero *redivivus* in the beast that 'once was alive and is alive no longer but has yet to ascend out of the abyss before going to perdition' – and he is distinctly said to be one of the seven, even though mysteriously he is to return as an eighth. He is linked too with the beast that 'appeared to have received a death-blow, but the mortal wound was healed' (13.3), that 'had been wounded by the sword and yet lived' (13.14). This, as we have seen, almost certainly refers to Nero's death by his own sword, and the cipher which gives his identity is specifically said to represent a man's name (13.18). It therefore becomes difficult to deny that there is *some* historical reference, and one which was intended to be well understood.

Now we know from both Tacitus[126] and Suetonius[127] that the belief that Nero was not really dead but would come back circulated within a very short time.[128] There have been elaborate attempts to trace stages in the development of this myth,[129] to show that at first it presupposed that he was physically alive and in hiding, later that he was dead but would return from the underworld. It is then argued that Rev. 17.8, in saying that he would 'ascend out of the abyss', reveals a late, non-historical form of it, which, supposedly, could not have arisen till the time of Domitian.[130] This surely is to misunderstand

[125] E.g. Beckwith; Lohmeyer, *Die Offenbarung des Johannes* (HNT 16), Tübingen 1926, [2]1953; M. Kiddle, *Revelation* (Moffatt NTC), 1940; Bowman, *IDB* IV, 60f.; Caird; and G. R. Beasley-Murray, *Revelation* (NCB), 1974.

[126] *Hist.* 2.8f.: 'About this time [early in 69] Achaia and Asia were terrified by a false rumour of Nero's arrival. The reports with regard to his death had been varied, and therefore many people imagined and believed that he was alive.' Tacitus goes on to describe an impostor who was caught and executed.

[127] *Nero* 57: 'A few faithful friends used to lay spring and summer flowers on his grave for some years . . .; they even continued to circulate his edicts, pretending he was still alive and would soon return to confound his enemies.'

[128] For other references, cf. Orac. Sib. 4.119–24, 137–9; 5.33f., 104–7, 139–54, 214–20, 361–70; Asc. Isa. 4.2–4; some of which at least are probably to be dated from the reign of Vespasian, and the last perhaps even earlier.

[129] E.g. Peake, *Revelation*, 123–33; Beckwith, *Apocalypse*, 400–3; Charles, *Revelation* II, 76–87.

[130] In fact even by the death of Domitian Nero would still not have been sixty and could well have been supposed to be alive – like Martin Bormann in South

the psychology of such expectation. There are some characters in history (Frederick Barbarossa and Hitler are other examples) who have been so feared or hated in their lifetimes that men cannot really believe that they have seen the last of them. At one level of their minds they know that they are dead, yet at another they cannot accept it. In what form these characters will reappear depends not on the passage of time but on the pattern of credulity. It did not take long for Herod to think that Jesus might be John the Baptist risen from the dead, and there is no ground for supposing that Christians, who shared the same ambiguity about whether Nero was *really* dead (contrast Rev. 13.3,12 and 14 with 17.8 and 11), should not very soon have envisaged him emerging from the abyss – which for this author is in any case primarily the abode of evil rather than the place of the departed.[131] So we may conclude not only that the reference to Nero is quite specific but that the expectation of his return may have early historical associations. Indeed there are other passages, to which we shall be coming back, which could reflect the entirely mundane fears that Nero would return to wreak his vengeance on Rome at the head of a Parthian host.

The other factor which a purely symbolic, non-historical interpretation of ch. 17 ignores is the parallel already mentioned with this kind of calculation to be found elsewhere in Jewish and Christian apocalyptic. In Orac. Sib. 5.1–50, each of the Roman emperors up to and including Hadrian[132] is listed under the thinnest of disguises. There is a similar passage in Ep. Barn. 4.4 where there are ten kings, including three under one, whom Lightfoot, I believe rightly, sees as referring to 'the association with himself by Vespasian of his two sons Titus and Domitian in the exercise of supreme power'.[133] But whatever the interpretation it is evident that some specific allusion is

---

America at a similar interval after the second world war. Indeed Dio Chrysostom, *Orat.* 21.10, in a passage almost certainly written under Domitian (cf. J. W. Cohoon (ed.), Loeb Classical Library, II, 1939, 271), says specifically: 'Even now everybody wishes he were still alive. And the great majority do believe that he is.' This is quoted in Prigent's admirably factual review of the expectation, *RHPR* 55, 227–32. Guthrie, *NTI*, 954, regards the use of the Nero myth as 'extremely inconclusive for a Domitianic dating'. In fact it is one of those arguments from 'development' constantly reiterated by New Testament scholars that needs exploding.

[131] Cf. Rev. 11.7, where the beast coming up out of the abyss is modelled on the beasts in Dan. 7.2f. coming up out of the sea.

[132] Or, if v. 51 is not an interpolation, Marcus Aurelius.

[133] *AF*, 240f. But cf. p. 315f. below for a fuller discussion.

intended. Similarly in II Esd. 11 we read of the vision of an eagle with twelve wings and three heads, the interpretation of which follows in 12.10–34. Again, it is palpably clear that particular historical references are intended. The three heads are once more the Flavian dynasty, whose identity this time is not in doubt:

> As for the greatest head, which you saw disappear, it signifies one of the kings who will die in his bed, but in great agony.[134] The two that survived will be destroyed by the sword; one of them will fall by the sword of the other, [135] who will himself fall by the sword in the last days[136] (12.26–8).

The historical perspective of II Esdras is provided by 12.17f.:

> As for the voice which you heard speaking from the middle of the eagle's body, and not from its heads, this is what it means: In the midst of the time of that kingdom[137] great conflicts will arise, which will bring the empire into danger of falling; and yet it will not fall then, but will be restored to its original strength.

Here the troubles following the death of Nero lie well in the past, and Domitian, whose evil reign is vividly depicted in 11.36–12.1, is dead. The central vision of II Esdras 3–14 dates itself (and there is no good reason to doubt it) in the year 100, 'in the thirtieth year after the fall of Jerusalem' (3.1), and the contrast with the perspective of Revelation could hardly be greater. In this book, as in I and II Baruch, the Epistle of Barnabas and the Sibylline Oracles, there are unmistakable allusions to the destruction of Jerusalem.[138] In Revelation there are none at all – in fact just the opposite. And whereas in II Esdras the tally of kings to date is twelve, and in the Epistle of Barnabas ten, in Revelation the sixth is still reigning. Yet we are asked to believe by those who hold to a Domitianic date that Revelation and II Esdras are virtually contemporary.

The contortions to which the commentators have been driven in the interpretation of ch. 17 are I am convinced self-imposed by the 'discrepancy', as Beckwith calls it,[139] between the clear statement that the sixth king is now living and what Torrey called their 'stubborn conviction'[140] that the book cannot be earlier than the time of

[134] I.e. Vespasian; cf. Suetonius, *Vesp.* 24.

[135] I.e. Titus. Strong rumours of his murder by Domitian are denied by Suetonius, *Tit.* 9.3; but cf. Dio Cassius, *Hist.* 66.26.2.

[136] I.e. Domitian; cf. Suetonius, *Dom.* 17.

[137] The NEB here follows the Latin version, 'after this second king's reign', which Box in Charles, *AP* II, 613, is surely correct in arguing is mistaken. The symbolism of the vision requires a word meaning 'in the midst', as in the Syriac and Armenian versions.

[138] For the details, cf. p. 316f. below.

[139] *Apocalypse*, 705.

[140] Torrey, *Apocalypse*, 73f.

Domitian. Drop this conviction and the evidence falls into place. With it too disappears the need for the aspersions which scholars have not hesitated to rain upon the head of the unfortunate author or his editor. Thus, Perrin[141] says bluntly:

> The conditions implied by the book as a whole simply do not fit. Either the author is reusing an earlier text or he does not know his emperors.

Charles excuses him by introducing a particularly crass reviser, whom he describes summarily as:

> profoundly stupid and ignorant, a narrow fanatic and celibate, not quite loyal to his trust as editor; an arch-heretic, though, owing to his stupidity, probably an unconscious one.[142]

Yet to be compelled, in the words of a recent commentator,[143] 'to write off as the interpolation of an imbecile anything which is inconsistent with one's own interpretation' scarcely inspires confidence.

So, if we drop the Domitianic hypothesis as itself the cause of confusion, can we come to any positive conclusion with regard to the dating of the book?

The simplest hypothesis is to take literally the indication of 17.10 that Galba is on the throne and to put the book late in 68, some six months after the suicide of Nero, when, with the public collapse of the structure of authority, the imminent end of 'Babylon' and all it stood for might plausibly have seemed in sight. This case is strongly argued by Henderson[144] writing as a Roman historian. Apart from its fitting 17.10f. (and he fails to see any reason why Galba, Otho and Vitellius should not be counted – especially Galba), he believes (*a*) that 9.14–16 and 16.12, with their reference to hordes coming from the east across the Euphrates, reflect the early expectation of Nero's return with the host of the king of Parthia, whose frontier with the Roman empire was formed by that river;[145] (*b*) that 11.2 (where the approaches to the temple area are in heathen hands) and 20.9 (where the hosts of Gog and Magog 'lay siege to the camp of God's people and the city that he loves') suit the current situation in Judaea;

141 *NTI*, 81.

142 *Revelation* I, xviii. His comments on the editor's efforts in 22.18f. are particularly pungent.

143 H. Richards, *What the Spirit Says to the Churches: A Key to John's Apocalypse*, 1967, 26.

144 *Nero*, 439–43. So also Torrey, op. cit., 58–89.

145 Cf. Tacitus, *Hist.* 1.2; Suetonius, *Nero* 57; and many of the references in the Sibylline Oracles given above. But it has to be admitted that the dating of the Parthian scare cannot with certainty be established so early. Cf. Peake, *Revelation*, 128, who criticizes Henderson at this point.

(*c*) that 17.16f. clearly imply internecine strife and civil war, which had 'an excellent basis of probability in the general outlook at the end of AD 68, but no such basis at all under Vespasian or Domitian'; and (*d*) that in 18.17f. the account of the burning of Rome, while 'the sea-captains and voyagers, the sailors and those who traded by sea, stood at a distance and cried out as they saw the smoke of her conflagration', is based on memories of the fire of Rome some four years earlier.[146]

Before however settling for this date it is perhaps worth bringing into the picture an ingeniously argued variation upon it. Edmundson[147] puts forward a reconstruction which he claims not only does better justice to the internal evidence but succeeds also in turning the external evidence to positive account. This, it will be remembered, said that John was banished by Domitian and restored by Nerva. Now in December 69 Vespasian was acclaimed emperor. But for the first half of 70 he was occupied in Alexandria, while his elder son Titus was engaged upon the siege of Jerusalem. His younger son, Domitian, the sole representative of the family in Rome, accepted the name of Caesar and the imperial residence[148] and was invested with full consular authority (consulare imperium), his name being placed at the head of all dispatches and edicts.[149] As Josephus puts it, he was ruler until his father should come,[150] and for over six months, with the backing of the army chief Mucianus, his writ ran.[151] In Edmundson's words,[152]

> Though but a boy of eighteen his head became filled with ambitious ideas, and he began, says Suetonius,[153] to use his power in so arbitrary a manner as to give proof of what he was to become later. To such an extent was this the case that Dion Cassius[154] tells us that Vespasian wrote to him from Alexandria 'I am much obliged to you, my son, for letting me still be emperor and for not having yet deposed me.'

In the repressive measures required after the chaos to restore law and order Edmundson suggests that the sort of inflammatory language used by the Christian prophet John could well have led, as Tertullian's tradition says, to his narrowly escaping death and to deportation from

146 Mr James Stevenson, the editor of *A New Eusebius*, has made the same point to me. He believes the description is coloured by the view from the port of Ostia. Similarly Eckhardt, *Der Tod des Johannes*, 63, who notes that the doom-song pronounced over Tyre in Ezek. 27, on which so much of the rest of Rev. 18 is modelled, contains no reference to a fire. He suggests that the transition to the past tense in vv. 17b–19 reflects actual memories.

147 Op. cit., 164–79. 148 Tacitus, *Hist.* 4.2; Suetonius, *Dom.* 1.

149 Tacitus, *Hist.* 4.3; Dio Cassius, *Hist.* 65.2.1f. 150 *BJ* 4.654.

151 Tacitus, *Hist.* 4.11, 44–7, 68, 86. 152 Op. cit., 170.

153 *Dom.* 1. 154 *Hist.* 65.2.3; cf. Tacitus, *Hist.* 4.51; Suetonius, *Dom.* 1.

Rome, early in 70, through a sentence passed in Domitian's name.[155] In June Domitian left Rome, and shortly afterwards Vespasian arrived, determined to conduct himself with great moderation and clemency.[156] The following year he took as his colleague in the consulship M. Cocceius Nerva, a lawyer and future emperor. Edmundson goes on:

> Nerva held office during the first *nundinum* of 71 AD, and it is permissible to believe that in accordance with tradition one of the sentences quashed by him was that which sent John to Patmos. If by an order of Nerva he were now released, his exile would have lasted almost exactly one year.[157]

So he was banished by Domitian and restored by Nerva, as the tradition says – but in 70–1!

It is undoubtedly clever (though his interpretation of Domitian and Nerva is not original).[158] But how then does Edmundson resolve the crucial calculation in 17.10 of the king now reigning being the sixth? He believes that the key to the understanding of this whole passage is that it deals simply with that period of Roman history which he calls 'the Neronian cycle' – for Nero is not simply one of the seven heads, he is the Beast itself. He takes the words 'five are fallen' (ἔπεσαν) to imply that

> in each of these five cases there was a violent death. Augustus and Tiberius could not be described as 'fallen', even had their reigns come within the Seer's purview. The five are Claudius, who adopted Nero as his son and heir, Nero himself, Galba, Otho and Vitellius.[159] 'The one who is' signifies the man for the moment invested with imperial power, Domitian, the acting Emperor, who banished the writer. 'The one not yet come' is the real Emperor Vespasian, who had not yet arrived at Rome to take into his hands the reins of government, and 'he will continue only for a short while,' for Nero – 'the beast that was, and is not, who is also an eighth, and is one of the seven' – will quickly return from the East whither he had fled, and once more seat himself on the throne. And 'his end is perdition,' for after his return will immediately follow the great struggle between Christ and Antichrist, when the latter will be overthrown and cast alive into the lake of fire.[160]

[155] One can only surmise that he was sent to Patmos because he belonged to the jurisdiction of the province of Asia before coming to the capital.

[156] Suetonius, *Vesp.* 8 and 10.

[157] Op. cit., 171f. For the details, see his references.

[158] Hort, *Apocalypse*, xxix, quotes B. Weiss for a similar view as far back as 1869 (cf. also Peake, *Revelation*, 74f.). It was adopted, tentatively, by Simcox, *Revelation*, l–li, followed by E. C. Selwyn, *Authorship of the Apocalypse*, 94–6; *Christian Prophets*, 120–2.

[159] Claudius, Galba and Vitellius were murdered, Nero and Otho committed suicide.

[160] Op. cit., 175f.

The ten horns with their ten diadems of 13.1 he takes (as others have) to be governors of the chief provinces of the empire and he sees in the prediction of 17.12, that 'for one hour' they 'are to share with the beast the exercise of royal authority', the fearful battering of Rome in the events of 68–9:

> They together with the beast will come to hate the whore; they will strip her naked and leave her desolate, they will batten on her flesh and burn her to ashes (17.16).

The writer, says Edmundson,[161]

> had seen it with his own eyes – the storming and burning of the Capitol by the foreign mercenaries of Vitellius, and the subsequent capture and sacking of the city by the infuriated Flavian army under Mucianus and Antonius Primus on December 19 to 21, 69 AD. At no other time, certainly not in the end of Domitian's reign, was it possible to speak of Rome as fallen, or for the Seer to have raised his triumphant cry 'Rejoice over her, thou heaven, and ye holy apostles and prophets; for God hath avenged you on her' (18.20).

To bear out the seer's description of the plight of Babylon in ch. 18 he sets the comments of Tacitus[162] on the burning of the Capitol and the capture of the city by the Flavian troops:

> From the foundation of the city to that hour the Roman republic had felt no calamity so deplorable, so shocking as that....
>
> The city exhibited one entire scene of ferocity and abomination.... Rivers of blood and heaps of bodies at the same time; and by the side of them harlots, and women that differed not from harlots – all that unbridled passion can suggest in the wantonness of peace – all the enormities that are committed when a city is sacked by its relentless foes – so that you could positively suppose that Rome was at one and the same time frantic with rage and dissolved in sensuality....
>
> Lamentation was heard from every quarter, and Rome was filled with cries of despair and the horrors of a city taken by storm.[163]

As he says, it is tempting to believe that 'both writers are describing one and the same unique event'. He further suggests that the scenes of the kings assembled at Armageddon (16.16) and of the hosts of Gog and Magog, countless as the sands of the sea, mustered for battle from the nations of the four quarters of the earth (20.8), are

161 Ibid., 169. 162 *Hist.* 3.72, 83; 4.1.

163 Op. cit., 169. He could have cited Josephus' account of the same events (*BJ* 4.645–54), reaching their climax in the death of Vitellius: 'Then issued from the palace Vitellius drunk and, knowing the end was come, gorged with a banquet more lavish and luxurious than ever; dragged through the mob and subjected to indignities of every kind, he was finally butchered in the heart of Rome. He had reigned for eight months and five days; and had fate prolonged his life, the very empire, I imagine, would not have sufficed for his lust' (4.651f.).

inspired in part at least by the battles earlier in 69 in which the armies of Vitellius and Vespasian contended for the mastery of the empire.

> On the one side were troops from Italy, Spain and Portugal, Gaul, the German Rhine frontier, even from far distant Batavia and Britain; on the other, legions from the Danube frontier, and behind these the armies of Syria, Judaea and Egypt, with auxiliaries from the furthermost East, from the borderlands of the Euphrates and Tigris.[164] The Seer is not describing these battles,[165] but he saw the medley of troops from every nation under heaven actually fighting in the streets of Rome, and the scenes he witnessed still so freshly imprinted in his mind are vividly reflected in the imagery of his vision.[166]

I have quoted Edmundson at some length[167] because it is a case that has been almost entirely ignored.[168] It has its weak spots like any other, but a number of his points are impressive. The sack and burning of Rome in 69 is a more convincing parallel than the fire of 64, and the proximity of the foreign troops to the temple area in 11.2 would suit the early months of 70 better even than 68. Above all the turning of the external evidence is clever – if not too clever. Yet to start the count of the emperors with Claudius is strained.

But, whatever the details of the events reflected, the Apocalypse is, I believe, intelligible only if, as Tertullian says, its author had himself been 'a partaker of the sufferings' (1.9) *in Rome* during and after the Neronian persecution.[169] In comparison with this, the precise dating (late 68 or early 70) is of secondary significance. There is in any case no need to suppose that all his visions, any more than those of the Old Testament prophets, came to him at once. Nevertheless there is, I suggest, much to be said for the hypothesis that in exile the seer was using his imagination, under the influence of scripture and the Spirit,

[164] For the details, cf. B. W. Henderson, *Civil War and Rebellion in the Roman Empire, A.D. 69–70*, 1908, 21–35; 128–44; and recently P. A. L. Greenhalgh, *The Year of the Four Emperors*, 1975, and K. Wellesley, *The Long Year AD 69*, 1975.

[165] In fact the forces of Gog and Magog in 20.9 are apparently marching upon Jerusalem.

[166] Op. cit., 177.

[167] He has still further parallels to offer (177–9) of earthquakes, pestilence, hurricane, and volcanic eruption, but these inevitably carry less conviction since they are not unique historical events.

[168] The only discussion of it I know is in Peake, *Revelation*, 82f., 95f., who is impressed but rejects it in favour of the traditional dating, adding (96): 'It may be granted that the case for a date in the reign of Domitian has sometimes been overstated. . . . The indications of earlier date are not to be denied'. Henderson, *Five Roman Emperors*, 45, welcomes Edmundson's support for his own early dating but does not say if it has shifted him from late 68 to early 70.

[169] This is strongly maintained by Eckhardt, though his case that John had also been in Jerusalem in 68–9 (*after* his exile in Patmos; cf. the 'I was' of 1.9) seems to me much more doubtful.

to reflect upon the terrible events of the latter 60s, both in Rome and in Jerusalem, and then dispatching his warning of what could lie ahead of them to those Asian churches whose spiritual state concerned him so intimately.[170] As it turned out, it was Jerusalem that fell in the autumn of 70 and Babylon that survived. The universal martyrdom of the Christian church did not materialize, neither did the shortly promised *parousia*. He himself was to be released before long, and he could well, as Clement's legend has it, have lived on to a ripe old age organizing the troublesome congregations of Asia Minor. But whether he was the same John of whom these and other stories are told, and what is his connection, if any, with the remaining Johannine writings, must be left to the next chapter.

[170] Selwyn, *Christian Prophets*, 212–21, held that Rev. 4–22 was written in Rome under Galba in 68–9 and *caused* the author's banishment, by Domitian, in the early part of 70 to Patmos, where he then wrote chapters 1–3 as a covering letter to the Asian churches. This is by no means impossible. Yet the continuity of ch. 1 with 4.1ff. and the unemended state of 17.10 ('one is now reigning') militate against it.

IX

The Gospel and Epistles of John

SO FINALLY AMONG the books of the New Testament we turn to the rest of the Johannine literature. It is appropriate and relevant to put it this way because whatever the relationship between the Apocalypse and the gospel and epistles traditionally ascribed to St John there are implications to be drawn. Fortunately there is no need here to seek to establish in advance the authorship of all or indeed any of the books mentioned – or this chapter would have to be far longer than in any case it is. Indeed one of the facts about the remarkable scholarly consensus which we shall be noting on the dating of the Johannine literature is that it cuts across almost every possible division. Those who believe that all five books – the Revelation, the gospel and the three epistles – are by one man, and that man the apostle John, and those who hold to none of these, or to almost every possible permutation of them, find common ground in dating both the Revelation and the gospel and epistles in the years ±90–100.

Hort, as we have seen, with Lightfoot and Westcott, believed that it was possible to hold that the Apocalypse and the remaining books came from the same pen only if they were *not* written at the same time. The Apocalypse, they contended, came from the late 60s, while the gospel and epistles must be assigned to the last decade of the first century 'and even to the close of it'.[1] They thus thought it possible to explain the great difference in their Greek styles, though this was not, as Hort insisted, a *reason* for the early dating of Revelation, which rested for him on independent grounds.[2] Baur indeed argued for the

[1] B. F. Westcott, *John*, xl; *The Epistles of St John*, 1883, xxxif. Westcott could not say which came first. Lightfoot, *Biblical Essays*, 198, held that the first epistle was intended to be circulated with the gospel, as an epilogue to it.

[2] Op. cit., xl: 'It would be easier to believe the Apocalypse was written by an

early dating, and apostolicity, of the Apocalypse in the clear understanding that it had nothing whatever to do with the gospel, which he and his Tübingen disciples dated up to a hundred years later. If one thing has become clear in the century since Lightfoot, Westcott and Hort, it is that common authorship of the Apocalypse and the gospel cannot credibly be argued on the interval of time needed for John to master the Greek language.[3]

The Greek of the Apocalypse is not that of a beginner whose grammar and vocabulary might improve and mature into those of the evangelist. It is the pidgin Greek of someone who appears to know exactly what he is about with his strange instrument and whose cast of mind and vocabulary is conspicuously different from, and more colourful than, that of the correct, simple but rather flat style of the gospel and the epistles.[4] Indeed what is astonishing is the number and the diversity of scholars who have clung to the tradition of common authorship – whoever that author may be. They include not only the more conservative Roman Catholics and English-speaking Evangelicals but such names as Harnack, Zahn, Lohmeyer, Preisker, Schlatter and Stauffer, and one is bound to weigh the final footnote which Beckwith appends to his long and balanced discussion of the issue:

> The present commentator ventures to say that his earlier conviction of the impossibility of a unity of authorship has been much weakened by a study of the two books prolonged through many years.[5]

For all that one wonders, if it were not for the strong testimony to common authorship in the external tradition[6] (which yet is no stronger

---

unknown John than that both books belong alike to St John's extreme old age. The supposition of an early date relieves us however from any such necessity, and the early date, as we have seen, is much the most probable on independent grounds.' But Armitage Robinson in his review of Hort's book, *JTS* 10, 1909, 8, had his doubts: 'I have long felt, and cannot get away from the feeling, that the adoption of the earlier date was primarily a result of apologetic controversy.' Yet it must also be remembered that Hort's lectures were first given in 1879, when this was the general view.

[3] Cf. Peake, *Revelation*, 57–63.

[4] For an exhaustive analysis of the stylistic differences, cf. Charles, 'A Short Grammar of the Apocalypse', *Revelation* I, cxvii–clix.

[5] *Apocalypse*, 362. Similarly C. F. Nolloth, *The Fourth Evangelist*, 1925, ch. 8, confesses that he still could not get away from seeing all the Johannine books as coming from the same mind over the same period.

[6] The only breach in it is the powerful counter-argument of Dionysius of Alexandria (*c.* 247–65) quoted by Eusebius, *HE* 7.25, which anticipates most of the points made by modern critics. But this is not ancient testimony (he produces none except the hearsay evidence of two graves of men called John at Ephesus) but an early, and notable, application of critical principles.

than that for apostolic authorship, which many even of those who accept common authorship agree in rejecting), whether critics would ever have thought of ascribing such superficially (and not so superficially) diverse writings to the same hand.[7] Nevertheless *some* association between them is ultimately undeniable. Even if they are not the product of the same 'school',[8] the Apocalypse seems to presuppose at the very least some familiarity with Christianity in the Johannine idiom. Since the writer has evidently had an association with the congregations of the Ephesus area over an extended period (cf. Rev. 2.4,19; 3.2; etc.), then, if the Apocalypse is to be dated between 68 and 70, this presupposes the presence of Johannine-type teaching in western Asia Minor at any rate in the early 60s, if not earlier. This, of course, carries no implications for the dating of the actual gospel or epistles of John, which could have been *written* a good deal later – or earlier. But it is a factor that must be taken into account in any overall hypothesis.

Meanwhile it will be better to begin at the other end and ask what is the evidence, external and internal, for dating the gospel and epistles. And of these, whichever way round they turn out to have been written, the gospel is clearly the determinative document: the evidence to be derived from the epistles has to be brought in to test any hypothesis framed for the gospel rather than *vice versa*.

If then we start, as we did with the Apocalypse, with the external evidence for the date of the gospel, we come up against the fact that it is much vaguer, and less secure, than it is for the Apocalypse. This is paradoxical because, while Lightfoot, Westcott and Hort declined to accept what Hort admitted to be the powerful external evidence for the dating of the latter in the time of Domitian, they, with all the other conservative scholars who argued for apostolic authorship, accepted virtually without question the traditional picture of the fourth gospel as the product of the last years of a very old man.[9]

Yet if we ask what is the origin and basis of this tradition, it is

[7] It is to be observed that even at the points of overlap their vocabulary is subtly different – e.g. Rev. 'the Word of God': John 'the Word'; Rev. 'the Lamb': John 'the Lamb of God'; Rev. ἀρνίον: John ἀμνός; Rev. Ἰερουσαλήμ: John Ἱεροσόλυμα; Rev. ἔθνη, the heathen: John ἔθνος, the Jewish nation.

[8] So e.g. J. Weiss, Bousset, Moffatt, Barrett, Brown. But it is certainly not fair, as some of these do, to regard the differences of style between the Apocalypse and the other Johannine writings and those within the latter group as comparable, as though they could all be put down to different disciples of the same master. The latter are differences of degree, the former of kind.

[9] Cf. Westcott, *John*, xxxvi. For a popular presentation of this picture, cf. J. Armitage Robinson, *The Study of the Gospels*, 1902, 151–7.

extraordinarily elusive. That the apostle John *lived* to a great age, into the reign of Trajan (98–117),[10] and that he was the last evangelist to *write*[11] are both well attested in the tradition. But that he wrote as a very old man is an inference which only appears late and accompanied by other statements which show that it is clearly secondary and unreliable. The Muratorian Canon describing the origin of the gospel[12] suggests no date, but it presupposes that John's 'fellow-disciples' including Andrew are still alive and with him, and thus argues against a very late period. The so-called Anti-Marcionite Prologue[13] records that 'the gospel of John was revealed and given to the churches by John while still in the body' (in some mss 'after writing the Apocalypse'). But it is improbable that this statement rests, as it claims, on the authority of Papias, since Eusebius quotes nothing from him on the fourth gospel and would surely have done so if he had had anything to say. It is even more improbable that, as the Prologue asserts, the gospel was 'dictated' to Papias, and quite impossible that Marcion (who taught in Asia Minor *c.* 130) was 'rejected' by John. Victorinus (died *c.* 304) also says that John wrote the gospel after the Apocalypse,[14] but sees it as written against (among others) Valentinus, who taught in the middle of the second century. Epiphanius (*c.* 315–403) says explicitly[15] that John, refusing in his humility to write a gospel, was compelled by the Holy Spirit to do so in his old age, when he was over ninety, after his return from Patmos and after living 'many years' (ἱκανὰ ἔτη) in Asia. Yet, as we have seen,[16] Epiphanius combined this with the confused statements that John's banishment took place 'under the emperor Claudius' (!) and that he prophesied under that emperor 'before his death.'[17] Later, Georgius Hamartolus in the ninth century says in his *Chronicle*:[18]

[10] Irenaeus, *Adv. haer.* 2.22.5; 3.3.4; quoted Eusebius, *HE* 3.23.3f. Jerome, *De vir. ill.* 9, places his death in 'the 68th year after our Lord's passion', i.e. *c.* 98.

[11] Irenaeus, *Adv. haer.* 3.1.1; Clement, apud Euseb. *HE* 6.14.7; and Eusebius himself, *HE* 3.24.7.

[12] Text in K. Aland (ed.), *Synopsis Quattuor Evangeliorum*, Stuttgart [6]1969, 538, or in translation in C. K. Barrett, *The Gospel according to St John*, 1955, 96f.

[13] Aland, op. cit., 533; Barrett, *John*, 96.

[14] Migne, *PL* 5.333; tr. Westcott, *John*, xxxvi. So too the Monarchian Prologue (Aland, op. cit., 538).

[15] *Haer.* 51.12. The Greek text is quoted by Zahn, *INT* III, 197f.; tr. Hort, *Apocalypse*, xviii. Zahn concedes that 'not one of the Church Fathers (Irenaeus, Clement, Origen, Eusebius) says that John wrote his Gospel after his return from Patmos and therefore after the completion of Revelation', but he regards this as confirmed by later tradition.

[16] P. 224 above.

[17] *Haer.* 51.33. [18] Text in Lightfoot, *AF*, 519; tr., 531.

> After Domitian Nerva reigned one year, who recalled John from the island, and allowed him to dwell in Ephesus. He was at that time the sole survivor of the twelve Apostles, and after writing his Gospel received the honour of martyrdom.

He is of interest only because he claims to base the martyrdom of John on a statement of Papias; but this is notoriously doubtful.[19] With regard to the date of the gospel he is merely repeating earlier tradition. The same is true, finally, of another very late version of the Papias legend,[20] which records that

> last of these, John, surnamed the Son of Thunder, when he was now a very old man, as Irenaeus and Eusebius and a succession of trustworthy historians have handed down to us, about the time when terrible heresies had cropped up, dictated the gospel to his own disciple, the virtuous Papias of Hierapolis, to fill up what was lacking in those who before him had proclaimed the word to the nations throughout all the earth.

But it is certain that Irenaeus and Eusebius did *not* say that John dictated his gospel either to Papias or 'when he was now a very old man'.

I have cited this evidence in some detail, most of it worthless, to show how thin is the external testimony for dating (in contrast with authorship). Even the tradition that John wrote *after* the Synoptists (at whatever date) is based on the theory that his purpose was either to complement them by giving the 'spiritual' as opposed to the 'bodily' facts (Clement) or to supplement them by additional matter at the beginning of the ministry (Eusebius). But neither of these is any more than a guess unsubstantiated by critical study.

There is in fact an alternative tradition about the writing of the gospel which is equally legendary, but since I have not seen it quoted in *any* discussion of the question it is perhaps worth inserting as an interesting corrective. It occurs in the Syriac *History of John*, which we had occasion to mention earlier as placing the banishment of John under Nero.[21] This puts the arrival of John in Ephesus quite early,

[19] It is unnecessary at this date to expose once again the weakness of the evidence for an early martyrdom of John; for it has ceased to be considered seriously as a factor in assessing the authorship or date of the Gospel. Cf. A. M. Hunter, 'Recent Trends in Johannine Studies', *ExpT* 71, 1959–60, 222: 'We agree with W. L. Knox that those who accept the early martyrdom of the Apostle show a quite monumental preference for the inferior evidence.'

[20] Catena *Patr. Graec. in S. Joan.* Prooem., first published by B. Corder, Antwerp 1690. Text in Lightfoot, *AF*, 524; tr., 535.

[21] Wright, II, 3–60 (see p. 224 above). It is to be distinguished from the *Acts of John* (Hennecke, *NT Apoc.* II, 188–259), whose only point of contact is with the account, in a separate Syriac manuscript of John's death (Wright, 61–8; Hennecke, 256–8). There is no other mention of the *History of John* in Hennecke, nor is it included in any other collection of apocrypha known to me. Whereas the Greek

the city being the first to receive the gospel of Christ (after, apparently, Edessa in eastern Syria, evidently the home of this tradition as of those mentioned in Eusebius, *HE* 1.13). He came as a youth, and even after a long interval, when the other gospels had been written (in the canonical order), John hesitated to write lest they should say, 'He is a youth'. But he was prevailed upon to do so after some days' persuasion by Peter and Paul, who visited him in Ephesus before going on to see James in Jerusalem. It also says that John lived on to the age of one hundred and twenty, yet combines this tradition and that of his writing last with a date for the gospel prior to the deaths of Peter and Paul (who, it agrees, were slain by Nero) and indeed of James. This totally independent and eccentric chronological tradition, though worthless as history, is nevertheless remarkable – at whatever date it comes from.[22]

The story of the dating of the fourth gospel in modern scholarship is an extraordinarily simple one. On the one hand, the conservatives have not had occasion (at any rate until very recently)[23] to shift their position and have consistently put the gospel in or about the last decade of the first century.[24] On the other hand, the radical critics like Baur began by dating it anything up to 170[25] and have since steadily come down. Thus, P. W. Schmiedel, who wrote the article on John, Son of Zebedee, in the *Encyclopaedia Biblica*, occupied a mediating position with a date between 132 and 140.[26] The upper of these two dates represented the first at which he believed the gospel was quoted (and that still not by name), the lower the revolt of Bar-Cochba, to whom he saw an allusion in John 5.43: 'If another comes

---

Acts of John are docetic and rather dreary (and contain no account of the writing of the gospel) the Syriac *History* is thaumaturgical and much more entertaining. John gets employed as an assistant attendant at the public baths at Ephesus, the takings immediately go up, the procurator's son is discovered bathing in the nude with a harlot, struck dead in judgment, resuscitated, and finally 39,205 persons are baptized by John in a single night and day!

22 R. H. Connolly, 'The Original Language of the Syriac Acts of John', *JTS* 8, 1907, 249–61, argues (against Wright) that it is an original Syriac composition and comes from the end of the fourth century or earlier.

23 Cf. p. 308 below.

24 Even H. P. V. Nunn, who polemizes against every other aspect of modern criticism of the gospel, accepts without question that the gospel and epistles of John were written 'late in the first century or early in the second century' (*The Authorship of the Fourth Gospel*, Eton 1952, 117).

25 The *terminus ad quem* was its first citation by name *c.* 180 by Theophilus of Antioch, *Ad Autolyc.* 2.22.

26 P. W. Schmiedel, *The Johannine Writings*, ET, 1908, 200f.

self-accredited you will welcome him.' There has been much discussion as to whether the gospel is quoted, or rather presupposed, in the language used by Ignatius and Justin Martyr. Certainly there are no direct citations, as there is (without acknowledgment) of I John 4.2f. in the epistle of Polycarp (7.1). Yet Johannine thought-forms unquestionably lie behind a number of passages,[27] and if the gospel itself had not been written by then one has to posit some other (unknown) form of the same tradition. It seems easier to believe that it is the document we know which is being presupposed.[28] But the issue has largely become academic from the point of view of dating the gospel. Thus, Bultmann, who asserts without hesitation (or argument) that 'without question Ignatius did not make use of it', agrees that it cannot be later than *c.* 120.[29] The decisive factor has been the discovery in Egypt of a papyrus fragment (𝔓[52]) of the gospel itself from the first half of the second century,[30] together with fragments of an unknown gospel[31] from *c.* 150, which almost certainly draws on John.[32] As

[27] Especially Ignatius, Magn. 7.1; 8.2; Philad. 7.1; Justin, *Apol.* 1.61; *Dial.* 63, 88, 91. The parallels are set out in Barrett, *John*, 93f., whose presentation is always admirably accurate and fair even when (though not here) I find myself dissenting from his conclusions. For a fuller discussion, cf. J. N. Sanders, *The Fourth Gospel in the Early Church*, Cambridge 1943; C. Maurer, *Ignatius von Antioch und das Johannesevangelium*, Zürich 1949; and especially F. M. Braun, *Jean le Theologien*, I: *Jean le Theologien et son évangile dans l'église ancienne*, Paris 1959.

[28] Cf. R. E. Brown, *The Gospel according to John* (Anchor Bible), New York 1966–70, I, lxxxi, who concludes: 'An objective evaluation would seem to indicate that the argument for the late dating of John because the Gospel was not used in the early second century has lost whatever probative force it may have had.'

[29] R. Bultmann, *The Gospel of John*, ET Oxford 1971, 12. The introduction to the ET from which these words and the dating are taken is by W. Schmithals.

[30] Cf. Brown, *John* I, lxxxiii: 'The dating of this papyrus to 135–50 has been widely accepted; and the latest attempt to date the New Testament papyri by K. Aland, *NTS* 9, 1962–3, 307, assigns to 𝔓[52] a date at the "beginning of the second century".'

[31] Egerton Papyrus 2; edd. H. I. Bell and T. C. Skeat, *Fragments of an Unknown Gospel*, 1935.

[32] So Dodd, 'A New Gospel' in *NT Studies*, 12–52; and Jeremias in Hennecke, *NT Apoc.* I, 95. It is significant that it appears to reflect the text of John's gospel but only synoptic-type tradition rather than quotations from the gospels themselves. By contrast exactly the opposite seems to be true of the 'Secret Gospel of Mark', which betrays clear knowledge of the text of Mark but (at most) echoes of the Johannine tradition. In fact, *pace* R. E. Brown, 'The Relation of the "Secret Gospel of Mark" to the Fourth Gospel', *CBQ* 36, 1974, 466–85, I am not persuaded of literary dependence in either direction. I would see in the Secret Gospel an independent version of the story of the raising of Lazarus, related to the gospel of John in the same kind of way in which I believe the parables in the Gospel of Thomas are related to those in the synoptic gospels. Its significance is that it sup-

Kümmel summarizes the present situation,[33]

> If John was known in Egypt in the first quarter of the second century, the beginning of the second century is a *terminus ad quem*. On the other hand, John's knowledge of Luke is extremely probable, so it could not have been written before *ca.* 80–90. The assumption that John was written probably in the last decade of the first century is today almost universally accepted.

Before turning to the *terminus a quo*, it is interesting to observe how remarkably general is the consensus at this point. With marginal variation at each end (and even Bultmann goes down as far as 80 for the first composition), the span 90–100 is agreed by Catholic and Protestant, by conservative and radical, by those who defend apostolic authorship and those who reject it, by those who believe that John used the synoptists and those who do not. It includes virtually all those who have recently written commentaries on the gospel,[34] not to mention other interpreters. It is one of the relatively few points at which over a span of two generations Hastings' *Dictionary of the Bible* and *The Interpreter's Dictionary of the Bible* agree, and the consensus includes now the redaction-critics.[35] Indeed many commentators (e.g. Schnackenburg) scarcely bother to discuss the issue of dating, and the space it occupies in introductions, whether to the New Testament or to the gospel, compared with that of authorship is minimal.[36] Kümmel's two-sentence summary quoted above is typical: the question appears to be settled.

Yet it is typical also that he does not advance a single positive reason why this date, roughly corresponding to the end of the reign of

---

plies us with an independent (albeit in this instance much inferior) version of a miracle that has hitherto stood alone and has indeed often been regarded as an invention of John's to illustrate his theological theme.

[33] *INT*, 246.

[34] E.g. J. H. Bernard (ICC), 1928; G. H. C. Macgregor (Moffatt NTC), 1928; E. C. Hoskyns (ed. F. N. Davey), 1940; ²1947; R. Bultmann (KEKNT 2), Göttingen 1941; ET Oxford 1971; A. Wikenhauser, Regensburg 1949; ³1961; H. Strathmann, Göttingen 1951; W. F. Howard in *The Interpreter's Bible*, New York 1952; C. K. Barrett, 1955; R. H. Lightfoot (ed. C. F. Evans), Oxford 1956; A. Richardson, 1959; R. V. G. Tasker (Tyndale NTC), 1960; A. M. Hunter, Cambridge 1965; R. Schnackenburg, I, Freiburg 1965; ET London 1968; II, 1971; R. E. Brown (Anchor Bible), New York 1966–70; J. N. Sanders (ed. B. A. Mastin; Black's NTC), 1968; J. Marsh (Pelican NTC), Harmondsworth 1968; J. C. Fenton (New Clarendon Bible), Oxford 1970; B. Lindars (NCB), 1972.

[35] Cf. Marxsen, *INT*, 259; Perrin, *NTI*, 229f.

[36] An exception, from an earlier period, is H. Latimer Jackson, *The Problem of the Fourth Gospel*, Cambridge 1918, who devotes two chapters (2 and 6) to arriving at a similar conclusion (*c.* 100 (?90)–125). But this was before the discovery of the papyri.

Domitian, is the right one. It is reached purely by a process of elimination. Yet if it is appropriate to the Apocalypse, then one would have thought that almost by definition it would not fit the fourth gospel (traditionally from the same circle in the same area) – or indeed the Johannine epistles, which breathe no hint of public persecution. It is therefore at least worth asking, since the ceiling is now more or less fixed, whether the floor is really as secure as hitherto it has seemed to conservative and radical alike.

The reason for it given by Kümmel is John's use of Luke. Similarly, Barrett writes with assurance:

> A *terminus post quem* may easily be fixed. John knew Mark; he not only knew it but had thoroughly mastered its contents, and expected his readers also to be familiar with them. There is wide agreement that Mark was written either not long before, or soon after, AD 70. We must allow time for Mark to reach the place in which John was written and to be studied and absorbed. This brings us to a date certainly not earlier than AD 80; 90 would perhaps be a safer estimate.[37]

Yet the confidence with which these statements can be made has diminished dramatically in the twenty years since Barrett wrote. For he is now[38] in a minority of Johannine scholars in holding to what used to be the critical orthodoxy, represented for instance by Streeter,[39] that John certainly used Mark, probably Luke and possibly Matthew. The work of P. Gardner-Smith[40] and Dodd[41] has convinced most recent scholars that, whatever the cross-fertilization between the traditions, John is not dependent upon the synoptists for his material and therefore does not *for this reason* have to be dated after them. But there is no need here to argue the case afresh, since it is not of itself decisive for dating purposes. Even if it could be shown that John could not have been written until after the publication of Mark, Luke or Matthew, we have already argued that there is no compelling reason to date these later than the early 60s. Equally, from the other side, those who have abandoned the argument for dependence still

[37] Op. cit., 108. It is interesting that Zahn, who argues strongly for apostolic authorship, makes an almost identical assessment, namely, that the presupposing of the synoptists by John brings the earliest date for the composition of the gospel down to 'the year 75, probably to some time between 80 and 90' (*INT* III, 335).

[38] For a recent reaffirmation of C. K. Barrett's position, cf. 'John and the Synoptic Gospels', *ExpT* 85, 1973–4, 228–33. He rightly observes: 'If the traditional date of the gospel is correct one wonders where the evangelist can have lived if indeed he knew none of the earlier gospels' (233). But he does not think to question 'the traditional date'.

[39] *FG*, ch. 14.

[40] P. Gardner-Smith, *St John and the Synoptic Gospels*, Cambridge 1938.

[41] C. H. Dodd, *Historical Tradition in the Fourth Gospel*, Cambridge 1963.

(as we have seen) wish to retain a dating towards the end of the century. This is true not only of the commentators listed above but of Dodd himself, who ascribes the gospel to an Ephesian elder writing between 90 and 100. He combines this view with the conviction that the tradition behind the gospels goes back a great deal further.[42] At all sorts of points, he maintains, it can be shown to be just as primitive as, if not more primitive than, comparable synoptic material and to reflect the religious, political and geographical conditions of Palestine and Jerusalem prior to the war of 66–70.

Since this is the position from which I myself began this investigation and which I have presupposed in previous publications on John,[43] and since in one form or another it looks like becoming the new critical orthodoxy, I should like to devote some space to saying why it has come to appear to me unsatisfactory. For it is this dissatisfaction that led me, as I explained at the beginning, to reopen the question of the dating of the New Testament as a whole.

Published in his eightieth year, Dodd's great study *Historical Tradition in the Fourth Gospel* marked a watershed in Johannine studies. It converted what I had noted as one of several 'straws in the wind' blowing in much the same direction[44] into a strong presumption that the tradition behind the fourth evangelist is potentially as near to source as that behind any of the others. Yet the question remains, What was the evangelist's own relation to that tradition? Dodd has no doubt that it was an external and second-hand relation. He speaks of the tradition on which he 'depended',[45] which he is 'following'[46] or 'drawing on',[47] as material that 'came into his hands'[48] in the form of 'information received',[49] which he then 'took over',[50] 'made use of'[51] and 'worked upon'[52] to his own purposes. It is a curiously passive relationship – though twice it is suggested that the evangelist 'sought for information'.[53] But, however he acquired it, the presupposition is

[42] Similarly, T. W. Manson, 'Materials for a Life of Jesus: The Fourth Gospel', *Studies in the Gospels and Epistles*, 105–22.

[43] 'The New Look on the Fourth Gospel' in *Twelve NT Studies*, 94–106; 'The Destination and Purpose of St John's Gospel', ibid., 107–25; 'The Relation of the Prologue to the Gospel of St John', *NTS* 9, 1962–3, 120–9 (reprinted in *The Authorship and Integrity of the NT*, 61–72); 'The Place of the Fourth Gospel' in P. Gardner-Smith (ed.), *The Roads Converge*, 1963, 49–74.

[44] 'The New Look', 94. [45] *HTFG*, 59, 431.

[46] Ibid., 138, 265, 288. [47] Ibid., 263, 387.

[48] Ibid., 228; 'came down to him', 138; 'reached him', 180, 217.

[49] Ibid., 244, 431. [50] Ibid., 329. [51] Ibid., 243.

[52] Ibid., 244; 'put his mark on', 226; 'developed', 431.

[53] Ibid., 24, 425.

that he was 'incorporating material which, at a distance of place and time, he did not fully understand'.[54]

And this distance is seen by Dodd as considerable. Indeed it is so great as to raise acutely the question of how the gulf was bridged and what was happening to the tradition in the interval. The evangelist himself and his gospel Dodd assigns to 'a Hellenistic environment' 'late in the first century'.[55] Though 'probably a speaker of Aramaic'[56] (though why, at such a remove of space and time, is not explained), his own interests were very different; and the argument is used more than once that he would have had no motive to invent the details he did. Dodd's concluding summary of John's account of the trial of Jesus is characteristic:

> I doubt very much whether a writer whose work we must place late in the first century and in a Hellenistic environment, could have invented such a persuasive account of a trial conducted under conditions which had long passed away. It is pervaded with a lively sense for the situation as it was in the last half-century before the extinction of Judaean local autonomy. It is aware of the delicate relations between the native and the imperial authorities. It reflects a time when the dream of an independent Judaea under its own king had not yet sunk to the level of a chimaera, and when the messianic idea was not a theologumenon but impinged on practical politics, and the bare mention of a 'king of the Jews' stirred violent emotions; a time, moreover, when the constant preoccupation of the priestly holders of power under Rome was to damp down any first symptoms of such emotions. These conditions were present in Judaea before AD 70, and not later, and not elsewhere. This, I submit, is the true *Sitz im Leben* of the essential elements in the Johannine trial narrative. This narrative is far from being a second-hand *rechauffé* of the Synoptics. While there is evidence for some degree of elaboration by the author, the most probable conclusion is that in substance it represents an independent strain of tradition, which must have been formed in a period much nearer the events than the period when the Fourth Gospel was written, and in some respects seems to be better informed than the tradition behind the Synoptics, whose confused account it clarifies.[57]

Essentially the same point is made of his material on the topography of Jerusalem,[58] his awareness of the geographical and psychological divisions of Palestine before the Jewish war,[59] and his use of metaphors and arguments which would be 'barely intelligible' outside a purely Jewish context in the earliest period.[60]

One may well ask why it should have been to this remote and neglected quarry that the evangelist went for his information or why he should have chosen to take it as 'a starting point for his theological adventure'[61] when his own interests and those of his public were con-

[54] Ibid., 94. [55] Ibid., 120, 243, 246. [56] Ibid., 424. [57] Ibid., 120.
[58] Ibid., 180. [59] Ibid., 243–6. [60] Ibid., 311f.; 332f.; 412f.
[61] Ibid., 312.

fessedly so different. But what needs greatest explanation is the gap in the history of the material itself. For it bears all the marks of having been shaped in Jewish–Christian circles in Judaea, very much in touch with the synagogue, prior to the rebellion of 66 – and then to have suffered from an extended period of cultural isolation and arrested development until it was reused in Hellenistic circles of Asia Minor in the 90s.

At two points only does Dodd see traces of development external to Palestine. First, he thinks that the reference in John 4.53 to the officer in the royal service 'becoming a believer' with 'all his household' seems to reflect the experience of the Gentile mission as recorded in Acts.[62] But this is very questionable.[63] The βασιλικός or king's man in Galilee is evidently a Herodian (not, as in the parallel synoptic tradition, a Roman centurion). Indeed the Gentiles (τὰ ἔθνη) are never mentioned in the gospel,[64] and there is no other sign of contact with the Gentile mission as described in Acts or of the controversies it occasioned.

Secondly, Dodd supposes that

> the 'Testimony of John', while it is well grounded in first-century Jewish belief and practice, and has only the slightest marks of the distinctively Johannine theology – and these readily separable – appears to reflect the situation such as that portrayed in Acts 18.24–19.7 for Ephesus, the probable home of this gospel.[65]

Even if this were so, the situation depicted dates from the period immediately before and after Paul arrived in Ephesus in 52.[66] As Dodd says,

> After that time the supply of such persons must have rapidly declined. I suggest that this gives a rough limit for the period to which we may assign the main development of the tradition here followed by the Fourth Evangelist. There can, I think, be no reasonable doubt that this tradition included very primitive material, but before it reached our evangelist it had undergone development in the environment indicated.[67]

Even therefore if we assume that this Asiatic environment (and not merely a Palestinian one) moulded the interest of the Johannine

[62] Ibid., 193, 426.

[63] I cannot detect, as Dodd argues, that the use of πιστεύειν in 4.53 differs from other examples of Johannine usage (e.g., to go no further, 4.41f.); and in the parallels in Acts (16.34; 18.8) the verb is not used absolutely, as here, but has 'God' or 'the Lord' as object.

[64] Cf. my 'Destination and Purpose', 109–12.

[65] *HTFG*, 426f.

[66] Ibid., 300. Dodd dates it 55–7, but it must be earlier than that.

[67] Ibid., 300.

tradition in Baptist–Christian relationships 'before it reached our evangelist', the influence is still remarkably early.

But when these two possible signs of external development have been noted, Dodd concludes:

> It is the more remarkable how comparatively little the traditional narratives have been affected by late non-Palestinian influences, and how much has come through, even in the report of the teaching, in which we can recognize the authentic atmosphere of early Palestinian Christianity.[68]

Yet this evidence of very early tradition in so late a document poses problems. Dodd gives several examples of bits of tradition that appear to have become 'frozen' in a very primitive state. Thus of the political background of the desert feeding vividly reflected in the attempt of the crowds to seize Jesus and make him king (6.15) he writes:

> At the next stage it would disappear altogether, but the form of tradition which John followed had crystallized at just this stage, and our evangelist has preserved it as it reached him.[69]

If it was locked away for half a century, how and where did it survive in this crystallized condition, with those 'almost forgotten elements in the background of the story which made it at the time so significant for the immediate followers of Jesus'?[70]

Again, he writes of 7.23 ('If a child is circumcised on the Sabbath to avoid breaking the law of Moses, why are you indignant with me for giving health on the Sabbath to the whole of a man's body?'), which he says faithfully reflects contemporary rabbinic disputes:

> The *Sitz im Leben* of such tradition must have been within a Jewish environment such as that of the primitive Church, and in all probability it belongs to an early period. Once the Church, by that time mainly Gentile, had ceased to have relations with the synagogue, such discussions would no longer be kept alive, and only isolated traces of them remain, embedded in the gospels.[71]

But again, we may ask, why and how this fossilized piece of Judaic tradition in a Hellenistic document of the late first century?

Finally, perhaps the most interesting and perplexing example of all is Dodd's suggestion that the predictions by Jesus of his going away and coming back in 14.3 and 16.16 antedate the development (already found in Mark) of such sayings into predictions of *either* resurrection *or parousia*.

> I suggest that John is here reaching back to a very early form of tradition indeed, and making it the point of departure for his profound theological interpretation; and further, that the oracular sayings which he reports have

[68] Ibid., 427. [69] Ibid., 217. [70] Ibid., 222. [71] Ibid., 333.

good claim to represent authentically, in substance if not verbally, what Jesus actually said to his disciples – a better claim than the more elaborate and detailed predictions which the Synoptics offer.[72]

Short of asserting *ipsissima verba* one could hardly make higher claims for any piece of gospel tradition. Yet again, how or why was this preserved apparently immune to subsequent influences or developments from the moment virtually when it left Jesus's lips till an Ephesian elder took it out of the deep freeze and 'incorporated' it two generations later?

If we ask by what route, or when, the evangelist received his material, Dodd is not very forthcoming. The most he will say is that it must have come 'directly or indirectly' from a circle of Jewish-Christian disciples in Judaea who were 'witnesses' to the tradition.[73] Again, if we ask in what form the tradition was received, we are not taken much further:

That some parts of it may have been written down by way of *aide-mémoire* is always possible, and such written sources may have intervened between strictly oral tradition and our Fourth Gospel. If so, I am not concerned with them.[74]

But there is a gap here which strains credibility – and the more primitive the tradition incapsulated in the gospel, the greater the gulf.

There are three possible ways out of this dilemma:

1. One can deny that the tradition is as near to the events in space or time as is claimed.

2. One can fill in the missing links and trace the continuities across the gulf.

3. One can refuse to assume that the evangelist is as remote or isolated from his tradition as is asserted.

1. The first approach really consists in showing that Dodd and others have not made their case and reverting to a situation in which there is no serious gap because there is no serious historical tradition going back to primitive times. I do not believe that this can easily be done. There is no need here to repeat the mass of evidence which in recent years has led to a major revaluation of the historical tradition behind the fourth gospel,[75] reinforcing the conclusion, argued by con-

[72] Ibid., 420. Cf. my *Jesus and His Coming*, 175 and ch.8 generally, where I suggested that if there were any authentic sayings of Jesus promising his own return they were probably something like those in John 14.3,18f.,28; 16.16,22. I argued that the Johannine presentation of a continuing *parousia* beginning on Easter day represented a very primitive (as well as a very profound and mature) form of the tradition, before it had undergone the process of apocalypticization found in the early Paul and the later states of the synoptic material.

[73] *HTFG*, 246f. [74] Ibid., 424.

[75] It is conveniently summarized in popular form in A. M. Hunter's *According*

servative scholars all along,[76] that it reflects intimate contact with a Palestinian world blotted off the map in AD 70. Indeed I have lately become persuaded that, historically and theologically, it is our single most reliable guide to the exceedingly intricate (and historically unrepeatable) relationships between the 'spiritual' and the 'political' in the ministry, trial and death of Jesus.[77]

Even those who have no inclination to regard John as early draw attention not simply to pieces of historical detail embedded in later material (which could come from isolated sources) but to theological categories integral to the gospel which appear to be strangely primitive. Thus Cullmann writes:[78]

> Except for the Gospel of John and the first (Jewish-Christian) part of Acts, no New Testament writing considers Jesus the eschatological Prophet who prepares the way for God.[79]

F. Hahn[80] too speaks of this 'antiquated Christology' in John which appeared at 'an early stage of the tradition' but was 'blurred and covered over by later Christological statements'. Referring to 'traditional material', not only in John 6.14f. (the prophet and king) but in 7.40–2 (the prophet and the messiah of David), 4.19 and 9.17 (a prophet), 4.25 (*Μεσσίας*) and 3.2 (a teacher sent from God), he says:

> We have to reckon with a very early Christological tradition of the primitive church. In such pieces of tradition as Mark 6.1–5, 14–16 and 8.28 this has already completely faded.[81]

---

to John, 1968. Cf. his bibliography, and E. Stauffer, 'Historische Elemente im vierten Evangelium' in E. H. Amberg and U. Kühn (edd.), *Bekenntnis zur Kirche: Festgabe für E. Sommerlath*, Berlin 1960, 33–51.

[76] From Lightfoot's lectures on 'The Authenticity and Genuineness of St John's Gospel' in *Biblical Essays*, 1–198, to L. Morris, *Studies in the Fourth Gospel*, 1969, especially 65–214. The external evidence is much stronger, I believe, than critics, e.g. like Barrett, *John*, 83–8, have allowed. Dodd, who thinks apostolic authorship improbable but not impossible (*HTFG*, 17), writes: 'His [Irenaeus'] evidence is formidable, even if it is not conclusive. Anyone who should take the view that in the absence of any cogent evidence to the contrary it is reasonable to accept Irenaeus' testimony is on strong ground. Of any external evidence to the contrary that could be called cogent I am not aware' (*HTFG*, 12).

[77] 'His Witness is True: A Test of the Johannine Claims' in Moule and Bammel, *Jesus and the Politics of his Day*.

[78] O. Cullmann, *The Christology of the New Testament*, ET ²1963, 38.

[79] For a full discussion of this category and its implications for an early dating of John, cf. F. L. Cribbs, 'A Reassessment of the Date of Origin and the Destination of the Gospel of John', *JBL* 89, 1970, 44–6, and the literature there cited.

[80] F. Hahn, *The Titles of Jesus in Christology*, ET 1969, 352.

[81] Ibid., 383.

With regard also to the gospel's central category of 'sonship' Hahn writes:

> The early view . . . is still clearly preserved in the Gospel of John. The after-effect also shows itself here and there elsewhere in the New Testament.[82]

I believe in fact and have argued[83] that we are nearer in this gospel to the original parabolic source of this father-son language and its Hebraic understanding in terms of character rather than status than in any other part of the New Testament.

As a further witness, the redaction critic J. L. Martyn, who sees John as anything but a source book for the Jesus of history, has to admit, not only that the attitudes which this evangelist records to 'the people of the land' (7.39; cf. 9.34) 'stand proudly among the most accurate statements of Jewish thought in the whole New Testament',[84] but that 5.27 appears in some respects to be the most 'traditional "Son of Man" saying in the whole of the New Testament'.[85] For it is unique in retaining *υἱὸς ἀνθρώπου* without the articles, as in Dan. 7.13;[86] and in its *καὶ ἐξουσίαν ἔδωκεν αὐτῷ* it echoes the *καὶ ἐδόθη αὐτῷ ἐξουσία* of Dan. 7.14.

That there is a connection of some sort to be drawn in John between genuine early tradition and late editing (and that the knot cannot merely be cut by denying the former) is after all the presupposition behind the problem that has most fascinated and perplexed recent interpreters and commentators, namely, the history of the Johannine tradition.[87] So without further argument we may pass to the second way in which the apparent gulf is to be bridged between the evidence for early source-material and the presumption of late composition.

2. As earlier we took as a sample the major contribution made by Dodd, so here we may select as a working model the impressive reconstruction of Brown. For in this he is representative, like Schnackenburg[88] too, of those who desire to establish a link or links between

[82] Ibid., 316; cf. Cullmann, op. cit., 302.

[83] *The Human Face of God*, 186–90; 'The Use of the Fourth Gospel for Christology Today' in Lindars and Smalley, *Christ and Spirit in the NT*, 69–74.

[84] J. L. Martyn, *History and Theology in the Fourth Gospel*, New York 1968, 93.

[85] Ibid., 131.

[86] Elsewhere even when there is direct allusion to this text it becomes '*the* Son of Man' (Mark 13.26; 14.62; and pars; cf. Acts 7.56), except, interestingly enough, in the other 'Johannine' writing, Rev. 1.13; 14.14.

[87] Cf. especially B. Noack, *Zur johanneischen Tradition*, Copenhagen 1954; R. Gyllenberg, 'Die Anfänge der johanneischen Tradition' in W. Eltester (ed.), *Neutestamentliche Studien für Rudolf Bultmann* (*ZNW* Beiheft 21), Berlin 1954, 144–7.

[88] *John*, 100–4.

an original apostolic tradition reaching back to the earliest times and what they take to be the necessity for a much later finished gospel.

Brown postulates five stages as a 'minimum' for the composition of the gospel:[89]

(*a*) A body of traditional material pertaining to the words and works of Jesus.
(*b*) The development of this material in 'Johannine' style and patterns through preaching and teaching, in oral and eventually written forms.
(*c*) The organization of (*b*) into a consecutive written gospel in Greek.
(*d*) A second edition by the same hand, expanding and adapting the material to meet new needs and groups of persons.
(*e*) A final redaction by another hand, though incorporating 'material stemming from the preaching days of the evangelist himself' (and therefore at points not differing in style or vocabulary from the rest of the gospel).

This process is envisaged as occupying a considerable period of time. Stage (*a*) is dated between 40 and 60; stage (*b*), 'lasting perhaps several decades', and therefore overlapping (*a*), goes on till *c.* 75; stage (*c*), the first edition of the gospel, is set in *c.* 75–85; (*d*), its revision, occupies the late 80s and early 90s; (*e*), the final redaction, takes place *c.* 100. As far as authorship is concerned, (*a*) is held to go back to John, son of Zebedee; (*b*)–(*d*) are the work of his disciples and in particular of 'one principal disciple' (the evangelist); (*e*) is the work of yet another disciple (the redactor) after the evangelist's death.

The question of authorship is not directly here our concern, though we shall have to return to it. Brown's dating itself requires a span covering the literary lifetime of more than one man, but the differences of hand (confessedly minute) do not of themselves require a late date. Indeed at this point he is very cautious and admits that even the work of the final redactor cannot be isolated with confidence, since he introduced material that may not be 'any less ancient than material that found its way into the earlier additions'. The reasons for separating (*a*) from (*b*), and therewith for the introduction of the unknown evangelist (in contrast with 'the beloved disciple', who Brown argues to be John),[90] are again not chronological. There is no gap, as in Dodd, between the evangelist and his source-material; for the disciple of the apostle is in close contact with him and belongs to his circle. Apart from the linguistic difficulty of believing that John, son of Zebedee, could himself have 'written these things', it is the later stages of composition, (*c*) and (*d*), that make it inconceivable for Brown that the finished form of the gospel could be the work of an eyewitness. Thus, he instances the final state of the story of the anointing in 12.1–7:

[89] *John* I, xxiv–ix, xcviii–cii. [90] Ibid., xcii–xcviii.

If modern criticism has any validity, then the anointing of Jesus' feet represents an amalgamation of diverse details from two independent stories, in one of which a woman anointed Jesus' head and in the other of which a sinful woman wept and her tears fell on his feet. . . . The process responsible for such development can only with the greatest difficulty be attributed to an eyewitness.[91]

But this judgment needs sifting. 'Modern criticism' has *not* shown this story to be an 'amalgamation' of two diverse stories, if by that is meant that it is dependent on the fusion of two other versions (viz. those of Mark and Luke) and is therefore secondary to them. Dodd and indeed Brown himself have shown that the case for such dependence has collapsed.[92] The Johannine version is from a literary point of view as independent and potentially near to source as the other two.[93] But this does not imply a claim that it describes 'exactly what happened', which, Brown asserts, an eyewitness 'presumably would remember',[94] or even that it is the most reliable version. John's account could well be a muddled reminiscence of the incident, or, as Brown supposes, of two separate incidents. In the course of teaching and preaching much assimilation, elaboration and adaptation can take place, even in the mind of an eyewitness. For, as Brown himself says, 'the conception of the apostolic eyewitness as an impartial recorder whose chief interest was the detailed accuracy of the memories he related is an anachronism'[95] – and in any case is far removed from the evident meaning of 'witness' in this gospel. Dodd makes the point,[96] in the course of his argument *against* apostolic authorship, that 'even if it were certain that the work was by a personal disciple, we could not proceed directly to the inference that his account is a transcript of the facts, or that he intended it to be such'; and he cites as an analogy Plato's account of the teaching of Socrates, whose personal disciple no one doubts he was.

This is not to argue that the fourth evangelist *was* the apostle John. It is simply to keep open the point that the sort of gradual process which Brown, like others, sees as lying behind the formation of the gospel does not of itself demand the interposition of a disciple at a further remove or a period of time exceeding the span of one generation. Indeed Brown himself sees the stages in the process as closely parallel to those which earlier we envisaged as lying behind the synoptists (where no one is contending for direct eyewitness), and in

[91] Ibid., c. [92] Dodd, *HTFG*, 162–73; Brown, *John* I, 449–54.

[93] Cf. Brown, *John* I, 452, who argues that in comparison with Mark 'the account of the incident at Bethany that underlies the present Johannine narrative gives evidence in some points of being close to the earliest tradition about that incident'.

[94] *John* I, xcix. [95] Ibid., c. [96] *HTFG*, 17.

fact he bases his datings of the various stages of John almost entirely on this parallel. He takes 40–60 to be the formative period for the traditions behind *all* the gospels, and having accepted 75–85 as the date for Matthew and Luke he uses this for the first edition of John (with the second and third editions trailing on to the end of the century). Yet in the case of the synoptists we saw no necessity for prolonging the whole process (from the first preaching and teaching summaries, through the earliest proto-gospels, to the gospels as we now have them) beyond the early 60s. In the light of that chronology, is there good ground for more than doubling the time-span in the case of the fourth gospel or should we not ask whether the *pari passu* development envisaged by Brown may not still hold?

3. This leads into the third way of resolving the dilemma posed by the apparent gap between the evangelist and his tradition – not simply by bridging it but by narrowing it. Why should the end-product be so late?

Beyond unargued inferences from what he calls 'the usual' datings for the synoptists, there is one date cited by Brown which he believes gives 'a reasonably precise indication' for the *terminus post quem* of John's gospel. And with this we may begin. In company with many other commentators, he holds that its use of ἀποσυνάγωγος (9.42; 12.42; 16.2), and in particular the statement in 9.22 that 'the Jewish authorities had already agreed that anyone who acknowledged Jesus as Messiah should be banned from the synagogue', reflects the formal exclusion of Christians from Judaism with the introduction in *c.* 85–90 of the twelfth of the Eighteen Benedictions, against 'the Heretics'. But this is an inference whose precarious basis it is desirable to expose in some detail, since it is so frequently made.

The wording of the Benediction, which has suffered such modification that the original form cannot be established with certainty, is in any case far from precise and contains no specific reference to excommunication:

> For the renegades let there be no hope, and may the arrogant kingdom soon be rooted out in our days, and the Nazarenes and the *minim* (heretics) perish as in a moment and be blotted out from the book of life and with the righteous may they not be inscribed. Blessed art thou, O Lord, who humblest the arrogant.[97]

Its addition was intended[98] as a test-formula, or shibboleth, which

[97] Reconstruction and translation by J. Jocz, *The Jewish People and Jesus Christ*, [2]1954, 51–7; quoted Barrett, *John*, 300. Cf. H. Strack and P. Billerbeck, *Kommentar zum Neuen Testament*, Munich 1922–8, IV, 293–333 (and especially 329–33); Martyn, op. cit., 31–40, 148–50.

[98] Cf. K. L. Carroll, 'The Fourth Gospel and the Exclusion of Christians from the Synagogues', *BJRL* 40, 1957–8, 19–32.

Christians who claimed to be Jews in every other respect could not recite. Since they would not withdraw from the community of Israel they had to be smoked out. It was directed against Hebrew Christians[99] of an extreme Judaizing kind, for whom the fourth gospel would have been anathema. There is nothing to connect it with the situation in the kind of Greek-speaking city which Martyn makes the setting and starting-point of his highly imaginative reconstruction of the history of the fourth gospel.[100] Unless one *begins* with a late date for the gospel, there is no more reason for reading the events of 85–90 into 9.22 than for seeing a reference to Bar-Cochba in 5.43, which has long since become a curiosity of criticism.[101]

A recent careful study by D. R. A. Hare[102] regards the connection as entirely unproven. He makes the point that exclusion was already a regular discipline at Qumran,[103] who used very similar language in anathematizing their heretics. Indeed the word describing the action in John 9.34f., ἐκβάλλειν to throw out, is so common as to be used in similar circumstances of Jesus himself (Luke 4.29), Stephen (Acts 7.58), Paul (Acts 13.50), and of Christians by other Christians (III John 10). The warning of John 16.2, 'they will ban you from the synagogue' (though the *term* ἀποσυνάγωγος is unparalleled anywhere else), says no more than Luke 6.22: 'How blest are you when men hate you, when they outlaw (ἀφορίσωσιν) you and insult you, and ban (ἐκβάλωσιν) your very name as infamous'.[104] It describes the kind of treatment recorded in Acts (13.45–50; 14.2–6,19; 17.5–9,13; 18.6f.,12–17) as meted out to Paul in the late 40s and early 50s and which in 50 Paul himself

[99] Jocz, op. cit., 52f., 57.

[100] Op. cit., 17–41. Commenting on this reconstruction W. H. Brownlee, 'Whence the Gospel according to John?' in J. H. Charlesworth (ed.), *John and Qumran*, 1972, 182f., holds that John 12.42 must describe an earlier situation such as *called forth* the Benediction: 'The evidence of the rabbinic malediction introduced in about AD 85 points rather to an earlier and not to a later date for the Fourth Gospel'.

[101] Thus Carroll, *BJRL* 40, 19f., asks: 'Why is it that John alone reports this development when the three earlier Gospels apparently know nothing of it? The answer to this question can be found in the late date at which the Fourth Gospel was produced and in the fact that the author, whoever he may have been, was a gentile'. Neither of these statements (the latter of which is entirely unlikely) is in any way derived from or based upon the evidence of the Benediction itself.

[102] D. R. A. Hare, *The Theme of Jewish Persecution of Christians in the Gospel according to St Matthew*, Cambridge 1967, 48–56.

[103] Cf. 1QS 5.18; 6.24–7.25; 8.16f.,22f.; CD 9.23; and Josephus, *BJ* 2.143, of the Essenes.

[104] So Dodd, *HTFG*, 410, who makes the comment: 'The prospect of such exclusion was before Christians of Jewish origin early enough, at least, to have entered into the common tradition behind both Luke and John.'

testifies in I Thess. 2.14f. to have been true not only of his converts but, from still earlier personal experience (described in Acts 9.29f. and 22.18?), of the Christians in Judaea:

> You have fared like the congregations in Judaea, God's people in Christ Jesus. You have been treated by your countrymen as they are treated by the Jews, who killed the Lord Jesus and the prophets and drove us out (ἐκδιωξάντων).[105]

This last passage is also relevant against those who say that John's use of 'the Jews' represents a late and non-Jewish perspective.[106] For here it is being used of the very earliest period by Paul, a Hebrew of the Hebrews, of his fellow-countrymen with the same grim objectivity and apparent externality as in John.[107] Whether or not we say with Brown that it is 'almost unbelievable' that the agreement of John 9.22 reflects a situation in Jesus' lifetime,[108] there is no compelling reason to assign it to a situation that obtained only at the end of the first century. Indeed there seems to be no ground even for placing it (with Brown) among the material added to the gospel at a later stage. In any case, as Dodd points out, the sanction of excommunication from the synagogue is 'a menace which would have no terrors for any but Jewish Christians'.[109] It underlines the presumption found, I believe, throughout the gospel that those to whom it is addressed are, primarily at any rate, Jews rather than Gentiles.

Indeed, the entire absence from the gospel, to which we have already alluded, of any reference to 'the Gentiles' (or even to individual Gentiles, apart from Pilate and his soldiers) is as remarkable as it is unremarked.[110] This of course proves nothing as to date, but it stands in notable contrast to the assumption reflected throughout the synoptists, Acts and Paul that the rejection of the Jews is to be followed by the in-coming of the Gentiles. It cannot be argued from this

[105] It is significant that no reference to this passage is made in the lengthy discussion of the question by Martyn, nor for that matter by Barrett, Dodd or Brown.

[106] For a recent estimate of this usage as part of the evidence that John betrays 'an intimate knowledge of Palestinian geography, history and religious thought', cf. Brownlee in Charlesworth, op. cit., 183.

[107] Cf. II Cor. 11.22–4, and the Jewish-Christian gospel of Matthew, 28.15.

[108] *John* I, 380. Like Martyn, op. cit., 19, 31f., he thinks that it implies a formal agreement of the Council and refers it indirectly to the ordinance of the Synod of Jamnia. But the only other uses of συνεπιτίθημι in the NT (Luke 2.25; Acts 23.20) do not support this. When John wishes to indicate a formal decision of the authorities he makes it clear (11.47,53,57).

[109] *HTFG*, 412.

[110] Oddly I have not noticed a reference to it in the introduction to any of the commentaries (though I could easily have missed it). For the evidence again, cf. my 'Destination and Purpose', 109–12.

that there was at the time no Gentile mission, but it certainly presupposes a milieu where concentration on the presentation of Jesus as the truth and fullness of Israel was the all-absorbing task of Christian apologetic. Of no conceivable milieu was this true after 70 except in isolated pockets of Ebionite Christianity which still saw Christianity as tied to the Jewish manner of living (the 'Nazarenes' of the twelfth Benediction). And if anything can be said with certainty of the fourth gospel, it is that John was no Judaizer or preacher of a narrow Jewish exclusivism. His Christ was the hope and light of the *world*, challenging and transcending all the legal and ritual limitations of Judaism, yet presented always in categories – of which the manna and the vine are typical – that would enable the *Jew* to come to this truth as the fulfilment of everything for which Israel stood.[111]

So universally is it taken for granted that the fourth gospel reflects the situation obtaining between Jews and Christians after 70[112] that it may seem bold – or even naive – to question it. The absence of reference to the Sadducees is frequently said to reflect their demise after 70: yet the chief priests and their party are certainly not absent, but still very much in the saddle. John never speaks of the scribes either – yet they certainly did not disappear after 70, but rather came to their own. In fact he appears remarkably well informed about the parties and divisions of Judaism before the Jewish war[113] – and repeated attempts to prove him ignorant or stupid tend to recoil upon those who make them.[114] While there are many things upon which in the absence of evidence it would be prudent to suspend judgment, there is nothing, as far as I know, which is plainly anachronistic or which positively requires a later perspective. Above all, there is nothing that suggests or presupposes that the temple is already destroyed or that Jerusalem is in ruins – signs of which calamity and of the difference in outlook it engendered are inescapably present in any Jewish or Christian literature that can with any certainty be dated in the period 70–100.[115]

[111] Cf. ibid., 109–12. To bear out what I said there, cf. Howard, *IB* VIII, 715, who, noting that the word in John 15.1 is that used in the LXX to translate Jer. 2.21 (a true as opposed to a degenerate vine), writes: '"The true vine" means the genuine vine, i.e., the vine which corresponds perfectly to its name (Israel).'

[112] Thus, in his latest treatment of the subject, *The Gospel of John and Judaism*, 1975, 40–58, C. K. Barrett simply takes over the traditional date of the gospel without further argument and proceeds to compare it with the Judaism *of that period*. For a statement of the contrary case, cf. Cribbs, *JBL* 89, especially 47–51.

[113] Cf. again my 'Destination and Purpose', 117f.

[114] Cf. Stauffer, 'Historische Elemente', 34f.

[115] Cf. ch. x below.

Of all the writings in the New Testament, with the exception perhaps of the epistle to the Hebrews and the book of Revelation, the gospel of John is that in which we might most expect an allusion (however indirect, subtle or symbolic) to the doom of Jerusalem, if it had in fact already been accomplished. For the focus of the gospel is on the rejection by metropolitan Judaism of the one who comes to his own people (1.11) as the Christ and King and Shepherd of Israel. This coming and this rejection must inevitably mean the judgment and the supersession of the old religion, represented by the law (1.17), the water-pots of purification (2.6), the localized worship of Gerizim and Jerusalem (4.21), the sabbath (5.10–18), the manna that perishes (6.31f.), and much else. Above all it means the replacement of the temple by the person of Christ himself (2.21). Yet, for all the capacity of this evangelist for overtones and double meaning and irony, it is hard to find any reference which unquestionably reflects the events of 70. The saying about the destruction of the temple, which in this gospel (2.19) is not a threat *by Jesus* to destroy the temple (as the false witnesses at his trial in the synoptists asserted) but a statement (such as well could be the original of what was distorted) that 'if this temple be destroyed'[116] he would rebuild it 'in a trice', is related to the events not of 70 but of 30. It is seen as a prophecy not of what the Romans would do in the rebellion but of what God would do in the resurrection. The *cleansing* of the temple with which, uniquely, it is associated in John occurs not in the politically explosive context of the synoptists at the close of the ministry, where it foreshadows the end of the nation, but is focused entirely upon Jesus' all-consuming concern under the influence of the Baptist's preaching for the religious purity of Israel.[117]

There is to be sure the explicit prophecy of Roman intervention placed on the lips of the Jewish leaders in 11.47f.:

> This man is performing many signs. If we leave him alone like this the whole populace will believe in him. Then the Romans will come and sweep away our temple and our nation.

Yet this is an unfulfilled prophecy. They did not leave him alone, and still the Romans came. Caiaphas indeed is represented in retrospect as prophesying truer than he knew – but this is not that the temple

[116] 'Destroy this temple and . . .' is widely recognized as a Hebraism for the conditional clause. So C. H. Dodd, *The Interpretation of the Fourth Gospel*, Cambridge 1953, 302, who argues that the Johannine form of the saying is more primitive than the Markan. He is supported by Lindars, *John*, ad loc.

[117] For an expansion of this, cf. my 'His Witness is True' in Moule and Bammel, op. cit.

and nation would be swept away but that Jesus should die for the people *rather than* the whole nation be destroyed (11.49–52). It is in fact remarkable that there is nothing in John corresponding to the detailed prophecies of the siege and fall of Jerusalem. And this is true despite the fact that every *other* feature of the synoptic apocalypses (apart again from the preaching to the Gentiles) is represented in the Johannine last discourses: the injunction against alarm, the forewarning against apostasy, the prediction of travail and persecution for the sake of the name, the need for witness, the promise of the Spirit as the disciples' advocate, the reference to 'that day', when, in an imminent coming, Christ will be seen and manifested, the elect will be gathered to him, and the world will be judged.[118]

Arguments from silence can, of course, never be conclusive. There are however two further indications in John that Jerusalem and its temple are still standing.

The first is in 2.20, when the Jews make the apparently unmotivated observation that Herod's temple has been a-building for forty-six years.[119] This comports very accurately with the date at which, according to John's chronology, Jesus must be presumed to be speaking.[120] The building was not finished till *c.* 63,[121] shortly before it was destroyed. Yet there is no presentiment of its destruction, as there is in the comparable comment on the temple buildings in Mark 13.2. But though the context would seem almost to cry out for such foreboding, it may still be said that there is no reason why it had to be mentioned. In any case, the point in time is intended to reflect the perspective of Jesus, not of the evangelist – though the constant assumption is that this is not a distinction that John cares to observe or preserve.

But in the second passage the reference is quite clearly to the time of the evangelist. In 5.2 he introduces the story of the healing of the cripple with the words:

118 For the detailed parallels, cf. my *Jesus and His Coming*, 172. I failed then to observe the significance of what is in the apocalypses but *not* in the last discourses.

119 Cf. Brown, *John*, ad loc. Barrett's insistence that the aorist οἰκοδομήθη must imply that the building had ceased (and that John mistakenly supposed that the temple was by then complete) ignores the exact parallel in Ezra 5.16, already cited by Bernard, *John*, ad loc., and earlier by C. H. Turner, *HDB* I, 405: ἀπὸ τότε ἕως τοῦ νῦν ᾠκοδομήθη καὶ οὐκ ἐτελέσθη. From manuscript notes of my father's taken from another student I find that it was also cited by Lightfoot, whom little escaped, in his lectures of 1873, in a section on the history of the temple's building which he evidently added to the 1867–8 course on the 'Internal Evidence for the Authenticity and Genuineness of St John's Gospel' reprinted in *Biblical Essays*, 168. John 2.20, he said, 'speaks volumes for the authenticity of the Gospel'.

120 Cf. again my 'His Witness is True'.

121 Josephus, *Ant.* 20. 219.

> Now at the sheep-pool in Jerusalem there is a place with five colonnades. Its name in the language of the Jews is Bethesda.

This is one of John's topographical details that have been strikingly confirmed in recent study.[122] Not only does it reveal a close acquaintance with Jerusalem before 70, when the evidence of the five porches was to be buried beneath the rubble only recently to be revealed by the archaeologist's spade; but John says not 'was' but 'is'. Too much weight must not be put on this – though it is the only present tense in the context, and elsewhere (4.6; 11.18; 18.1; 19.41) he assimilates his topographical descriptions to the tense of the narrative. Of course too it is always open to the critic to attribute it to a source, which the evangelist has not bothered to correct – though such editorial introductions are usually regarded as the latest links. The natural inference, however, is that he is writing when the building he describes is still standing.[123]

Let us then proceed to test out the hypothesis that the gospel of John reflects the situation before 70 because that is when it was written. And let us begin by looking at what is universally agreed to be the latest element in it, the epilogue of ch. 21.

There can be no doubt that this chapter is an addendum or afterthought to the gospel as a whole, which reaches a rounded close at 20.31. It is unnecessary for our purpose to decide whether it was added by the same hand. Investigators are more or less evenly divided on this.[124] There are small variations in the style,[125] though the similarities are so great[126] as to presuppose either deliberate imitation or a single author writing after a lapse of time or in different circum-

[122] J. Jeremias, *The Rediscovery of Bethesda, John 5.2*, ET, Louisville 1966; 'The Copper Scroll from Qumran', *ExpT* 71, 1959–60, 228. Cf. more generally, W. F. Albright, *The Archaeology of Palestine*, Harmondsworth 1949, 244–8; 'Recent Discoveries in Palestine and the Gospel of John' in Davies and Daube, *The Background of the New Testament and its Eschatology*, 153–71; R. D. Potter, 'Topography and Archaeology in the Fourth Gospel', *Studia Evangelica* I (TU 73), Berlin 1959, 329–37 (reprinted in *The Gospels Reconsidered*, Oxford 1960, 90–8); A. J. B. Higgins, *The Historicity of the Fourth Gospel*, 1960, 78–82; Hunter, *According to John*, 49–55; Brownlee in Charlesworth, *John and Qumran*, 167–74.

[123] Cf. Bengel, *Gnomon*, ad loc.: 'Scripsit Joannes ante vastationem urbis.' So too Eckhardt, *Der Tod Johannes*, 57f., citing E. Schwartz and Schlatter to the same effect.

[124] Cf. Brown, *John* II, 1080.

[125] They are clearly set out by Barrett, *John*, 470f., who concludes that they 'are not in themselves sufficient to establish the belief that chapter 21 was written by a different author' – though he thinks it was.

[126] Cf. Lightfoot, *Biblical Essays*, 194f.

stances. It is clear in any case that 21.24, or at least the second half of it, represents the endorsement of the Johannine community:

> It is this same disciple who attests what here has been written. It is in fact he who wrote it, and we know that his testimony is true.

Again we need not stop to decide the question whether this is to be taken to mean what it appears to mean, namely, that this disciple wrote the gospel, or whether this conclusion may be avoided, either by taking γράψας to mean 'caused to write'[127] or ταῦτα to refer only to what has just been said or to the appendix as a whole,[128] or by regarding the verse as a mistaken attribution added in good faith.[129] From the point of view of dating, the present participle μαρτυρῶν ('attests') suggests, until proved otherwise, that the disciple in question is still alive, and Zahn[130] insisted strongly on this. Nevertheless this has frequently been denied, on the basis of the preceding verses 18–23, whose interpretation is crucial.

In this passage two sayings of the Lord are recorded, the first of which is referred to the death of Peter, the second to the death of the beloved disciple. The first runs:

> When you were young you fastened your belt about you and walked where you chose; but when you are old you will stretch out your arms, and a stranger will bind you fast, and carry you where you have no wish to go.

In itself this is capable of wide interpretation. But the evangelist's comment, 'He said this to indicate the manner of death by which Peter was to glorify God', especially when taken in conjunction with his similar comments in 12.33 and 18.32 on the manner of Jesus' death and with the evidence that stretching out of the arms was itself a symbol of crucifixion,[131] leaves little doubt that he intended it to be seen as a specific reference to Peter's death by crucifixion; and the passage is so understood as early as Tertullian.[132] One may therefore agree with Brown, and the commentators generally, that the passage

[127] So Bernard and Brown, on the basis of 19.19, where Pilate presumably got someone else to write the *titulus* (though even this cannot be proved). Yet its use of a private individual to mean anything more indirect than the employment of a secretary (which would still make the disciple the author of the gospel as much as Paul is of Romans) cannot be demonstrated.

[128] So Dodd, 'Note on John 21.24', *JTS* n.s. 4, 1953, 212f. Yet this is an unnatural way of taking it; and it is difficult to avoid an echo of the ταῦτα γέγραπται of 20.31.

[129] So Barrett and Lindars. There is of course no evidence for this except that *they* think it is mistaken.

[130] *INT* III, 239f. [131] Cf. Bernard, *John*, ad loc.

[132] *Scorp.* 15: 'Tunc Petrus ab altero cingitur, cum cruci adstringatur.'

almost certainly presupposes the death of Peter. This puts it some time after 65, according to when we date that event.

There then follow these words:

> Peter looked round, and saw the disciple whom Jesus loved following – the one who at supper had leaned back close to him to ask the question, 'Lord, who is it that will betray you?' When he caught sight of him, Peter asked, 'Lord, what will happen to him?' Jesus said, 'If it should be my will that he wait until I come, what is it to you? Follow me.' That saying of Jesus became current in the brotherhood, and was taken to mean that that disciple would not die. But in fact Jesus did not say that he would not die; he only said, 'If it should be my will that he wait until I come, what is it to you?'

From this Brown goes on to draw the deduction:

> Seemingly at a considerable interval after Peter's death, a long-lived eyewitness of the ministry of Jesus passed away – an eyewitness who was intimately connected with the Fourth Gospel.[133]

But this is to read in a great deal. In the case of Peter the circumstantial detail gives good ground for believing that the saying of Jesus is being interpreted after the event. In the case of the beloved disciple all that is said is that Jesus' words were misunderstood to mean that that disciple would not die. This could certainly imply that his death had shown that that could not be their true interpretation and that a different explanation was therefore called for. Yet this is only an inference, and Brown admits that 'Westcott, Zahn, Tillmann, Bernard, Hoskyns and Schwank are among the many scholars who do not agree'.[134]

But Brown also makes two other statements, namely, that the eyewitness was 'long-lived' and that the time of writing was separated 'seemingly at a considerable interval' from Peter's death. Neither of these has any support in the text. It is not the beloved disciple but Peter who is referred to as 'growing old' (*γηράσῃς*), and we have the testimony of Irenaeus[135] that in the ancient world this was an appropriate description for anyone over forty or fifty: in fact Peter

[133] *John* I, lxxxv. The death of this eyewitness is to be distinguished from that of the evangelist (not for Brown the same man) who *also* apparently had died shortly before the epilogue was written (I, xxxix). Apart from the need to postulate another hand for ch. 21, there would seem to be no evidence for this death either.

[134] *John* II, 1119. He could have added Lightfoot (*Biblical Essays*, 195f.). Nor was it the inference of the ancients, who are unanimous that the gospel was written and published by John 'himself' (Irenaeus, *Adv. haer.* 3.1.1), 'in his own name' (Muratorian Canon), 'while still in the body' (Anti-Marcionite Prologue).

[135] *Adv. haer.* 2.22.5: 'That the age of thirty years is the prime of a young man's ability, and that it reaches even to the fortieth year, everyone will allow; but after the fortieth and fiftieth year, it begins to verge towards elder age' (tr. Lightfoot, *AF*, 554).

would presumably have been in or near his sixties when he died. With regard to the beloved disciple, it might today be a reasonable inference that if it was supposed of someone that he would never die it would indicate that he was hanging on interminably. But the perspective of the early Christians was very different: whether or not one would die depended on whether the *parousia* would supervene first. At the beginning all Christians expected not to die, and as far as we can tell Paul first entertained doubts on this subject for himself in the mid-50s.[136] By the time of Philippians, which we dated in 58 but which cannot in any case be very much later, he is seriously debating (1.25) whether he would 'remain' (μένειν) – the very term used in John 21.22f. (cf. also I Cor. 15.6) – though he is still convinced that he should. The debate has nothing to do with old age: Paul might by then have been in the latter forties or early fifties if he was a 'young man' (Acts 7.58) about the year 33. The same uncertainty about John (assuming, with Brown, that this is the intended identity of the disciple whom Jesus loved) need not presuppose a 'considerable interval' after Peter's death.[137] On the contrary, all the evidence suggests that the latter 60s of the first century (not unnaturally in the light of what was happening both in Rome and Jerusalem) saw a quickening of the expectation that the end could not now be long delayed (I Peter 4.7) but that Christ would come very soon to his waiting church (Rev. 1.7; 3.3; 22.7, 20), in fulfilment of the promise that that first, apostolic generation would live to see it all (Mark 9.1; 13.30; etc.). When therefore all the other 'pillars' (Gal. 2.9) had been removed by death (James in 62, Peter and Paul in 65+) and John only 'remained', a supposed promise of Jesus that he would not die, but that the end would come first, must have fed fervid expectations of an imminent consummation. There is no reason to think that the correction of the error would have waited another thirty years. On the contrary, the association in our passage of this hope of 'staying on' with the *parousia* and the death of Peter strongly suggests that all three were closely linked.[138] It was damping false hopes of an

[136] In I Thess. 4.15–17 he uses the phrase 'we who are left alive until the Lord comes' in distinction from 'the dead', and says again in I Cor. 15.52, 'the dead will rise immortal, and we shall be changed'. But in II Cor. 4.12 he writes that 'death is at work in us, and life in you' and in 5.1 contemplates the possibility that 'the earthly frame that houses us today' could well be 'demolished'. The events of 55–6, which made him despair even of life itself (II Cor. 1.8), appear to have had a decisive effect. Cf. Dodd, 'The Mind of Paul: II', *NT Studies*, 109–18.

[137] Cf. Brownlee in Charlesworth, op. cit., 194: 'In so far as 21.22 relates to believers generally, it could be very early. Cf. I Thess. 4.13–18'.

[138] Cf. Gaston, *No Stone on Another*, 458: 'There can be . . . no question of a

apocalyptic intervention (from which consistently the John both of the gospel and of the epistles desires to detach the presence or coming of Christ),[139] not correcting idle speculation based on longevity, which occasioned the need for an epilogue to the gospel – that and concern for the pastoral ministry of the church (21.15–17), another marked characteristic of the later 50s and 60s.[140] So provisionally we may date the epilogue shortly after the death of Peter in 65+. This would mean that not only does it not reflect the destruction of Jerusalem but it could antedate the outbreak of the Jewish revolt, of which there are no more signs in John than I believe there are in the synoptists and Acts. Relations with Rome (represented in the person of Pilate) are still courteous and sycophantic to the point of irony (18.28–19.16).

Though it is not so clear nor so clean an addition, it can, I believe, be shown that the prologue is likewise a subsequent introduction, built like a porch into the original structure of the gospel.[141] Its function, like that of the prologues to the first and the third gospels, is to provide the setting in which the theological history that forms the heart of the *kerygma* may be understood in its full cosmic context. Round what I believe to have been its original opening, 'There appeared a man named John sent from God' (1.6), closely parallel to the historical starting-points of the other gospels,[142] has been built the hymn or meditation which we know as the prologue.[143] I see no reason to suppose that it was non-Christian in origin or to attribute

---

continual postponement of the parousia; it was expected at the end of the first generation, and then when it did not occur the church adapted with little difficulty to the longer perspective required by the Gentile mission. We can state here but by no means demonstrate our conviction that all of the New Testament writings which indicate a persecuted church with a heightened expectation of the nearness of the end: Mark, Rev., Hebs, I Peter, were written in the sixties of the first century' (note that Revelation is included). He thinks that John 21.23 and II Peter 3.3ff. are the only post-70 exceptions. But we have already seen reason to put the latter in the 60s.

[139] Cf. not only John 14–16 but I John 2.18,22f., 28–3.30; 4.1–3.

[140] Cf. the Pastoral Epistles *passim*. For the stress in particular on tending the flock, cf. Acts 20.28f.; I Peter 5.2–4. Attempts to read into the stylistic (and textual) variations, ἀρνία, πρόβατα, προβάτια, latter-day ecclesiastical divisions, or even the age-groups of I John 2.13f., are entirely misguided (so Brown, *John*, ad loc.). There is nothing here to suggest or require a late date.

[141] For substantiation of what follows, cf. my 'Relation of the Prologue to the Gospel of St John', *NTS* 9, 120–9.

[142] Cf. Mark 1.4; Luke 1.5; 3.2 (which could well have been the original opening of Luke).

[143] 1.1–5,10–14,16–18, though vv. 7–9 have doubtless also been recast in the light of it.

it to another hand, though I believe it probable that, like the epilogue, it was added to the first edition of the gospel after an interval. How long that interval was can be estimated only after taking into account the evidence of the epistles, since the opening of the first epistle (I John 1.1–3) shows a number of obvious similarities with it and reads indeed as if it could be a first draft for it.

First, however, the prologue gives us occasion to ask, and indeed compels the question, whether its language and thought-forms, supremely among the Johannine writings, do not suggest or require a considerably later stage of development, and therefore date, than that with which we are now working. Arguments from development, even more than those from distribution or dependence, are, as we have already seen, extremely difficult to handle. How long should we allow for the kind of theological sophistication about the significance of Christ which the prologue unquestionably evinces? Is it thirty, forty, sixty, or a hundred years? It is impossible to quantify. One can only make comparisons; and here the relative fixity of the Pauline yardstick again is valuable. The nearest parallels for the pre-existence Christology of John's prologue are to be found in Philippians and Colossians (which we dated in 58), and also in Hebrews (67) and Revelation (68+). Simply from within the internal dynamics of Christian theology there appears to be no reason, as far as I can see, for demanding more time for the maturation of the Johannine idiom. The same upper limit as for the latter two books, permitting the best part of forty years' 'distancing' from the events, would appear sufficient. At any rate to *require* more time demands specific reasons or additional evidence which I cannot see are forthcoming.

But what about external criteria in the history of ideas in the surrounding world? The trouble here is that most of the influences or parallels suggested for the background of the Johannine thought-forms are themselves more difficult to date than the gospel. This is certainly true of the five main backgrounds surveyed by Dodd[144] – the Hermetic literature, Philonic Judaism, rabbinic Judaism, gnosticism and Mandaism. Of these only the evidence from Philo may be pinned down to a period which can constitute a probable background, as opposed to a possible environment, for the ideas of the fourth gospel. The material from the other milieux, whatever their influence, cannot be used for *dating* the gospel. Philo, even if he could be shown to be a direct source, died not later than *c.* 50, and cannot therefore argue for a late date. In fact it is coming to seem much more likely that Philo and John shared a common background in the Wisdom

144 *Interpretation of the Fourth Gospel*, 10–130.

literature of the Old Testament, to which Philo gave a philosophic twist entirely absent from John. Brown[145] accepts Braun's summary that 'if Philo had never existed, the Fourth Gospel would most probably have not been any different from what it is'.

The more recent evidence, which has come to light since Dodd wrote, from the Qumran scrolls and the gnostic library at Chenoboskion, has merely had the effect of undermining the grounds for putting John late. The Qumran material comes from the heart of southern Palestine before the Jewish war.[146] Though certainly not suggesting or establishing any *direct* contact with or influence upon John,[147] it has killed any dogmatism that the fundamental Johannine categories must be Hellenistic and must be late. Equally study of the new gnostic material has served to demonstrate the gulf rather than the similarities between the fourth gospel and the second-century gnostic systems.[148] John's is at most what Reicke has, correctly I think, designated 'pre-gnostic' language,[149] and there is every reason to suppose that the kind of Judaism that formed a natural seed-bed for this way of thinking, with its speculative and mystical developments of the Old Testament and intertestamental Wisdom themes,[150] went back well before 70. In fact the other evidence for this strain of gnosticizing Judaism in the New Testament – in Colossians, the Pastorals, Jude, II Peter and Rev. 1–3 – all suggests that the late 50s and the 60s saw a burgeoning of it which was to create urgent new problems for the Christian church.

I do not therefore believe that there is anything in the language even of the Johannine prologue which demands a date later than the 60s of the first century. But this may best be tested by turning aside at this point from the gospel to look at the evidence of the Johannine

[145] *John* I, lviii.

[146] Amid the mass of literature on its relation to John, cf. Charlesworth, *John and Qumran* (with its lengthy bibliography), and for a popular summary, Hunter, *According to John*, 27–33. See also the earlier estimate of the thoroughly Jewish character of the gospel by Neill, *Interpretation of the NT*, 308–24.

[147] There could be indirect contact through the disciples of John the Baptist, especially if the unnamed companion of Andrew in 1.35–40 is intended to be John son of Zebedee, as I believe is likely (so Zahn, strongly, *INT* III, 209–12, 224f.). Cf. my 'The Baptism of John and the Qumran Community' in *Twelve NT Studies*, 11–27; and Morris, 'The Dead Sea Scrolls and St John's Gospel', *Studies in the Fourth Gospel*, 321–58 (particularly 353f.); Brownlee in Charlesworth, op. cit., 174.

[148] Brown's assessment at this and similar points is very judicious (*John* I, lii–lvi).

[149] B. Reicke, 'Traces of Gnosticism in the Dead Sea Scrolls?', *NTS* 1, 1954–5, 137–41.

[150] For the Wisdom literature as the best background for understanding John, cf. Brown, *John* I, cxxii–cxxv.

epistles, which, like the rest of the Johannine literature, have usually been regarded as belonging to a later generation.

Dodd dates them between 96 and 110, on the grounds that they are subsequent to the gospel and that 'the general tone of the epistles offers the strongest contrast to that of the Revelation, which shows us a Church enduring severe persecution and looking forward to yet worse'.[151] Since Dodd puts the gospel, as we have seen, in the 90s and says that 'we may take it for granted that the Revelation belongs to the reign of Domitian', it follows that since 'these epistles were written in the same province of Asia' they must come from a good deal later – though he allows that a date *before* Domitian's persecution is 'not excluded'. This reasoning illustrates how relative are the arguments for much New Testament dating. And with writings apparently so timeless as the three brief Johannine letters this is inevitably true whatever one's chronological schema. But it suggests also that there are few solid obstacles to stand in the way of reopening the question.

In what follows I shall presuppose the setting of the epistles for which I argued in my article 'The Destination and Purpose of the Johannine Epistles',[152] though there I was still assuming a date at the end of the first century. The epistles were, I believe, written to reassure Jewish Christian[153] congregations in Asia Minor, who were the product of the Johannine mission and in danger of being shaken from their faith and morals by false teachers of a gnosticizing tendency. In other words, the situation is remarkably parallel to that which we postulated for Jude and II Peter. Indeed we have observed earlier that Jude seems to stand to II Peter much as II John stands to

[151] C. H. Dodd, *The Johannine Epistles* (Moffatt NTC), 1946, lxvii–lxxi (lxviii). R. Bultmann, *Die drei Johannesbriefe* (KEKNT 14), Göttingen 1967, 9f., similarly argues that I John is later than John (and by a different hand) and II and III John subsequent to that. J. L. Houlden, *The Johannine Epistles* (Black's NTC), 1973, 1, also believes that the epistles were written later than the gospel by another hand and is content to say (without argument) that it is 'almost certain that all these writings date from the very end of the first century after Christ or the early decades of the second'.

[152] *Twelve NT Studies*, 126–38.

[153] For this aspect, cf. ibid., 130–3. Their essential Jewishness has been reinforced by close parallels with the language of Qumran (cf. especially Boismard, 'The First Epistle of John and the Writings of Qumran' in Charlesworth, op. cit., 156–65). Not only is there still no reference to Gentiles in the church but in III John 6f. ἐθνικός is used in the typically Jewish contemptuous sense of 'the heathen', with the same *contrast* between the ἐκκλησία and the ἐθνικοί as in Matt. 18.17: 'If he will not listen even to the congregation, you must then treat him as you would a pagan.'

I John. II John is a particular rather than a general pastoral letter, and its purpose may have been to give early warning of the new heresy ('If anyone comes to you', II John 10). In I John the false teachers, who are evidently peripatetic prophets (4.1–6), have clearly done their damage and have already persuaded some to leave (2.19).

The teaching indeed has much in common with that combated in Jude and II Peter. It evidently involves a denial of Jesus as the Christ and Son of God (2.22f.; 4.15; 5.1,5; cf. Jude 4; II Peter 2.1) and particularly of his coming in the *flesh* (4.2; II John 7). This docetic emphasis is new, and it leads both to doctrinal error – repudiation not only of the incarnation but of Jesus's coming 'with the blood' (5.6), i.e., probably, the reality of his sacrificial death (1.7; cf. 2.2; 4.10) – and to moral error. For if matter is unreal one can soon claim to be beyond morality – beyond sin (1.8–10), beyond law (2.3–5; 3.4) and beyond the material needs of the neighbour (1.9–11; 3.17; 4.20). It is this distortion of the teaching which his charges received, from a moral to a metaphysical dualism (with matter as indifferent or evil), that the writer sees as the root heresy, and this is characteristically gnostic. There is the familiar claim by the false teachers to give esoteric initiation and knowledge, which has to be countered by the Christian claim to the true knowledge and understanding (2.20f., 26f.; 5.20). We have already noted the similarity between the promise in II Peter 1.4 of coming to share in the very being of God and that in I John 3.2 of being like God because we shall see him as he is. The pretension of the heretics is evidently to be 'advanced' Christians (II John 9), going beyond both Judaism and the Christianity they have received. Yet there is no evidence here again of the developed gnostic systems of the second century.[154] So far from teaching a myth of a heavenly redeemer or of multiplying intermediaries like the Colossian heretics, they appear to have proffered an unmediated God-mysticism, promising possession of

[154] I should be much less confident than I was in my article on the Johannine epistles (op. cit., 134–6) that I John 5.6 contains specific reference to the heresy of Cerinthus, that the divine Christ came upon the human Jesus at his baptism but left him before his crucifixion (Irenaeus, *Adv. haer.* 1.26.1). Cf. R. M. Grant, 'The Origin of the Fourth Gospel', *JBL* 69, 1950, especially 308–16: 'The precise relation of these statements to Cerinthus is so unclear that it seems difficult to believe that John had Cerinthus in mind' (315). Cerinthus' teaching, as represented by Eusebius (*HE* 3.28.1–5), of a carnal kingdom of Christ on earth, is very different, and whatever John's later opposition to this heretic (Irenaeus, *Adv. haer.* 3.3.4; cf. Eusebius, *HE* 3.28.6; 4.14.6), he is here best seen as attacking an adumbration of a more developed docetism, which is not yet as explicit as that combated by Ignatius (Smyrn. 1–3). So R. Schnackenburg, *Die Johannesbriefe*, Freiburg [2]1963, 15–23; Kümmel, *INT*, 441f.; Guthrie, *NTI*, 870f.

the Father without the Son (2.23; 5.12; II John 9). The teaching is also connected, as in II Peter, with a false eschatology. It looks as if they too denied the Christian hope, repudiating the eschatological as well as the ethical dualism which marks the fourth gospel. So John is forced to insist upon it – while at the same time reinterpreting the truth distorted in its popular apocalyptic presentation:

> My children, this is the last hour! You were told that Antichrist was to come, and now many antichrists have appeared; which proves to us that this is indeed the last hour (2.18).

> Every spirit which does not thus acknowledge Jesus is not from God. This is what is meant by 'Antichrist'; you have been told that he was to come, and here he is, in the world already! (4.3)

It is a different (more profound) way of turning the denial from that employed in II Peter. Yet John too is led into an uncharacteristic use of the same phrase 'his *parousia*' (2.28; cf. II Peter 3.4).

The other link between the Johannine epistles and II Peter and Jude[155] is the notable absence of any reference to persecution – beyond the hatred that Christians must always expect from 'the world' (3.13). In this they stand in great contrast, as we have already noted, to the letters to the seven churches of Revelation (with which otherwise they have a number of similarities), and also to I Peter and Hebrews. These last three we dated between 65 and 68+, but Jude and II Peter we saw reason to put earlier, in 61–2. There would therefore seem to be much in favour of placing the Johannine epistles provisionally in this same period of the early 60s. II John was perhaps written shortly before I John. III John deals not with heresy but with the conflict over authority in the church's ministry, which also marks Jude and II Peter (and the Pastoral Epistles). There is no ground either from the use of 'the Elder' in v. 1 or from the (very uncertain) position of Diotrephes in v. 9, for assigning III John to the period of transition to the Ignatian monepiscopacy of the second century.[156] We can only guess from their almost identical endings ('I have much to write to you, but I do not care to put it down in black and white. But I hope to visit you and talk with you face to face'; II

[155] Oddly there is also a common reference to Cain (3.12; Jude 11) – the only proper name in I John.

[156] For the objections to Käsemann, 'Ketzer und Zeuge', *ZTK* 48, 292–311, who argues this, cf. Schnackenburg, *Johannesbriefe*, 299f.; Kümmel, *INT*, 448f.; Guthrie, *NTI*, 897; and the literature there cited. Bultmann, *Johannesbriefe*, 95, though putting I John late, describes Käsemann's view that the Elder of III John was excommunicated by Diotrophes as 'phantastisch'.

John 12; cf. III John 13f.) and other repetitions[157] that II and III John come from very much the same occasion. Indeed it is not at all impossible that the 'letter to the congregation' referred to in III John 9 may actually be II John.[158] Their subjects are not the same (there is no claim that they are); but there is the common issue of Christian hospitality (II John 10f.; III John 8–10). If so, then we should set the epistles in the order II John, III John, I John, but in quick succession.

If then tentatively we put the Johannine epistles in the early 60s and the epilogue in the latter 60s, with the prologue (perhaps) somewhere between, this would fit well with the many points of contact between the epistles and the distinctive features of the prologue and epilogue when compared with the body of the gospel. We have already suggested that the opening of I John reads like a preliminary sketch for the *Logos* theology of the prologue. There are obvious similarities. In both 'that which was from the beginning' was 'the word of life', and 'the life was manifested' (I John 1.1f.; John 1.1, 4, 14). Yet in the first epistle there is still not the absolute or fully personal use of 'the Word' found in the gospel prologue, and the latter is far more carefully constructed and richly orchestrated. In the epilogue too we have observed the same concern for the pastoral ministry of the church that marks all the Johannine epistles, and the same reference to eschatological expectations in current circulation which are yet given no encouragement in their popular form. There is the same use of *ἀδελφοί* to characterize the Christian brotherhood (John 21.23; I John 3.13f., 16; III John 3, 5, 10) and of *παιδία* in the address of Christians (John 21.5; I John 2.18). Then in the penultimate verse of the epilogue (21.24), the 'we know that his witness is true' echoes both the 'we' of I John and the 'you know that our witness is true' of III John 12.

Finally, there is another distinctive feature of the epistles which strangely is not noticed among the fifty 'peculiarities' of the first epistle listed by Holtzmann[159] nor is it mentioned by Dodd[160] among those differences from the gospel that lead him to posit a separate author for the epistles.[161] Indeed it does not seem to have been

[157] 'Whom I love in the truth' (II John 1; III John 1); 'Joy that your (my) children are living by the truth' (II John 4; III John 4).

[158] So Zahn, *INT* III, 378; G. G. Findlay, *Fellowship in the Life Eternal*, 1909, 8; McNeile-Williams, *INT*, 307. But the majority of scholars decide against this.

[159] Set out by A. E. Brooke, *The Johannine Epistles* (ICC), Edinburgh 1912, xiii–xv.

[160] *Johannine Epistles*, xlvii–lvi.

[161] For the contrary position, cf. W. F. Howard, 'The Common Authorship of the

observed by any commentary to which I have had access.[162] In the gospel, except on two occasions, 'Christ' is not a proper name (as it already is for Paul) but always a title, the Christ or Messiah.[163] In the epistles on the contrary the situation is exactly reversed. On two occasions it is a title (I John 2.22; 5.1); once it is ambiguous (II John 9); but for the rest it is always part of the proper name 'Jesus Christ'. Now, of the two exceptions in the gospel, one occurs in the prologue (1.17), and the other looks suspiciously like a later addition:

> After these words Jesus looked up to heaven and said: . . . 'This is eternal life: to know thee who alone art truly God, and Jesus Christ whom thou hast sent' (17.1–3).

To represent Jesus as talking to the Father about 'Jesus Christ' is the sort of crude anachronism that John conspicuously avoids. May it be that the clause 'and Jesus Christ whom thou hast sent' is inserted (whether by the same hand or another) precisely to counteract the false interpretation which had been put by John's opponents on the first clause taken by itself, that eternal life was to be had by knowledge of the Father without the Son? Certainly I John 2.22–25 and 5.11f. could suggest this. If so, the proper name 'Jesus Christ' here, as in the prologue, will reflect the usage of the epistles and be subsequent to that of the body of the gospel.

In my article on the epistles I argued that they presuppose not only the gospel but an extended interval between the two. The Johannine epistles are intelligible only on the assumption that their readers, who have evidently been their writer's pastoral charge from 'the beginning' (2.7,24; 3.11; II John 6), have been nurtured in 'Johannine Christianity'. The fundamentals alike of faith and morals to which they are being recalled are clearly the kind of teaching embodied in the fourth gospel.[164] The ἐπαγγελία, which the writer also received

Johannine Gospel and Epistles', *JTS* 48, 1947, 12–25; W. G. Wilson, 'An Examination of the Linguistic Evidence Adduced against the Unity of Authorship of the First Epistle of John and the Fourth Gospel', *JTS* 49, 1948, 147–56. In the light of this 'searching criticism', Williams, in McNeile-Williams, *INT*, 305, concludes that 'the verdict reached after careful linguistic analysis by R. H. Charles and A. E. Brooke that the fourth gospel and all three Johannine epistles were penned by the same person has not been overthrown'. I would agree.

[162] Though cf. M. de Jonge, 'The Use of the Word *ΧΡΙΣΤΟΣ* in the Johannine Epistles' in *Studies in John: Presented to Professor Dr J. N. Sevenster* (*Nov Test* Suppl. 24), Leiden 1970, 66–74.

[163] Burton, *Galatians*, 397, comments on the usage of the fourth Gospel in contrast with most of the rest of the New Testament but oddly omits all reference to the Johannine Epistles, as does Cribbs, *JBL* 89, 42, who quotes him.

[164] Westcott, *Johannine Epistles*, xli–xliii, clearly sets out the many parallels.

from Christ himself, can be summed up, as throughout the gospel, in terms of 'eternal life' (2.25). This does not of course necessarily mean that they have had that gospel in writing. Common themes such as the 'new commandment' of I John 2.7 and John 13.34 or the description of Christianity as a state of having 'passed from death to life' in I John 3.14 and John 5.24 need imply no more than oral teaching. The same could apply to the apparent background of the argument in I John 5.9f. (about human testimony and the testimony that God has borne to his Son) in the words of Jesus in John 5.31–40. But in I John 3.8–15 there is a connected series of themes which also occur in John 8.40–7 (the difference between being 'born of God' and not; the sinner being a child of the devil, who has always been the same 'from the beginning'; and the only two occurrences of ἀνθρωποκτονός, murderer, in the New Testament). It is surely easier to believe that the writer is taking for granted a knowledge that these connections have already been made in material with which his readers are familiar.[165]

The priority of the gospel (without the prologue and epilogue) to the epistles must fall short of proof. Yet this is also the order which seems to be presupposed in the closely parallel statements of their respective purposes. Of the gospel it is said:

> These [things] are written that *you may believe* that Jesus is the Christ, the Son of God, and that believing *you may have* life in his name (John 20.31).

Of the first epistle it is said:

> I write this *to you who believe* in the name of the Son of God, that *you may know that you have* eternal life (I John 5.13).

Even if the present subjunctive πιστεύητε in John 20.31 is pressed to mean 'go on believing' or 'hold the faith' (NEB) rather than 'come to believe', it is clear that the purpose of the gospel is primarily *furtherance of the faith* (and I should be perfectly prepared to agree that it was for the use of *Christians* in the Jewish mission), while that of the epistles is *reassurance of the faithful.*[166] They are a defence of the truth of the gospel against those who would distort its teaching. There is no

[165] The priority of the gospel to the epistles is argued on these grounds by Brooke, *Johannine Epistles*, xix–xxvii, and accepted by Dodd, *Johannine Epistles*, lv. But he has difficulty in accommodating the prologue, which he does not recognize to be a later addition to the gospel in the light of the epistles.

[166] Nine times in the first epistle the writer offers his readers tests, beginning with the words 'by this we know' or 'by this we may be sure' (2.3,5; 3.16,19,24; 4.2,6,13; 5.2), with which to assure themselves of the truth. For this emphasis, cf. R. Law, *The Tests of Life: A Study of the First Epistle of St John*, Edinburgh 1909.

need to assume that the gospel itself goes right back to 'the beginning' of the missionary activity to which the writer recalls his flock. Indeed this is always associated with what they 'heard'. Yet that its *writing*[167] was intended to serve as an instrument of evangelism and teaching there can, I think, be little doubt.

But since those early days much water has passed under the bridges. Considerable evangelistic labour had been put in: Take care, pleads the writer in II John 8, that you do not lose 'all that we worked for'. I John 2.12–14 presupposes an established Christian community with a full range of age-groups; II and III John a number of Christian centres, thick enough on the ground for travelling Christian missionaries to have no need to live off the heathen (II John 1, 13; III John 5–9). Heresy and schism alike have assumed dangerous proportions, and there is the same silver-age stress on sound doctrine, especially in II John 9f., that we meet in the Pastorals and again in Jude and II Peter. We shall hardly be wrong therefore in surmising that at least a decade has passed since 'the form of teaching to which they had been handed over', to use Paul's phrase (Rom. 6.17), had been in their possession. If then epistles do come from the early 60s we are back at any rate to the early 50s for some form of the gospel message.

But who and where were these Christians whom the writer calls his 'children' (I John 2.1), a form of address which appears to carry the same implication as when Paul uses it to his converts in Gal. 4.19, namely, that he had begotten them in the faith and been in a continuing, though not necessarily continuous, parental relationship to them ever since? We have been assuming that they are in Asia Minor, though there is no more certainty about this than that about the equally anonymous recipients of Jude and II Peter. But there is (*a*) the strong (and unchallenged) external tradition associating the gospel and the pastoral care of John with Ephesus and Asia Minor; (*b*) the fact that a Johannine type of Christianity is presupposed in the Apocalypse, which is indubitably associated with this area; (*c*) the similarity with the kind of gnosticizing teaching which, from the evidence of Colossians, I and II Timothy and the letters to the seven churches in Revelation, has already led us to place Jude and II Peter there; and (*d*) the fact that, admittedly much later, the first evidence for the use of I John comes from Smyrna (Ep. Polyc. 7). So we may accept this location until proved otherwise.

Now the tradition says that Asia was 'allotted' to John at the

[167] The word γράφειν occurs more often in the gospel and epistles of John (and also in the Apocalypse) than in any other New Testament writer.

dispersion of the apostles and disciples at the time of the Jewish war.[168] Yet Peter's preaching in Pontus, Galatia, Bithynia, Cappadocia and Asia mentioned in the same context must have occurred (if it occurred at all) earlier; and in any case the 'assignment' of Asia to John, if not purely legendary, like that of Scythia to Andrew[169] and Parthia to Thomas, would suggest previous association with the area. But the tradition is equally clear that John's missionary activity, like Peter's, did not start in Asia Minor but in Jerusalem and Samaria (Acts 3.1–4.31; 8.14–25). So too the epistles point back beyond the point which marked 'the beginning' for their readers to 'the beginning' of the events in which the writer, with his associates, claims to have had a very personal and tangible share (II John 5; cf. I John 1.1–3,5; 2.25) and indeed behind that to the *ἀρχή* in which eternally those events were grounded (I John 1.1; 2.13f.; cf. John 1.1). His message would be worthless if it were not already rooted and shaped in Palestine. So at this point we are driven back again from the epistles to the evidence supplied by the gospel.

I argued in my earlier article, 'The Destination and Purpose of St John's Gospel', that in its present form the gospel was an appeal to the Greek-speaking *diaspora* Judaism of Asia Minor, the sort of persons whom Paul addresses there as 'men of Israel and those who worship God' (Acts 13.16), to accept as the Christ him whom 'the people of Jerusalem and their rulers' (13.27), 'the Jews' of this gospel, had refused to acknowledge. All through the gospel there is an outer circle, of those who do not belong to 'the nation' (*τὸ ἔθνος*; always for this writer metropolitan Judaism), namely, 'the scattered children of God' (11.51f.), those of 'his own' (1.11) at present in dispersion. These are 'the Greeks' of 12.20, i.e. Greek-speaking Jews, whose representatives are present to 'worship at the festival', and who are spoken of so disparagingly by the Jerusalem crowds in 7.35.[170] Similarly they are 'the other sheep of mine, not belonging to this fold' who will also 'listen to my voice' and come to form one flock under the one shepherd (10.16) – as in the classic prophecies of the restora-

[168] Eusebius, *HE* 3.1.1.

[169] According to the Muratorian Canon Andrew is said to be with John at the time of the writing of his gospel. If there is anything at all in these traditions it could point to a period for the composition of the gospel prior to the dispersion. Cf. Brownlee in Charlesworth, *John and Qumran*, 189: 'Perhaps one should consider the Muratorian Canon as attesting the tradition that John at least began to write his Gospel before the dispersion of the apostles from Jerusalem.'

[170] For defence of this interpretation, cf. my 'Destination and Purpose', 116–22. The Greek *diaspora* was especially despised compared with the Babylonian (cf. the quotations given by Lightfoot, *Biblical Essays*, 157).

tion of Israel (Ezek. 34; 37.21–8; Jer. 23.1–8; 31.1–10). Chapter 17 too is a prayer 'not for these only', that is, for those already faithful to Jesus in Palestine, but for those who shall come to believe through their word (17.20), that is, for those who have not seen and yet find faith (20.29). The prayer 'may they all be one' is on Jesus' lips not (anachronistically) a prayer for broken Christendom but for scattered and disrupted Judaism, viewed as the true Israel of God. Throughout the gospel we can hear the anxiety of the evangelist and pastor that of those who have been 'given' (cf. Isa. 8.18) none should be lost (6.39; 10.28f.; 17.12; 18.9). This theme is introduced first in 6.12f., where importance is attached to the care with which the fragments must be collected after the feeding. Filling as they do twelve baskets, they symbolize the fullness of Israel still to be gathered in after 'the Jews' (or Judaeans) have been satisfied.

Yet though this clearly indicates the missionary outreach of the gospel, it is significant – and this I did not observe earlier – that in every case except one the movement envisaged is not of going out but of coming in. The climax to the ministry of Jesus which sets in motion his glorification and the world's judgment (12.23,31) is when the Greek-speaking Jews who have 'come up' to Jerusalem ask to see Jesus (12.20f.). This marks the beginning of the harvest (12.24), in which the reaper 'gathers' a crop for eternal life (4.36), and of the 'drawing' of all men to the Christ (12.32; cf. 6.44). The sheep are to be 'brought in' (10.16), the scattered fragments and children of God 'gathered together' (6.12f.; 11.52). The one exception is in 7.35, where the Jews ask: 'Where does he intend to go, that we should not be able to find him? Will he go to the Dispersion among the Greeks, and teach the Greeks?' Like other uncomprehending remarks in this gospel, and especially those a few verses later about Galilee and Bethlehem (7.40–42,52), this is both a total misunderstanding and the ironic truth. Of course Jesus will not go to the Greeks of the Dispersion (he is going to the Father) – yet they will find him (unlike the disbelieving Judaeans). Though the missionary motive of the evangelist is unquestionable, his perspective again is that characteristic of late Judaism (cf. Isa. 60; etc.), that the world would 'come in' to Jerusalem, not that it should go out to the world.

If this is so, then we may have an important clue to the original milieu of the Johannine preaching and teaching. The gospel shows the marks of being *both* Palestinian *and* Greek – in contrast with the Qumran literature which is Palestinian and Hebrew. I am not convinced that this simple difference has been given sufficient weight. I believe there is much to be said for the hypothesis that the Johannine tradition first took its characteristic form in Jerusalem, precisely in contact with those circles of Greek-speaking Judaism who feature at the climactic point of the gospel. Particularly at the feasts, which occupy such a dominant place in the tradition, their numbers would be greatly swollen by 'Jews from the province of Asia' and others (Acts 21.27). But in the intervals there were those 'devout Jews from every nation under heaven' who lived permanently (κατοικοῦντες) in Jerusalem (Acts 2.5).[171] These were the Greek-speaking Jews or Hellenists,[172] with whom the bilingual Paul 'talked and debated' when he 'moved about freely in Jerusalem' after his conversion (9.28f.). They were also those who earlier had 'argued with Stephen' and belonged to the so-called 'Synagogue of the Freedmen, comprising Cyrenians and Alexandrians and people from Cilicia and Asia' (6.9).

Now there is a widespread impression that the Greek-speaking Jews were 'more liberal-minded' (17.11; RSV) than the narrow Hebraists. But whatever may be the evidence for this outside Palestine (and Paul did not find much of it), those in Jerusalem were clearly determined to prove themselves more papal than the pope[173] or certainly than Gamaliel! They hauled Stephen before the Council and ended by killing him (7.8–60), and twice they planned to murder Paul (9.29; 21.27–36). There is no reason to think that the 'Hellenists' were *per se* Hellenizers (i.e. Graecophiles)[174] – any more than the

[171] Cf. Brownlee in Charlesworth, op. cit., 184: 'Here was a witness who needed Greek as well as Aramaic. The Evangelist who preached so eloquently in Palestine may therefore have been concerned with Greek-speaking Jews who went to Jerusalem at festival time (12.20). Wherever else this Evangelist preached, the substance of his message seems to have been worked out in the living context of the varied population of the land of Israel, and there he proclaimed Jesus as the prophet-king and Saviour of Israel.' For the assimilation of Palestinian and *diaspora* Judaism at this period, cf. W. D. Davies, *Paul and Rabbinic Judaism*, 1948, 1–16. There is not the gulf that is usually supposed, foı instance still by Morris, op. cit., 356: 'The more firmly it is demonstrated that the ideas and the language are basically Palestinian the more difficult it is to claim that the Gospel is essentially Hellenistic. It makes an appeal to Hellenists, but that is another matter.' But *is* it another matter, if the Hellenists were in Palestine?

[172] That the Hellenists were a linguistic group and not Gentiles (as Cadbury argued, *Beginnings* V, 59–74) is now generally accepted. Cf. Moule, 'Once more, Who were the Hellenists?', *ExpT* 70, 1958–9, 100–2; Fitzmyer, 'Jewish Christianity in the Light of the Qumran Scrolls' in L. E. Keck and J. L. Martyn (edd.), *Studies in Luke-Acts: Essays . . . in Honor of Paul Schubert*, Nashville 1966, 237f.; and *CBQ* 32, 515; Sevenster, *Do You Know Greek?*, 28–38.

[173] The members of the Synagogue of the Freedmen could also have been compensating for a social as well as a geographical sense of inferiority.

[174] Cullmann, 'A New Approach to the Interpretation of the Fourth Gospel',

'Hebrews' with whom they are contrasted in Acts 6.1 were necessarily Judaizers. Some of them may have been, but the word itself implies no more than that they spoke Greek (as their first, if not their only, language). Nor is there any reason to suppose, with Cullmann, that they were as such heterodox or nonconformist Jews on the fringes of Judaism, sitting loose to the law and the temple cult. Again some may have been – but certainly not those who attacked Stephen so vehemently, who were evidently at the very opposite end of the ecclesiastical spectrum.

Again, it is necessary to distinguish clearly between the Jewish Hellenists with whom Paul disputed[175] and the Christian Hellenists round Stephen. Nor should we assume that all Christian Hellenists shared the theology of Stephen. In fact when Hengel[176] refers to the bilingual 'Graeco-Palestinians' he cites men like Barnabas, John Mark and Silas/Silvanus; and when he asks 'whether the Gospel of Matthew might not come from such Greek-speaking Jewish-Christian circles in Palestine,'[177] he certainly has not in mind the group round Stephen whose outlook was quite evidently different from that of the first gospel. He does not mention the gospel of John in this connection, but I believe the same applies. *Pace* Cullmann, I see no reason to think that the 'Johannine circle', any more than the author to the Hebrews, had any special connection with the disciples of Stephen.[178] The theological emphasis that Jesus was the fulfilment and therefore the replacement of everything for which Israel stood, which is indeed so marked in John, is after all common to Paul (Rom. 10.4; etc.) and Matthew (12.6; etc.), not to mention the epistle to the Hebrews. Though in John worship is clearly not tied to the temple, it is very much 'from the Jews that salvation comes' (4.21f.), and far from being fringe Judaism ('Randjudentum') to which the Johannine

---

ExpT 71, 1959–60, 8–12, 39–43, argues that behind the noun lies the verb ἑλληνίζειν, which he says, 'does not mean to speak Greek but to live after the manner of the Greeks' (10). For this he is severely criticized by Sevenster, op. cit., 28f.: 'Any larger Greek dictionary could have convinced Cullmann that this pronouncement in no way obtains without exception.' But he makes no attempt to meet this criticism in his latest presentation of the same case, *The Johannine Circle*, ET 1976, 41.

[175] It is notable that Paul's encounter with these Hellenists in Acts 9.29 is passed over altogether by Cullmann in his recent study.

[176] 'Christologie und neutestamentliche Chronologie' in Baltensweiler and Reicke, *Neues Testament und Geschichte*, 59.

[177] *Judaism and Hellenism* I, 105.

[178] *Johannine Circle*, 39–56. Trocmé, *Formation of Mark*, 253–8, even makes them responsible for Mark 1–13!

mission appealed, it is a Judaism centred firmly in Jerusalem and its festivals. Moreover, it is not Philip the evangelist and those round Stephen with whom the Johannine tradition has links – *his* contacts are rather with Luke and Paul (Acts 21.8) – but Philip the apostle and Andrew, Greek-speaking Galileans from the cosmopolitan city of Bethsaida-Julias (John 12.20–2). Finally, if the Johannine circle was connected with that of Stephen, why was John left free when the persecution occasioned by the death of Stephen dispersed the others (Acts 8.1,14–17)?

The debate of the Johannine group, with its contacts with the high-priestly household (John 18.15), seems rather to have been with the inner core of the Jerusalem leadership. The distinctive Johannine dialogue is with those who claim to be rulers and teachers of Israel (3.1,10) or with those repudiated by them (7.49; 9.22). Its mission to 'the circumcision' (cf. Gal. 2.9) included in its appeal members of the Sanhedrin and others of the ruling class. A few of these were evidently sympathetic (7.50f.; 12.42) but the great majority implacably hostile (7.26,48; 12.37–43). If then this is the kind of background against which the Johannine mission was conducted, it is hardly surprising that a note of acrimony creeps so frequently into the debates which constitute the hard core of its gospel tradition. Yet the Johannine preaching and teaching was also very much concerned for 'the Jews who believed' (8.31), and we may hear this concern coming through the last discourses and especially such a passage as:

> I have told you all this to guard you against the breakdown of your faith. They will ban you from the synagogue; indeed, the time is coming when anyone who kills you will suppose that he is performing a religious duty. . . . I have told you all this so that when the time comes for it to happen you may remember my warning (16.1–4).

There is really no reason to think that such a passage reflects any greater distance in place or time than the Jerusalem of the first two decades of the Christian church. Wherever later this gospel was to be taken, expanded and edited, here I believe is where it began. And it is here that we may place the formative stage of the tradition, corresponding to the early stages of the synoptic traditions. Indeed I detect a growing readiness to accept that the first draft of the gospel itself (what before we called the proto-gospel stage) may have been written in Palestine.[179] In fact with this author, in contrast with the synop-

[179] Cf. Brown, *John* I, lxxiii: 'It is not impossible that the first edition of John was directed to the Palestinian scene and the subsequent edition(s) adapted for an audience living outside Palestine'; Charlesworth, 'A Critical Comparison of the Dualism in 1QS 3.13–4.26 and the "Dualism" Contained in the Gospel of John'

tists, and especially Luke, I doubt if much meaningful distinction can be drawn between his 'sources' and his own first composition – for, unlike Dodd, I am persuaded that he stood in an internal rather than an external relationship to his tradition. The unity of style has rendered unconvincing all attempts to analyse out written sources.[180] I would agree with the comment of Brownlee[181] on a recent attempt to do this:[182]

> A more valid goal, it seems to me, is the recovery of a proto-Johannine narrative, which (since it is by the same author as much else) it will never be possible to separate completely from the other Johannine contributions.

Even this, however, is a highly arbitrary procedure, as another recent piece of writing shows[183] in its attempt to isolate an original (and *very* primitive) Aramaic core expanded later by another hand. Indeed I would question whether there is, as Brownlee argues,[184] following Burney and Torrey, any real evidence for saying that the Johannine tradition was originally written in Aramaic[185] and then translated by another hand, whether in Palestine or elsewhere.[186] Though the Aramaic 'accent' of the writer is constantly apparent, there would seem no compelling reason to suppose that the stories and discourses

---

in Charlesworth (ed.), op. cit., 105: 'It is more probable at the present time that John was written, perhaps only in first draft, in Palestine.' Cf., earlier, W. F. Albright, 'Some Observations Favoring the Palestinian Origin of the Gospel of John', *HTR* 17, 1924, 189–95.

180 Cf. the remark of Pierson Parker, which I have quoted before, 'Two Editions of John', *JBL* 75, 1956, 304: 'It looks as though, if the author of the fourth Gospel used documentary sources, he wrote them all himself'!

181 In Charlesworth, op. cit., 181.

182 R. T. Fortna, *The Gospel of Signs*, 1970. The damaging criticisms of this in Lindars, *Behind the Fourth Gospel*, 1971, ch. 2, would seem to me to apply to any theory, including his own, that presupposes that the evangelist used external sources.

183 S. Temple, *The Core of the Fourth Gospel*, 1975.

184 Op. cit., 185–8.

185 For a survey of this issue, cf. Schuyler Brown, 'From Burney to Black: The Fourth Gospel and the Aramaic Question', *CBQ* 26 1964, 323–39; also Barrett, *John and Judaism*, ch. 2.

186 Brownlee's supposition (op. cit., 189–91) that the gospel was composed in Alexandria (and even that the apostle John may have preached there) seems to me to fall down, like other versions of this hypothesis, on the fact that it is inconceivable that had there been any association of the fourth, like the second, gospel with Alexandria, Clement and Origen (who prized it above all) would have known and made nothing of it. The evidence for Ephesus is far stronger and, *pace* Brownlee, does *not* 'depend' on 'an alleged claim of Papias to have known the apostle himself during his residence at Ephesus'.

that make up the gospel were ever written in anything but Greek. Nicodemus with his Greek name may stand for the typical educated Jewish Hellenist, in debate with whom the gospel tradition originated. As Nigel Turner has pointed out, the pun in 3.3–8 on ἄνωθεν (over again, from above) works only in Greek,[187] the language indeed in which, he maintains, Jesus himself could originally have conducted the discussion. Yet this is a Greek-speaking Palestinian milieu unaffected by the issues and conflicts which quickly arose within the church in a frontier-situation like that of Antioch.[188] Nor is there any evidence of a charge against John such as Paul had later to face from the Jews in Jerusalem, of selling Judaism short in order to accommodate the Gentiles (Acts. 21.27f.) But by that stage it seems that John, like Peter, was no longer in Jerusalem (21.17f.).

At this point we can postpone no longer the question of who the writer of this gospel was. For, though the dating in no way depends on the hand or hands involved, an early date also renders many of the arguments for an indirect and extended chain of authorship much less plausible or necessary. Indeed Brownlee, though himself still supposing the gospel to have been translated and 'put together from the manuscripts left behind by the original evangelist',[189] says:

> The Gospel according to John is in my view substantially the testimony of the apostle John.... If what one is looking for as apostolic is a fresh and independent witness, John has it – and not as fabrications of the imagination stemming from

[187] *Grammatical Insights into the NT*, 182. He also draws attention to the play on αἴρει . . . καθαίρει in 15.2.

[188] I have indicated ('Destination and Purpose', 115f.) why I would differ from Dodd in his belief that the dialogue of John 8.35–58 presupposes the same Antiochene background as Galatians. John is not faced with the question whether one should live as a Jew or as a Gentile. Indeed, I see no solid evidence for the view that the Johannine tradition reached Ephesus from Jerusalem *via* Antioch and Syria (T. W. Manson, *Studies in the Gospels* 118–21; Schnackenburg, *John*, 152). However Syria and Antioch are not simply to be equated. Cf. G. Quispel, 'Qumran, John and Jewish Christianity' in Charlesworth (ed.), op. cit., 138: 'Many other indications suggest that Syrian Christianity came from Palestine and not from Antioch, the centre of Gentile Christianity.' As long as this important distinction is maintained, one can be open to the possibility (though it is pretty tenuous) that the connections between John and the Odes of Solomon (cf. Charlesworth, 'Qumran, John and the Odes of Solomon' in Charlesworth (ed.), op. cit., 107–36) suggest 'northern Palestine and Syria for the provenance of the Odes and of at least one recension of John' (136). He believes that the two are contemporaneous (*c.* 100). Cullmann, op. cit., 98f., argues for Syria, and still more Transjordan, but discounts Ephesus. But this is because he dissociates the gospel from John son of Zebedee altogether. Yet the links between a Johannine-type Christianity and the Apocalypse still have to be explained.

[189] Op. cit., 191.

some later period of the Gospel tradition, but as the voice of a living witness from the cultural context of the early decades of Christianity in Palestine![190]

But rather than become involved in going over once again the well-worn case for attributing the gospel to John son of Zebedee,[191] we may begin at the other end by sketching the kind of author to whom the internal evidence points.

G. D. Kilpatrick has attempted this exercise in an article called 'What John Tells us about John'.[192] This is his conclusion:

> What have we learned about him? A poor man from a poor province he does not seem to have been a bookish person. In Greek terms he was uneducated with no contact with the Greek religious and philosophical literature of his day. This creates a problem: how does a man without these contacts have so many apparent similarities to a writer like Philo in his thought? As his material conditions as far as we can elicit them indicate a man of Palestinian origin it seems reasonable to look for the background of his presentation of the Gospel there. Our sources of information will be the LXX and related works, the literature of the Qumran and the Rabbinic texts especially the traditions of the Tannaim. On other counts we are being forced to recognize that notions we have associated with Hellenistic Judaism were not unknown and not without influence in Palestinian Judaism in the first century AD.[193]

Now whatever affinities John may have had with Philo, they were not literary. For Kilpatrick himself shows[194] that John's vocabulary is much nearer that of the LXX and Josephus than of Philo or the Hermetica.[195] Indeed the vocabulary and style of the gospel point to a man whose first language was evidently Aramaic and who wrote correct though limited Greek, with Semitisms but not solecisms.[196]

[190] Ibid., 184f.

[191] One can still hardly improve on the marshalling of the external and internal evidence by Lightfoot, *Biblical Essays*, 1–122, and Westcott, *John*, v–xxxii. Their case is presented afresh in the light of subsequent criticism by Morris, *Studies in the Fourth Gospel*, 215–80.

[192] G. D. Kilpatrick, in *Studies in John* (see n. 162 above), 75–87.

[193] Ibid., 85f. [194] Ibid., 77f.

[195] Earlier he had written, 'The Religious Background on the Fourth Gospel' in F. L. Cross (ed.), *Studies in the Fourth Gospel*, 1957, 43: 'We can discard the Hermetica along with the Mandaean texts and other evidences of Gnosticism. They constitute no significant part of the background of the Gospel, they do not provide the key to its interpretation.'

[196] For the linguistic evidence, cf. still Lightfoot, *Biblical Essays*, 16–21, 126–44. He argues that especially in the towns and in centres of commerce like the Lake of Galilee and Jerusalem 'the Palestinian Jew resembled a Welshman on the borderland, a Fleming in the neighbourhood of the half-French towns of Flanders, a Bohemian in Prague' (128) and that John's vocabulary and syntax are just what one would expect of such a person writing in the language he did not normally speak. Schnackenburg, *John*, 105–11, surveys the evidence in the light of modern

The evidence therefore for the person we are seeking, so far from ruling out a relatively poor and uneducated Palestinian, points suspiciously towards the kind of man that John, son of Zebedee, might have been.[197] There is in fact no reason to suppose that his family was particularly poor and uneducated. His mother Salome (cf. Mark 15.40 with Matt. 27.56) was among those who ministered to Jesus in Galilee (Mark 15.41), as Luke adds (8.3), 'out of their possessions'. In Zahn's words,[198]

> As regards its prosperity and social position, the family of Zebedee is to be compared with that of Chuza (Luke 8.3), the financial officer of Herod, or even of Joseph of Arimathea,[199] rather than that of Joseph and Mary (Luke 2.24; cf. 2.7).

The often observed fact that Zebedee's household ran to 'hired servants' (Mark 1.20) suggests that his status may not have been incomparable with that of the father of the prodigal in the parable (Luke 15.11–32), who also had two sons as well as a number of hired servants and was evidently a man of moderate substance (15.12,22f., 29). In more than one of John's parables the point of contrast is between the position in the household of servants and sons (8.35; 15.15), and the 'hireling' of 10.12 is the same word as is used for the hired servants in Mark 1.20.

Again, the lack of education attributed to John and Peter by 'the Jewish rulers, elders and doctors of the law' in Acts 4.13 need indicate no more than that in their professional eyes these were 'untrained

---

study and concludes that it leaves open the possibility, among others, that the author 'must have spoken Aramaic and some Hebrew in his youth, but was a Jew of the Diaspora, whether he was born there or moved there' (111).

[197] For a forceful statement to the contrary, cf. Parker, 'John the Son of Zebedee and the Fourth Gospel', *JBL* 81, 1962, 35–43. But it is possible to dispute many of his points (as I do below), and the psychological gap between the picture of the son of Zebedee in the synoptists and the presumed author of the fourth gospel is certainly no greater than that between their different portraits of the same man Jesus. The omission from the fourth gospel of all mention of the apostle John *unless* he is the author is much more difficult to explain, as is its distinctive designation of the Baptist as 'John' without qualification or fear of confusion. Parker's own preference for John Mark as author ('John and John Mark', *JBL* 79, 1960, 97–110) seems to me to raise many more problems than it solves.

[198] *INT* III, 187.

[199] In the different traditions Salome, Joseph of Arimathea ('a man of means', Matt. 27.57) and Nicodemus are all associated with procuring the spices for the burial of Jesus (Mark 16.1; John 19.39), which, if John's quantities are in any way to be trusted, must have cost a considerable sum.

laymen' (NEB), a view shared by the authorities both of Jesus (John 7.15; cf. 9.29) and of Paul (Acts 21.37f.). The astonishment was that *despite* this they showed themselves so articulate. Indeed John in particular must have had personal qualities that brought him rather rapidly to the fore. He starts as the younger of two brothers, who in Mark and Matthew is invariably mentioned second as 'James's brother John'. But from the beginning of Acts (1.13) he is given precedence (an order reflected back on one occasion in Luke 8.51), and the last mention of James is as 'the brother of John' (Acts 12.2). Both in Paul (Gal. 2.9) and in Acts (1.13; 3.1; 8.14; etc.) he stands second only to Peter in the Jerusalem church.

But not merely in stature does he, and he alone within the circle of the twelve or among any known to us outside it, meet the requirements of the role we are seeking, but both his background and his subsequent sphere of work are singularly appropriate.

It is often said (e.g. by Dodd[200]) that the fourth gospel shows an 'indifference' to the Galilean ministry which counts against its author being a Galilean. But this is surely an exaggeration. Purely statistically the word 'Galilee' actually occurs more often in John than in any other gospel. For all the additional Jerusalem material, it is clear that Galilee is still Jesus's base, where he 'remains' and from which he 'goes up' for the feasts (cf. especially 7.1–9); and the basic pattern of the story 'from Galilee to Jerusalem' (Acts 10.37; cf. Luke 23.5), with its watershed in Galilee (ch. 6), is unaffected. Moreover, in an interesting way John confirms the otherwise unsupported statement by Matthew that 'leaving Nazareth he [Jesus] went and settled at Capernaum' (4.12), with its implication that during the period of the ministry Capernaum was Jesus' home-town (τὴν ἰδίαν πόλιν Matt. 9.1; cf. Mark 2.1, ἐν οἴκῳ 'at home') in contrast with his place of origin (τὴν πατρίδα αὐτοῦ Matt. 13.54; cf. Luke 4.16).[201] For in a passage which reads like an entirely motiveless piece of travel diary[202] John records that from Cana (where Jesus had arrived independently of his family)

[200] *HTFG*, 16, 245f.; cf. Parker, 'John the Son of Zebedee', *JBL* 81, 37, 41f.

[201] There may be a comparable distinction, differently expressed, in the fourth gospel, where τῇ ἰδίᾳ πατρίδι (4.44) designates Judaea as his 'own land' (τὰ ἴδια), *to* which he came and where they did not receive him (1.11), in contrast to Galilee, the land *from* which he came (7.40–52) and where they did receive him (4.45). Cf. W. A. Meeks, 'Galilee and Judaea in the Fourth Gospel', *JBL*, 85, 1966, 165.

[202] Cf. Dodd, *HTFG*, 235: 'This passage is completely out of relation to any other topographical data supplied, and does not in any way contribute to the development either of the narrative or of the thought of the gospel. . . . [It] is not the product of any particular interest of the evangelist.'

> he went down to Capernaum in company with his mother, his brothers, and his disciples, but they [i.e., evidently, Jesus and his disciples][203] did not stay there long (2.12).

The natural inference is that Capernaum was then his home, and that he was paying a short visit on the family with his new disciples. In fact, apart from Cana, Capernaum is the only Galilean town Jesus is specifically recorded in John as visiting, although as in the synoptists he still goes about in Galilee generally (4.45; 7.1). In 6.15, after the feeding of the five thousand, the disciples naturally start rowing back to Capernaum as if this were home, though in Mark Jesus orders them to Bethsaida (6.45) while they actually land up at Gennesaret (6.53). The following day, in John, the crowds also set out for Capernaum, evidently expecting to find Jesus there (6.24),[204] which indeed they do (6.25), for the dialogue that follows takes place in its synagogue (6.59). Capernaum with its synagogue, which also features in the synoptists (Mark 1.21 [and 3.1; 5.21f.?]; Luke 7.5) and could perhaps be said to be the equivalent of Jesus' parish church,[205] is mentioned more frequently in John than in any of the other gospels. It is not insignificant therefore that John son of Zebedee himself probably lived in Capernaum as well. At any rate we are told that Peter's house was there (Mark 1.21,29),[206] which Jesus first enters with James and John, whom he had just found 'a little further on' from where Simon and Andrew were at work (1.19). And if, as Luke informs us in a passage independent of the Markan tradition, these pairs of brothers were in partnership (5.10), it looks as if Zebedee and sons also had their fishing business in Capernaum. I cite these connections, however inferential, because at any rate they do not show indifference to or ignorance of Galilean detail.

Yet it is in Samaria and above all in Jerusalem and its environs that the distinctive topographical interest of the fourth evangelist is centred. John is recorded as being associated later with the Samaritan

[203] For there is no suggestion that his *family* travelled round with him (cf. 3.22; 4.8–38; 6.3–24; 7.1–10; etc.).

[204] The extraordinarily circumstantial account of the itineraries in 6.15–24, though complicated, has the lucidity of a detective story. The mention of Tiberias, which had then recently been founded, is confined to John and is introduced for no apparent motive apart from factual accuracy. This does not read like the work of a man who had no knowledge of or interest in Galilee.

[205] A part of it may actually have survived beneath the ruins of the later synagogue. Cf. J. Finegan, *The Archaeology of the New Testament*, Princeton 1969, 51–4.

[206] Peter, like Philip and Andrew, originally came from Bethsaida (John 1.45; cf. 12.21), but there is no evidence (*pace* Lightfoot, *Biblical Essays*, 128) that John did too.

mission not only in authorizing the work of others (Acts 8.14–17) but in evangelizing 'many Samaritan villages' (8.25). Cullmann has indeed derived the meaning of Jesus' words in John 4.38, 'others toiled and you have come in for the harvest of their toil', solely from this later setting. I should question this,[207] but would not doubt that the church's Samaritan mission gives John the interest to devote such attention to Jesus' work in these parts (4.4–42), so that in this gospel he is even accused in insult of being a Samaritan (8.48). Moreover, there are a number of scholars who with greater or less probability have traced connections between the gospel of John and Samaritan theology.[208]

But it is the Jerusalem connections and interests that have most to be explained. And here it seems to me that the evidence points strongly to the apostle John.[209] Not only is he based there from the beginning by Acts (1.13–8.25) and subsequently by Paul (Gal. 2.1–10), but both Acts and Paul record him as being devoted to the Jewish rather than to the Gentile mission, which is precisely what we should deduce from the Johannine writings.

Indeed it seems to me that this last passage in Galatians may hold a neglected clue to the composition of the fourth gospel. Up to the time to which Paul is referring (on our dating 48) John had as far as we know lived and worked exclusively in Jerusalem and Samaria. For the best part of twenty years his dialogue and that of his circle had been with the Jews of the capital, and it is this engagement during this period that, we have argued, basically shaped his tradition. Yet subsequently the evidence points to the *diaspora* and particularly to Ephesus and Asia Minor as the sphere of the Johannine mission. How and when did this transition occur?

[207] Cf. my article, 'The "Others" of John 4.38' in *Twelve NT Studies*, 61–6.

[208] Cf. J. Bowman, 'Samaritan Studies: I. The Fourth Gospel and the Samaritans', *BJRL* 40, 1957–8, 298–327 (especially 298–308); W. A. Meeks, *The Prophet-King: Moses Traditions and the Johannine Christology*, Leiden 1967; G. W. Buchanan, 'The Samaritan Origin of the Gospel of John' in J. Neusner (ed.), *Religions in Antiquity: Essays in Memory of E. R. Goodenough* (*Numen* Supplementary Studies 14), Leiden 1968, 148–75; E. D. Freed, 'Samaritan Influence in the Gospel of John', *CBQ* 30, 1968, 580–7; and 'Did John write his Gospel partly to win Samaritan Converts?', *NovTest* 12, 1970, 241–6; Brownlee in Charlesworth, op. cit., 179, 183; Cullmann, *Johannine Circle*, 46–51.

[209] Nothing must be made to rest on the connections with the high priest of the unnamed 'other disciple' in 18.15f., though with Zahn, *INT* III, 190, 215f., I think it is more likely than not that he is intended to be identified with the beloved disciple (cf. 20.4), and this would certainly fit with the over-all picture. So Lightfoot, *Biblical Essays*, 128. Cullmann, op. cit., 71f., also argues for the equation of the disciples of 1.35 and 18.15 with the beloved disciple – but of none of them with John.

I had originally surmised that the change of location coincided with the great dispersion occasioned by the Jewish war.[210] Yet this is a pure assumption, though, as Eusebius says, these events may later have caused this area to be 'assigned' to him. I now believe that the clue to the transition is to be found in Gal. 2.6–9. There Paul says that the 'men of repute' at Jerusalem (i.e. James the Lord's brother, Peter and John) first

> acknowledged that I had been entrusted with the Gospel for Gentiles as surely as Peter had been entrusted with the Gospel for Jews. For God whose action made Peter an apostle to the Jews, also made me an apostle to the Gentiles.

Thus far the reference is to the past and is limited to the two leaders who, as far as we know (Acts 10–11; 13–14), had by that time broken the confinement of the church's preaching to the Jews of Palestine. But now a new stage seems to open up, marked appropriately by a fresh paragraph in the NEB:

> Recognizing, then, the favour thus bestowed upon me, those reputed pillars of our society, James, Cephas, and John, accepted Barnabas and myself as partners, and shook hands upon it, agreeing that we should go to the Gentiles while they went to the Jews.

The resolution looks to the future and should, I believe, be read as a new concordat for missionary policy, for which the gathering for the Council provided the occasion and opportunity. Though the verb 'should go' has to be supplied, it is most naturally taken as a decision to go out from Jerusalem in a fresh wave of expansion, which now was to affect not simply Peter and Paul (with Barnabas) but James and John as well. Paul and Barnabas were to go to the ἔθνη, Peter, James and John to the διασπορά.

It may be a sheer coincidence, but it is in the writings attributed to these latter designated for mission among the Jews that the only three occurrences of the word διασπορά occur in the New Testament (James 1.1; I Peter 1.1; John 7.35). Now we know from I Corinthians that Peter must in all probability have been at Corinth not long afterwards in the early 50s, and perhaps subsequently in Rome. Of James' movements we know nothing, but there is, as we have seen,[211] a *possible* pointer in the priority given to the Lord's brothers over Peter in I Cor. 9.5 to the fact that he too was involved at this same time in missionary travelling.

What of John? Again, with Acts silent, we are working almost

[210] 'Destination and Purpose', 125. Similarly Lightfoot, *Biblical Essays*, 51f., who describes it as 'a very probable conjecture'.

[211] Cf. p. 137 above.

totally in the dark. But I suggest that the facts are best explained on the hypothesis that John too first started missionary work among Jewish congregations in Asia Minor at the beginning of the 50s – and was out of Jerusalem, like Peter, when Paul returned there in 57, only James and the local elders appearing to be in the city (Acts 21.18). One of the interests of the author of the fourth gospel is evidently the incorporation into Christianity of those (like himself – the unnamed disciple of John 1.35–40?) who started as followers of John the Baptist. I believe there is no basis for the view that it was written against groups who claimed John as Messiah (of whom we hear nothing till the late second century).[212] But, as Dodd recognized, it would fit the sort of situation in Ephesus described in Acts 18.24–19.7 (though I suspect that the real basis of this interest goes back to earlier connections with Baptist groups in Judaea and Samaria). The 'disciples' who had known only the baptism of John were there, as we have seen, before Paul began his Ephesian ministry (probably in the late summer of 52). It is somewhere about that period that I would suggest John was independently in 'dialogue' with the synagogue (cf. Acts 18.4; 19.8) in the Ephesus region although, unlike Paul, he assuredly did not after three months 'separate' his disciples (the same word ἀφορίζειν used to describe the reverse process in Luke 6.22) to Gentile premises (19.9).

The obvious objection is that, if all this activity was going on in the same area at the same time, why do we not hear about it? Yet our sources are very limited. Acts has by then simply become a record of the Pauline mission, and is in any case exceptionally thin at this period even for that. It is worth remembering that neither in Acts nor in Paul should we have any notion of Peter's work in Corinth,[213] the congregation, after all, whose history we know far better than that of any other, were it not for the facts that (*a*) he was married and (*b*) he was seen by a faction there as a rival to Paul – neither of which as far as we know applied to John. Of the churches in the Ephesus area (not excluding Ephesus itself) we gather practically nothing from the Pauline letters except Colossae, which, to judge from Rev. 1–3, was not among the centres of Johannine Christianity. Similarly, there also were Petrine groups in the province of Asia (I Peter 1.1 – *whoever* was the author of this epistle); yet we have no idea how they originated. It would therefore go far beyond the evidence to conclude

[212] Cf. my 'Elijah, John and Jesus', *Twelve NT Studies*, 49–51, and Dodd, *HTFG*, 298: 'To base a theory upon the evidence of the late and heretical Clementine romance is to build a house upon sand.'

[213] The incidental reference to Barnabas in I Cor. 9.6 is equally characteristic.

that John was not then working in Asia too. Indeed, if as we have argued, the Apocalypse comes from the latter 60s, then some form of Johannine presence had certainly been established for a considerable time before that, at any rate in Ephesus itself (Rev. 2.4f.). This would also fit with the deduction we drew from I–III John that by the early 60s the beginning of the Johannine mission in Asia Minor already lay a decade or more back.

So the pieces are starting to fall into place. When the gospel itself was first committed to writing we still cannot be sure. But I believe we shall not be far wrong in seeing the stages as closely parallel to those which we observed for the synoptists. Here we may agree with Brown, though on a different time-scale. For like him I believe the various gospel traditions developed more or less concurrently. While not presupposing the synoptic gospels, John certainly presupposes the common oral tradition. 'In fact', as Brownlee says,

> one should conceive of this Johannine witness as born within a milieu where many people were intimately acquainted with the deeds and words of Jesus not mentioned in the Gospel (20.30f.).[214]

This of course would apply particularly to Palestine. Brownlee draws attention to the fact that in his speech at Caesarea Peter starts:

> I need not tell you what happened lately over all the land of the Jews, starting from Galilee after the baptism proclaimed by John. You know about Jesus of Nazareth (Acts 10.37f.).

John is not using (or correcting) anyone else's account, but he is taking for granted the same facts and their assimilation in the common life of the church. He gives the impression that he is writing the tradition for the first time and is looking over his shoulder at no one. This seems to be an altogether more credible account of affairs than that which is presupposed by the traditional dating. As Nolloth expressed it,[215] who, though dating the synoptic gospels between 50 and 60, still put John *c.* 95:

> Is it not a most perplexing thing that about the close of the first century, when all but one of the original witnesses of our Lord's life had passed away, a fresh account of him should suddenly be launched upon the Church, containing so much that, to men familiar with the existing tradition, appeared to give quite a different version of the facts?

If we envisage the various gospels coming into being more or less concurrently, and in the case of John largely independently, there is no objection to seeing, as Brown does, some limited cross-fertilization

[214] Op. cit., 184. [215] *Rise of the Christian Religion*, 25.

– in either direction – between the Johannine and the other developing traditions, particularly the Markan and Lukan. Indeed the so-called 'Western non-interpolations' in Luke 24.12,36 and 40, whether original to the text of Luke or not,[216] look to be influenced by the Johannine tradition, though there is no need to postulate dependence on the actual gospel of John, from which there are significant differences of detail. Yet, while the gospels were being formed concurrently, the span of development seems to have been somewhat more prolonged in John than with the synoptists, making John still the last gospel to be finished – though possibly also the first to be put down in a consecutive form. For the units of its tradition are not so much isolated *pericopae* as ordered wholes shaped by a single mind, originally no doubt, as Eusebius says, for preaching purposes.[217]

We might therefore hazard the following very rough and tentative timetable:

30–50 formation of the Johannine tradition and proto-gospel in Jerusalem
50–55 first edition of our present gospel in Asia Minor
60–65 II, III and I John
65+ the final form of the gospel, with prologue and epilogue.

Despite the solidarity of commentators cited earlier for a date late in the first century, there have always been isolated voices claiming John as a primitive gospel, or at least questioning whether it need be so late.[218] But they have not till very recently been backed by any

[216] K. Snodgrass, 'Western Non-Interpolations', *JBL* 91, 1972, 369–79, argues strongly that this tendentious category invented by Westcott and Hort should be 'relegated to history' and, with Jeremias and Aland, that these and similar passages form part of the original text of Luke.

[217] Cf. Eusebius, *HE* 3.24.27: 'John, who all the time had used unwritten preaching, at last came to write.' It would also fit, for entirely independent reasons, with the dating in the legendary Syriac *History of John* (cf. pp. 258f. above).

[218] Thus Goguel, *INT* II, 530, quotes six quite forgotten names who put it before the fall of Jerusalem: Gebhardt, Delff, Draeseke, Küppers, Wilms and Wuttig, whom I mention *honoris memoriae causa*! From recent times, cf. V. Burch, *The Structure and Message of St John's Gospel*, 1928, 228 (original contents near in date to the crucifixion; final editing before 70); C. C. Torrey, *Our Translated Gospels*, 1937, x (no necessity for a date after 50); P. Gardner-Smith, *St John and the Synoptic Gospels*, Cambridge 1938, 93–6 (perhaps contemporary with Mark); A. T. Olmstead, *Jesus in the Light of History*, New York 1942, 159–255 (shortly after the crucifixion); E. R. Goodenough, 'John a Primitive Gospel', *JBL* 64, 1945, 145–82 (from one of the Hellenistic synagogues of Jerusalem or by a Palestinian Jew in exile); C. C. Tarelli, 'Clement of Rome and the Fourth Gospel', *JTS* 48, 1947, 208f. (pre-70?); H. E. Edwards, *The Disciple who Wrote these Things*, 1953, 129f. (for Jewish-Christian refugees at Pella, *c.* 66); S. Mendner, 'Die Tempelreinigung', *ZNW* 47, 1956, 111 (75–80?); B. P. W. Stather Hunt, *Some Johannine Problems*,

substantial arguments. Now, despite the fact that even scholars like Brownlee still argue for a later final date, it looks as if we may stand on the point of a fresh break-through in what I called 'the new look on the fourth gospel'. Thus Charlesworth, though himself dating John *c.* 100, says:

> F. L. Cribbs is certainly correct in urging us 'to make a reassessment of this gospel in the direction of an earlier dating and a possible origin for John against the general background of Palestinian Christianity'.[219]

This article by Cribbs, 'A Reassessment of the Date of Origin and the Destination of the Gospel of John',[220] is in my judgment much the weightiest statement so far of the case for an early dating. He concludes that it was written 'by a cultured Christian Jew of Judaea during the late 50s or early 60s' – though still not by the apostle John. There would appear indeed to be a new convergence on a pre-70 dating between those who have given most study to the Jewish background of the gospel and the newer conservative evangelicals.[221] It will be interesting to see if and when others join them.

Over the span of time that we have predicted for the creation of the Johannine corpus, and allowing for considerable intervals between the stages in the writing of the gospel and epistles[222] and for the effect

---

1958, 105–17 (in Alexandria, just before 70); Hunter, 'Recent Trends in Johannine Studies', *ExpT* 71, 1959–60, 164–7, 219–22 (*c.* 80 or a decade earlier); Mitton, 'The Provenance of the Fourth Gospel', *ExpT* 71, 1959–60, 337–40 (early but no firm date); Eckhardt, *Der Tod des Johannes*, Berlin 1961, 88–90 (between 57 and 68); R. M. Grant, *A Historical Introduction to the New Testament*, 1963, 160 (around the time of the Jewish war of 66–70, or probably not long after it, for Jewish sectarians in Palestine or the dispersion); and *The Formation of the New Testament*, 1965, 159f. (not much later than 70, perhaps in Asia Minor); G. A. Turner, 'The Date and Purpose of the Gospel of John', *Bulletin of the Evangelical Theological Society* 6, 1963, 82–5 (prior to the Jewish revolt); G. A. Turner and J. R. Mantey, *John*, Grand Rapids 1964, 18 (possibly, if not probably, contemporary with the Pauline epistles); M. C. Tenney, *New Testament Times*, 1965, 321 (perhaps immediately after 70); W. Gericke, 'Zur Entstehung des Johannesevangelium', *TLZ* 90, 1965, cols. 807–20 (*c.* 68); E. K. Lee, 'The Historicity of the Fourth Gospel', *CQR* 167, 1966, 292–302 (not necessarily after Mark); Albright, *New Horizons in Biblical Research*, 1966, 46 (late 70s or early 80s); Morris, 'The Date of the Fourth Gospel' in *Studies in the Fourth Gospel*, 1969, 283–92 (nothing that demands a date later than 70); and *John*, 1972, 30–5 (pre-70 date probable); Temple, *The Core of the Fourth Gospel*, 1975, viii (35–65, on the basis of a still earlier record *c.* 25–35); M. Barth, in an unpublished statement (cf. Temple, op. cit., 306) (pre-70, the earliest gospel).

[219] 'Qumran, John and the Odes of Solomon', op. cit., 136.

[220] *JBL* 89, 1970, 38–55.

[221] Cf. Guthrie, *NTI*, 285: 'There are considerations in support of such a theory which have not received the attention which they deserve.'

[222] The Apocalypse is a different matter. I think it is probably better to

of new issues and influences, I see no changes of style and substance which are not better put down to the development of one large mind than to a disciple or disciples slavishly imitating the voice of their master. Above all it seems to me that the creation *ex nihilo*, as the real evangelist, of what Brown calls a 'master preacher and theologian',[223] a 'principal disciple . . . marked with dramatic genius and profound theological insight',[224] who was yet 'not famous'[225] raises far more problems than it solves. And to say casually, with Barrett,[226] that 'the evangelist, perhaps the greatest theologian in all the history of the Church, was now forgotten. His name was unknown' is to show an indifference to evidence (or rather to the lack of it) that makes one wonder how with others he can possibly appeal to the silence on the use of John in the second century as a powerful argument against apostolic authorship. Nor can it really help to bring in the shadowy figure of John the Elder[227] who, even if he was separate from the apostle,[228] is nowhere stated to have been a disciple of John son of

---

attribute it to another John, a prophet in the same circle, whose identity later became lost in that of the great apostle. The first evidence for this identification, *c.* 155, in Justin (*Apol.* 1.28; *Dial.* 81), allows after all for a tunnel-period of nearly ninety years following the last of the Johannine writings, in which much could happen. There is nothing in the Apocalypse itself to suggest apostolic claims. Indeed the authority of the prophet who says in the name of Christ, 'If you do not repent, I shall come to you' (Rev. 2.5), and that of the apostle who says in his own name, 'If I come, I will bring up the things he is doing' (III John 3.10) are subtly different. For an apostle describing himself as an elder (II John 1; III John 1), cf. I Peter 1.1 and 5.1.

[223] *John* I, xxxv.

[224] Cf. Howard, *IB* VIII, 441: 'He stands out as a religious genius of the first order.'

[225] *John* I, ci. [226] *John*, 114.

[227] Eusebius, *HE* 3.39.4, quoting Papias. This well-known passage is given in full by Barrett, *John*, 89, whose interpretation of it however I believe to be highly questionable.

[228] For a recent statement of the case to the contrary, cf. G. M. Lee, 'The Presbyter John: A Reconsideration' in E. A. Livingstone (ed.), *Studia Evangelica* VI (TU 112), Berlin 1973, 311–20. His strongest point, also made long ago by Zahn (*INT* II, 452), is that Eusebius himself, who disputes the identity of apostle and elder, implicitly acknowledges shortly afterwards in 3.39.7 that what Papias meant by 'the discourses of the elders' was 'the discourses of the *apostles*'. (Zahn's presentation is not helped by the crucial slip, also in the original German [II, 222], of misquoting the latter passage as τοὺς τῶν πρεσβυτέρων λόγους instead of τοὺς τῶν ἀποστόλων λόγους!) Cf. also C. S. Petrie, 'The Authorship of "The Gospel According to Matthew": A Reconstruction of the External Evidence', *NTS* 14, 1967–8, 15–24, who argues persuasively that ὁ πρεσβύτερος Ἰωάννης (not Ἰωάννης ὁ πρεσβύτερος) means, when the name is repeated with the article, 'the (aforementioned) ancient worthy John' (for πρεσβύτεροι as 'the men of old', cf. Heb. 11.2). He too is convinced that a

Zebedee, or (*pace* Eusebius) to have lived in Ephesus, or indeed to have written a word, though Eusebius *guessed* that he could have written the Apocalypse. With regard to the gospel, Armitage Robinson's comment is sufficient: 'That mole never made such a mountain.'[229] I find it much easier to believe that the role of the disciples of John was basically confined to that of which we have direct evidence, namely their certificate in 21.24 that this disciple himself 'wrote these things', and that this certificate, given in his presence (μαρτυρῶν), is true.

To sum up on the question of authorship, perhaps I can make the point by comparison and contrast. Brown, as we saw earlier, argues for the identity of the beloved disciple with John son of Zebedee but denies the identity of the beloved disciple with the evangelist. Cullmann[230] *per contra* argues for the identity of the beloved disciple with the evangelist but denies the identity of the beloved disciple with John. He believes he was an anonymous Judaean disciple, a former follower of the Baptist, in part an eye witness, but not one of the twelve. Why he should ever have been identified with John or how the gospel or 'the Johannine circle' ('for want of a better name'!) was so called remains a mystery. It is these self-created *aporiai*, or perplexities, in Johannine studies which seem to me so much more baffling than the breaks and discontinuities at which the critics balk.[231] I believe that both men are right in what they assert and wrong in what they deny. Further I think they are both wrong in assuming that the evangelist is dead at the time of composition and therefore introducing yet another divide between him and the final redactor (or redactors). In fact ironically it is the *lack* of final redaction to which the evidence most powerfully points. The faulty connections and self-corrections do not of themselves argue a multiplicity of hands. They merely show that what was first written, perhaps very early, as homiletic and apologetic material for various occasions has still not at the end been knit into a seamless robe.

But whatever the actual authorship and the precise limits of other

---

second John is simply 'wished on' Papias by Eusebius, who in his own interest in finding a separate author for the Apocalypse wants to believe that Papias 'proves their statement to be true who have said that two persons in Asia have borne the same name, and that there were two tombs at Ephesus, each of which is still to this day said to be John's' (3.39.6). Of course Papias does nothing of the sort; but he could certainly have expressed himself more clearly!

229 *The Historical Character of St John's Gospel*, ²1929, 102.

230 *Johannine Circle*, 74–85.

231 Cf. Lindars, *Behind the Fourth Gospel*, 14–16.

hands at work (on which there will remain scope for unending diversity and debate), I believe that John represents in date, as in theology, not only the *omega* but also the *alpha* of New Testament development. He bestrides the period like a colossus and marks out its span, the span that lies between two dramatic moments in Jerusalem which boldly we may date with unusual precision. The first was when, on 9 April 30, 'early on the Sunday morning, while it was still dark', one man 'saw and believed' (John 20. 1–9). And the second was when, on 26 September 70, 'the dawn of the eighth day of the month Gorpiaeus broke upon Jerusalem in flames'.[232] Over those forty years, I believe, all the books of the New Testament came to completion, and during most of that period, if we are right, the Johannine literature was in the process of maturation. It gradually took shape, in meditation and preaching, in evangelism and apologetic, in worship and instruction, and in that decisive translation into writing (John 20.31; I John 5.13) which fixed it, alone of the early Christian traditions, in the form of both gospel and epistles – as well as in those pastoral dealings for which 'pen and ink' (II John 12; III John 13) could be no substitute.

This does not mean that at this point the Johannine any more than any of the other streams of tradition ceased to flow or to grow. On the contrary, there is mounting evidence that for a considerable period, before the writings of the New Testament came to be cited as authoritative, the oral tradition and the 'living voice', of which Papias quotes John as a last survivor,[233] continued to hold the field. But this raises the problem of the sub-apostolic age. If the New Testament was essentially complete by 70, was it succeeded simply by a literary desert? What of those decades, especially between 80 and 100, which scholars have seeded so freely with their second sowings of deutero-Pauline and other latter-day literature? Are they merely left vacant? One cannot redate the New Testament without giving some attention, however sketchily, to this shadowy period in which any secure landmarks are still more scarce.

[232] Josephus, *BJ* 6.407. [233] Apud Euseb. *HE* 3.39.4.

X

A Post-apostolic Postscript

IF THE CANONICAL books of the New Testament are all to be dated before 70 the question naturally arises: What happens to the space in the last third of the first century previously occupied by so much Christian literature? Is there not an unexplained gap between the end of the New Testament writings and the first productions of the sub-apostolic age? And does not history, like nature, abhor a vacuum?

The possibility, if not the probability, must indeed be faced that there was not a steady stream of early Christian writings but that an intense period of missionary, pastoral and literary activity, culminating in the desolation of Israel and the demise of all the 'pillars' of the apostolic church except John, was followed by one of retrenchment and relative quiescence. A 'tunnel period' in which there was no evidence of literary remains would therefore be perfectly explicable – in fact more explicable, and less extended, than that which the traditional dating has presupposed prior to the emergence of the gospels in written form.

Yet it may also be that the gap to be accounted for is largely artificial. It may have been created by pushing the sub-apostolic literature late so as to leave room for meeting the supposed requirements of New Testament development. In other words, because the latter part of the first century is already occupied, other documents must belong to the second. Remove the initial presupposition and what happens? A look at the dating of some of the earlier sub-canonical literature will help to test and to set in perspective our previous conclusions.

The first thing that strikes one is the still greater lack in this twilight area of any fixed points or solid obstacles. Indeed there can really only be said to be two which are generally accepted, and they are by no means as secure as is usually assumed.

The first is the first epistle of Clement to the Corinthians, which is regularly dated in 95 or more often 96. Clement's episcopate at Rome, it is agreed, roughly coincided with the nineties of the first century,[1] and the assumption is that the opening reference to 'the sudden and repeated calamities and reverses which have befallen us' (1.1) and the admonition 'we are in the same lists [as the martyrs Peter and Paul], and the same contest awaiteth us' (7.1) refer to persecution of Christians at the close of Domitian's reign. Yet this *is* an assumption, however widely accepted. For the time being, however, let us leave it in possession of the field.

The second fixed point is the martyrdom of Ignatius and dependent upon it the dating of his epistles shortly before, and the epistle of Polycarp (at any rate in part) shortly after.[2] Lightfoot was able to place this event 'with a high degree of probability . . . within a few years of AD 110, before or after',[3] and except for those who question the genuineness of the entire Ignatian corpus there is no serious disagreement with this estimate. Harnack[4] favoured 110–17, Streeter[5] 115.

A third possible stable point of reference is provided by the so-called Epistle of Barnabas, which is held by the majority of scholars, with greater or lesser assurance, to be datable around 130. But here there is much more dispute, and a consideration of it will introduce discussion of a number of factors relevant to the larger scene.

This Epistle is noteworthy as the first Christian document explicitly to mention the fall of Jerusalem in the past tense:

> Because they [the Jews] went to war it [the temple] was pulled down by their enemies (16.4).

This is the kind of statement conspicuously absent from the New Testament and it clearly dates the Epistle after 70. But since there is no mention of the final Jewish rebellion and the reconstruction of Jerusalem as a pagan city under Hadrian (132–5), it is generally agreed that it is to be placed somewhere between these (wide) limits. But where?

[1] Eusebius, *HE* 3.15 and 34, dates it as 92–101, but Hippolytus, probably more correctly, 88–97. Cf. Lightfoot, *AF* I. 1, 67 and 343; Harnack, *Chron.*, 718. There is unanimity among the various episcopal lists that it lasted nine years.

[2] Cf. Lightfoot, *AF* II.1, 583; and also P. N. Harrison, *Polycarp's Two Epistles to the Philippians*, Cambridge 1936.

[3] *AF* II.1, 30. [4] *Chron.*, 406. [5] *PC*, 273–6.

Some have seen in the context of the same passage a reference to proposals by the Romans to rebuild the temple in *c.* 130:

> Furthermore he saith again: 'Behold they that pulled down this temple themselves shall build it.' So it cometh to pass; for because they went to war it was pulled down by their enemies. Now also the very servants of their enemies shall build it up (16.3f.).[6]

But there is much uncertainty about such a plan, if it existed. Some[7] refer it to a promise in the early days of the emperor Hadrian (117+) to rebuild the Jewish temple.[8] Yet the evidence for this is extremely sketchy[9] and to see a reference to the Jews themselves in 'the servants of their [the Jews'] enemies' is very difficult. Schürer concludes,[10] 'The historical value of the legend is nil', and Prigent,[11] 'One must abandon this explanation and its promoters.' Others[12] see an allusion to the building of a pagan temple on the site in Hadrian's new city of Aelia Capitolina, which is said by Dio Cassius to have been planned in 130 before the Jewish revolt and indeed to have been its occasion.[13] Again, the evidence for the site of this temple is very doubtful,[14] and it is surely incredible that if this is the reference it should not be seen by a Christian writer as a sign of judgment on the infidelity of the Jews.[15]

But in fact all such speculation is beside the point. It is clear from the subsequent context (16.7–10) that the new temple that *is* being built is a spiritual one in the heart: its agents are Christians, viewed as the loyal subjects of the Roman empire. As Lightfoot argued long ago,[16] 'the passage has no bearing at all on the date' of the Epistle,

[6] There is a textual variant, 'they and the servants of their enemies', but the text given is preferred by almost all editors.

[7] Cf. L. W. Barnard, 'The Date of the Epistle of Barnabas: A Document of Early Egyptian Christianity', *JEA*, 44, 1958, 101–7.

[8] Epiphanius, *De mens. et pond.* 14. But the account is highly unreliable.

[9] Cf. Gen. Rabbah, 64.10: 'In the days of Rabbi Joshua ben Hananiah the [Roman] State ordered the Temple to be rebuilt. Pappus and Lulianus [*sic?*] set tables from Acco as far as Antioch and provided those who came up from the Exile [i.e., Babylon] with all their needs'; H. Freedman and M. Simon (edd.), *Midrash Rabbah: Genesis* II, 1939, 579f.

[10] *HJP* I, 535.

[11] P. Prigent, *Les Testimonia dans le christianisme primitif: l'Épître de Barnabé I–XVI et ses sources*, Paris 1961, 76.

[12] E.g. Harnack, *Chron.*, 423–7; Windisch, 'Der Barnabasbrief' in Lietzmann's HNT, Erganzungsband III, Tübingen 1920, 388f.; Schürer, *HJP* I, 536.

[13] *Hist.* 69.12.1f.; contrast Eusebius, *HE* 4.6.4, who places it after the rebellion.

[14] P. Prigent, *La fin de Jérusalem*, Neuchâtel 1969, 121f.

[15] So Prigent, *Testimonia*, 78.

[16] *AF* 241.

and this is agreed by the two latest commentators.[17] Naturally the Jews *hoped* all along that the temple would be rebuilt physically,[18] but the response of this writer is to see all the ordinances of Judaism fulfilled in Christ in a spiritual manner (6–17). And this is true whatever the date.

The other reference to a possible dating is in 4.4–6, where there is an obscure allusion to contemporary history in the traditional apocalyptic mode:

> Ten reigns shall reign upon the earth, and after them shall arise a little king, who shall bring low three of the kings under one. In like manner Daniel speaketh concerning the same: And I saw the fourth beast to be wicked and strong and more intractable than all the beasts of the earth, and how there arose from him ten horns, and from these a little horn, an excrescence, and how that it abased under one three of the great horns. Ye ought therefore to understand.

It must be conceded at once that it is hazardous to build anything firm on this.[19] The reference is not as clear as it is even in the comparable passage Rev. 17.7–18. But it is evident that the fourth beast of Daniel stands here for the Roman empire, and the 'little horn' who is 'from' the ten kings is probably again Nero *redivivus*. Prigent[20] supports Lightfoot[21] in saying that the most likely reference of 'the three kings under one' is to the three Flavian emperors, Vespasian and his two sons Titus and Domitian, who shared the rule even during Vespasian's lifetime.[22] The passage is therefore to be dated before the death of Vespasian in 79, since he has still to meet his doom, with his sons, at the hand of the returning Nero (which he did not).[23] Whereas, as we have seen, in Revelation in 68 the sixth emperor is on the throne, and by 100 in II Esdras twelve have already reigned, here the tally to date is ten.[24]

Prigent is at pains to stress that this tells us no more than the date

[17] R. A. Kraft in R. M. Grant (ed.), *The Apostolic Fathers* III, New York 1965, 42f.; and P. Prigent, *L'Épître de Barnabé*, Paris 1971, 191.

[18] Cf. e.g. I Bar. 4.21–5.9; II Bar. 6.9; 68.4–6; II Esd. 10.41–55; Orac. Sib. 5.414–33.

[19] Cf. the discussion in Harnack, *Chron.*, 418–23, whose conclusion is 'non liquet'.

[20] *Testimonia*, 151f.; *Épître de Barnabé*, 97.

[21] *AF* 240f.; I.2, 509–12.

[22] Cf. the very similar expressions in II Esd. 11.29f.; 12.22f.

[23] For another such unfulfilled prophecy in regard to Titus, who it was predicted would die as soon as he set foot on Italian soil after sacking Jerusalem, cf. Orac. Sib. 5.408–11.

[24] In the latter two cases Julius Caesar is already included in the reckoning, as in Orac. Sib. 5.1–51.

of this particular passage, which indeed he thinks goes back to *c.* 70. Yet there is no real evidence for supposing that it is not homogeneous with the rest[25] and it fits with what can be gleaned from contemporary Jewish apocalypses. A brief comparison with these will be instructive.

I Baruch (in the Apocrypha) claims to be written in 'the fifth year after the Chaldeans had captured and burnt Jerusalem' in 586 BC (1.2; cf. II Kings 25; Jer. 52). Yet it is clear that this is but a thin disguise for the similar action of the Romans in AD 70, and the book, whatever earlier material it may incorporate, thus dates itself in 75. The Jews are urged to 'pray for Nebuchadnezzar king of Babylon and for his son Belshazzar' (sc. Vespasian emperor of Rome and his son Titus) (1.11).[26] There are allusions to recent calamities notably absent from the New Testament apocalypses – to parents eating their children in the extremities of the siege (2.3),[27] to the burning of the city (1.2), and to the deportation of captives to Rome (4.6,15f.,31f.; 5.6). The references to the doom of 'Babylon' in 4.30–5 are strikingly similar to those in Rev. 18, but here the fall of Rome is seen as direct retribution for the sacking of Jerusalem ('The same city that rejoiced at your downfall and made merry over your ruin shall grieve over her own desolation', 4.33) in a way that we should expect but significantly do not get in Revelation. There is possibly also a reference to the Christians in 4.3, 'Do not give up your glory to another or your privileges to an alien people', corresponding to the reference to the Jews in the Epistle of Barnabas.

Again in parts at any rate of II Baruch (the Syriac Apocalypse of Baruch)[28] we seem to be in the same period. There are similarly circumstantial references to the overthrowing of the walls of Jerusalem and the burning of the temple (7.1; 80.3), and to the despoiling of the sanctuary:

> And I saw him descend into the Holy of Holies, and take from thence the veil, and the holy ark, and the mercy-seat, and the two tables, and the holy raiment of the priests, and the altar of incense, and the forty-eight precious stones, wherewith the priest was adorned, and all the holy vessels of the tabernacle (6.7).[29]

There is also the same prediction of the reversal of judgment upon Rome and particularly upon Vespasian:

[25] Contrast, for instance, II Esd. 1–2 and 15–16 which are fairly evidently separate from the main body of the book.

[26] Contrast the very different attitude towards Domitian in II Esd. 11.36–46.

[27] Cf. Josephus, *BJ* 6.201–3. There is no such reference in our accounts of the events of 586.

[28] Charles, *AP* II, 470–526, from which the translation is taken.

[29] Cf. Josephus, *BJ* 148–151, 161f.

> The king of Babylon will arise who has now destroyed Zion, and he will boast over the people, and he will speak great things in his heart in the presence of the Most High. But he shall also fall at last (67.7f.).

If in the passage from the Epistle of Barnabas we examined earlier there were a Christian riposte to Jewish hopes of a literal restoration of the temple and its worship, it could equally come from this same period. Witness the muted promise given to the apocalyptist:

> After a little interval Zion will again be builded, and its offerings will again be restored, and the priests will return to their ministry, and also the Gentiles will come to glorify it. Nevertheless, not fully as in the beginning (68.5f.).

One could go on citing parallels. Thus there is the passage in the Apocalypse of Abraham 27:[30]

> And I looked and saw: lo! the picture swayed and from it emerged, on its left side, a heathen people, and these pillaged those who were on the right side, men and women and children: some they slaughtered, others they retained with themselves. Lo! I saw them run towards them through four entrances, and they burnt the temple with fire, and the holy things that were therein they plundered.

And there are comparable references in the somewhat later book of II Esdras, especially in 10.21–3:

> You see how our sanctuary has been laid waste, our altar demolished, and our temple destroyed. Our harps are unstrung, our hymns silenced, our shouts of joy cut short; the light of the sacred lamp is out, and the ark of the covenant has been taken as spoil; the holy vessels are defiled, and the name which God has conferred on us is disgraced; our leading men have been treated shamefully, our priests burnt alive,[31] and the Levites taken off into captivity; our virgins have been raped and our wives ravished, our godfearing men carried off, and our children abandoned; our youths have been enslaved, and our strong warriors reduced to weakness. Worst of all, Zion, once sealed with God's own seal, has forfeited its glory and is in the hands of our enemies.

I quote these passages as the contrast with the New Testament is so glaring, and it is surely incredible that if parts of it too came from the same period nothing of the kind is reflected in it. But that the Epistle of Barnabas should come from these traumatic years following the fall of Jerusalem is entirely possible; and several of those who put it in the reign of Hadrian or suspend judgment admit that the internal evi-

[30] *The Apocalypse of Abraham*, ed. and tr. G. H. Box, 1918. Box contends (xvi) that the description suggests that the events are fairly recent. Similarly D. S. Russell, *The Method and Message of Jewish Apocalyptic*, 1964, 37, dates it between 70 and 100.

[31] Cf. Josephus, *BJ* 6.280, who specifically mentions two leading men among the priests who threw themselves into the fire and were burnt together with the holy house.

dence would naturally suggest an earlier dating.[32] Indeed there are many other pointers to this.

From early times the Epistle achieved near-canonical status, being included with the Shepherd of Hermas immediately after the book of Revelation in Codex Sinaiticus. Yet it makes no claims to apostolic authorship characteristic of later pseudepigrapha. In fact the writer disavows even the authority of a 'teacher', addressing his audience simply as 'one of yourselves' (1.8; 4.6,9). There is no reference to any specific order of ministry apart from that of teacher – merely to 'every one who speaks the word of the Lord to you' (19.9) and to those 'in higher station' (21.2), which, however, almost certainly refers in the context to those who are economically better off ('Keep amongst you those to whom ye may do good'). He calls his readers on their own initiative to 'assemble yourselves together and consult concerning the common welfare' (4.10). The whole approach is strikingly different from the second-century appeal in the Ignatian epistles to the authority of the bishop. And unlike these, and still more the epistle of Polycarp, this epistle makes no reference to any other Christian writing,[33] not even to the epistle to the Hebrews with whose argument it has so many affinities. Its appeal is to the Old Testament and Jewish tradition.[34] The sole apparent reference to any saying of Jesus, though not by name, is in 4.14: 'As it is written, Many are called, but few are chosen.'[35] But since this is entirely isolated the commentators are rightly inclined to doubt whether it is a citation from the gospel tradition, seeing in it rather 'a popular Jewish apocalyptic saying also known to (Jesus and) the author of Matthew'.[36] There are indeed allusions to the gospel tradition about Jesus (5.8f.;

[32] Cf. Eltester, *IDB* I, 358: 'Even though the letter suggests an earlier dating'; J. Lawson, *A Theological and Historical Introduction to the Apostolic Fathers*, New York 1961, 201: 'The evidence would well accord with the early date [70–79].'

[33] There are phrases in the 'two ways' material at the end which have been said to reflect knowledge of the New Testament, but these are also in the Didache and are much more likely to have come from the source behind them both (see below). Again, Barn. 15.4 represents not a quotation from II Peter 3.8 but a common use of Ps. 90.4.

[34] Despite assertions to the contrary, Barn. 11.9 cannot establish literary dependence on II Bar. 61.7, nor Barn. 12.1 on II Esd. 5.5. The phrases are part of the common stock of late Jewish imagery.

[35] Cf. Matt. 22.14.

[36] Kraft, ad loc.; similarly Windisch and Prigent. For the idea in Judaism, cf. II Esd. 8.1–3. I Tim. 5.18 similarly cites as 'scripture' not only Deut. 25.4 ('You shall not muzzle a threshing ox') but, apparently, Matt. 10.10 = Luke 10.7 ('The labourer is worthy of his hire'); but the latter too is probably a proverbial Jewish saying rather than an original word of Jesus.

7.3; 8.3) (as well as to an unwritten saying)[37] but nothing that demands dependence on our written gospels. In 15.9 there is a reference to the ascension having taken place on Easter day, contrary to the tradition in Acts. The epistle contains no developed doctrine of the person of Christ, still less of the Spirit, and remains within the purview of Jewish-Christian theology. The 'gnosticism' of the author is a naive and primitive one, exegetical, ethical and eschatological[38] rather than systematic, heretical or polemical. It stands in strong contrast to the gnostic Gospels of Thomas and Philip and the Gospel of Truth, which really do seem to belong to the mid-second century from which the Epistle of Barnabas has been supposed to come.

In sum, there is nothing here that could not have been written, as Lightfoot said, about 75. It does not begin to reach the heights of the New Testament, and the church was obviously right to exclude it from the canon. But in date there is no reason to think of it coming far behind.

With the Epistle of Barnabas must be considered its nearest associate, the Shepherd of Hermas. This again has regularly been placed in the middle of the second century, but solely on the ground of one piece of external evidence, the Muratorian Fragment on the Canon:[39]

> Very lately in our times Hermas wrote 'The Shepherd' in the city of Rome while his brother Pius, the bishop, was sitting in the chair of the Church of the city of Rome, and therefore it ought to be read; but it cannot, to the end of time, be placed either among the prophets who are complete in number, nor among the Apostles, for public lection to the people in church.

Pius was bishop of Rome from *c.* 140–155.

The Muratorian Canon is usually held to be the work of Hippolytus and to come from Rome *c.* 180–200,[40] though recently it has been asserted to be not a second-century Roman product but a fourth-century eastern list.[41] In any case for no other book should we take its unsupported evidence seriously, and it is full of palpable mistakes. With regard to Hermas in particular there are good grounds for questioning its statements. Thus Irenaeus, who resided in Rome less

[37] 'Thus, he saith, they that desire to see me, and to attain unto my kingdom, must lay hold on me through tribulation and affliction' (7.11; cf. Acts 14.22).

[38] Cf. Kraft, op. cit., 22–9.

[39] There is a similar reference in the fourth century Liberian Catalogue (cf. Lightfoot, *AF* I.1, 254) but it evidently goes back to the same common source.

[40] Cf. Lightfoot, *AF* I.2, 405–13, who dated it before 185–90; Hennecke, *NT Apoc.* I, 42–5.

[41] A. C. Sundberg, 'Canon Muratori: A Fourth Century List', *HTR* 66, 1973, 1–41. His argument in questionable at many points.

than twenty years after the death of Pius, quotes the opening sentence of the first Mandate of the Shepherd as 'scripture',[42] which would scarcely be likely if it was known to have been composed within living memory. Not much later Tertullian[43] strongly disparages Hermas in contrast with Hebrews and it seems improbable that he would not have deployed against it the argument of its late composition. Origen, who freely cites the Shepherd as scripture, attributes it indeed in his *Commentary on Romans* to the first-century Hermas greeted by Paul in Rom. 16.14. In his early work on the Shepherd[44] Zahn seriously challenged the evidence of the Muratorian Canon, and Edmundson argued that its attribution to the bishop's brother arises from a sheer blunder.[45] It is on the face of it highly unlikely that one who tells us he was a foster-child sold into slavery in Rome (Vis. 1.1.1), probably from Arcadia in Greece (Sim. 9.1.4),[46] should have had a brother in Rome called Pius who was head of the church there at the time but whom he never mentions, despite several references to his family. But elsewhere[47] we are told that this Pius was 'the brother of Pastor' and it looks very probable that the Shepherd of Hermas, which in its Latin version, possibly dating from the end of the second century and therefore perhaps contemporary with the Muratorian Fragment, is called 'Liber Pastoris' (or the Book of the Shepherd), has by a natural confusion been attributed to the brother of the bishop.

But the external evidence can in any case only be as strong as the internal, and this latter suggests a considerably earlier date. In Vis. 2.4.2f. the seer is told:

> When then I shall have finished all the words, it shall be made known by thy means to all the elect. Thou shalt therefore write two little books, and shalt send one to Clement, and one to Grapte. So Clement shall send to the foreign cities, for this is his duty; while Grapte shall instruct the widows and the orphans. But thou shalt read (the book) to this city [Rome] along with the elders that preside over the Church.

There is general agreement that unless this reference is a pseudonymous fiction (which there is no other reason to suppose) it must be to the Clement who was bishop of Rome in the last decade of the first

[42] *Adv. haer.* 4.34.2. [43] *De pudic.* 20.

[44] *Der Hirt des Hermas*, Gotha 1868.

[45] *The Church in Rome*, 208–15. Cf. Streeter, *PC*, 202–13, who however detects anti-Montanist polemic at work. But if the Shepherd was favoured by the Montanists, why does Tertullian slate it as lax in its attitude to post-baptismal sin in comparison with Hebrews?

[46] Cf. J. A. Robinson, *Barnabas, Hermas and the Didache*, 1920, 27f.

[47] *The Acts of Pastor and Timothy.* For the detailed evidence, see Edmundson, op. cit., 210–2.

century. But Edmundson argues cogently that it relates to a time before Clement held that office. He seems to have an appointment which, in Lightfoot's words 'constituted him, as we might say, foreign secretary of the Roman Church'.[48] But, says Edmundson,[49]

> such a description surely implies that at the time Clement was occupying what can only be described as a subordinate position, since he was charged with secretarial duties entrusted to him by others. The particular charge was one that might very well be assigned to a younger member of the presbyterate distinguished among his colleagues for wider culture and greater familiarity with literary Greek. The mere fact that his name is here coupled with that of Grapte, apparently a deaconess, is of itself a proof that the Clement of Hermas' second Vision had not yet become at the close of a long and honoured career the venerated bishop of 96 AD.

Edmundson himself dates the Shepherd of Hermas in the first decade of the reign of Domitian (81–91),[50] pointing out that the allusions to past sufferings correspond closely with the records of the Neronian persecution (Vis. 3.2.1; Sim. 8; 9.19.1; 9.28). A fair amount of time has elapsed, which now makes possible a forgiving attitude towards previous betrayals (Vis. 2.2.4; Sim. 9.26.6). Yet the references to the Christian ministry still presuppose a relatively early period. Thus Vis. 3.5.1 speaks of

> the apostles and bishops and teachers and deacons, who walked after the holiness of God, and exercised their office of bishop and teacher and deacon[51] in purity and sanctity for the elect of God, some of them already fallen on sleep, and others still living.

This passage appears to imply that some of the original generation of church leaders were still alive.[52] In Sim. 9.15.4 there is a distinction made between the first 'foundation' generation, who are represented by ten stones (not, be it noted, as in Revelation, twelve), a second generation of 'righteous men', represented by twenty-five stones, and a third group of thirty-five 'prophets of the Lord and his ministers'. Yet the 'apostles and teachers of the preaching of the Son of God' are not, as we might expect, identified with the first, but are yet a fourth group, forty in number. Except in Sim. 9.17.1 the term 'apostles' is

[48] *AF* I.1, 348. [49] Op. cit., 203f

[50] Ibid., 203f., 215–21. W. J. Wilson, 'The Career of the Prophet Hermas', *HTR* 20, 1927, 21–62, while agreeing that Zahn discredited the testimony of the Muratorian Canon for a date *c.* 140, opted with him, Salmon and Bigg for one *c.* 95, but only because of the reference to Clement, who was simply assumed to be bishop at the time. Similarly Streeter, *FG*, 528, put it *c.* 100.

[51] Note that he does not say bishop, presbyters and deacons, as in Ignatius.

[52] Cf. Sim. 9.16, which does not say that *all* the apostles and teachers had fallen asleep, but speaks of those who had.

still being used at this stage, as in some passages of the New Testament, in the wider sense of missionaries. As in the Didache, to be discussed below, 'prophets' for this writer appear to be in a category apart. Though they do not feature in the list of ministries in Vis. 3.5.1, Mand. 11 gives careful criteria for distinguishing true prophets from false. He himself claims the gift of prophecy and with it the authority, like the seer of Revelation, to deliver charges and admonitions to the church and its rulers (Vis. 2.2.6; 2.4.2f.; 3.8.11; 3.9.7–10; Sim. 9.31.3–6). These are called the 'chiefs' or 'leaders' of the church, the same terms that are used in Hebrews and I Clement.[53] He speaks of 'the elders that preside over (προϊσταμένων) the church' (Vis. 2.4.3) in exactly the same way as the Pastoral Epistles (I Tim. 5.17; cf. I Thess. 5.12; Rom. 12.8), and the qualities commended in such 'bishops' are again the same (Sim. 9.27.2; cf. I Tim. 3.2–7; Titus 1.6–9). There is no sign yet of a monarchical episcopate, even in Rome (Vis. 2.4.3), such as would have been enjoyed by Pius I in the mid-second century, though there are indications of struggles for 'first places and a certain dignity' (Sim. 8.7.4; cf. Vis. 3.9.7). Lightfoot himself recognized that these references suggested an earlier date.[54] Still there are no direct quotations from or references to Christian books, and its 'spirit' or 'angel' Christology remains within the limits of primitive Jewish-Christianity.[55]

There thus seems nothing against and everything in favour of the sort of date proposed by Edmundson. In his chronological table[56] he finally plumped, without having argued it, for *c.* 90. But this depends on his belief that Clement did not become bishop of Rome till 92. If with Lightfoot we put that back to 88 or even 86[57] then perhaps *c.* 85 would be a better estimate. Indeed this is an upper limit; it could be earlier, and may well have been composed over a period.[58] This would allow a twenty years' interval after the Neronian persecution, and put the Shepherd a decade later than the Epistle of Barnabas.

So we turn to the third of three writings that have been closely linked and indeed held to be mutually dependent – the Didache, or the Teaching of the Twelve Apostles, discovered in 1875 and pub-

[53] Cf. p. 209 n. 45 above. [54] *AF* 294; cf. Lawson, op. cit., 224f.

[55] Cf. A. Grillmeier, *Christ in Christian Tradition*, ET 1965, 41–66.

[56] Op. cit., 241. [57] *AF* I.1.343.

[58] W. Coleborne, 'A Linguistic Approach to the Problem of Structure and Composition of *The Shepherd of Hermas*', *Colloquium* (*The Australian and New Zealand Theological Review*) 3, 1969, 133–42 (especially 141f.), thinks that it was written, by several hands, between 60 and 100 and that the older parts could well go back to the Hermas at Rome mentioned in Rom. 16.14. I doubt the spread at either end, but the authorship is not impossible chronologically.

lished in 1883. Of no other Christian book have the dating-estimates shown a wider or a wilder swing – ranging between 50 and the fourth century. It is significant that Edmundson,[59] who opts for an early dating of everything else, is inclined, though without any adequate discussion, to concur with Bigg[60] (who thought II Peter apostolic!) in placing it at the latter extreme. In Armitage Robinson's words,

> It does not seem to fit in anywhere, in either time or place. The community which it presupposes is out of relation to all our knowledge of Church history.... We still ask, Was there ever a Church which celebrated the Eucharist after the manner here enjoined? Was there ever a Church which refused to allow Apostles more than a two days' stay?[61]

His conclusion was that it was an artificial and imaginative construction of an ideal apostolic era which affords no reliable historical information of that or any other time. But his own question, 'What after all was the writer's object in composing the book?', remained unanswered.[62]

But, if we cannot fit it into any period of liturgy or ministry for which we have written evidence, is it possible that it belongs to a period before such documentation? This is the thesis that has boldly been advanced by the massive recent commentary by the French Canadian J.-P. Audet, who concludes that it was composed, almost certainly in Antioch, between 50 and 70.[63] Coming to this only after reaching my own conclusions on the chronology of the New Testament, I cannot but concur with the remarkably sympathetic review by Kelly[64] in regarding it as a most persuasive thesis argued in a masterly manner.

If one thing is now probable it is that the material on 'the two ways' which comprises the first half of the Didache (1.1–6.2) is not, as Armitage Robinson, Vokes and others argued, dependent upon the

[59] Op. cit., 187. [60] C. Bigg, *The Doctrine of the Twelve Apostles*, 1898.

[61] J. A. Robinson, 'The Problem of the Didache', *JTS* 13, 1912, 340, reprinted in *Barnabas, Hermas and the Didache*, 86.

[62] *Barnabas, Hermas and the Didache*, 103. Streeter, *PC* 283, says that his theory is 'one that I cannot bring myself to take seriously'. Yet the theory persists in one form or another. F. E. Vokes, *The Riddle of the Didache*, 1938, similarly regards it as a fictitious reconstruction, but thinks its object is to present and defend the 'new prophecy' of the Montanist movement as 'apostolic'. He places it at the end of the second century or the beginning of the third (216–20). W. Telfer, 'The "Plot" of the *Didache*', *JTS* 45, 1944, 141–51, thinks it is a pseudepigraph which is 'supposed to be the work of the apostolic council of Jerusalem, narrated in Acts 15' (142). C. C. Richardson, *Early Christian Fathers* (Library of Christian Classics I), 1953, 165, holds it to be 'the first of those fictitious Church Orders which edit ancient material and claim apostolic authorship'. He dates it *c.* 150.

[63] *La Didachè: Instructions des Apôtres*, 219. [64] *JTS* n.s. 12, 1961, 329–33.

Epistle of Barnabas (18–20) with which it has many close parallels, but that both go back to common Jewish sources. The evidence of the Qumran Manual of Discipline, which preserves very similar material,[65] has tilted the balance again in favour of the latter view.[66] The same applies to the much weaker case for the Didache's dependence on Hermas.[67]

More contentious is the relationship between the Didache and the New Testament. It was characteristic of an earlier period to see every echoed phrase as denoting direct citation and literary dependence. Thus, even the 'Amen' in Did. 10.6, says Armitage Robinson, 'doubtless comes from I Cor. 14.16',[68] and Vokes holds that the Didache is based on 'the whole of our New Testament, with the possible exception of the very late II Peter and the unimportant Mark and Philemon'.[69] But there is an increasing tendency to recognize that apparent quotations in this period are far more likely to reflect oral tradition,[70] and Audet argues that the Didache is completely independent of our written gospels.[71] Though he believes it to have been written at two stages (by the same hand), even the allusions at the second stage to a written 'gospel' do not, he contends, refer to our Matthew but to a sayings-collection of ethical teachings. Moreover, the passage in 1.3b–5, which contains the closest parallels of all and which with most others he agrees to be an interpolation,[72] still, he believes (unlike Koester), represents common oral tradition rather than a conflation of Matthew and Luke. The Didache, in other words, is valuable evidence for the prehistory of the synoptic tradition, and particularly of the Matthean: it does not reflect later quotations from it.

[65] 1QS 3.18–4.26; cf. also Test. Asher 1.3–6.6 and, behind all, such passages as Deut. 30.15–20; Ps. 1; and Prov. 2.9–22; 4.18f.

[66] Cf. J.-P. Audet, 'Affinities littéraires et doctrinales du Manuel de Discipline', *RB* 59, 1952, 219–38; *Didachè*, 122–63; Kraft, op. cit., 4–16; L. W. Barnard, 'The Dead Sea Scrolls, Barnabas, the *Didache* and the Later History of the "Two Ways"' in his *Studies in the Apostolic Fathers and their Background*, Oxford 1966, 87–107.

[67] Cf. Audet, *Didachè*, 163–6.

[68] *Barnabas, Hermas and the Didache*, 96. [69] Op. cit., 119.

[70] Cf. The Oxford Society of Historical Theology, *The New Testament in the Apostolic Fathers*, Oxford 1905, especially 24–36; Koester, *Synoptische Überlieferung bei den apostolischen Vätern*, especially 159–241; E. P. Sanders, *Tendencies of the Synoptic Tradition*, 36f.

[71] *Didachè*, 166–86. Similarly R. Glover, 'The Didache's Quotations and the Synoptic Gospels', *NTS* 5, 1958–9, 12–29. To the contrary: Streeter, *FG*, 507–11; B. C. Butler, 'The Literary Relations of *Didache* Ch. XVI', *JTS* n.s. 11, 1960, 265–83; J. P. Brown, 'The Form of "Q" known to Matthew', *NTS* 8, 1961–2, 41f.

[72] Cf. B. Layton, 'The Sources, Date and Transmission of *Didache* 1.3b–2.1', *HTR* 61, 1968, 343–83, who puts it at *c.* 150 while conceding with Audet that the rest *could* be early. Glover, *NTS* 5, 12–29, denies it is an interpolation at all.

None of this can be more than a matter of probability. It is impossible to be dogmatic about the source of quotations. But I find the presumption against literary dependence to be strong. Yet, though dependence could knock out a very early dating (depending of course on the date of the gospels), independence cannot establish it.[73] The case must rest on the genuine primitiveness of the many indications in the Didache which point to a stage in the life of the church which is still that of the New Testament period itself.

Audet examines these at length[74] and we cannot go over his arguments in detail, some of which are more convincing than others.[75] The prayers and thanksgivings are full of archaic terminology, echoing not only the servant (παῖς) Christology of the early speeches of Acts (Did.9.2f.; 10.2f.; cf. Acts 3.13,26; 4.27,30), later abandoned, but what I have ventured to call[76] 'the earliest Christian liturgical sequence' (Did. 10.6; cf. I Cor. 16.22–4). In Did. 9.1–3 the eucharistic cup still precedes the bread, as in I Cor. 10.16 and Luke 22.17–19. Audet argues that the terminology relating to baptism (7.1; 9.5) is similarly primitive, and that the regulations about food (6.3) presuppose a period and a milieu where the dietary question is still genuinely posed:

> We are in the first Christian generation born of the Gentile mission, at little distance, it seems, in time if not in space, from I Cor. 8–10; Rom. 14; Col. 2.16, 20–3; and I Tim. 4.3.[77]

Above all, we are in an age of itinerant apostles, prophets and teachers (11–13), where 'apostles' designate not a closed body but any men commissioned as missionary preachers and 'prophets' exercise a high charismatic ministry (10.7; 13.3) more honoured than that of local appointments. It is still the world reflected in such incidents as that of Acts 19.13–20, where strolling Jewish exorcists might be encountered by any congregation. But we are also 'at a point of transition from the ministry of prophets and teachers to that of bishops and deacons'[78] when the former are not available for regular ministry in the local church:

[73] Any more than the fact that the Gospel of Thomas may contain parallel tradition independent of our gospels proves that it was written early – though I should be prepared to see the date-span of that, as of a good deal else, reopened.

[74] *Didachè*, 187–206.

[75] I cannot see, for instance, that the expression 'hosanna to the *house* of David' (even if the correct reading in 10.6) is 'almost unthinkable after the events of 70' (*Didachè*, 189f.).

[76] 'The Earliest Christian Liturgical Sequence?', *JTS* n.s. 4, 1953, 38–41; reprinted in *Twelve NT Studies*, 154–7.

[77] *Didachè*, 199. [78] Ibid., 195. Similarly Streeter, *PC*, 149–52.

> Appoint for yourselves therefore bishops and deacons worthy of the Lord, men who are meek and not lovers of money, and true and approved; for unto you they also perform the service of the prophets and teachers. Therefore despise them not for they are your honourable men along with the prophets and teachers (15.1f.).

This is not the later transition from a presbyteral to a monepiscopal ministry but the much earlier one from the primacy of the charismatic to the recognition (and that by congregational appointment) of an established ordained ministry. It is a transition already presupposed by Philippians (1.1) and the Pastorals in the later 50s. In an astonishingly percipient review-article of Harnack's original edition of the Didache, first published in the *Church Quarterly Review* of April 1887, C. H. Turner said:[79]

> The 'Teaching', then, represents a stage or organization intermediate between the Corinthian and the Ephesian letters: parallel, let us say roughly to the Epistle to the Philippians with its earliest mention of episcopi and deacons. It follows from this, that, if the 'Teaching' is to be a factor in the series of the full current of Church development, it ought to be placed about the year 60.

He hastened to guard himself by saying that 'it does not follow that so early a date is inevitable' but said 'a date between 80 and 100 AD is as late as we are prepared to admit'.

With the state of the ministry goes the general theological character of the book. It is content (like the epistle of James) to leave doctrinal issues on one side. There is no polemic (as, for instance, in the Pastorals) against heterodox or gnostic tendencies within the church – merely a concern to maintain a practical mark of difference between Christians and Jews.[80] The final chapter on eschatology breathes much the same apocalyptic atmosphere as I and II Thessalonians (with which it has many parallels) and may represent one of the many fly-sheets of this kind, combining dominical and traditional Old Testament materials, which seem to have been produced by the early church between 40 and 70.[81] Yet in contrast with the synoptic apocalypses (but not Thessalonians), there is no attempt to fuse this material with predictions of the destruction of the temple or the fall of Jerusalem. This

[79] C. H. Turner, 'The Early Christian Ministry and the Didache', reprinted in his *Studies in Early Church History*, 1–32 (31).

[80] Cf. 8.1: 'Let not your fastings be with the hypocrites, for they fast on the second and fifth day of the week; but do ye keep your fast on the fourth and on the preparation (the sixth) day'.

[81] Cf. my *Jesus and His Coming*, 118–27. I did not at that time recognize that Did. 16 might be another such example. It reflects many of the same common features that I noted between I and II Thessalonians and Matt. 24 and looks like an important clue which I missed to the development of the *parousia* doctrine.

suggests that it is composed well before or well after these events. But, in notable distinction from the Epistle of Barnabas or the Jewish apocalypses of Baruch or II Esdras, there is no hint of any such event lying in the past. It seems much easier to see it as early rather than late. Indeed of the book in general I would agree with the assessment of J. A. Kleist:

> If we admit an early date of composition, all the evidence is in favour of it; if we insist on a late date, we have to face a mass of conjectures and hypotheses.[82]

In conclusion, I believe that we are here in a thoroughly primitive situation and though the Didache, as Audet says, was probably formed, like the gospels, over an extended period, I should be inclined to put it between 40 and 60 rather than between 50 and 70. For there is little or nothing of the signs of persecution or 'falling away', and with it the concern for consolidation in doctrine and structure, so characteristic of the 60s. If this is its period, then there are a number of features in the New Testament itself which cannot be argued, as they usually are, to demand a date in the latter part of the first century (if not later). Among these may be mentioned the instruction to 'baptize in the name of the Father and the Son and the Holy Spirit' (Matt. 28.19; cf. Did. 7.1,3); the doxology to the Lord's Prayer (Did. 8.2) later incorporated into Matthew (6.13, marg.); the qualifications of bishops and deacons in the Pastorals (I Tim. 3.2–13; Titus 1.5–9; cf. Did. 15.1); the instructions about Christian hospitality in the Johannine epistles (II John 10f.; III John 8–10; cf. Did. 11–12); the use of the term 'the Lord's day' (Rev. 1.10; cf. Did. 14.1); and perhaps the phrase 'the apostles and prophets' in Ephesians and Revelation (Eph. 2.20; 3.5; Rev. 18.20; cf. Did. 11.3). In general, if the Didache is really to be set before 60 then the placing of the whole of the New Testament before 70 may turn out not to be the wild hypothesis that at first sight it appeared.

Finally, I return, with some hesitation, to the first epistle of Clement. The consensus for a date of 95–6 is so strong, backed by the magisterial

[82] J. A. Kleist, *The Didache*, etc., in *Ancient Christian Writers* 6, edd J. Quasten and J. C. Plumpe, Westminster, Md., and London 1948, 10. He puts it 'before the end of the first century'; but this *is* early on the usual New Testament chronology. Cf. H. Chadwick, *The Early Church*, Harmondsworth 1967, 46f.: 'The situation regarding Church order presupposed in the *Didache* makes it hard to find any plausible niche for it in early Christian history other than the period between about 70 and 110. It may be odd there, but it is much odder anywhere else.' Similarly Bartlet, *HDB* V, 449, opted for 80–90. Streeter, *PC* 279–87, argued that it could not be later than 100 nor earlier than 90; but the lower limit derived from his dating of the gospel of Matthew, on which he held it was dependent.

authority of Lightfoot's arguments,[83] that it might seem temerarious merely to question it. 'It has even been said', writes Cullmann, 'that it is the document of ancient Christianity which can be dated with the greatest certainty.'[84] Yet in fact its basis is a great deal weaker than it appears and the case against it has been powerfully stated by Edmundson,[85] whose book seems to have been ignored at this point as at others. It is particularly remarkable that he is nowhere referred to in *The Primitive Church* by Streeter, who would have been at Oxford during his Bampton Lectures.

He begins by agreeing that this epistle, though anonymous, is genuinely by the Clement who became bishop of Rome in the last decade of the century. The sole question is whether he wrote it when he was bishop or at an earlier stage. Edmundson argues strongly that the evidence points to the latter alternative.

At no point in the epistle is appeal made to episcopal authority. Indeed Lightfoot himself says:

> Even the very existence of a bishop of Rome itself could nowhere be gathered from this letter. Authority indeed is claimed for the utterances of the letter in no faltering tone, but it is the authority of the brotherhood declaring the mind of Christ by the Spirit, not the authority of one man, whether bishop or pope.[86]

Not only is the author not writing as a bishop, but the office of bishop is still apparently synonymous with that of presbyter (42.4f.; 44.1,4f.; 54.2; 57.1), as in the New Testament and all the other writings we have examined. As Streeter says,[87]

> As in Philippians, bishops and deacons are the names of two kinds of officers. These two offices are spoke of by Clement in a way which excludes the possibility that presbyters is the name of a third and intermediate office. . . . There is nothing to call forth surprise in this evidence that in Rome and Corinth a system still prevailed not very far removed from that established by Paul.

If this is really the state of affairs in Rome in 96, then we are faced with a very remarkable transition within less than twenty years to that presupposed by the epistles of Ignatius. For he, while addressing the church of Rome in the salutation of his epistle to it with the utmost veneration, says elsewhere that apart from the three orders of bishop, presbyters and deacons 'there is not even the name of a church' (Trall. 3), and he speaks of bishops, in his sense, as being by then 'settled in the farthest parts of the earth' (Eph. 3; cf. Eph. 4f.; Magn. 3, 6f.; Trall. 2f.; Philad. 4; Smyrn. 8). It is easier to believe that I Clement, like the Shepherd of Hermas, reflects an earlier period.

[83] *AF* I.1, 346–58. [84] *Peter*, 90. [85] *The Church in Rome*, 188–202.
[86] *AF* I.1, 352. [87] *PC*, 215.

The main reason for placing it in the 90s is the assumption that the opening words refer to the persecution of the church under Domitian:

> By reason of the sudden and repeated calamities and reverses which have befallen us, brethren, we consider that we have been somewhat tardy in giving heed to the matters of dispute that have arisen among you (1.1).

Often indeed the opening words of I Clement have actually been cited as *evidence* for a Domitianic persecution. Yet, as Merrill says,[88]

> It is quite preposterous to claim that the innocent sentence with which it starts bears manifest and conscious witness to a persecution of the Church in Rome by Domitian.

The evidence for any such persecution at all is, as we have seen,[89] extraordinarily thin. But even supposing Clement had just passed through a persecution in which Christians of illustrious rank had suffered, and with whom as bishop he must have had intimate relations, is it conceivable, Edmundson asks, that

> none of their examples should have been brought forward, but only those of an already distant persecution, whose memory more recent events must have tended to throw into the background?[90]

Rather, he contends, 'the sudden and repeated calamities and reverses' which have befallen 'us' refer to the chaotic political situation in Rome during the year 69. He quotes again Philostratus' *Life of Apollonius of Tyana* for the impact of the successive shock-waves of that fateful year:

> Galba was killed at Rome itself after grasping at the Empire; Vitellius was killed after dreaming of empire; Otho, killed in lower Gaul, was not even buried with honour, but lies like a common man. And destiny flew through all this history in one year.[91]

I Clement, he argues, was written in the early months of 70.

I confess that when I first read that I thought that if he can persuade me of that he can persuade me of anything. But I am convinced that his case merits the most serious consideration.

The Epistle, he says, presupposes that the temple sacrifices in Jerusalem are still being offered:

> Not in every place, brethren, are the continual daily sacrifices offered, or the freewill offerings, or the sin offerings or the trespass offerings, but in Jerusalem alone. And even there the offering is not made in every place, but before the sanctuary in the court of the altar; and this too through the high-priest and the aforesaid ministers (41.2).

[88] *Essays in Early Christian History*, 161. Merrill himself argues for a much *later* date. Cf. p. 334 below, n. 107.

[89] Pp. 321–3 above. [90] Op. cit., 191.

[91] *Vit. Apol.* 5.13 (tr. Phillimore, II, 58).

Lightfoot[92] maintained that this provides no evidence of dating, since Josephus, writing in 93, also speaks of the sacrificial system in the present tense.[93] But Josephus is giving a summary description of the Old Testament ordinances contained in the Mosaic Law. Clement is appealing, like the author to the Hebrews, to actual practice. He claims its divine sanction for the good ordering of the Christian liturgy, and this could hardly fail to have been undermined by its total disruption. The parallel therefore is far from exact. And the same applies to the other passages that Lightfoot adduces: the Epistle of Barnabas 7f., which is concerned with the typology of Old Testament sacrifice fulfilled in Christ, and the Epistle to Diognetus 3, which contrasts the presuppositions behind Greek, Jewish and Christian understandings of worship. Yet one must admit that this argument cannot in itself be decisive or so important as Edmundson claims.

More significant is his contention that Clement's references to the Neronian persecution point to events still fresh in the memory:

> But, to pass from the examples of ancient days, let us come to those champions who lived nearest to our time. Let us set before us the noble examples which belong to our generation. . . . Let us set before our eyes the good Apostles [Peter and Paul]. . . . Unto these men of holy lives was gathered a vast multitude of the elect, who through many indignities and tortures, being the victims of jealousy, set a brave example among ourselves. By reason of jealousy women being persecuted, after that they had suffered cruel and unholy insults as Danaids and Dircae, safely reached the goal in the race of faith, and received a noble reward, feeble though they were in body (5.1–6.2).

He comments:

> If anyone were to read those paragraphs for the first time without any presuppositions or *arrière-pensées*, would they doubt that they told of scenes of horror which not only the author but all those in whose name he wrote had literally before their eyes, and which still haunted the minds of the witnesses?[94]

This, I believe, is a fair observation, though again it cannot be decisive.

Furthermore, the metaphor in the subsequent words, 'we are in the same lists, and the same contest awaiteth us' (7.1), which takes up that of the 'athletes' or champions of the faith in 5.1f., need have no reference to renewed persecution, whether in Rome or Corinth, but, as in the New Testament generally (I Cor. 9.24–7; Heb. 12.1f.; cf. II Clem. 7, 20), may be a summons to the common Christian struggle. Indeed, in very similar words Paul had called the Philippians to 'contend as one man for the gospel faith', saying: 'You and I are engaged in the same contest: you saw me in it once, and, as you hear, I am in

[92] *AF* I.2, 124f. [93] *Ant.* 3.224–57. [94] Op. cit., 191.

it still' (Phil. 1.27–30). But we do not conclude from that that they too are in prison. Similarly, the prayer in I Clem. 59.4, 'release our prisoners', in which Streeter[95] saw a reference to the Domitianic persecution, may, like the clauses on each side of it, 'feed the hungry', 'raise up the weak', be entirely general – or could equally well allude to the situation Edmundson envisages in early 70, when the author of Revelation was among those in detention.

There are, however, two main passages which have regularly been held to presuppose a later date. The first is 44.1–3:

> Our apostles[96] knew through our Lord Jesus that there would be strife over the name of the bishop's office. For this cause, therefore, having received complete foreknowledge, they appointed the aforesaid persons [viz. bishops and deacons; cf. 42.4] and afterwards they laid down a rule[97] that if these should fall asleep, other approved men should succeed to their ministration. Those therefore who were appointed by them, or afterward by other men of repute with the consent of the whole Church, and have ministered unblameably to the flock of Christ in lowliness of mind, peacefully and with all modesty, and for a long time have borne a good report with all – these men we consider to be unjustly thrust out from their ministration.

It is however a fallacy to suppose that a second- or third-generation ministry implies a *span* of two or three generations. The first presbyters (by definition 'elderly') could have been appointed by Peter in Rome in the mid-50s (if not the mid-40s) and by Paul in Corinth in the early 50s. Even by 70 there must have been many subsequent creations and some of these men could have been long established in office. (I recently took part in the consecration of a new bishop of Woolwich, and by the end of the service there were present four holders of that see, my predecessor and I and two successors, all within a span of less than twenty years!) Nor does the reference in 63.3 to the Roman delegates as 'faithful and prudent men that have walked among us from youth unto old age unblameably' necessarily mean that they had been *Christians* all that time – even though this would not have been impossible. For, according to Acts 2.10, there were converts from Rome on the day of Pentecost, and in Rom. 16.6f. Paul greets Andronicus and Junia(s) as eminent among the apostles, adding: 'They were Christians before I was.'

The other passage is in 47.1–6:

[95] *FG*, 528; *PC*, 201.

[96] I.e., in all probability, Peter and Paul, who were subsequently regarded as joint founders of the churches of Corinth and Rome.

[97] Following the Latin 'legem dederunt', which is probably the sense of ἐπινομήν (the reading of Codex Alexandrinus). Lightfoot amended to ἐπιμονήν, 'provided a continuance'. But it does not affect the argument here.

> Take up the epistle of the blessed Paul the Apostle. What wrote he first unto you in the beginning of the Gospel (ἐν ἀρχῇ τοῦ εὐαγγελίου)? Of a truth he charged you in the Spirit concerning himself and Cephas and Apollos, because that even then ye had made parties. Yet that making of parties brought less sin upon you; for ye were partisans of Apostles that were highly reputed, and of a man approved in their sight. But now mark ye, who they are that have perverted you and diminished the glory of your renowned love for the brotherhood. It is shameful, dearly beloved, yes utterly shameful and unworthy of your conduct in Christ, that it should be reported that the very steadfast and ancient (ἀρχαίαν) Church of the Corinthians, for the sake of one or two persons, maketh sedition against its presbyters.

This has been interpreted to mean that the church of Corinth was by the time of writing regarded as an 'ancient' foundation. But evidently in the context the meaning of ἀρχαίαν is determined by the phrase 'the ἀρχή of the Gospel', which is precisely that used by Paul to the Philippians of the period when he first preached to them – after an interval of only a decade (Phil. 4.15; cf. also Luke 1.2; Acts 11.15; I John 2.7,24; 3.11; II John 6). Similarly, in Acts 15.7 ἀφ' ἡμέρων ἀρχαίων is used at the council of Jerusalem of 'the early days' less than twenty years previously, and Mnason, 'a Christian from the early days' is described already by Luke in the early 60s as an ἀρχαῖος μαθητής (Acts 21.16).

The objections therefore to placing I Clement in 70 cannot be regarded as decisive. Its references to Hebrews in the exhortation of ch. 36, so far from arguing, as has been claimed, a late date for Hebrews, on the ground that I Clement quotes from a recent document, would be entirely natural if Hebrews had been addressed to the Roman church but two or three years earlier. And there are other positive indications which Edmundson adduces in favour of an early date:

1. The continued use in the liturgical passage of 59.2–4 of the primitive description of Jesus as the παῖς, the servant or child of God, common to the Acts speeches and the Didache.

2. The fact that, as Lightfoot recognizes,[98] the quotations from the gospel tradition 'exhibit a very early type'. The author does not introduce them (as he does citations of the Old Testament) with the words 'It is written' or 'The scripture says'. Indeed on the only two occasions (13.1f.; 46.7f.) he cites such material he employs precisely the same formula that Luke places on the lips of Paul in Acts 20.35: 'Remember the words of the Lord Jesus, which he spake.' And once more in all probability the quotations are not from our gospels but

[98] *AF* I.1, 353.

from oral tradition or 'some written or unwritten form of "Catechesis" . . . current in the Roman Church'.[99]

3. In a later letter to Soter, Bishop of Rome, Dionysius, Bishop of Corinth, says:

> This day, therefore, we spent as a holy Lord's day, in which we read your epistle; from the reading of which we shall always be able to obtain admonition, as also from the former epistle written to us through (διά) Clement.[100]

Though Edmundson, following Bigg, thinks that this is parallel to I Peter 5.12, we have seen reason to doubt whether Silvanus is there designated as more than the carrier of the letter. The closest parallel would seem to be in the Martyrdom of Polycarp 20.1, where the church in Smyrna writes an account of Polycarp's death to the church at Philomelium 'through our brother Marcianus'. He is not simply the amanuensis (Euarestus is that; 20.2), but he is the church's agent. Similarly, says Edmundson, Clement is 'only the servant, not the head of the Church acting on his own initiative'.[101] In fact he is fulfilling precisely the role which Hermas (Vis. 2.4.3) says was his assignment (ἐπιτέτραπται), that of correspondent of the Roman church in its external relations (εἰς τὰς ἔξω πόλεις). He is not (yet) its bishop. The assumption that if I Clement is by Clement it must have been written during his episcopate,[102] that is, in the last nine years of his life, no more follows than it does of most bishops' literary productions, despite Lightfoot's fantastic achievement in working on the completion of his own revised edition of Clement up to within three days of his death as Bishop of Durham.[103]

4. Finally, and of least importance, the concluding reference in 65.1 to Fortunatus, who, unlike Claudius Ephebus and Valerius Bito, appears not to be a Roman envoy but a member of the Corinthian church, would fit the Fortunatus whose coming from Corinth to Ephesus so relieved Paul in 55 (I Cor. 16.17f.), if the epistle was written in 70. It is, however, as Edmundson says,[104] extremely unlikely that he 'was still active and travelling to and fro as an emissary between his native town and Rome in 96 AD, more than forty years later'. Of course it may not have been the same Fortunatus – though the fact that the only two we know of both came from Corinth looks more than a coincidence.

99 *NT in the Apostolic Fathers* (see n. 70 above), 61. Similarly, W. K. Lowther-Clarke, *I Clement*, 1937, 11f.; Koester, op. cit., 12–19; Grant and H. H. Graham in Grant, *The Apostolic Fathers* II, ad locc.; D. A. Hagner, *The Use of the Old and New Testaments in Clement of Rome*, Leiden 1973, 171.

100 Quoted Eusebius, *HE* 4.23.11.

101 Op. cit., 202.

102 First asserted (though still not explicitly) by Irenaeus, *Adv. haer.* 3.3.3.

103 Cf. Westcott's preface to Lightfoot, *AF* I.2, v–viii.

104 Op. cit., 199.

There are other points that Edmundson makes, including some intriguing speculation on the occasion of the Corinthian dissensions following the drafting by Nero of 6,000 Jewish prisoners to dig the Corinth canal in 67–8.[105] None of his arguments is in itself decisive. The over-all balance of probability will be assessed differently by different people. But if the case Edmundson makes is not proven,[106] it shows at least how fluid and uncertain is the dating of one of the so-called 'landmarks' of the sub-apostolic age.[107]

To conclude, there would seem to be very little *against* the following sequence:

[105] Op. cit., 195f. According to Eusebius, *HE* 3.16, who himself put I Clement under Domitian (following Irenaeus?), Hegesippus had evidence of a dissension which took place at Corinth at that time. But we know nothing else of this.

[106] His dating of I Clement, though largely ignored, was accepted, most notably, by Henderson, *Five Roman Emperors*, 45, despite his earlier adoption of Lightfoot's dating in *Nero*, 443, 484. It was also supported by Badcock, *Pauline Epistles*, 133, 186f., 208; and by L. E. Elliott-Binns, *The Beginnings of Western Christendom*, 1948, 101f., 225, as 'much more probable'. Lowther-Clarke, *I Clement*, 11f., while disagreeing, conceded that it was 'not impossible'. A. E. Wilhelm-Hooijbergh, 'A Different View of Clemens Romanus', *HJ* 16, 1975, 266–88, also contends (without any reference to Edmundson) for a date of 69. Some (but not all) of his arguments merit further consideration.

[107] All Lake was prepared to say for certain for the date of I Clement was 'between 75 and 110' (*The Apostolic Fathers*, Loeb Classical Library, 1912, 5). My colleague J. V. M. Sturdy, in an acutely argued article, soon to be published, on 'Clement, Ignatius and Polycarp', also starts from the quite insubstantial basis of the traditional dating. But he proceeds, with Merrill, op. cit., 217–41, to put it much later, *c.* 140, arguing back from the Muratorian Canon's dating of the Shepherd of Hermas with its reference to Clement. The corollary of his position is that 'the Ignatian Epistles are pseudepigraphical, from a date late in the second century, and that the Epistle of Polycarp is also pseudepigraphical, from yet a later date, perhaps in the third century, but possibly even later', and that the Martyrdom of Polycarp is no longer a contemporary account but comes from later in the second century. I cannot possibly enter into the details of his arguments (which include the usual cumulative one from pseudonymity), but, as when Knox throws over most of the Acts evidence, it would seem a weakness of any position to be required to jettison so much. Like Merrill, he denies that Clement was ever bishop of Rome (Merrill also disputing, op. cit., ch. 11, that Peter had ever been there!). But he does bring out very clearly the inconsistency we observed in Perrin (p. 9 n. 21 above), and which comes out also in Streeter's remark (*PC*, 108) that 'in Asia monepiscopacy antedates the writing of the Pastoral Epistles', of putting 'the "early catholic" books of the New Testament like the Pastorals' after or about the same time as 'the "definite catholic" books like I Clement and Ignatius'. With these last banished to the mid-second century and beyond, he observes that 'the strongest check on the dating of the New Testament books is removed' – and, apart from the genuine Pauline epistles, Mark and Colossians, he puts *everything* (even if only tentatively) after 110!

The Didache	40–60
I Clement	early 70
The Epistle of Barnabas	*c.*75
The Shepherd of Hermas	—*c.*85

But even if I Clement were still to be placed last, *c.*96, we should have a perfectly intelligible series. The pressure to push any of them into the second century has, I believe, largely been created by their natural place having been usurped by books of the New Testament. Conversely, if these non-canonical documents do *not* belong to the second century, then their affinities with certain features in the canonical writings cannot be used to relegate the latter to the same period. The arguments for dating the Pastorals and II Peter, let alone I Peter and Acts, in the second century begin to look less and less substantial. Obviously there is a circularity here, and only if the chronology of the sub-apostolic literature as a whole, including that of the crucial Ignatian epistles,[108] were being established in its own right could this be used to argue for an early dating of the New Testament. All that I have attempted in this postscript is to remove some of the objections to such a dating arising from the vacuum it could appear to leave in the last quarter of the first century.

[108] Sturdy regards these with their evidence for monepiscopacy in the early second century as 'the Piltdown man of the history of the Christian church'!

XI

Conclusions and Corollaries

BEFORE SUMMARIZING OUR own conclusions and looking to the consequences from them, it will be useful to set down certain general observations that have emerged from the survey of the evidence and of other positions built upon it.

1. We may start with the fact, which I confess I did not appreciate before beginning the investigation, of how *little* evidence there is for the dating of *any* of the New Testament writings. Moreover, there are no fresh facts – like the introduction of carbon-14 datings into archaeology – which have clearly changed the picture or which have caused me to reopen the question. It is surprising to be made to realize that there is only *one* reasonably secure absolute date (and that within a year or so either way) in the life of St Paul, which in turn can be used to fix the chronology of his writings. And this – that of the proconsulship of Gallio in Achaia – relates not to any statement of Paul himself but to a minor incident recorded of him in Acts. There are other events, such as the famine under Claudius, or the deportation of Jews from Rome, or the arrival of Festus in Judaea, or the alleged execution of Paul under Nero, which can provide very approximate supports. But the evidence for their dating is extraordinarily elusive, and none again turns upon anything that Paul himself wrote. The chronology of his life and letters has to be pieced together from a large number of statements and inferences – though the material for *relative* dating, both in the epistles and Acts, is far richer than for any other part of the New Testament literature. Yet at the end we have to confess that we cannot settle with any precision or finality the date of his birth, his conversion, his visits to Jerusalem, his various missionary journeys, his arrival in Rome, his death – or any of his letters. And if

we know so little about Paul, how much less can we say about Peter or John? There is not a single book of the New Testament that dates itself from the internal evidence. And important recent discoveries – e.g. of new papyrus fragments or the Dead Sea scrolls or the gnostic library at Chenoboskion – have done little more than tilt the balance *against* guesses which rested in any case upon very questionable judgments. In the case of the fourth gospel, which they chiefly affect, they do not *of themselves* require any change in the estimates made, for example, by Lightfoot and Westcott a hundred years ago.

The conclusion to be drawn from this first point is not that there is nothing, or nothing new, to be said. It is that the consensus of the textbooks, which inform the student within fairly agreed limits when any given book of the New Testament was written, rests upon much slighter foundations than he probably supposes.

2. When we turn to the external evidence in the testimony of the early church the situation is not very different. Compared with the plethora of ancient tradition, good, bad and indifferent, with regard to authorship, it is surprising to discover, as we have seen, that only one book of the New Testament, the Apocalypse, is dated in early Christian writings. Irenaeus sets it 'towards the end of the reign of Domitian', a statement which, if one combines it (as Irenaeus does not) with what evidence there is for a Domitianic persecution, puts it at about 95. Yet we have found no more reason to accept this statement than most scholars have found to accept the other two with which Irenaeus associates it, namely, that the book of Revelation was composed by John the apostle and by the same man who wrote the fourth gospel. For the rest, the traditions (to take a selection) that the gospel of John was written when the apostle was a very old man, or that Mark was written during the lifetime – or after the death – of Peter, or that Matthew was written 'while Peter and Paul were preaching and founding the church in Rome', have been shown to be worthless, self-contradictory or ambiguous. Moreover, such statements as that John wrote his gospel 'last of all' or 'after the Apocalypse' or that the Pastoral Epistles come from a period following Paul's first Roman imprisonment or that the first epistle of Clement was composed during his episcopate turn out to be little more than guesses. The conclusion must be that, as with authorship, the external evidence is only as good as the internal, and cannot prevail over it. Indeed in contrast with the evidence for authorship, which sometimes, I believe, has to be taken seriously (e.g. on Mark, Luke–Acts, the gospel and epistles of John, and, in one instance, Hebrews), the external testimony on dating, with the single exception of the Apocalypse

(where it is significant though far from unanimous), is virtually worthless.

3. Closely connected with the last is the evidence of first attestation by name to the existence of a New Testament book in the early church. The first thing that needs to be said is that one is dealing here almost totally with an argument from silence. The one exception that can be dated within the first century is the explicit reference in I Clement to I Corinthians (though described simply as Paul's 'epistle' to that church). This does nothing to help with the dating of I Corinthians, which if it is genuine (as no one now doubts) must in any case have been written years earlier. When later the Apocalypse is mentioned by Justin or the gospels by Papias or Irenaeus, we have, for what it is worth in any given instance, a certain ceiling for dating purposes. But the *absence* of such mention is a very different matter. The small quantity of early Christian literature and its occasional character make the argument from silence, that such and such a book of the New Testament was not in existence or was not known, precarious in the extreme. We should not even guess from Acts that Paul wrote any letters, but at whatever date we put Acts – from the early 60s to the mid-second century – it would be highly hazardous to conclude that its author did not know of them – let alone that they did not exist. The argument from attestation, whatever its weight in regard to authorship, is relevant for dating only if there is ground for supposing that the book in question was written so late that its first mention provides a *terminus a quo* and not merely a *terminus ad quem*. This *could* be so with the Shepherd of Hermas, if we can trust the Muratorian Canon, and it has in the past been supposed to be so with regard to the fourth gospel, first cited by name only *c.* 180. But the more reason there is for pushing the date of a book back, the less relevant becomes the argument from its earliest attestation. That the Apocalypse is first mentioned by Justin in 150 does nothing to help us decide whether it was written in the late 60s or the mid-90s. And the same applies to the dating, say, of the gospels and epistles of John, or even of Jude and II Peter. The gap is usually in any case so great – and the bridge so thin – that an extra thirty years or so can make little difference.

4. More relevant, and much more difficult to decide, is the question of quotation for establishing literary dependence and therefore temporal posterity. This applies both to literary dependence within the New Testament itself and to its subsequent citation. Though practically no one would question the fact of literary interrelationship between the synoptists, it is less clear than it was fifty years ago that

the first three gospels can be set in a simple chronological series or that we know what the order of the sequence is. Equally it is much less evident than it once seemed that John is dependent upon, and *for that reason* later than, the synoptists. Confident assertions too that James quotes Paul or Matthew, or that there is a direct literary connection, whichever way, between Ephesians, I Peter and Hebrews, or that the author of Revelation knows and uses most of the other books of the New Testament, are more muted than they were. The work of the past two generations has made us far more conscious of the common tradition both of preaching and teaching within the apostolic communities and sensitive to the processes of oral transmission. Direct citation from previous documents known to be available requires to be argued with much greater precision than earlier scholars who spotted similar phraseology assumed, particularly in the first part of this century – the heyday of source criticism. And this applies equally to the sub-apostolic period. The readiness to assert specific quotation from canonical books of the New Testament in the Apostolic Fathers has been much chastened and modified. Particularly in relation to the gospel traditions, it is becoming clearer that other channels of transmission, both oral and written, continued to function well after the latest probable date of any of our gospels. Studies of the quotations in I Clement and even in the Didache far from compel the conclusion that their authors used our synoptic gospels, while the discoveries of the Egerton papyrus of an unknown gospel, or of the Gospel of Thomas, or even of the 'Secret Gospel' of Mark (with its witness to a non-Johannine (?) version of the raising of Lazarus), testify to parallel traditions in written form that may go back earlier and certainly go on later than our canonical gospels.

All this suggests a much greater rigour and reserve in the use of the argument from quotation as an indicator of dating. This applies both positively and negatively. We cannot say positively that *on these grounds* James must be later than Romans, or Ephesians than I Peter (or *vice versa*), or the Apocalypse than Luke, or the Didache than Matthew. Nor can we say, negatively, that the gospel of John was unknown to Ignatius or Justin because they do not specifically quote it. Since both of these arguments have, paradoxically, been used in the interests of late dating, it is relevant to remind ourselves how precarious is their foundation. Indeed I would think it safe to say that there is no certain argument for dating to be drawn from the use of any one New Testament book by any other – and this applies even where there is undoubted literary interrelationship, e.g., between the synoptic gospels or between Jude and II Peter. Moreover, with the exception of the clear allusions to Hebrews and I Corinthians in I Clement (36, 47, 49), I doubt whether any of the references in the four sub-apostolic writings which we have ventured to set in the first century can unquestionably be said to show dependence on any of our canonical New Testament books or on each other. This does not of course prove that the apostolic or later writers wrote in mutual ignorance or isolation (which is highly improbable), nor is it in itself any argument for early datings. It is merely a salutary warning against misplaced dogmatism based on arguments from literary dependence.

5. A similar chastening would seem to be appropriate in the assurance with which scholars have pronounced on prophecy after the event. That such activity was a stock-in-trade, especially of apocalyptists, cannot be doubted. Daniel's 'prophecy' in ch. 7 of the four beasts, to depict the progress of the Babylonian, Median, Persian and Greek empires, is an obvious paradigm. And the later apocalypses of Baruch and Ezra (ostensibly set in the period after the capture of Jerusalem by Nebuchadnezzar) describe the capture of Jerusalem by Vespasian and Titus, while the Sibylline Oracles use the device of the Sibyl to 'predict' the detailed pattern of world history to date (and where they go beyond that they start getting it wrong). But the very detail of these, which could have deceived or been intended to deceive no one, must make us pause before assuming that every prophecy in the gospels and elsewhere, and particularly of the fall of Jerusalem and the destruction of the temple, must come into this category. On the contrary, we have seen reason to question very closely the prevailing assumption that this is so in regard to the gospels of Matthew and Luke (the nearly parallel statements in the Markan apocalypse have not, rather surprisingly, led most scholars to the same conclusion). At any rate prophecy *ex eventu* has to be demonstrated, and demonstrated by minute and strict criteria, rather than simply assumed.

This is *not* of course to say that subsequent reflection on events or the later experiences of the church have not shaped or conditioned the gospel tradition as we have it. John's looking back on the manner of Jesus' death, or of Peter's, obviously presupposes the former and in all probability the latter. Equally the predictions of the rejection, crucifixion and resurrection of the Son of Man in the synoptic tradition are clearly influenced in lesser or greater degree by the knowledge of what happened. Again, the synoptic apocalypses and the Johannine last discourses have evidently placed on Jesus's lips warnings to the church that have been conditioned by the church's own sufferings. Indeed there is not a saying or a story in the gospel tradition that has not reached us through the sieve of the community's needs and uses. Yet it is quite another matter to say that these sayings or stories have simply been created by the history of the church and then put back into the mouth or the life of Jesus, or to say that Jesus could not have foretold what would befall his followers or his nation. Moreover, in Christian apocalyptic, whether set on the lips of Jesus or of John, there is no hint of the convention of pre-casting predictions so as to make it appear that occurrences within the readers' time were foreknown from the distant past. While the Christian prophet might indeed shape his oracles, as John evidently did, out of his own experiences, the very limits of those experiences indicate where events had *not* yet reached. Thus, there is nothing in Revelation that speaks of the fall of Jerusalem or that certainly reflects anything beyond the late 60s, just as there is nothing in the predictions of Paul in Acts that certainly reflects the situation beyond the point at which its story ends – or the subsequent organization of the Roman Empire or of the Christian church. Whether the gospels, Acts, or the Apocalypse *were* written after the fall of Jerusalem must be assessed on the merits of each case. The argument from prophecy, like the argument from quotation, must take its place within the larger context and must in each instance be deployed with the most exacting critical discrimination.

6. It is sobering too to discover how little basis there is for many of the dates confidently assigned by modern experts to the New Testament documents. The argument advanced by so great an authority as Harnack that when Matthew says that the coming of the Son of Man would occur 'immediately' upon the tribulation in Judaea this means that his gospel could not have been written more than five years after 70 is, to say the least, a disconcertingly tenuous deduction. We have observed also how not only Harnack and Lightfoot but the vast majority of scholars take over the assumption that the Neronian persecution (and therefore, if it is apostolic, I Peter) is to be dated in the year 64 – when the sole piece of evidence for its association with the fire of Rome (in the *Annals* of Tacitus) clearly points to its being at the earliest in the spring of 65. We have noted too how incredibly limited is the evidence (depending on the passing reference in its opening sentence to our recent local difficulties) on which I Clement has almost universally been assigned to the year 95–6. Similarly the Domitianic persecution of the church which has been the basis for dating so much (either because the writing in question is held to reflect it or because it must ante-date or post-date it) has itself turned out to be virtually a non-event. In the same way, the dating of the gospel of Mark, when it has not merely been held to reflect the pro-

gress of the Jewish war, whether finished or unfinished, has been made to turn on the report that it was written after the death of Peter – or even on the *a priori* assumption that the death of Peter would (only then?) have led to the need for a written record – whereas the tradition that it was written during the lifetime of Peter is just as strong, if not stronger. Finally, as examples of how much has been built on so little – yet constantly reiterated by commentators till their weaknesses were exposed – we may mention the alleged use of Josephus by Luke to put Acts after 93, or the mention of the founding of the church of Smyrna in Ep. Polyc. 11.3 to date Revelation late, or the reference in John 5.43 to 'another coming in his own name' to the revolt of Bar-Cochba in 135. Dare we think that the allusion to the issuing of the twelfth of the Eighteen Benedictions in 85–90 still found in scholar after scholar to explain the language of expulsion from the synagogue in the same gospel will turn out to be a similar curiosity of criticism?

7. Then there is the apparently almost wilful blindness of investigators to the seemingly obvious. Thus Harnack chided scholars – and himself – for failing to take seriously the explanation which stared them in the face of why Acts ends where it does. They could not believe it, because of previous assumptions about the dating of Mark and therefore of Luke. In the same way, the absence of all reference in the gospels, Acts, epistles or Apocalypse to the fall of Jerusalem in the past tense is a phenomenon that should have raised far more questions than it has. Even – or especially – a deliberate rewriting of history to conceal it must surely have left more trace than it has. It is not enough to say, however loudly, that its 'importance . . . is impossible to exaggerate', and that 'much of the subsequent literature both of Judaism and Christianity took the form it did precisely in an attempt to come to terms with the catastrophe of AD 70',[1] and then to give no specific evidence. The assumption that the epistle to the Hebrews could have been written as it is without reference to this cataclysmic event (so specifically mentioned in the comparable Epistle of Barnabas) is surely quite astonishing. So too is the blindness to the obvious interpretation of the statement in Rev. 17.10 that it was written during the reign of the sixth Roman emperor. While certainly not ruling out more complicated explanations or resort to purely symbolic interpretation, the consistent evasion by modern commentators of a solution they have already prejudged to be impossible contrasts strikingly with the openness of an earlier age (of whatever school of thought). And of the Apocalypse in general the marked contrast with the post-70 Jewish apocalypses, not least in their predic-

[1] Perrin, *NTI*, 40.

tion of the doom of 'Babylon' as direct revenge for its sack of Jerusalem, is passed over extraordinarily lightly. Another blind spot, on which we have already touched, is the way in which commentators have blandly assumed that Matthew is deliberately writing for the *interval* between the fall of Jerusalem and the *parousia* when he *alone* inserts the statement that the latter will subvene 'immediately' upon the former. Finally I believe one must insist that most liberal scholars have allowed themselves to be insensitized, whether by the climate of critical opinion or for other reasons, to the very considerable strength of the external – and internal – evidence for the apostolic authorship of the fourth gospel, and that all students of it (including myself) have until very recently too hastily *assumed* that the relations it depicts between Judaism and Christianity can only reflect a situation after 70.

8. We have drawn attention to the way in which so much dating of New Testament books has been determined more by a process of elimination than by positive indications. This is particularly true again of St John's gospel. There is really not a single positive reason for associating it with the years 90–100. Indeed the reign of Domitian has, as we pointed out, become the repository, for one investigator or another, of *every* book of the New Testament (and several outside it) with the exception of the undisputed epistles of Paul: even the gospel of Mark has recently been put there by Trocmé and II Peter by Reicke. But there cannot be *that much* which this period has in common – except our convenient ignorance of it. For here we are in an age with few firm landmarks and with correspondingly few objections to almost any dating. Writing of the book of Revelation in relation to the gospels of Matthew, Luke and John, Austin Farrer has said with characteristic charm:

> The datings of all these books are like a line of tipsy revellers walking home arm-in-arm; each is kept in position by the others and none is firmly grounded. The whole series can lurch five years this way or that, and still not collide with a solid obstacle.[2]

And to show how fluid the situation is he himself proceeds to ignore the only remotely fixed point (the association of the Apocalypse with the last years of Domitian) and to set it in the reign of Trajan! The received schema of New Testament chronology scarcely convinces by its own internal logic. As Farrer says, each book is held in place by the other, yet negatively rather than positively. They coexist rather than cohere. There is no compelling reason why Matthew or John, James or Jude, should belong where they do. Perhaps it is wrong to

[2] A. M. Farrer, *The Revelation of St John the Divine*, Oxford 1964, 37.

ask that there should be. But the accepted pattern is the outcome of a protracted period of shunting and jostling until the pieces have settled in a certain contiguity. It is remarkable how little it itself tells us about the course of church history – unless with a Baur or a Perrin we superimpose an *a priori* pattern upon it and force the pieces to fit.

9. Another factor which we have observed is the subjectivity in assessing the intervals required for development, distribution or diffusion. There is a close parallel here, as we saw, with what has been going on in archaeology. What Renfrew calls the 'archaeological bellows' can be moved in or out at will. And there is a kind of Parkinson's law that takes over: the intervals will contract or expand to fill the time available. Thus, we have watched Ogg stretching the intervals in Paul's activities (even by having him off sick for a year), with Barrett compressing them equally violently – all to fit the space they regard as available between two points. While indeed certain points may be determinable (within whatever margin of error), the intervals tend to be indeterminable – and can therefore be treated freely. One is reminded of the dumpy lady who concluded that she had the same vital statistics as Marilyn Monroe – apart from the spaces in between: and these no one thinks to measure or to mention.

Estimates of how long it takes, say, for doctrines to develop or structures to become institutionalized, for a golden age to decline into a silver, or for documents to travel, vary wildly. Some can squeeze the whole of church history up to the conversion of Paul into a single year, others require decades for the emergence of the conditions in I Peter. And nothing is so slippery as the relation between Christology and chronology. The greater the stress on the part of the early Christian communities in the formation of the tradition, the longer the 'tunnel period' tends to be. Yet the procedures to which the form critics and redaction critics draw attention carry in themselves no implications for dating. The whole process could be speeded up or slowed down, as in a film, without being essentially affected. The assumption that it was slow or steady is purely arbitrary. In fact it is inherently probable that, as in the creative ferment of any new movement, it was swift and took place in spurts – with periods of retrenchment and consolidation in between. The only reliable canon or measure of development is the Pauline corpus. For there within a testable period of less than a decade we can see something of what could go on in one creative mind and within a shorter space still what could change in the condition of a single congregation at Corinth. Moreover, if we accept the basic reliability of the Acts outline – which for Corinth certainly holds – there is a great deal more to go on. For if all the developments described in Acts – in theology, organization and ethos – could come into being between 30 and 62, it is difficult, on developmental grounds alone, to demand more time for the formation of the gospel tradition. Moreover, if the Didache is really also evidence for the stage that discipline and liturgy had reached in this period, practically nothing is foreclosed.

10. Closely connected with the supposed requirements of development is the manifold tyranny of unexamined assumptions. Even (perhaps most of all) in their reactions *against* each other, different schools of critics take these over from their predecessors, and of course individual commentators and writers of introductions take them over from each other. Fashions and critical orthodoxies are established which it becomes as hard to go against in this field as in any other. A notable instance of this was the swing, about the turn of the century, among New Testament (but not classical) scholars in the dating of the Apocalypse; but the fashions on the fourth gospel – or the epistle of James – have not been far behind. Again, it seems to have been 'respectable' in critical circles till recently to put Hebrews late – with few appearing to question how improbable this is. Solutions of the synoptic problem (including the relation of John to the synoptists) have tended to become accepted for extended stretches as assured – and therefore reassuring – results. Some of this is sheer scholarly laziness. We all respond to the urge *quieta non movere*; and I confess to a long reluctance to reopening the synoptic problem for what it might force one to reconsider. There is also an understandable temptation to depreciate or lose patience with the lower reaches of 'mere' introductory questions of date and authorship. Those who press on to the more constructive work of building theologies of the New Testament tend to be content to assume and incorporate the foundations laid by others. It is noticeable as one visits the literature of the past hundred years how much more thoroughly grounded in these questions was the work of the older generation – most of whom were brought up on the classics – and how much more rigorous in the dating of evidence, as well as attentive to the evidence of dating, than some of their successors. This, one has to say it, has been true of many, though not all (R. H. Lightfoot was an honourable exception), of the form critics and redaction critics. Their world has been a world without fences, where words and ideas, myths and movements, Hermetic, gnostic, Mandean and the rest, have floated freely with no very noticeable tethering to time or place. Many of the circles and communities of the early church with their tensions and tendencies are frankly creations of the critics or highly subjective reconstructions.

Yet this has not prevented the fixing and the indeed freezing of a number of powerful assumptions. We may instance three.

One has been that the period of oral tradition preceded, and was in turn succeeded by, the period of written tradition. In a broad sense this is obviously true. Where it becomes dangerous is when it hardens into two presumptions. (*a*) The first is that the writing down of traditions did not begin until *after* a considerable stretch of oral transmission – the transition being marked, it is also often *assumed*, by the passing of the first apostolic generation or by the fading of the hope of an early *parousia*. Ellis in an important and refreshing article on 'New Directions in Form Criticism'[3] observes that the supposition that

> writing would begin only when the expectation of an imminent end of the age subsided foundered with the discovery of the Dead Sea Scrolls: the Qumran sect viewed itself to be in the 'last generation' (1Q pHab. 2.7; 7.2), expected an imminent end, but, nevertheless, produced a large body of literature.

Moreover he makes the obvious point, when one comes to think about it, that

> the circumstance that gave rise to written teachings in early Christianity was not chronological distance but geographical distance. This is evident in the case of Paul's letters and of the Jerusalem Decree (Acts 15), but a similar situation on a smaller scale was also present in the mission of Jesus.

Indeed he argues for 'a considerable degree of probability for some written transmission of Gospel traditions from the time of Jesus' earthly ministry'. (*b*) The second presumption is that once the period of writing did begin the traditions were transmitted, and mutually influenced, almost exclusively by the processes of literary dependence, as one writer 'used', 'copied' or 'altered' another. On the contrary, there is every reason to think that both oral and literary processes went on concurrently for most of the first hundred years of the Christian church. The writing was earlier and the reign of the 'living voice' longer than we have tended to suppose. If the preaching material of Peter or the eucharistic prayer of the Didache came at a certain point to be written down, that *per se* is to say nothing about dating.

A second assumption has been that Aramaic-speaking Christianity was prior to Hellenistic Christianity. Again in a general sense this is true. But I believe it is misleading, if the deduction is then drawn that Greek was not spoken in Palestine from the very earliest days of the

[3] E. E. Ellis in G. Strecker (ed.), *Jesus Christus in Historie und Theologie: Neutestamentliche Festschrift für Hans Conzelmann zum 60. Geburtstag*, Tübingen 1975, 299–315 (304, 306, 309).

church and indeed that the spiritual majority was not in the first instance made up of those who also (or most naturally) spoke Greek, whether they were from Galilee, Jerusalem or the *Diaspora*. The mere fact that *all* the surviving Christian literature is in Greek while *all* the surviving Qumran literature is in Hebrew (or to a small extent in Aramaic) must say something about the relative provenance of the two movements. The testimony of the New Testament itself, not to mention the growing weight of contemporary evidence from outside it, suggests that the assumption that Hellenistic Christianity, with the use of the Septuagint, was a secondary phenomenon confined to the Gentile churches is far too facile. Certainly the assumption that Peter would have needed Greek only in addressing Gentiles, or James would not have been able to write it at all, or that the Johannine tradition must have passed through the medium of translation, demands challenge and scrutiny. This does not in itself affect the question of dating, but, unless questioned, the assumption tends to work uncritically in the direction of identifying what is Hellenistic with what is late. There is nothing inherently impossible about the notion that both the epistle of James and the first draft of the gospel of John could be very Jewish *and* very early *and* be written in Greek.

The third assumption I would mention primarily concerns authorship, though it regularly recurs in conjunction with dating. This is that there was an indefinite number of totally unrecorded and unremembered figures in the history of early Christianity who have left absolutely no mark except as the supposed authors of much of its greatest literature. This creates relatively minor problems when the writings in question are either anonymous or of secondary significance. Thus, who wrote the Epistle of Barnabas or II Clement or even the epistle to the Hebrews can ultimately be left unanswered without the overall picture being affected – though it is noticeable that all attempts to answer these questions in the early church turned upon names, like those of Paul or Luke, Barnabas or Clement, that we have already heard of: no one thought to postulate *ex nihilo* some forgotten spiritual genius. (Even the ghostly figure of John the Elder is not recorded *in the tradition* as the author of anything. Eusebius merely guessed that he might have written the Apocalypse: Dionysius was more judicious.) It is when we are dealing with the conjuring out of thin air of major theologians or spiritual giants, like the authors of the fourth gospel and the epistle to the Ephesians, who not only died as if they had never been but also claimed to be the apostles who overshadowed them, that credibility begins to be stretched. Pseudonymity is invoked as if it were an accepted and acceptable way of life at a date and to an extent for which we simply have no evidence. Indeed the fact of pseudonymity is frequently just assumed: it is the explanation for it alone that is argued. I Peter, II Peter, Jude, James, the Pastoral Epistles and Ephesians, not to mention Colossians and II Thessalonians are freely, and for very diverse reasons, attributed to men who were well known to be dead – without this practice being remarked upon or noticed *except negatively* in *any* early Christian writers. The most that is suggested by way of acceptable literary explanation is that two Johns may have been confused, not that one was purporting to *be* the other.

None of this is to say that the question of authorship is to be settled in a simplistic or fundamentalistic way. For we know that there were from the middle of the second century pseudo-apostolic writings both among the heretics and within the main stream, which when exposed were rejected. The Christian fathers were well familiar with the categories of genuine, disputed and spurious literature. But there has been insufficient discrimination in modern scholarship between hypotheses of secretaries (like Tertius for Romans), ghost-writers (such as, supposedly, Silvanus for I Peter), agents (such as possibly for the Pastorals or II Peter) and impostors (on the usual explanation of II Peter). In particular, it is important from the point of view of dating to distinguish between theories which presuppose that the document is being written with the authority and within the lifetime of the apostle in question and those which presuppose a purely fictional and subsequent setting. The peopling of the sub-apostolic era with a penumbra of pseudo-Pauls, pseudo-Peters, pseudo-Johns (and even pseudo-Judes!) on no evidence which is not drawn out of the documents themselves is really an astonishing confidence trick. Surely a Clement or an Ignatius, a Justin or an Irenaeus, might have expected to refer to them either positively or negatively. But we hear nothing of them. And it makes one gasp the more that these same critics are entirely prepared to use the absence of external attestation to question the genuineness or even the existence of the same documents.

The observations made so far may have appeared excessively negative and critical. Before passing to my own conclusions I should like to correct that impression. No one working in this field – least of all one like myself who came to it so ignorant – can fail to be conscious of the overwhelming debt one owes to those who have worked in it before and to the introduction to so many valuable studies one has received. There is nothing that I have put into the pool that I have not first taken out. And delving back into the history of the work has revealed labours and labourers all too easily forgotten or ignored by the modern surveyor of the scene. In particular, there was a generation of scholars astride the turn of this present century whose erudition was matched by a judgment which must still command immense respect even when one dissents from their conclusions. What for me has come from this work has been the rediscovery – or in some cases the discovery – of men like Lightfoot and Hort, Harnack and Zahn, C. H. Turner and Armitage Robinson, Mayor and Chase, Edmundson and Peake, to name but a few, and those chiefly from my own heritage.[4] I say this in no way to depreciate contemporaries – for who could be more richly endowed in their scholarly equipment than a Bultmann or a Dodd, a Jeremias or a Käsemann, a Kümmel or a Hengel? – but because one cannot help observing how the caravan of New Testament scholarship has tended to move on to fresh sites, attracted by different and exciting questions, but leaving behind the

[4] Since the others have left their memorials behind them, the reader's interest may by now have been aroused, as has mine, to enquire what if anything is known about George Edmundson. In spite of holding no high academic or professional office he was sufficiently distinguished to rate a substantial entry in *Who's Who*. The son of a Yorkshire parson and lord of the manor, he was born in 1848. After taking a double first in mathematics at Magdalen College, Oxford, as well as a university scholarship in mathematics and prize in the Greek Testament, he was ordained to the title of a fellowship at Brasenose, of which College he was mathematical lecturer, tutor and junior bursar until 1880. Then at the age of 32 he left Oxford, to enter upon two incumbencies covering forty years, first at Northolt and then at St Saviour's, Upper Chelsea, which were to last until his retirement to the south of France, where he lived on till 1930. He received no visible recognition from the church, not even an honorary canonry, though at the very end of his career he reached the heights of becoming war-time Rural Dean of Chelsea. In the world however it was a rather different story. Apart from an Oxford D.Litt., he was a Fellow of the Royal Historical and of the Royal Geographical Societies, as well as being an honorary member of two Dutch learned bodies. He was twice employed by the Government in boundary-arbitrations in British Guiana and by the historical department of the Foreign Office. His literary productions were equally varied and included books on Milton, Archbishop Laud, Anglo–Dutch rivalry in the seventeenth century (the Ford lectures at Oxford), the chapter on Spain and Portugal in the eighteenth century in the *Cambridge Modern History*, a history of Holland, and the editing of the manuscript of an early Spanish journal from the Amazon. None of this or his mathematical training would prepare one for his Bamptons, at the age of 65, on *The Church in Rome in the First Century*, which disclose an extensive and intensive knowledge of classical and patristic learning, as of modern German, French and especially Italian literature and excavation – prompting one of its rare reviewers (*TLS*, 19 February 1914, 86) to the back-handed compliment: 'The learning and erudition shown on every page is quite unusual in an English work.' Yet it received no discussion in any classical, historical or theological journal that I have been able to discover. Shall we again see the like of such a clerical career?

other workings in the state in which they then were and taking over their results to date, without further re-examination, as the presuppositions of the new work. This I suggested happened, notably in regard to the synoptic problem, both when the form critics took over from the source critics and when the redaction critics took over from the form critics. These newer disciplines have had much illumination to shed. But they become dangerously unrelated to reality when they ignore detailed investigation of the 'introductory' questions – and still more when they claim that these can be settled by the answers to their own questions. Thus, it is frankly nonsense to say, as I have recently heard claimed, that the priority of the gospel of Mark can be demonstrated by its theology alone. In the study of chronology the argument from development may be a useful servant but it is a bad master. Used with great discrimination and delimitation – e.g. within the Pauline corpus – it can sometimes help towards establishing the sequence of the New Testament documents (though 'the argument from order', while it looks the most objective in synoptic studies, can be made to prove almost anything). What it cannot do, except within the very broadest limits, is itself to determine the span of time over which the development takes place. There is no more reason to suppose that the history of the synoptic tradition (or the Johannine) as delineated by the form critics requires a canvas of sixty years rather than thirty, or that the questions and answers of the redaction critics are not just as valid if the entire process took place before the fall of Jerusalem rather than after it. These issues can only be decided by the historical evidence; and of course the signs of doctrinal or organizational development, in so far as we can pin them down to time or place, are one important part of this. Naturally, too, this evidence can never be investigated 'without presuppositions'. But the presuppositions must continually be re-examined and tested. The chronology of the New Testament documents, however fundamental to other studies, has tended to lie too long at the bottom of the agenda – in fact for the three-quarters of a century since Harnack. Each new student enters a field already marked out for him by date-lines which modesty as well as sloth prompts him to accept, and having accepted to preserve. The mere fact that 'New Testament introduction' tends to occupy his earliest and most inexperienced years has a formative effect, for good or for ill, on all his subsequent work.

But having questioned the basis of much that passes for assured results in this field, it behoves us now to state in summary form what we would put in its place. The arguments for the conclusions reached on each particular book of the New Testament have already been set out and it would be tedious to condense them here. All that is necessary is to bring together the results and make some comment on the inferences to be drawn, and not to be drawn, from them.

The dating of any document must stand or fall primarily on its own merits, though inevitably the strength of some datings will depend – on any chronology – upon how they cohere with others. Yet, if a coherent or more coherent pattern emerges, its truth cannot be made to rest simply on its self-consistency. For it would be possible to devise many such patterns. Each dating must be grounded in the requirements of the internal and external evidence in so far as this points to a particular period or even year. Again it has to be said in reminder that every date is more approximate than it looks – though relatively few (and those mainly for the gospels) require, I believe, a margin of error of more than two years either way. This may seem extraordinarily small, but with an overall span of not much more than twenty years to which we have found ourselves working for the completion of the New Testament documents, it is proportionately high.

First, then, I would set out the results in a simple chronological table, for comparison with the tables in the opening chapter. Yet there is an important factor which can only be brought out in the subsequent graph, namely, that while some books, notably epistles, are written over a short period for a specific occasion, others, notably gospels (but also the Didache), must be seen as the product of a much longer period of gestation in which there are at least three stages (represented in the diagram by dots, dashes and continuous lines), corresponding to the traditions behind them, the first drafts, and the final writing and rewriting. Obviously these stages, which run into each other, can be represented only very approximately, but the last term (which is itself only the starting-point for textual and other accretions) gives but an inadequate and misleading idea of the date of composition. We cannot simply say that Mark was written in the year '*x*' as with fair precision we can say that I Corinthians was written in the year '*y*'.

So, bearing this in mind, I first list the books of the New Testament and of the immediate sub-apostolic age in what I believe (with qualifications and alternatives again omitted) to have been their approximate order of completion. Then I try to give a conspectus of their overlapping development in the order in which they appear in the New Testament canon and in Lightfoot's collection of the Apostolic Fathers.

James	*c.* 47–8
I Thessalonians	early 50
II Thessalonians	50–1
I Corinthians	spring 55
I Timothy	autumn 55
II Corinthians	early 56
Galatians	later 56
Romans	early 57
Titus	late spring 57
Philippians	spring 58
Philemon	summer 58
Colossians	summer 58
Ephesians	later summer 58
II Timothy	autumn 58
The Didache	*c.* 40–60
Mark	*c.* 45–60
Matthew	*c.* 40–60+
Luke	–57–60+
Jude	61–2
II Peter	61–2
Acts	–57–62+
II, III and I John	*c.* 60–65
I Peter	spring 65
John	*c.* –40–65+
Hebrews	*c.* 67
Revelation	late 68 (–70)
I Clement	early 70
Barnabas	*c.* 75
The Shepherd of Hermas	–*c.* 85

What corollaries then should be drawn from these conclusions?

1. There is, first of all, the observation that all the various types of the early church's literature (including the Didache, a version of its 'manual of discipline') were coming into being more or less concurrently in the period between 40 and 70. This, I believe, is what we should naturally expect. The notion that all the Pauline epistles, with the theology they imply, were prior to all the gospels, with the theology they imply, is not one that we should derive from the documents themselves. Laymen are always surprised to be told it, and I believe they are right to be surprised. I suggest that what has emerged is a more credible pattern.

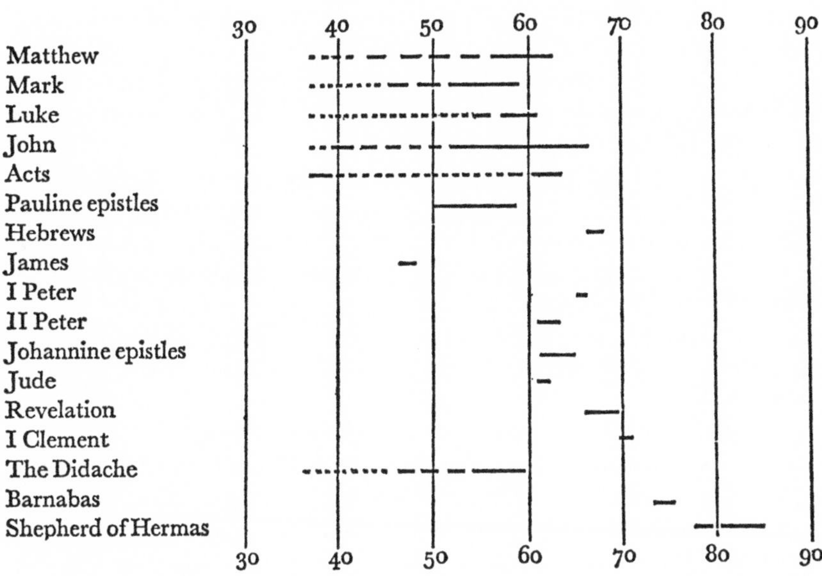

2. The pattern of early church history suggested by the New Testament documents now reinforces that which we should independently deduce from the Acts narrative (up to the point that it takes us). This could approximately, decade by decade, be plotted as follows:

30–40 early mission in Palestine and Syria
40–50 consolidation of bases for the next thrust
50–60 rapid expansion into Asia Minor and Europe
60–70 testings from within and from without
70+ reorientation and reappraisal

The epistle of James affords us a glimpse into the period prior to 50. But the really creative period of the primitive church, its 'Elizabethan era' from the point of view of literary output, was undoubtedly the 50s. These saw the full flowering of the preaching and teaching traditions in the gospels and the Didache and the creation of the Pauline corpus. The 60s mark the beginning of the silver age (already foreshadowed by the Pastorals), with its concern for the confirmation and defence of the faith against the threats of heresy and schism, persecution and defection (Acts, Jude and II Peter, the Johannine epistles, I Peter, the prologue and epilogue of the fourth gospel, Hebrews and Revelation). Yet the glow remains till the end of the first apostolic generation, fed by the fire of the martyrs and reflected in I Clement. Thereafter the spiritual temperature drops and the literary production of the church falls away, both in quantity and quality (Barnabas and Hermas), till it begins to emerge again with the martyrs and apologists of the second century (Ignatius and Polycarp, Justin and the Epistle to Diognetus). In the first century as in every other age of church history there were periods of rapid social change and of relative quiescence, of carefree ferment and of careful consolidation. The pattern of dating that has emerged helps us plot these without unnatural forcing. In particular, we can see a reason why the books we have assigned to the 60s belong together and belong there (in a decade full of events at each end of the empire that we know a great deal about) in a way in which there is no visible rationale for the books usually consigned to the reign of Domitian.

3. Thirdly, and most difficult to interpret aright, there are the deductions to be drawn from the contraction of the overall span. Just as the shrinking of the span from 50–150+ to one from 50–100+ resulted in discrediting some of the extremer forms of scepticism about the Christian tradition, so a further reduction in final datings by more than half from −50 to −70 must tend to reinforce a greater conservatism. Yet it is important to define this rather carefully. The last inference to be drawn is that it renders otiose or invalid the critical work done on the documents of the New Testament over the past two hundred years. For it is by applying the same critical methods and criteria that the conclusions have been reached. In particular the recent light thrown on the history of the tradition by form criticism and redaction criticism is, as we have stressed, by no means to be repudiated. It is merely that unexamined assumptions have tended to lead to the unwarranted conclusions that the more the documents tell us about the early church (*a*) the less they tell us about Jesus and (*b*) the longer they took to develop. But neither conclusion necessarily follows. As George Orwell showed in his *Critical Essays*,[5] it is possible to put questions to all sorts and levels of literature – from Dickens to seaside postcards – to get it to yield information (in his case, about the socio-economic attitudes of its authors) which it was never written to provide. Yet it does not follow that the more it tells us of this, the less it tells us of what it is meant to be about. In fact the more we recognize the standpoint and prejudices of the writers, the more we are in a position to discount these when assessing their contribution to their subjects. Thus, in relation to the gospels, Jeremias has demonstrated in his *Parables of Jesus* and his *New*

[5] George Orwell, *Critical Essays*, 1954.

Testament Theology how it is possible to use all the tools and techniques of critical scholarship not to induce historical scepticism but by a gradual peeling back of the layers superimposed by the church to expose with the greater confidence what is likely *not* to come from it but from Jesus himself.

In the same way there is no necessary correlation between the wealth of knowledge the documents can be made to yield about their setting in the life of the church and the *duration* of the period for which these processes give evidence. In logic this is obvious. Yet the 'tunnel period' between the events of the life, death and resurrection of Jesus and the moment when, as it were, the train emerges, laden with ecclesiastical baggage, in our canonical documents has been viewed as so extended that almost anything could have happened on the way. To shorten the tunnel in principle changes nothing. For much can overtake and overlay a tradition (especially about a storied and creative character) in a remarkably brief time. But obviously there is less likelihood of distortion the shorter the interval. Moreover, there is a critical point of transition. If one is dealing with a gap, say, of thirty years (the distance that separates us, at the point of writing, from the end of the second world war), there is a good deal of built-in control in the form of living memory – whereas if the distance is doubled the controls are much less than half as strong. Without access to public records, when parents or grandparents die folklore takes over. And what applies to the gospel stories applies also to the history researched by the author of Acts. His claim to have 'gone over the whole course of events' for himself will obviously be affected by whether, as the 'we' passages imply, he has personally shared in much of it. This does not mean that we must simply take him at his word. The scholarly checks remain, to test whether in any given instance the tradition (of whatever date) is good tradition, or whether the documents present us with a picture that is evidently unreliable or palpably anachronous. The results of such tests will continue to be a matter of degree and of judgment, on which scholars will properly differ. But it is worth reminding New Testament theologians of the friendly chiding they have received, for instance, from the classical historian Sherwin-White for not recognizing, by any contemporary standards, what excellent sources they have. This judgment does not depend on dating – as far as I know he would accept the traditional datings of the gospels and Acts – but it is obviously strengthened if the gap between the records and the events is that much shorter.

Perhaps I may be allowed to insert at this point a somewhat naughty comment, quoted by others before me, from a book by a layman on the fourth gospel which with a light touch takes the academics to task:[6]

> There is a world – I do not say a world in which all scholars live but one at any rate into which all of them sometimes stray, and which some of them seem permanently to inhabit – which is not the world in which I live. In my world, if *The Times* and *The Telegraph* both tell one story in somewhat different terms, nobody concludes that one of them must have copied the other, nor that the variations in the story have some esoteric significance. But in that world of which I am speaking this would be taken for granted. There, no story is ever derived from facts but always from somebody else's version of the same story. . . . In my world, almost every book, except some of those produced by Government departments, is written by one author. In that world almost every book is produced by a committee, and some of them by a whole series of committees. In my world, if I read that Mr Churchill, in 1935, said that Europe was heading for a disastrous war, I applaud his foresight. In that world no prophecy, however vaguely worded, is ever made except after the event. In my world we say, 'The first world-war took place in 1914–1918.' In that world they say, 'The world-war narrative took shape in the third decade of the twentieth century.' In my world men and women live for a considerable time – seventy, eighty, even a hundred years – and they are equipped with a thing called memory. In that world (it would appear) they come into being, write a book, and forthwith perish, all in a flash, and it is noted of them with astonishment that they 'preserve traces of primitive tradition' about things which happened well within their own adult lifetime.

Such a statement can be used – and has been used – to buttress, if not the fundamentalism of the fearful, at any rate the conservatism of the committed.[7] Yet it would be sad if the conclusion were to be drawn from this study that I was giving any comfort to an obscurantist or literalist approach to the New Testament. Since the passage quoted was written *à propos* the fourth gospel and since it is on this gospel above all that my argument for early dating and apostolic authorship could well be interpreted in this direction, it may be worth indicating very briefly what in my judgment this conclusion does, and does not, imply.

It does not imply a return to a position in which John is held to be reporting the *ipsissima verba* of Jesus (whether he catches what Jeremias distinguishes as the *ipsissima vox*[8] is a very different matter). His theological purpose is unaffected by whether he is writing late or early, from sources or from source. If we conclude that 'his witness is true' we are not back at a purely physical understanding of witness or at a verbalistic understanding of truth – both of which are decisively

[6] A. H. N. Green-Armytage, *John Who Saw*, 1952, 12f.

[7] For an expansion of this and other attitudes to the Bible, I would refer to a forthcoming popular book of mine, *Can We Trust the New Testament?*, 1977.

[8] For this important distinction, cf. his *New Testament Theology* I, ET 1971, 37.

repudiated by the gospel itself. Nor are we denying, in this gospel or any other, the processes of community tradition – fostered by the needs of apologetic and preaching, catechesis and liturgy – in favour of an individualistic understanding of the channel of transmission as the memory of one old man. Indeed, while nowhere more than in the Johannine corpus are we so aware of the authoritative note, 'La tradition c'est moi',[9] nowhere else is the 'we' of the community so explicit or the overtones of worship and the sacraments[10] (to mention no others) so clearly to be heard. Nor are we saying that the Johannine tradition, if or because it goes back to one who claimed to rest on his master's breast, is for that reason always reliable or in isolation the whole truth. In fact the more one becomes convinced of the complex and complementary nature of the synoptic relationships and dissatisfied with a simple pattern of literary dependence and temporal sequence, the more persuaded also one becomes of the distortion involved in the academic isolation of 'the synoptics' from 'the fourth gospel'. And this distortion has its effects in both directions. John has to be complemented by the other traditions and the other traditions by John for a 'stereoscopic' view. And nowhere, I believe, is this more true than in interpreting the literally crucial meeting between Word and flesh, theology and history, πνεῦμα and κόσμος, that comes to its climax in the trial and death of Jesus.[11] What *is* being asserted is that John has just as much right to be taken seriously on the history as well as on the theology, that his tradition reaches continuously back at least as far as that of the others, and that his claim to be heard, if indeed he *is* John the son of Zebedee, is certainly no less than that of Matthew, Mark or Luke. And yet, if Plato may be said to have *understood* his master best, the Socrates of Xenophon, or even of Aristophanes, is an indispensable supplement and indeed corrective to the portrait he paints.

In closing I would return to the position from which I began, that all the statements of this book should be taken as questions. It certainly makes no claim to represent a conclusive redating of the New Testament – if only because I am aware of how often I have changed my mind in the course of the work. It is an irritant and incentive to further exploration, and, I should like to think, to the

[9] Cf. P. H. Menoud, *L'évangile de Jean d'après les recherces récentes*, Neuchâtel [2]1947, 77.

[10] Cf. Cullmann, *Early Christian Worship*, ET 1953 – however exaggerated on occasion.

[11] Cf. again for the outworking of this theme my article, 'His Witness is True' in Moule and Bammel, *Jesus and the Politics of his Day*.

opening up of fresh questions. For, as again in archaeology, settled positions, even if they prove to be vindicated, can by the very weight of their consensus deaden dissatisfaction and deter discovery. But if the chronology of the documents and the pattern of development should turn out to be anything like what I have suggested, then there will be scope for numerous new trajectories to be drawn and for the rewriting of many introductions to – and ultimately theologies of – the New Testament. For dates remain disturbingly fundamental data.

ENVOI

Since completing this manuscript I have found a letter from Dodd, whose contents I had entirely forgotten. It was written evidently in response to a first intimation of my rethinking the date of the gospel of John, in which I must have adumbrated the implications as I began to see them for the chronology of the whole New Testament. Since I have presumed to put some questions to Dodd's own views – he did not live to see these – I thought it would be fair, as well perhaps as interesting to others, to reproduce a letter which reveals what, at the age of eighty-eight, openness of mind in a very great scholar can mean. Could any author ask for more?

1 Wellington Road,
St Giles',
Oxford

19 June, 1972

My dear Robinson,

It is a long time now since I received from you a letter, very kindly written, which gave me much pleasure, and also aroused no little interest. In the meantime I have been through a rather rough patch, when I was not much in the way of serious letter-writing. I had to go into hospital for an operation, and came out to lead a semi-invalid existence. That however has not prevented me from thinking much about the challenging views on the Fourth Gospel which you put forward. For all I know, you may already have published these in some form, but I am simply going on your letter. Your *volte face* takes one's breath away, though you may well say that you prepared the way by various articles, starting with the 'New Look'. As you know, I am very much in sympathy with a view which makes it possible to derive from John not only valuable light on the primitive church, but even authentic information about the Jesus of history. But I can't help thinking that you will find it difficult to persuade people of the very early date which you now wish to assign. It is true that Bultmann was prepared to date it early, but that was on his presupposition that Christianity began as a kind of gnosticism, and was only later 'Judaized' and so historicized. For myself, with every motive for assigning an early date, I found this encountered too many difficulties for me to get over. However, I am open to conviction. You are certainly justified in questioning the whole structure of the accepted 'critical' chronology of the NT writings, which avoids putting anything earlier than 70, so that none of them are available for anything like first-generation testimony. I should agree with you that much of this late dating is quite arbitrary, even wanton, the offspring not of any argument that can be presented, but rather of the critic's prejudice that if he appears to assent to the traditional position of the early church he will be thought no better than a stick-in-the-mud. The whole business is due for radical re-examination, which demands *argument* to show, e.g., that Mark *must* be post-70 – or *must* be so because anything earlier than that could not present such a plain, straightforward story: that would be to neglect the findings of the fashionable *Redaktionsgeschichte*. It is surely significant that when historians of the ancient world treat the gospels, they are quite unaffected by the sophistications of *Redaktionsgeschichte*, and handle the documents as if they were what they professed to be (Sherwin-White, with all his limitations, is the latest instance). But if one approaches them in that way, does not the case for late dating collapse? I look forward therefore to your damaging assault on the system of late date. But I still feel that the Fourth Gospel has reasons of its own for resisting attempts to place it very early in the time-scale. But you will be airing the whole discussion in published form – or may already have done so; I am so out of touch. I hope I have not darkened counsel by words without knowledge, or wearied you with the product of muddled thinking (for I am conscious that I do get muddled nowadays).

With kind regards,

Yours sincerely,

C. H. Dodd

INDEX OF NAMES